Planning Better Cities

"From understanding what makes great cities to the techniques of strategic planning, this book provides invaluable guidance for students, policy makers and established practitioners. Accessible and packed with interesting case study examples, Halvard Dalheim has drawn on his exemplary and varied career to share essential insights on planning with and for new and changing communities. I recommend this book to anyone seeking an insider's manual for navigating the strategic planning process that is equally instructive and inspiring."

—Professor Nicole Gurran, *Professor of Urban and Regional Planning, The University of Sydney*

"Halvard Dalheim is amongst the very best of Australian urban and regional planners. He has plied his trade across all spheres of government and in most jurisdictions for decades. Dalheim has distilled this immense experience into a great textbook on applied strategic planning. It's a must for practitioners and scholars alike."

—Dr. Marcus Spiller, *Principal & Partner, SGS Economics and Planning*

"Teaching students how to be good strategic planners is a challenging task. Part of the problem has been the lack of good teaching materials. There is a lot of scholarship criticizing strategic plans but until this book very little good writing about how to "do it". This book is an excellent combination of scholarship and practical advice based on the author's deep experience of writing plans for major cities. It is an invaluable resource for teachers, students and strategic planners trying to improve their practice."

—Emeritus Professor Peter Phibbs, *School of Architecture, Design and Planning, University of Sydney*

"This text is brilliant. Strategic planning is a combination of the art of planning, predicting the future, and the science of planning – knowing what the future will bring. Halvard has developed an approach that is practical and deeply rooted in experience and most importantly that deals with the paradox of predicting and knowing! Sydney is a better and more equitable city because of him."

—Geoff Roberts AM, *Chief Commissioner, Greater Cities Commission*

"Halvard Dalheim's Planning Great Cities: A Practical Guide assembles a vast amount of information on cities and their planning in a well-organised and readable book. It begins with a clearly articulated and comprehensive sense of the history of cities and of planning which leads into a dissection and explanation of the strategic planning process. The early sections are enriched with references in books, articles and to web sites and include pointers for further development of the ideas and cases discussed.

The second part of the book follows the strategic planning process through some l-defined and illustrated stages applied across a wide scale of issues from metropolitan areas to local precincts. Here Dalheim's personal experience provides a strong foundation.

In short this book explains the issues in a process that few people see as a whole, buried as they usually are in local scale or short term issues. It is likely to be the go-to book not only in planning education but also a valuable refresher for those engaged in strategy planning exercises of all kinds."

—Professor Emeritus Kevin O'Connor, *Urban Planning, University of Melbourne*

Halvard Dalheim

Planning Better Cities
A Practical Guide

What I think about when I think about cities

Halvard Dalheim
University of Sydney
Sydney, NSW, Australia

ISBN 978-3-031-33946-2   ISBN 978-3-031-33947-9 (eBook)
https://doi.org/10.1007/978-3-031-33947-9

© The Editor(s) (if applicable) and The Author(s) 2023

This work is subject to copyright. All rights are solely and exclusively licensed by the Publisher, whether the whole or part of the material is concerned, specifically the rights of translation, reprinting, reuse of illustrations, recitation, broadcasting, reproduction on microfilms or in any other physical way, and transmission or information storage and retrieval, electronic adaptation, computer software, or by similar or dissimilar methodology now known or hereafter developed.
The use of general descriptive names, registered names, trademarks, service marks, etc. in this publication does not imply, even in the absence of a specific statement, that such names are exempt from the relevant protective laws and regulations and therefore free for general use.
The publisher, the authors, and the editors are safe to assume that the advice and information in this book are believed to be true and accurate at the date of publication. Neither the publisher nor the authors or the editors give a warranty, expressed or implied, with respect to the material contained herein or for any errors or omissions that may have been made. The publisher remains neutral with regard to jurisdictional claims in published maps and institutional affiliations.

Cover credit: Maremagnum; VOJTa Herout; JaySi

This Palgrave Macmillan imprint is published by the registered company Springer Nature Switzerland AG
The registered company address is: Gewerbestrasse 11, 6330 Cham, Switzerland

Cities are in a permanent state of flux, there is no end state.
Collaboration is the key to successful city planning.

To Brenda,
Who always believed

Preface

Why this book. Around 35 years ago, my first employer, Dr. Jeff Wolinski, encouraged me to undertake further study—and I soon realised there were no courses in city planning or strategic planning. This was a challenge, as my business card said I was a 'strategic' planner.

Dr. Wolinski suggested I enrol in a course in project management, as it would provide skills in dealing with a core aspect of strategic planning—juggling multiple complex activities. Now 35 years on, practical courses on strategic planning still appear to be few and far between.

This book seeks to fill that gap. It is a book about city planning, particularly the process of influencing change within a city—strategic planning. This book is a how-to guide for all those involved in the shaping of cities, particularly those involved in land use and transport planning (you cannot have one without the other).

This book started as the insights I gained—and recorded—after finishing a major town centre plan and wanting to reflect on the experience. The latent teacher in me thought there may be a benefit in sharing this knowledge. My early reflections have evolved into this textbook, which focuses on a 7-Step Strategic Planning Process.

Furthermore, my focus on metropolitan and regional planning over the last decade crystallised my perspective away from thinking only about traditional land use planning issues to wider questions about the dynamics of cities. Plans for cities, if they are to fulfil the needs of the community and protect and enhance natural systems, cannot be constrained by a single focus on land use issues.

Finally, in putting pen to paper, I have found the best way for me to consider how to go about city (strategic) planning is when I ask myself—what do I think about when I think about cities?

Acknowledgements

I would like to thank all the people who have influenced my learning over the past 38 years. First and foremost, Dr. Jeff Wolinski, who still has a profound influence on how I approach city planning and my love of learning. Secondly to all my colleagues, team members and peers over the years—thank you for the many insights and for raising my awareness of many different issues on my journey of learning about cities, which continues today.

I am also grateful to Elle Davidson, a Balanggarra woman, for her valued contributions, outlining how the 7-Step Strategic Planning Process aligns with First Nations Country, community and culture and for reviewing how First Nations issues are addressed throughout the book.

Writing some thoughts in a notepad is one thing but turning them into something to share requires more deliberate steps. For me, this means acknowledging and thanking a few people. Firstly, Dr. Marcus Spiller, for encouraging me to pursue the task. Secondly, Professor Peter Phibbs and the Henry Halloran Research Trust for creating the opportunity to make it happen. Thirdly, Dr. Michael Bounds, of the Trust, for providing the right advice at the right time as drafts evolved.

Finalising a manuscript is a major task and I thank Tara Madden for editing and Max McMaster for compiling the index. I also acknowledge and thank Leanne Terrington for typing the original draft which allowed me to share my initial thoughts.

Finally, and most importantly, this book would not have happened without the encouragement, support and first edit of Brenda.

The subtitle for this book was inspired by the title of the book by Haruki Murakami.
What I talk about when I talk about running.

About This Book

This book is a how-to guide to city planning—specifically, the strategic planning processes required to develop city plans, from whole metropolitan areas to town centre plans.

My experience suggests cities vary too much to approach how we plan them with a preconceived view of what a city should be. Thus, this book is about the steps involved in creating a vision that can be implemented while maximising the opportunities for what a city could be, in the context of the relevant community's aspirations.

Ultimately, the objective is to provide the reader with sufficient understanding of what to do and the reasons for doing it, including a structured how-to framework for preparing city plans—the 7-Step Strategic Planning Process. The book also aims to provide advice as to how to adapt this process to the circumstances of each city or place, recognising that at a fundamental level all cities are different.

This book is structured into discrete chapters to allow the reader to jump in at any point. Moreover, the book is organised into three parts to make it accessible to different audiences.

Parts I and II are for the student or recent graduate starting the journey into planning, or the practitioner looking to move into strategic planning. Part III is for the practitioner looking to enhance their knowledge of research methods for strategic planning.

Contents

1 **Introduction** 1
  1.1 City Planning Context 1
      1.1.1 The Nature of Strategic Planning 2
      1.1.2 Cities—Where Change Is the Constant 2
      1.1.3 Typology of City Plans 3
      1.1.4 Jurisdictional Context 4
      1.1.5 First Nations Heritage, Culture and Country 4
  1.2 Content Overview 5
      1.2.1 Part I: Why and How to Plan Cities 5
      1.2.2 Part II: A 7-Step Strategic Planning Process 7
      1.2.3 Part III: Approaches to Research 8
      1.2.4 Insights and Case Examples 9
  1.3 Definition 9
      1.3.1 Definitions 9
      1.3.2 Acronyms 13
  1.4 Summary 13
  References 13

Part I Why and How to Plan Cities

2 **What Are Great Cities?** 19
  2.1 Introduction 19
      2.1.1 Warm-Up Exercise 20
  2.2 What Is Special About Cities? 20
      2.2.1 The Emergence of Cities 20
      2.2.2 The First Cities 22
      2.2.3 Cities Through the Ages 23
      2.2.4 The Urban Form of Cities 24
      2.2.5 Insights for a Strategic Planning Framework 30
  2.3 Great Cities: Various Perspectives 30
      2.3.1 What Makes Great Cities? 30
      2.3.2 Great Streets 31
      2.3.3 Public Spaces and Great Cities 34
      2.3.4 Accessibility: At the Core of Great Cities 36

		2.3.5	City Leader Boards	37
		2.3.6	Who Defines 'Great'?	38
		2.3.7	Insights for a Strategic Planning Framework	38
	2.4	Summary		39
	References			40
3	**What is Planning About?**			43
	3.1	Introduction		43
		3.1.1	Warm-Up Exercise	43
	3.2	The Emergence of Modern Planning		44
		3.2.1	A Response to the Urban Ills	44
		3.2.2	The Australian Experience	46
		3.2.3	Evolving Planning Eras in Australia	46
	3.3	Reflections on Planning Eras in Australia		46
		3.3.1	Evolving Planning Eras in Australia	46
		3.3.2	Events From 2000 to 2020	51
		3.3.3	Insights for a Strategic Planning Framework	53
	3.4	Contemporary City Planning		56
		3.4.1	Insights from Australian City Plans	56
		3.4.2	Insights From International City Plans	58
	3.5	The Rationale for Planning Cities		59
	3.6	The Scope of City Planning		62
		3.6.1	Legislation Requirements	63
		3.6.2	Common Issues from Australian Contemporary Plans	63
		3.6.3	Common Themes from Contemporary International Plans	68
		3.6.4	Drivers of Change in the Twenty-First Century	71
	3.7	Summary		77
	References			78
4	**The Purpose of Strategic Planning**			83
	4.1	Introduction		83
		4.1.1	Warm-Up Exercise	84
	4.2	The Purpose of Strategic Planning		84
		4.2.1	Is Business As Usual Acceptable?	85
		4.2.2	Needs of the Community—A Research Framework	85
		4.2.3	Temporal Considerations in Strategic Planning	88
	4.3	What is Important to People's Lives and Places?		89
		4.3.1	People and Households	89
		4.3.2	Socio-Economic Characteristics	90
		4.3.3	Characteristics of Places and Country	90
		4.3.4	City Setting	91
		4.3.5	Needs of People and Households	91
		4.3.6	Quality of Life	92

		4.3.7	Needs of Businesses	92
		4.3.8	Growth and Change Equation	93
		4.3.9	Transport and Digital Accessibility and Performance	94
		4.3.10	Qualities of Places	95
		4.3.11	Urban and Suburban Communities	96
		4.3.12	City Design	97
	4.4	Planning for Places		97
		4.4.1	Defining Places	98
		4.4.2	Creating Places	98
		4.4.3	Responding to Community Values	99
		4.4.4	Integrated Place Planning	99
	4.5	It's About Delivery		103
		4.5.1	The Issues	103
		4.5.2	Selected Strategic Intervention	104
		4.5.3	Intervention Levers	105
		4.5.4	Funding the Delivery of City Plans	107
	4.6	Summary		111
	References			111
5	**A Strategic Planning Process**			113
	5.1	Introduction		115
		5.1.1	Warm-Up Exercise	115
	5.2	A 7-Step Strategic Planning Process		116
		5.2.1	Rationale for a Framework	116
		5.2.2	The Model	119
		5.2.3	Implications of Differing City Planning Typologies	120
		5.2.4	From Plans to Planning	122
	5.3	Common Threads and Considerations		122
		5.3.1	Planning Systems	123
		5.3.2	*Communityand Stakeholder Engagement*	125
		5.3.3	First Nations Country, Community and Culture	133
		5.3.4	Politics and Planning	136
		5.3.5	Planning and Decision-Making	137
		5.3.6	Confidentiality	138
		5.3.7	Project Management	139
		5.3.8	Sustainability	140
		5.3.9	Complexity, Cities and A Systems View of Planning	142

		5.3.10	The Challenge of Planning for Change	143
	5.4	Summary		145
		5.4.1	Insights	147
	References			148

Part II The 7-Step Strategic Planning Process

6 Getting Started 155
	6.1	Introduction		155
		6.1.1	Warm-Up Exercise	156
	6.2	Purpose of Step 1: Project Establishment		156
	6.3	Principal Activities		157
		6.3.1	The Tasks	157
		6.3.2	An Iterative Process	159
		6.3.3	The Project Brief	160
		6.3.4	First Nations and Project Establishment	162
	6.4	Establishing Working Relationships		162
		6.4.1	Why It Is Important?	162
		6.4.2	Identifying Your Project Partners Across Government	163
		6.4.3	Establishing Informal Working Relationships	163
		6.4.4	Engaging Outside Government	165
	6.5	Auditing the Planning Context		165
		6.5.1	What Are We Seeking to Achieve?	165
		6.5.2	Reviewing Existing Background Material	166
		6.5.3	The Outputs for the Project Brief	167
	6.6	Establishing the Project Objectives and Scope		167
		6.6.1	Be Clear on the Objectives	167
		6.6.2	Approach	168
		6.6.3	Outputs for the Project Brief	169
	6.7	Developing the Project Methodology		169
		6.7.1	What Are We Seeking to Achieve?	169
		6.7.2	Approach	169
		6.7.3	Timing	171
		6.7.4	Resourcing	173
		6.7.5	Other Considerations	173
		6.7.6	Outputs for the Project Brief	176
	6.8	Governance, Sign-Off and Project Initiation		176
		6.8.1	What Are We Seeking to Achieve?	176
		6.8.2	Governance Arrangements	177
		6.8.3	Outputs for the Project Brief	177
	6.9	Implications for Other Planning Typologies		178
	6.10	Summary		181
		6.10.1	Insights	182
	References			186

7	**Gathering the Evidence**		187
	7.1	Introduction	187
		7.1.1 Warm-Up Exercise	188
	7.2	Purpose of Step 2	188
	7.3	Principal Activities	189
		7.3.1 First Nations and Research and Analysis	190
	7.4	Finalising the Research Briefs	192
		7.4.1 Research Briefs	192
		7.4.2 Research Activities	193
		7.4.3 Research Methods	194
		7.4.4 Approach for Each Research Area	195
	7.5	Community Engagement Activities	201
		7.5.1 Purpose of the Engagement Activities	201
		7.5.2 Approach and General Considerations	202
		7.5.3 Coordinating the Activities	202
	7.6	Coordinating the Research Initiatives	203
	7.7	Distilling the Research Findings into Narratives	204
	7.8	Implications for Other Planning Typologies	205
	7.9	Summary	205
		7.9.1 Insights	206
	References		211
8	**Synthesis and Direction Setting**		213
	8.1	Introduction	213
		8.1.1 Warm-Up Exercise	214
	8.2	Purpose of Step 3	214
		8.2.1 Principal Activities	214
	8.3	Synthesis of the Research Findings	217
		8.3.1 Principal Activities	217
		8.3.2 Integration and Interdependencies	219
		8.3.3 First Nations and Synthesis and Direction Setting	221
		8.3.4 The Importance of Narratives	223
	8.4	Scenario Development and Evaluation	224
		8.4.1 The Evaluation Process	224
		8.4.2 The Multi-Criteria Analysis Method	227
		8.4.3 The Base Case: Business as Usual	228
		8.4.4 Importance of the Growth and Change Equation	229
		8.4.5 An Evaluation Framework	230
		8.4.6 Net Community Benefit	233
	8.5	Scenario Typologies	234
		8.5.1 Housing Scenarios	234
		8.5.2 Employment Scenarios	235
		8.5.3 Transport Scenarios	236
	8.6	Direction Setting	237
		8.6.1 Directions (Objectives) Setting	237

		8.6.2	A Vision Statement	240
	8.7		Implications for other planning typologies	243
	8.8		Summary	244
		8.8.1	Insights	245
	References			248
9	**Preparation of a Draft Plan**			251
	9.1	Introduction		251
		9.1.1	Warm-Up Exercise	252
	9.2	Purpose of Step 4		252
	9.3	Principal Activities		252
		9.3.1	Phase 1: Plan Development	253
		9.3.2	Phase 2: Plan Refinement	255
		9.3.3	Phase 3: Sign-Off and Exhibition Ready	256
		9.3.4	First Nations and Preparation of a Draft Plan	258
		9.3.5	Supporting Activities	258
	9.4	Report Role, Structure and Content		258
		9.4.1	Core Plan Elements	262
		9.4.2	Optional Plan Elements	262
	9.5	The Structure Plan		264
	9.6	Finalising Objectives and Strategies		266
		9.6.1	A Hypothetical Sequence of Thinking, from Findings to Objectives	266
		9.6.2	A Worked Example	267
	9.7	Development of Actions		268
	9.8	Implications for Other Planning Typologies		270
	9.9	Summary		270
		9.9.1	Insights	272
	Further Reading			273
10	**Exhibition and a Final Plan**			275
	10.1	Introduction		275
		10.1.1	Warm-Up Exercise	275
	10.2	Step 5: Exhibition of a Draft Plan		276
		10.2.1	Purpose of Step 5	276
		10.2.2	Principal Activities	277
		10.2.3	First Nations and Exhibition	277
		10.2.4	Pre-exhibition: A Community Engagement Plan	279
		10.2.5	The Exhibition: Eliciting Submissions	282
	10.3	Step 6: Plan Finalisation		283
		10.3.1	Purpose of Step 6	283
		10.3.2	Principal Activities	283
		10.3.3	First Nations and Plan Finalisation	286
		10.3.4	Submissions	286
		10.3.5	Finalising the Plan	287
		10.3.6	Annual Monitoring and Reporting	289

	10.4	Implications for Other Planning Typologies	290
	10.5	Summary	291
		10.5.1 Insights	292
	Further Reading		294
11	**Plan Delivery and Ongoing Planning**		**295**
	11.1	Introduction	295
		11.1.1 Warm-Up Exercise	296
	11.2	Purpose of Step 7	296
	11.3	Principal Activities	297
		11.3.1 Plan Delivery—Principal Activities	297
		11.3.2 Ongoing Research—Principal Activities	299
		11.3.3 Plan Updates—Principal Activities	300
		11.3.4 First Nations and Plan Delivery and Ongoing Planning	300
	11.4	Implementing the Approved Plan	301
		11.4.1 An Implementation Plan	301
		11.4.2 Plan Delivery	301
		11.4.3 Promoting the Plan	302
		11.4.4 Strategic Alignment	302
	11.5	An Ongoing Strategic Planning Process	303
		11.5.1 Book of Knowledge	304
		11.5.2 Ongoing Research	306
		11.5.3 Ongoing Engagement	307
		11.5.4 Targeted Policy Review and Updating Plans	308
	11.6	Implications for Other Planning Typologies	308
	11.7	Summary	309
		11.7.1 Insights	310
	References		311
12	**City Planning Typologies**		**313**
	12.1	Introduction	313
		12.1.1 Warm-Up Exercise	314
	12.2	Local Government Area Planning	314
		12.2.1 Purpose	314
		12.2.2 Spatial Planning	315
		12.2.3 Research Framework	316
		12.2.4 Growth and Change Equation	317
		12.2.5 Community Engagement	318
		12.2.6 Levers for Change	318
		12.2.7 Governance	319
	12.3	Town Centre Planning	319
		12.3.1 Purpose	319
		12.3.2 Spatial Planning	320
		12.3.3 Project Establishment	322
		12.3.4 Research Framework	322

		12.3.5	Growth and Change Equation	324
		12.3.6	Scenarios and Evaluation	324
		12.3.7	Draft Plan Elements	325
		12.3.8	Community Engagement	325
		12.3.9	Levers of Change	326
		12.3.10	Governance	326
	12.4	New Greenfield Community Planning		327
		12.4.1	Purpose	327
		12.4.2	Spatial Planning	327
		12.4.3	Research Framework	328
		12.4.4	Growth and Change Equation	329
		12.4.5	Temporal Considerations	329
		12.4.6	Draft Plan Elements	330
		12.4.7	Community Engagement	330
		12.4.8	Levers of Change	331
		12.4.9	Governance	331
	12.5	Neighbourhood Community Planning		331
		12.5.1	The Challenge	331
		12.5.2	Purpose	332
		12.5.3	Project Establishment	332
		12.5.4	Spatial planning	333
		12.5.5	Research Framework	333
		12.5.6	Growth and Change Equation	334
		12.5.7	Direction Setting	334
		12.5.8	Community Engagement	336
		12.5.9	Levers of Change	336
		12.5.10	Governance	336
		12.5.11	The Plan	337
	12.6	Summary of Approaches to Research		337
	12.7	Summary		340
	Reference			340

Part III The 12 Research Areas

13	Part A: The People and the Place			343
	13.1	Introduction		343
	13.2	Characteristics of People and Households		343
		13.2.1	Demographic Profiles	343
		13.2.2	Household Characteristics	344
	13.3	Socio-economic Characteristics		345
		13.3.1	Research Considerations	345
		13.3.2	Research Objectives	345
		13.3.3	Approaches to Research	346
	13.4	Characteristics of Places and Country		346
		13.4.1	Land Use Activities and Transport Networks	346

		13.4.2	Physiography and Climatic Conditions	348
		13.4.3	Country	349
	13.5	City Setting		350
		13.5.1	Research Consideration	350
	13.6	Summary		351
	References			351
14	Part B: Needs of People and Business			353
	14.1	Introduction		353
	14.2	Needs of People and Households		353
		14.2.1	Improving the Level of Housing Choice	353
		14.2.2	Enabling the Financial and Economic Independence of Households	357
		14.2.3	Enabling the Economic Self-Determination of First Nations Communities	360
		14.2.4	Urban Amenity: Improving the Level of Access to Goods, Services and Jobs	362
		14.2.5	Improving the Health of Individuals and Communities	365
		14.2.6	Reducing the Cost of Living	367
	14.3	Quality of Life		368
		14.3.1	Improving Individual and Community Wellbeing	368
		14.3.2	Enabling Cultural and Artistic Expression, Participation and Appreciation	370
		14.3.3	Providing Access to Natural and Developed Public Places	372
		14.3.4	Protecting the Physical Amenity of Homes	374
	14.4	Needs of Businesses		375
		14.4.1	Enabling Businesses to Grow, Flourish and Innovate	375
		14.4.2	The Economy and Spatial Economic Structure	376
		14.4.3	Protecting the Physical Amenity of Businesses	377
		14.4.4	Transport and Telecommunication Access to Support Business Activities	378
		14.4.5	Protecting Natural Resources	379
	14.5	The Growth and Change Equation		380
		14.5.1	Population and Demographics	380
		14.5.2	Dwellings	382
		14.5.3	Commercial Activities	384
		14.5.4	Industrial Development	384
		14.5.5	Retail	385
		14.5.6	Offices	387
		14.5.7	Health and Education Precincts	389
		14.5.8	Agriculture and Mining Activities	390
		14.5.9	The Growth and Change Equation	390

		14.6	Summary	391
		References		391
15	Part C: Qualities and Performance of Place			393
	15.1	Introduction		393
	15.2	Accessibility, Transport and Digital Performance		393
		15.2.1	Transport Network Performance	394
		15.2.2	Transport Service Provision	397
		15.2.3	Trade Gateways and Freight	399
		15.2.4	Digital Coverage and Performance	400
		15.2.5	City Structure—Spatial Equity and Mode Choice	401
		15.2.6	The City in its Region	403
	15.3	Qualities of Places		404
		15.3.1	A Sense of Place and Community	404
		15.3.2	First Nations Country, Community and Culture	405
		15.3.3	Post-European Contact Heritage	407
		15.3.4	Quality, Aesthetics (Beauty) and Amenity	408
		15.3.5	Healthy Natural Systems	411
		15.3.6	Responding to Climate Change	412
		15.3.7	City Hinterlands	416
	15.4	Urban/Suburban Communities		417
		15.4.1	Urban Infrastructure	417
		15.4.2	Natural Hazard Risks	418
		15.4.3	Choice in Local Neighbourhoods	420
		15.4.4	Adaptation, Change and Innovation	421
	15.5	City Design		422
		15.5.1	Introduction	422
		15.5.2	A Definition	424
		15.5.3	City Design Scope	424
		15.5.4	Understanding Place	425
	15.6	Summary		427
	References			427
Afterword				429
Index				433

List of Figures

Fig. 1.1	Overview of the chapters	6
Fig. 2.1	Cities and specialisation: choice	22
Fig. 3.1	Land use and transport, two sides of one coin	68
Fig. 4.1	The three-part strategic planning research framework	87
Fig. 4.2	City planning at the intersection of people and place	88
Fig. 4.3	Positive and negative experiences when walking in the public domain	100
Fig. 4.4	Eleven intervention levers for city planning	106
Fig. 5.1	Principal insights	117
Fig. 5.2	A conceptual framework for a 7-step strategic planning process	118
Fig. 5.3	The relationship between the fundamental elements and the 7-Step Strategic Planning Process	119
Fig. 5.4	Project management triangle	139
Fig. 6.1	Project establishment: A highly iterative process	160
Fig. 6.2	The project brief: inputs and outputs pivot off the problem statement	161
Fig. 6.3	Governance layers	178
Fig. 7.1	Step 2: Research and analysis: principal activities	191
Fig. 8.1	Step 3: Integrating the findings and setting the direction: principal activities	216
Fig. 8.2	Integrating the findings	217
Fig. 8.3	Overlay of economic data sets for Greater Sydney	222
Fig. 8.4	Integrating themes - understanding housing #1 - housing development data	225
Fig. 8.5	Integrating themes: a housing narrative	226
Fig. 8.6	Population changes over time for selected local government areas across Melbourne	230
Fig. 8.7	The decline of the Victorian Plains Grasslands, pre 1780–2005	231
Fig. 8.8	Plan on a page: greater Sydney region plan	239
Fig. 8.9	Vision diagram from the City of Casey's 2002 strategy Casey C21: a vision for the future	242
Fig. 9.1	Step 4: Preparing the draft plan: Principal activities	253

Fig. 9.2	Structure Plan for Greater Sydney	263
Fig. 9.3	Presentation options: Stylistic and accurately showing the transport network	265
Fig. 10.1	Step 5: Exhibition: Reaching out	278
Fig. 10.2	Step 6: Plan finalisation: Principal activities	284
Fig. 11.1	An ongoing strategic planning framework: from plans to planning	298
Fig. 11.2	Step 7: Plan delivery	299
Fig. 11.3	Strategic alignment of delivery activities	303
Fig. 11.4	Building the book of knowledge	304
Fig. 12.1	Convergence of community and government activities: Action delivery model	335
Fig. 12.2	Doveton/Eumemmerring neighbourhood renewal: management framework	338
Fig. 12.3	Summary of typical research areas for differing city planning typologies	339
Fig. 14.1	Accessibility: The intersection of a three-way tussle	362

List of Tables

Table 3.1	Basic chronological framework of Australian metropolitan planning	47
Table 3.2	The emergence of planning interventions since the 1880s across the globe	53
Table 3.3	Australian and international metropolitan plans: Variability in content	60
Table 3.4	Planning objectives as outlined in NSW and Victorian legislation	64
Table 3.5	Common policy issues across contemporary Australian capital city plans	66
Table 3.6	Policy themes across four international metropolitan plans	69
Table 6.1	Applying Step 1 to other planning typologies	179
Table 7.1	Part 1: Overview of research activities	196
Table 7.2	Part 2: Overview of research activities	197
Table 7.3	Part 3: Overview of research activities	199
Table 7.4	Planning for places: issues for consideration	201
Table 7.5	Applying the Step 2 approach to other planning typologies	204
Table 8.1	Nomenclature of capital city plans	238
Table 8.2	Nomenclature of international plans	238
Table 8.3	Applying the Step 3 approach to other planning typologies	243
Table 9.1	Principal elements of capital city plans across Australia	260
Table 9.2	Principal elements of four international metropolitan plans	261
Table 9.3	Applying Step 4 to other planning typologies	271
Table 10.1	Capital city comparison: Monitoring and reporting	290
Table 10.2	Applying the Step 5 and Step 6 approach to other planning typologies	291
Table 11.1	Applying Step 7 to other planning typologies	308
Table 12.1	Applicability of research areas to the planning areas for local government areas	316

Table 12.2	Applicability of research areas to various spatial considerations for town centres	321
Table 15.1	Assessment of the scope of climate change issues addressed in capital city plans	413
Table 15.2	Variability of wording for common issues in the capital city plans	414
Table 15.3	Assessment of the scope of climate change metrics addressed in capital city plans.	415
Table 15.4	Comparative assessment of the approach to design for Australia's capital cities plans	423

About the Author

Halvard Dalheim has more than three decades of experience as a strategic planner covering state and local government and the private sector, including roles as an executive in the NSW and Victorian government planning departments and the then Greater Sydney Commission.

During his time in state government Halvard led metropolitan plans for Greater Sydney and Melbourne. Most recently he led the development of the Greater Sydney Region Plan, *A Metropolis of Three Cities*. Halvard's experience in spatial planning also includes regional, growth area and town centre plans across NSW, Victoria, Queensland and Tasmania.

Halvard's collaborative approach to strategic planning has been acknowledged by his peers—in Victoria he received the Department of Transport's inaugural award for an external stakeholder for '*inspirational contribution to the work and people of the Department of Transport*'.

Recently Halvard has participated in expert panels for the planning of Ho Chi Minh City in Vietnam.

In 2020, Halvard established his consultancy, with a focus on executive leadership in city planning and building strategic planning capacity across the planning field. He is also an Adjunct Associate Professor in the School of Architecture, Design and Planning at the University of Sydney, where he regularly teaches.

HALVARD DALHEIM

Introduction 1

I begin by acknowledging the Traditional Owners of the land on which I sit and write this book, the Dja Dja Wurrung people and pay my respects to Elders past and present.

I also acknowledge the learnings I have gained from my reflections on First Nations peoples' approach to planning, the complexity and intent behind how they engaged and continue to engage with Country. Our first planners.

1.1 City Planning Context

Before starting the journey of strategic (or city) planning it is worthwhile providing some context to the task, including:

- A brief introduction as to what strategic planning for cities really means;
- The important underlying notion that there is no end state for a city—change is the only constant;
- The view that strategic planning is undertaken at various spatial geographies, not just a whole metropolitan area;
- The concept that strategic planning for cities, as a discipline, is generally universal across jurisdictions worldwide and
- The context, that despite at least 65,000 years of Aboriginal and Torres Strait Islander occupation in Australia, there is generally little reflection of this in city plans.

1.1.1 The Nature of Strategic Planning

This book outlines the process of strategic planning to develop a city plan. My approach to understanding and thinking about strategic planning is influenced by the learnings I gained during my first decade of planning working for Dr. Jeff Wolinski. He instilled in me that the process of strategic planning is quite different from the processes behind development approvals (statutory planning).

Statutory planning starts with a set of rules where the purpose is to assess a development proposal against those rules and determine whether the proposal should be approved.

In comparison, strategic planning is a process to determine if we should change the rules or make other interventions to set a course for an alternate future, which may allow different types of development.

In this context, Dr. Wolinski had a clear view of strategic planning that I have carried with me throughout my career; and, in the context of lifelong learning, I have sought to enhance the narrative he first put forward.

Thus, for those looking for a simple description of the nature of strategic planning, I present the following:

> Strategic planning is a pattern of decision-making aimed at optimally allocating limited resources to achieve social, economic, environmental and amenity objectives.
>
> Strategic planning requires engagement with the community and a collaborative process across all levels of government.
>
> Strategic planning requires a systems analysis and evaluation process.
>
> Strategic planning implies the selection of a pathway/s or sequence/s of actions.
>
> Strategic planning implies knowledge of intended outcomes, which raises the need for the concept of benchmarking.
>
> Strategic planning requires an implementation framework.

1.1.2 Cities—Where Change Is the Constant

A fundamental assumption when embarking on strategic planning—one that is not always recognised—is that strategic planning is not seeking to achieve some utopian end state. Instead, strategic planning seeks to identify a range of actions that can move the trajectory of a city away from a business-as-usual future towards a future more aligned with the aspirations of the community in terms of how they live, work and play, while at the same time respecting the intrinsic value of the places on which our cities now stand.

This question of continual improvement is emphasised by Alexander Garvin in the preface to his book—*What Makes a Great City*—where he emphasises "… a great city, unlike a great painting or sculpture, is not an exquisite, completed artefact" (Garvin 2016, p. xxii).

1.1 City Planning Context

Further, Garvin (2016, p. 11) points out that:

> Remaining a great city depends on people continuing to want to be there, to enjoy being there, and to remain there, and that depends on **continuing** to make improvements to the public realm – improvements that meet the needs of future generations. (Author's emphasis)

Jacobs (1995, p. 6) also emphasises the notion of continual change in his work of understanding great streets. He highlights how streets continually change over time, such as repaving and new landscaping or they are reshaped due to upgrades to underground services.

The significance of this ongoing evolution forms the central tenet of why I advocate that the last step in strategic planning is to establish a deliberative process for ongoing monitoring, research, review, and updating a plan. This is outlined in Chapter 11.

1.1.3 Typology of City Plans

There are several different types of city plans. Their typology generally reflects the focus and activities of governments in managing growth and change in cities and regions. The typologies include:

- **Metropolitan plans**, which, in Australia, include the capital cities plus larger regional cities. Australia's metropolitan areas generally incorporate many local government areas; consequently, to ensure a coordinated view across several councils, planning is a state government-led activity.
- **Regional city plans**, which vary in size. Compared to metropolitan areas regional cities are, in the main, covered by a single local government area.
- **Whole of local government area plans**, which vary in size, both spatially and in terms of population. They also vary in land use activities, which could include substantial rural areas for fringe councils or significant employment areas.
- **Town centre plans** that have been, in Australia's capital cities, a focus for planning policy since the first plans for capital cities 70 years ago.
- **New greenfield community plans,** often led by state governments due to the high need for state-funded infrastructure.
- **Neighbourhood community plans,** a fusion of local land use planning with community development activities and often at the spatial geography of a suburb.
- **Urban renewal plans**, a substantial element of managing growth and change in major cities.

The approach for preparing these different city plans is generally in line with a metropolitan plan; however, aspects of each typology warrant consideration. Chapter 12 addresses the issues of difference for each city planning typology.

The important message here is that the proposed 7-Step Strategic Planning Process is scalable to each of these typologies.

1.1.4 Jurisdictional Context

As a framework for the strategic planning of cities, this book can be adapted to the local jurisdictional context of any city.

This recognises that planning systems differ significantly across Australia, let alone the world. Despite this, the approach to strategic planning is generally universal across Western countries. Stein (2017, p. 8), in his exposé on urban land use planning activities across the globe, states that "Western countries or those with a Western institutional history have all developed, with local variations, a strategic planning system based on a similar logical, structured hierarchy."

The scope of this book reflects my experience in strategic planning across multiple jurisdictions in Australia. To address the question of the universal applicability of the 7-Step Strategic Planning Process, as outlined in Part II, I have undertaken a comparative assessment of contemporary strategic planning, specifically looking at case studies of:

- contemporary plans for Australia's capital cities (Sect. 3.5.2); and
- four international contemporary plans: Greater Toronto (Greater Golden Horseshoe), London, Metro Vancouver, and New York City (Sect. 3.5.3).

The comparative assessments are referenced through the textbook, in the areas of:

- Common themes—Sect. 3.5.2 and 3.5.3;
- Nomenclature of plans Sect 8.7.1
- Principal elements of a plan—Sect. 9.4;
- Monitoring and reporting—Sect. 10.3.5;
- Climate change—Sect. 15.3.6; and
- City design—Sect. 15.5.

1.1.5 First Nations Heritage, Culture and Country

Plans for Australia's capital cities are only now acknowledging Aboriginal and Torres Strait Islander people, the First Nations people of Australia—a people who have cared for the Country for more than 2,500 generations before Europeans arrived only nine generations ago.

In responding to First Nations Country, community and culture in city planning, we have a long way to go. The Australian Bureau of Statistics' Catalogue number 3105.0.65.001 *Australian Historical Population Statistics* has the population of Australia in 1788 as 859 people, **even though research suggests the First Nations population at the time was approximately 1.0 million people** (Smith 2002).

Moreover, the recognition of First Nations people as citizens was not finally enshrined in Australian law until 1984 when First Nations people gained full equality with other electors and were required to enrol and vote at elections (refer National Museum Australia website).

Effective planning for First Nations issues starts with a dialogue and engagement and, importantly, ongoing dialogue and engagement—a partnership. Critically, it must also include learning to see the world (Country) in a different way and actioning responses that reflect the issues raised.

This book is intended to continue the emerging response of city planning and First Nations people. In Australia, this requires a more overt recognition of the significance of First Nations culture and the First Nations peoples' relationship with Country. This should lead the built environment industry valuing First Nations Knowledges and perspectives in their work to achieve more respectful and informed decisions for our future.

1.2 Content Overview

This book is structured so the reader can focus on elements relevant to their day-to-day activities in strategic planning or in their role as an educator. There are 15 chapters presented across three parts (Fig. 1.1). Each chapter also includes a further reading section.

1.2.1 Part I: Why and How to Plan Cities

Part I provides a conceptual framework for why we plan cities, and what needs to be considered when we undertake strategic planning. This leads to the 7-Step Strategic Planning Process. These issues are covered in four chapters.

- **Chapter 2: What are great cities?** This chapter describes the elements that make a great city and the attributes, setting the scene for our aspirations as we going about planning better cities.
- **Chapter 3: What is planning about?** Planning is said to be about intervention (Gurran 2011). However, to establish a structured approach to city planning, we need greater clarity as to why intervention is required compared to the simple economic mantra of addressing negative externalities. This chapter explores interventions in cities through the ages. It shows that a more considered view of the rationale for intervention can be established, raising the question of the scope of planning. The chapter concludes with a discussion on the scope of planning, including some drivers of change in cities that have emerged over the last 20 years.
- **Chapter 4: The purpose of strategic planning.** This chapter builds on the findings of Chapter 3 by examining the purpose of city planning. It draws on the premise that if planning is about intervention, then the underlying purpose of strategic planning must be to determine whether a future based on business-as-usual activities (existing planning regulations and government commitments) is acceptable to the community, now and in the future. Moreover, understanding business as usual implies the need to understand what is acceptable to people, their lives and the places they live in, now and in the future. The chapter then

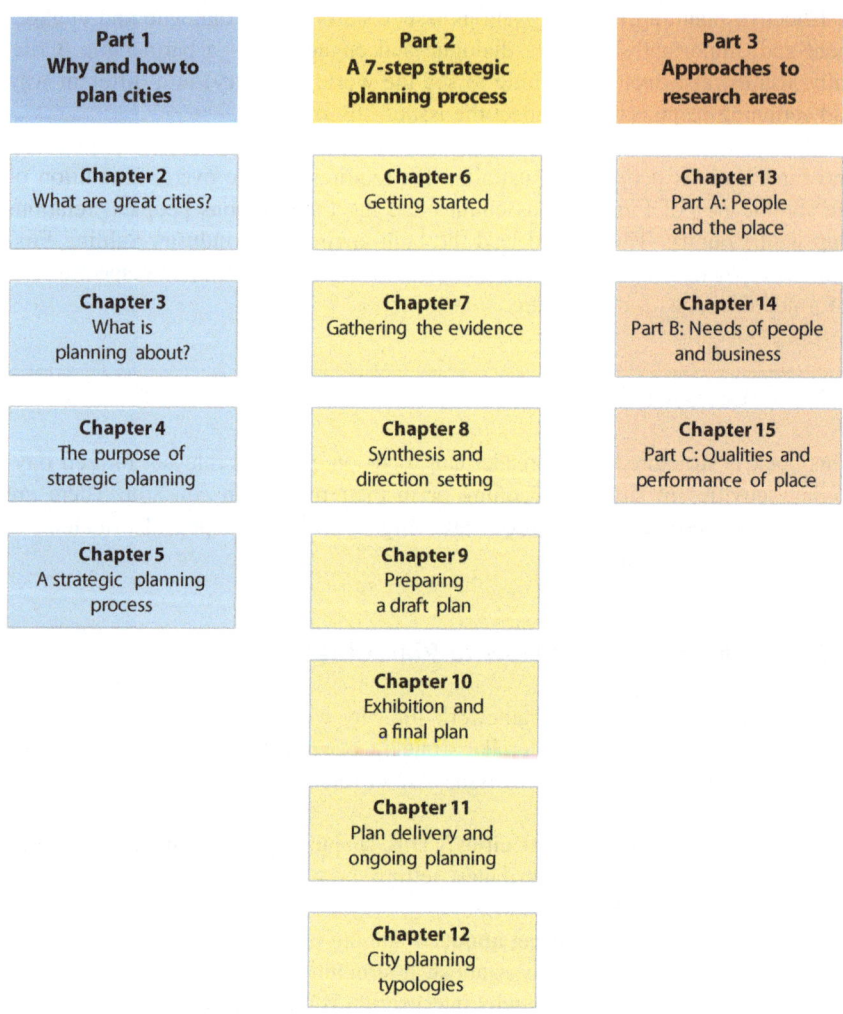

Fig. 1.1 Overview of the chapters

explores the implications of answering questions such as what we mean by the needs of the community, the future and an achievable vision.
- **Chapter 5: A strategic planning process.** This chapter is in two parts. The first brings together the insights from Chapters 3 and 4 and uses a series of conceptual frameworks to build the rationale for the 7-Step Strategic Planning Process. The second part examines common threads and considerations that underpin or flow through all the activities of the 7-Step Strategic Planning Process, including planning systems, community and stakeholder engagement, politics and planning, planning and decision-making, confidentiality, project management, First Nations Country, community and culture, sustainability, complexity and a systems view of planning, and the challenge of change.

1.2 Content Overview

1.2.2 Part II: A 7-Step Strategic Planning Process

Part II is the core of the book. It outlines how to go about the strategic planning process required to develop a city plan. Each of the six chapters uses a similar structure that outlines the purpose, principal activities, and issues for consideration for each step in the 7-Step Strategic Planning Process.

With Chapters 6 through 11 relating to the strategic planning process to prepare a metropolitan plan, an additional chapter addresses how the process can be adapted to respond to differing city planning typologies.

- **Chapter 6: Getting Started (Step 1)**. Before embarking on a strategic planning project, it is beneficial to have a plan for tackling the task. This chapter examines the range of considerations and pre-planning required. While the purpose of Step 1 is to write the project brief, the examination of the issues reveals that this step requires 10 distinct tasks. Completing each is an iterative and integrated process.
- **Chapter 7: Gathering the evidence (Step 2)**. The quality of research and the evidence obtained has a major influence on the quality of a plan. This chapter gets to the heart of the research and analysis phase and details areas such as preparing research briefs, undertaking research, commencing community engagement, and the challenging task of coordinating research activities.
- **Chapter 8: Synthesis and setting directions (Step 3)**. Synthesis is often categorised as being about a SWOT analysis (strengths, weaknesses, opportunities and threats) but it is much more. Synthesis is a journey towards strategic directions and a vision, which requires a deliberative approach that includes identifying interdependencies and choices. The chapter examines the three principal activities of synthesising research findings, developing and evaluating scenarios, and setting directions.
- **Chapter 9: Preparing a draft plan (Step 4)**. The purpose of Step 4, in one sense, is simple—preparing a draft plan for exhibition. This step begins with plan development, which extends the direction setting activities and includes developing a report structure, creating a structure plan; finalising objectives and strategies; and developing actions. These activities are then refined, and a preliminary implementation plan is developed. Finally, we need to prepare to place the plan on public exhibition, a substantial task requiring formal sign-off.
- **Chapter 10: Exhibition and a final plan (Steps 5 and 6)**. Step 5 focuses on engaging with the community to seek their participation and feedback. The feedback informs Step 6, which is about finalising and releasing an approved plan that clarifies a delivery approach that will ensure the plan is implemented.
- **Chapter 11: Plan delivery and ongoing planning (Step 7)**. Typically, the release of the final plan marks the end of the strategic planning process. Experience suggests that implementation is enhanced when there is a final step directed at embedding the implementation activities into the day-to-day activities of the relevant delivery agencies. Furthermore, the dynamic nature of cities and the impacts of unforeseen events such as the Global Financial Crisis or the

COVID-19 pandemic suggests that the concept of city plans being prepared at a single point in time is insufficient to meet the needs and aspirations of the community. This chapter addresses these issues.
- **Chapter 12: City planning typologies**. Strategic planning activities occur at multiple spatial geographies from a metropolitan area to a town centre. This chapter examines how to adapt the 7-Step Strategic Planning Process for differing spatial geographies or city planning typologies. It examines four typologies: local government area plans, town centre plans (including regional city plans), new greenfield community plans and neighbourhood community plans.

1.2.3 Part III: Approaches to Research

A major innovation in the 7-Step Strategic Planning Process is the introduction of the Strategic Planning Research Framework, which seeks to provide structure to the task of investigating and understanding the dynamics and attributes of a city. Part III provides detail on the methodological approach for each of the 42 research topics across 12 research areas, with a focus on outlining research considerations, research objectives and approaches to research in each case.

The intent is not to provide a detailed methodology for each research topic; rather, it is to provide a sufficient understanding of why each research topic is important and what needs to be the focus of the investigation. This information is provided as the foundation to directly undertake research or enhance the practitioner's ability to engage with specialists and communicate the specific needs of individual projects.

The Strategic Planning Research Framework has three parts, each includes four research areas.

- **Part A: People and the place** (Chapter 13) covers six research topics in the research areas of:
  – characteristics of people and households;
  – socio-economic characteristics;
  – characteristics of places and Country; and
  – city setting.
- **Part B: People and business** (Chapter 14) covers 19 research topics in the research areas of:
  – needs of people and households;
  – quality of life;
  – needs of businesses; and
  – growth and change equation.
- **Part C: Qualities and performance of place** (Chapter 15) covers 17 research topics in the research areas of:
  – transport and digital accessibility and performance;
  – qualities of places;

- urban and suburban communities; and
- city design.

1.2.4 Insights and Case Examples

As I began noting my insights into the learnings from the planning projects I had undertaken in my career, I also shared the notes with Marcus Spiller, a nationally recognised urban economist. Marcus suggested that a practical handbook for strategic planners was missing as a resource for planners.

That is the foundation of this book on strategic planning for planners. I feel that many of the original notes are of practical use to students of planning; consequently, my original insights appear at the end of each relevant chapter, primarily in Part II. For ease of recognition, they are boxed to differentiate them from the narrative of each section.

In addition, through the book, I have included small snapshots of working case studies from my experience in day-to-day strategic planning. They are indented and italicised.

1.3 Definition

Planning, as with most professions, has its own set of jargon and common phrases that may not be seen as plain English.

1.3.1 Definitions

To assist the reader some of the principal words and phrases used in this book include:

- *Aboriginal people*: Refer to First Nations people.
- *Base case*: When looking at scenarios as part of an options assessment or modelling process, the base case is the business-as-usual option against which other options are evaluated.
- *Benchmarking*: This is the process of measuring the performance of an outcome, such as vehicles per dwelling, which usually requires the establishment of a base position or aspiration to measure against.
- Blue-green grid: A more recent phrase in planning to describe the network of waterways (blue) and linear open space (green). Embedding this approach is part of responding to Country in strategic planning.
- *Business as usual*: These are the activities in a city that occur under current planning rules and within the current commitments of a government (such as building a specific road).

- *Cadastre*: Refers to a map that outlines land titles, roads and often railway lines. The level of detail included generally reflects the scale of an area. For example, a town centre plan would include title information, whereas a metropolitan plan would not.
- *Capital city names*: When describing the capital cities of Melbourne and Sydney, the nomenclature used for Sydney is 'Greater Sydney'. This reflects how the city is described in its government approved plan and, more importantly, acknowledges that the community of Western Sydney does not perceive that 'Sydney' sufficiently covers their perception of their community. Reference to Melbourne refers to the whole metropolitan area. For both cities, the area assumed reflects the area as outlined in their metropolitan plan.

For the other capital cities, the names used reflect those in the approved plans such as Perth and Peel for the greater Perth area and South East Queensland (SEQ), which covers a greater Brisbane area extending to the Sunshine Coast in the north, Gold Coast in the south and to Toowoomba in the west.

- *Centre* (activity centre, town centre): This is usually a place where a range of commercial, community and government activities are co-located, typically clustered around a concentration of retail activities. Surprisingly, there is not a standard nomenclature for such a place as often scale, geographic location—city versus regional—and type—internalised mall versus main street—results in different terminology.
- *Circular economy*: This is about decoupling economic growth from virgin resource use. The circular design of products, services and systems keep resources in the market longer, enabling sharing and reuse business models to become business as usual.
- *Clean (dark) pipes*: This new expression means an empty conduit installed to allow digital cables to be threaded into the conduit later.
- *Country*: First Nations people see the environment, people and stories as intrinsically connected. Country refers to the natural systems of the land, water and skies that bind us together, which humans rely on to live and function.
- *Crosstabs*: This expression relates to the analysis of two data sets. For planning, it is often about analysing data sets from the Australian Bureau of Statistics' Census.
- *Dark restaurant*: A restaurant that prepares meals, which are then supplied to customers via a courier service, thus there are no customers at the restaurant itself.
- *Decision-maker*: In the context of writing a metropolitan plan, the decision-maker is usually the planning minister, though it could be a Cabinet committee or full Cabinet. In local government, it would be the mayor, council or a committee. This book uses decision-makers to emphasise decisions of the elected official of government (local, state or federal).
- *Districts*: Several capital city plans divide the metropolitan area into districts or sub-regions. This book uses the term 'district'.

1.3 Definition

- *First Nations*: Throughout this book the term First Nations is used as an inclusive term to cover both Aboriginal and Torres Strait Islander peoples of Australia. Exceptions are when quoting text from another source or as part of a formal heading such as Aboriginal Land Councils.
- *Footloose knowledge worker*: Richard Florida's research and publication of the Creative Class talks about a new type of worker who is not bound to one place or one employer—they are footloose and will move to the area that best fulfils their work and lifestyle needs.
- *Governance of metropolitan areas*: In Australia, metropolitan areas are managed by multiple local governments. For example, in Melbourne and Greater Sydney, there are more than 30 in each case.
- *Greenfield/broadacre development*: Refers to undeveloped land, generally rural in nature and on the fringe of a city that is developed for urban purposes. This is sometimes called broadacre land.
- *Green infrastructure*: Refers to natural features which are utilised as part of the infrastructure to support a city and often linked to resilience planning and includes elements such as the urban tree canopy as a mitigation against heat.
- *Growth and change equation*: I have developed this equation to express the land use and population changes that need to be accommodated when planning for a city or place (refer to Sect. 4.3.8).
- *Infill development*: Redevelopment of an existing development generally occurs on a site-by-site basis in an ad hoc manner driven by the landowner.
- *Land banking*: This describes a process by which land, that is ready for development, is held for development later.
- *Marchetti's constant*: This is the average time spent commuting each day. Through the ages, up to the beginning of the industrial revolution, it had been relatively constant at one hour.
- *Precinct (structure) plan*: Strategic plans for different types of areas have different terminology in different state jurisdictions. For a greenfield area, a plan for a new suburb in NSW is a precinct plan, whereas in Victoria it is a precinct structure plan. These names change over time—for example, when I prepared my first such plan in Victoria 30 years ago, they were called local structure plans.
- *Predict and provide*: This phrase reflects the approach for modelling transport outcomes, where the focus is to assess new options against current circumstances. The alternative is the vision and validate method, which starts with a transport structure to support a long-term vision that is then delivered by reverse engineering the desired outcome.
- *Principal stakeholders*: The organisations, agencies, peak bodies and community groups that have a direct 'stake' in a plan's preparation according to its scope and objectives. As the scope and objectives change for each project, so does the list of principal stakeholders.
- *Social housing*: Housing provided by a government for low-income households, also referred to as public housing

- *Structure plan*: The principal element of a city plan. A spatial plan that outlines the principal spatial outcomes, thus highlighting their interrelationships. Each Australian planning jurisdiction has its own preferences as to which terminology reflects what type of plan.
- *Sweating the asset*: A term utilised in infrastructure planning which denotes that the utility of an infrastructure asset should be maximised before consideration of building new infrastructure.
- *SWOT analysis* (strengths, weaknesses, opportunities, and threats): An evaluation technique used to synthesise the principal issues arising from research and analysis.
- *Torres Strait Islander people*: refer to First Nations people.
- *Urban renewal*: The redevelopment of an area, as distinct from a single parcel, where the redevelopment is generally in line with a strategic plan.
- *Viewsheds*: What people can see from a public area (generally), which may warrant planning protection.
- *Vision and validate*: A method that starts with a transport structure to support a long-term vision, then is achieved by reverse engineering the desired outcome.
- *Word clouds*: A concept that has emerged with the use of social media tools to evaluate single-word responses to issues. Word clouds calculate how often a word is used and creates a 'cloud' of the words, where the size of each word reflects how often it was referenced. As discussed in Sect. 10.3.3.2, word clouds can be visually compelling, but often do not relate to a valid sample and can thus distort perceptions of what is valued.

In addition:

- There is some repetition across chapters to enable each to be read independently.
- References and website links are provided at the end of each chapter to support independent reading.
- The general commentary throughout the book reflects an Australian context unless otherwise stated.
- There may appear to be a small bias on some matters towards NSW phraseology, which is accidental and purely reflects my most recent working environment. This includes the use of the term 'development approval' (or DA as locally stated) instead of planning permit as used in Victoria.
- There is a small bias when it comes to providing examples, with the focus being Melbourne and Sydney, where I have spent much of my working career. Hence, there is a deliberate attempt to review all the capital city plans across Australia to draw relevant examples from across the country. In addition, four international plans have been reviewed: Greater Toronto (the Greater Golden Horseshoe), London, Metro Vancouver and New York City.

Throughout this book, there are references to the 2018 plan for Greater Sydney, which was prepared by the then Greater Sydney Commission (GCC). More recently their remit has expanded and the organisation is now called the Greater Cities Commission. As relevant, this change in name will be acknowledged.

1.3.2 Acronyms

As in many professions, planners use acronyms. I seek not to as they disempower those outside the planning community. Sometimes glossaries are provided, but often you need to find the original reference to determine the meaning, and this can be difficult. This book does not include acronyms, except for three that I believe are now part of the plain English vocabulary: CBD (Central Business District), NSW (the state of New South Wales, in Australia) and SWOT (the research method which stands for strengths, weaknesses, opportunities and threats).

A couple of times I use one technical acronym—SIDRA. It is an acronym for a traffic engineering software tool used to assess the performance of an intersection. Even though it has been around for my whole career I only recently learnt it stands for Signalised & Unsignalised Intersection Design and Research Aid. As can be expected, it is used in specific circumstances, where its purpose is usually explained.

1.4 Summary

This chapter introduces the reader to the nature of strategic planning, the city planning typologies to which it can be applied and the notion that in cities change is the only constant. An outline of the content and some clarifications regarding terminology is also provided.

The next chapter provides a context in line with the title of this book—*Planning Better Cities, A practical guide*. That is, what is a great city?

References

Garvin, A (2016), *What Makes a Great City*, Island Press Washington DC.
Gurran, N (2011), *Australian Urban Land Use Planning. Principles, Systems and Practice. Second Edition*. Sydney University Press, Australia
Jacobs, AB (1995), *Great Streets*, MIT Press US
Smith, L 2002. *How many people had lived in Australia before it was annexed by the English in 1788?* In G. Briscoe, L. Smith (Eds.). The Aboriginal population revisited, vol. 10. Canberra: Aboriginal History Monograph, 9–15.
— Provides an insight into the First Nations population in Australia in 1788.
Stein, LA (2017), *Comparative Urban Land Use Planning, Best Practice*, Sydney University Press

Website Links

Australian Bureau of Statistics' Catalogue number 3105.0.65.001 *Australian Historical Population Statistics,* Historical population, 2016 | Australian Bureau of Statistics (abs.gov.au).

Ministry for Housing, Communities & Local Government *Plain English guide to the planning system*, Plain English guide to the planning system - GOV.UK (www.gov.uk).

National Museum Australia *Indigenous Australian's right to vote* Indigenous Australians' right to vote | National Museum of Australia (nma.gov.au).

Part I
Why and How to Plan Cities

The policies, regulations and activities of all planning jurisdictions across Australia suggest that governments see the need to influence the outcomes of the market, to best meet the needs of the community and the places they live in now and in the future. A review of metropolitan plans for Greater Toronto (the Greater Golden Horseshoe), London, Metro Vancouver and New York City suggests these jurisdictions also see the benefits of preparing strategic plans for their cities.

Part I builds a case for a framework for the process of strategic planning directed at preparing a plan for a city. If we can articulate why we plan and what planning is about, we should be able to create a common framework for how we approach strategic planning.

This then provides a consistent basis for everyday strategic planning activities, one that can be easily adapted to reflect local considerations and differing spatial geographies.

A consistent framework provides a more robust basis for outlining to the community why a plan is needed, how the task of planning will be approached, what is to be achieved and how it will be achieved.

This is outlined in four chapters:

- Chapter 2: **What are great cities**? Sets the scene to introduce what is special about cities and different perspectives of what a 'great' city means.
- Chapter 3: **What is planning about?** Considers what is special about cities before exploring planning through the ages, specifically since the 1880s when modern planning is considered to have started and assesses contemporary plans for Australian and selected international cities.
- Chapter 4: **The purpose of strategic planning.** Builds on the principal conclusion of Chapter 3, that planning is about intervention to achieve a public good, to establish a structured approach to intervention and whether there are building blocks that can inform a planning framework.
- Chapter 5: **A strategic planning process.** Concludes the investigations of why and how to plan better cities with an outline of the 7-Step Strategic Planning Process, the proposed framework to guide city planning. The chapter also includes discussion of several common threads or considerations that run through the 7-Step Strategic Planning Process.

Part I: Summary

The underlying narrative in Part 1 is that planning is essentially about interventions to achieve a public good, whether that be positive economic, social or environmental outcomes. What has evolved over the last 140 years since the emergence of modern planning is why and how we intervene.

Why we intervene increasingly reflects:

- the demands of the community to enhance or augment the quality of the 'good life' in the face of pressures on cities created by population growth and change
- a recognition of inequities of choice (economic and social), created by long-standing structural differences across our cities
- opportunities to harness market forces to drive change in complex urban locations
- the importance of leaving a positive legacy for the next generation, such as responding to climate change
- the continued need to deal with negative externalities arising from actions of the marketplace
- a recognition that the delivery of basic utilities (from sewer to transport systems) can no longer be 'basic'; they need to meet wider societal objectives reflecting both long-term sustainability objectives and community expectations on expanded definitions of purpose (for example, a road is much more than a space for transporting vehicles).

Contemporary capital city plans in Australia reflect the latest expression of the scope of planning and highlight that there are areas of high commonality and equally some areas that relate to only one city. The issues addressed across all the plans include infrastructure, housing, urban renewal, walkability, heritage, industrial lands, centres, agricultural and mining activities, biodiversity, open space and water.

I argue that interventions should be a response to the question—is a business-as-usual future acceptable, and if not, then is there an alternative that is acceptable, and, importantly, achievable? The answer to these questions needs to reflect what is important to people, their lives and the places they live in, now and in the future.

Determining what is important to people requires a framework that draws from 12 areas, and importantly in the context of issues that influence land use and transport outcomes. They are:

- characteristics of people and households
- socio-economic characteristics
- characteristics of places and Country
- city setting
- needs of people and households
- quality of life
- needs of businesses
- growth and change equation

- transport and digital accessibility and performance
- qualities of places
- needs of urban and suburban communities
- city design.

These considerations are generally directed to the management of places. Planning needs to consider how to define places (such as the extent of the hinterland); what is important when creating places; and what the community values about their place.

With planning for intervention, there is a need to understand delivery. There are 11 types of levers available for planners when addressing the aspirations of the community:

- advocacy
- governance
- policy
- public works
- financial
- investment attraction
- regulation
- targeted research
- business and community development
- asset management
- digital accessibility.

From these considerations, I conclude that there are several fundamental elements or building blocks that need to be included in any strategic planning process. They are:

- clarity in why intervention is required
- evidence
- community participation
- a deliberative and transparent process
- a plan
- an approval process
- a designated delivery agency.

From these elements, I propose the 7-Step Strategic Planning Process.

- Step 1: Project establishment
- Step 2: Research and analysis
- Step 3: Synthesis and direction setting
- Step 4: Draft plan preparation
- Step 5: Exhibition
- Step 6: Plan finalisation

- Step 7: Plan delivery and ongoing planning.

In outlining these seven steps I recognise that there are several common threads or considerations that influence/relate to all the steps from community engagement to project management.

The details of the seven steps are the focus of Part 2.

What Are Great Cities? 2

2.1 Introduction

This book is about planning better cities. Therefore, it's worthwhile, initially, exploring cities and in particular, what makes great cities. What emerges is that there are several dimensions to what makes a great city. For example:

- Hall (1998) examines cities that were the standout city of their time in terms of the quality of what they produced, from commerce to culture.
- Garvin (2016) and Jacobs (1993) examine the features of the city that make it a great place such as the public realm and the streets.
- My own experience, after undertaking strategic planning for more than 100 places (from metropolitan cities to town centres), tells me it is the quality of the accessibility that allows people to work, rest and play that is integral to great cities.
- Communities, however, are not all the same, hence defining what is a great city may need a first step of asking the community what is important to them.

In this context, I note that Giovanni Botero, a sixteenth-century philosopher suggested, against the sentiment of the time, that it was the people of a city, not the built form, that created greatness (Kostof 1992, p. 8).

These differing perspectives are the focus of this chapter, with the discussion also including the activity of scoring cities, leader boards. But first a brief introduction to cities and city form.

2.1.1 Warm-Up Exercise

As you journey through your career as a strategic planner, your political leaders (the decision-makers) will most likely ask, even assume, that your plan will achieve a better city or great place—and rightfully so.

Consequently, there is a good chance you will be asked to define what makes a great city or place.

So, before reading this chapter, jot down a few points on what you think makes a great city or place.

2.2 What Is Special About Cities?

This section provides a brief introduction to cities themselves.

2.2.1 The Emergence of Cities

Mumford's *The City in History* (1961, pp. 11–69) outlines the journey from hunter-gatherer to farmer to urban dweller, a journey that took 10,000 plus years, and with each step, greater specialisation in the activities of daily life. For those interested in learning more of this journey I recommend *After the Ice* by Steven Mithen (2003).

The emergence of agriculture through cropping, animal domestication, food storage (especially the invention of containers) and food processing was a central requirement of moving to a sedentary lifestyle and part of the driving force towards fixed settlements, in villages then towns. Mumford (1961, p. 18) contends that:

> … even before the city is a place of fixed residence, it begins as a meeting place to which people periodically return: the magnet comes before the container …

Furthermore the:

> … first germ of the city, then, is in the ceremonial meeting place that serves as the goal for pilgrimage …

and (p. 47):

> What I would suggest is that the most important agent in effecting the change from decentralised village economy to a highly organised urban economy was the king, or rather, the institution of kingship.

Ultimately, Mumford suggests no single definition exists as to what is a city in terms of its emergence, as we can only access the physical remains—too much evidence is not available, such as language and rituals. Though Mumford (1961, p. 41) does provide a useful description:

2.2 What Is Special About Cities?

From its origins onwards, indeed, the city may be described as a structure specially equipped to store and transmit the goods of a civilisation sufficiently condensed to afford the maximum amount of facilities in a minimum space, but also capable of structural enlargement to enable it to find a place for the changing needs and more complex forms of a growing society and its cumulative social heritage. The invention of such forms of written record, the library, the school, and the university is one of the earliest and most characteristic achievements of the city.

One last comment on the emergence of cities from Mumford (1961, pp. 45–46):

There is nevertheless one outstanding difference between the first urban epoch and our own. ... This technological explosion has produced a similar explosion of the city itself: the city has burst open and scattered its complex organs and organizations over the entire landscape.

... Just the opposite happened with the first great expansion of civilisation: instead of an explosion of power, there was rather an *implosion*. ... The city was the container that brought about this implosion, and through its very form held together the new forces, intensified their internal reactions, and raised the whole level of achievement.

Kostof (1991, pp. 37–40), in his examination of the urban form of cities, provides an expanded definition of what is a city. He outlines nine elements:

1. Cities are places where a certain energised crowding of people takes place.
2. Cities come in clusters. A town never exists unaccompanied by other towns.
3. Cities are places that have some physical circumscription, ...
4. Cities are places where there is a specialized differentiation of work ... and where wealth is not equally distributed among the citizens.
5. Cities are places favoured by a source of income—trade, ... a natural geomorphic resource like a natural harbour, or a human resource like a king.
6. Cities are places that must rely on written records.
7. Cities are places that are intimately engaged with their countryside, that have a territory that feeds them and which they protect and provide services for.
8. Cities are places distinguished by some kind of monumental definition that is where the fabric is more than a blanket of residences.
9. Finally, cities are places made up of buildings and people.

What I like about this definition is that it provides a hint of the issues that planners should investigate when planning a city.

A final point on the emergence of cities comes from Vance as cited in Kostof (1991, p. 40):

The most enduring feature of the city is its physical build, which remains with remarkable persistence, gaining increments that are responsive to the most recent economic demand and reflective of the latest stylistic vogue, but conserving evidence of past urban culture for present and future generations.

2.2.2 The First Cities

The first cities arose in Mesopotamia (modern day Iraq) approximately 6000 years ago, and with cities came numerous changes including governance, from elders to kingship; a rise in rituals, including ceremonies concerning the dead; the invention of writing, which allowed improved management through documentation; and the enormous expansion of human capabilities and specialisation (Mumford 1961).

Specialisation and innovation provided choice—choice in what people ate, wore, participated in, and in how they lived and worked and where they lived.

Choice, as a driver of specialisation and as a magnet for the population of cities, can be seen in the observation of Aristotle as he describes the role of the *polis*. "It comes into existence for the sake of mere life, but exists for the sake of the good life" (cited in Hall 1998, p. 5). In line with this, Glaeser (2011, p. 15) suggests that behind choice is collaboration and it is this collaboration that has driven the success of cities and is, in fact, why they exist.

Today, specialisation continues to influence the activities that define and shape cities. Figure 2.1 is my best example of what specialisation is about today, and thus what cities provide in terms of choice.

The photograph emphasises the influence of a desire for choice of one small element of some people's daily lives—the consumption of bread. Specifically, the research of Transport for NSW (2018) shows that in one short section of a street in the Sydney CBD there was a consumer choice of 230 different types of bread for sale. The collaborative activities required to achieve this outcome (transportation, production, including sourcing raw material and sales) reflect the influence

Bread by numbers:
- 1 side of the street in a 220 metre CBD block
- 21 shops and cafes selling bread
- 35 bread suppliers
- 80 delivers each day

Fig. 2.1 Cities and specialisation: choice
(*Source* Transport for NSW [Published with permission from Transport for NSW])

that consumer demand and supplier innovation has on providing choice through specialisation.

Cities soon became the focus of civilisation and today are the dominant settlement pattern and growing rapidly. But, up to very recently, villages were the dominant settlement form. Mumford (1961, p. 69) notes that around 1960, 80 per cent of the world's population still lived in villages. In May 2018 the United Nations Department of Economic and Social Affairs publication *Revision of World Urbanization Prospects* stated that 55 per cent of the world's population lived in urban environments. This means that 45 per cent of the world's population still live in villages and towns.

However, the increase in specialisation in food, clothing, manufacturing, transportation, trade and the arts meant cities attracted more and more people. The growing size of cities brought pressures on necessities such as drinking water and sanitation, and innovations in these areas came early in the life of cities—thus prompting a need for planning.

2.2.3 Cities Through the Ages

There is a rich collection of works on the history of cities and from a planning perspective it is hard to surpass Mumford's *The City in History* (1961). The original bibliography went for 58 pages. It was the definitive textbook when I was a planning undergraduate and one I recommend today to any student of city planning.

A brief examination of cities since their emergence 6000 years ago suggests some observations can be made about the types of actions that have been taken to support the 'planning' of cities. I use the word 'planning' generously in the context of what we today appreciate as modern planning.

- **The emergence of cities**. The first cities emerged in Mesopotamia, modern-day Iraq. It is estimated that Uruk, regarded as the first city, had a population of around 40,000 people (Crawford ed. 2013).
- **Safety, health and worship**. Fortification, sanitation and religious precincts were part of cities from the outset. Mohenjo-Daro in the Indus Valley, of modern-day Pakistan, had complex sanitation works and a water supply 4,500 years ago. Interestingly, Mumford (1961, p. 24) notes that sanitation infrastructure brought about the loss of the ecological connection between human and animal dung in agriculture.
- **The emergence of structure**. Gridded cities, inter-city roads and scholarly works emerged 2500 years ago. The first grid-based town design is attributed to the Hippodamus of Miletus (ancient Greece) 2450 years ago (Kirkpatrick 2015). Some consider him the father of European urban planning. The first inter-city roads were built by the Roman Empire. In Italy, the Via Appia (Appian Way), which runs 261 kilometres, was built 2310 years ago (Mumford 1961, p. 250). It was after this that roads were built across Europe. Also, 2200 years ago, civic,

cultural and religious facilities were built as large complex precincts, such as in the Greek city of Pergamon (in modern-day Türkiye), where facilities included an amphitheatre, library, school and temples.

About 2050 years ago, a set of architectural books was published on a range of issues including town planning by the Roman Marcus Vitruvius Pollio. For a translation from Latin refer to Gwilt (1874). The works included the triad of characteristics associated with architecture—*utilitas, firmitas and venustas* (utility, strength and beauty). His 10-volume work—*De Architectura*—discussed the perfect proportion in architecture and the human body, which led to the famous drawing of Vitruvian Man 1500 years later by Leonardo da Vinci.

- **The re-emergence of cities**. The fall of the Roman Empire saw the decline of cities 1600 years ago. Their prominence re-emerged 600 years later with strong population growth during the high Middle Ages, with an initial focus on fortification.
- **City design**. The Renaissance brought grand architectural vision, such as the geometrically structured city design influenced by fortifications, such as Palmanova in Italy 600 years ago or the work of Pope Sixtus V, whose placement of a series of obelisks within Rome established a long period of transformation that created built form structure to transport patterns; this in turn influenced urban form outcomes. At that time (530 years ago) Biagio Rossetti, regarded as one of the first urbanists, commenced work on planning and enlarging the city of Ferrara in Italy during the Italian Renaissance.
- **The industrial revolution: the catalyst for modern planning**. The industrial revolution began around 260 years ago, bringing significant population growth to cities and significant challenges from pollution to urban poverty. The vast public works and urban renewal program of Paris 160 years ago, undertaken by Georges-Eugene Hausmann as directed by Emperor Napoleon III, is one of the most notable city-shaping projects of the modern age. In England, the *Royal Commission on the Housing of the Working Classes* in 1885 (Hall 1996) was one of the catalysts for the emergence of modern planning as, in response to the urban ills of the industrial revolution, a wave of planning activities began across the globe.

2.2.4 The Urban Form of Cities

Strategic planning typically starts with the question of the structure of the city, particularly whether the existing structure will meet community needs.

When it comes to looking at the structure of a city, or its urban form, I connect with Garvin (2016, p. xxvi):

> … you cannot understand any physical landscape – urban, suburban, or rural – without familiarity with how it got to be that way.

2.2 What Is Special About Cities?

This requires us to look at urban structure and the elements that make up a city. This section draws on the two works of Spiro Kostof:

- The City Shaped, Urban Patterns and Meanings Through History (1991).
- The City Assembled, The Elements of Urban Form Through History (1992).

Kostof emphasises that the two books are a set, and that they have been written to assist the practitioner in their work (Kostof 1992, p. 9).

2.2.4.1 Urban Patterns and Meanings

The first book examines five approaches to urban form used throughout history. Kostof outlines the variations of each urban form including why and how they evolved, providing a deeper understanding of the significance of variations and the intent of each. The five urban typologies examined are:

1. **'Organic' patterns**: "It is presumed to develop without the benefit of designers, subject to no master plan but the passage of time, the lay of the land, and the daily life of the citizens. The resultant form is irregular, non-geometric, "organic," with the incidence of crooked and curved streets and randomly defined open spaces" p. 43.
2. **The grid**: "The grid – or gridiron or checkerboard – is by far the commonest pattern for planned cities in history. It is universal both geographically and chronologically (though its use was not continuous through history)" p. 95.
3. **The city as a diagram**: "By their nature, these cities are the most often transposed into design in perfect geometric shapes, circles, and focused squares and polygons of various kinds, and they obey rigid modes of centrality – radial convergence or axial alignment" p. 162.
4. **The grand manner**: "The Grand Manner is not the currency of little towns. It is neither practical nor modest. Perceived as an expansive pattern of sweeping vistas, its relation to topography and prior urban arrangement is arbitrary, its effects often grandiloquent. Typically, behind designs in the Grand Manner stands a powerful, centrist state …" p. 240.
5. **The urban skyline**: "Skylines are urban signatures. They are shorthand of urban identity, and the chance for urban flourish. Cities of all descriptions and periods raise aloft distinctive landmarks, to celebrate faith and power and special achievement. The landmarks focus city forms and highlight city portraits. The presentation itself is contrived" p. 296

For the more curious reader
There are several takeaways on urban typologies which are worth highlighting.

The Evolution of Urban Form

- "The tendency too often is to see urban form as a finite thing, ... City walls are pulled down and filled in; once rational grids are slowly obscured; a slashing diagonal is run through close-grained residential neighbourhoods; railroad tracks usurp cemeteries and water fronts; wars, fires, and freeway connectors annihilate city cores." p. 13
- "The shape of many cities in history represents a serial growth of planned increments grafted to an original core, and one of the most revealing aspects of the urban landscape has to do with the ways in which these additions are meshed with, or purposely discriminated from, the older fabric." p. 36

The formation of towns and cities

- "The administrative coming together of several proximate villages to form a town, what Aristotle calls 'synoecism,' is repeatedly attested to in history" p. 59.
  - "When several villages are united in a single complex community," Aristotle writes, "large enough to be nearly or quite self-sufficient, the *polis* comes into existence" p. 60.
  - "... indeed, synoecism is beginning to prove itself as one of the commonest origins of towns coming out of a rural context, along with one other process – the cohesion of an urban core around an important institution like a religious centre or a fort" p. 62.
- Kostof also outlines how urban form has been influenced by "social structure and the limits of public control" p. 62. The streets of a Muslim city such as Baghdad, in Iraq, evolve "subject only to the respect of custom, ownership, and the Muslim's right to privacy". ... Therefore, "...the labyrinth medina proves to be quite rational after all" p. 63.
- "Towns are built by and for people. Their regional and local sitings [sic] are the result of decisions taken by people and not of some inevitable physical control. ... Whatever the initial reasons for a town's foundation on a particular site, once established it generates its own infrastructure, transport network and so on" p. 33.

2.2 What Is Special About Cities?

The rationale behind urban forms

- The gridded city has come in and out of favour in the modern planning era. "Olmstead wrote, in contrast to straight streets which implied 'eagerness to press forward, without looking to the right or left.' Riverside was called 'a suburban village' and openly touted as being for 'the more intelligent and more fortunate classes'" (Note: Riverside was a suburb designed by Olmstead) p. 74.
- From Le Corbusier (1924) as cited in Kostof "The pack donkey 'meanders along. Meditates a little in his scatter-brained and distracted fashion, he zigzags in order to avoid large stones, or to ease the climb, or to gain a little shade; he takes the line of least resistance.' That cannot be the way of humans. 'Man walks in a straight line because he has a goal and knows where he is going'" p. 95.
- "Urbanism, according to Sitte, is precisely the science of relationships. And the relationships must be determined according to how much a person walking through the city can take at a glance. Streets and squares must be considered in three dimensions, as volumes. 'The ideal street must form a completely enclosed unit.' It must avoid bilateral symmetry: it must avoid cross streets that come into it at intervals and at right angles to its line" p. 84.

Social outcomes

- "It is strange twist that 'organic' patterns in antiquity and the Middle Ages were intricate frames where the rich and poor were woven together. The organic of the modern suburb is exclusive: this is a private world peopled with one's own kind" p. 75.
    - "Such distinctions became more feasible in the United States as zoning – first de facto, then, since the 1920s *de jure* – brought about the separation of residence and workplace, and created the possibilities of exclusive, single-purpose urban divisions.
- The notion of the urban skyline is a recent addition to the elements of urban form, first noted in 1876 and referred to commonly by the 1890s. In part they are a privatised skyline as rival claims seek to lay dominance for their owners. There are also public beacons of religion of government or simply of technological progress, such as the Eiffel Tower. p. 279.

Unintended outcomes of controls

- "… it was the Federal Housing Administration, organised in 1934 to provide mortgage insurance to local banks for loans on privately built housing, that set out both construction standards and desirable street

patterns, to make sure that the housing was marketable and the risks kept down." The Federal Housing Administration "virtually assured the nationwide replication of 'organic' townscapes during an era of explosive suburban growth" p. 80.
- "… the Public Health Act of 1875 which spawned the 'bye-law street' with its minimum 40-foot (12 m.) width and the obligatory open space between rows, gave the Victorian speculative builders the excuse they needed to fix on a standardised formula of broad straight monotonous rows of near-identical houses separated from the back neighbours by small gardens" p. 149.
- The well-intentioned Tenement House Act of 1879 gave birth to what Catherine Bauer was later to call 'probably the worst legalized building form in the world' This was the 'dumbbell' tenement, so called from the shape of its floor-plan" p. 150.

Concluding points

- "Symbols are carriers of meaning. Urban symbols are presumably carriers of some collective meaning of those who live and work there. Who should be allowed to design a city's skyline? Who should have the privilege to represent us on the horizon? These are fundamental questions" p. 335.
- Finally, while Kostof provides a detailed grounding in the attributes and influences on and of urban form he does not distinguish any urban form to be greater than another.

2.2.4.2 Elements of Urban Form

In *The City Assembled*, Kostof's approach to exploring and understanding variations continues, with the focus on the elements that make up all cities, irrespective of the urban pattern. This covers:

- The city edge;
- Urban divisions;
- Public places;
- The street; and
- Urban process.

2.2 What Is Special About Cities?

For the more curious reader
Again, there are take-home messages on these urban elements:

- The city edge for much of history was well defined by a fortified wall that allowed control of entry to markets and thus customs collection. "The industrial era proved to be the unmaking of insular city form and centripetal forces that had driven the growth of cities. The advent of railways allowed factories and suburbs to leap the constricting city bounds and with them the fundamental notions of urbanity that these had contained" p. 16.
- Within cities there are lines drawn by public authorities that are either political or administrative. Either way they influence how the city is managed. "And because they deal with people, the divisions were often coincident with deep social schisms, and their very existence brought about the tensions and open conflict" p. 72.
- "Since piazzas are areas in villages or cities, empty of houses and other such things and of obstructions, arranged for the purpose of providing space or set up for meetings of men, it should be remarked that in general through piazzas the condition of man in this world can be discovered." Petrus Berchorius, fourteenth century French mythographer, cited p. 123.
- Kostof further states that "without ringing declarations on the subject, cities of every age have seen fit to make provision for open spaces that would promote social encounters and serve the conduct of public affairs" p. 123.
- On streets, Kostof makes several observations:
  - "The street is an entity made up of a roadway, usually a pedestrian way, and flanking buildings. How each one of these is articulated, how they interact, in what ways the design of the street walls is controlled and guided – these are questions of form pure and simple."
  - "Categories that remain in within the esthetic realm include the hoary distinction between curved and straight streets, which so preoccupied the post-Sitte planning debate in modern Europe."
  - "Beyond its architectural identity, every street has an economic function and social significance. The purposes of the street have been traffic, the exchange of goods, and social exchange and communication" p. 189.
- Kostof emphasises that cities "are long-lived artifacts". While he states that, if left unattended, "the artifact decays and disintegrates" he also notes that "as long as there are people in residence, the city will renew itself without letup in unrehearsed ad hoc procedures or more methodically" p. 250.

2.2.5 Insights for a Strategic Planning Framework

Up to the end of the nineteenth century, managing growth and change, in most cases, focused on interventions to allow cities to continue to function, such as water and sanitation, protection of the community, or transport infrastructure (from roads to ports), as distinct from issues of equality and liveability.

Today, the challenges of transport, urban services (utilities), and health (though expanded in scope) remain the dominant infrastructure costs for governments in managing the land use implications of growth and change. So, while modern planning seeks in many cases to enhance quality of life the fundamentals of providing for the basics remain core to the activities of planning.

Urban form and the elements of a city can be distilled into a framework that can inform the practitioner as to how the understanding of a city's built form influences its dynamics and opportunities.

2.3 Great Cities: Various Perspectives

Just as great art is said to be in the eye of the beholder, this section reveals differing perspectives of what makes a great city.

2.3.1 What Makes Great Cities?

Sir Peter Hall's seminal work *Cities in Civilisation: Culture, innovation, and urban order* (1998) asks what makes great cities? It is a mammoth read, but well worth it. In his words, the questions he seeks to address are (p. 9):

> … why should great cities have such golden ages, these belles époques? Why should the creative flame burn so especially, so uniquely, in cities and not in the countryside? What makes a particular city at a particular time, suddenly become immensely creative, exceptionally innovative? Why should this spirit flower for a few years, generally a decade or two at most, and then disappear as suddenly as it came? Why do so few cities have more than one such golden age? How is it that they fail to recapture the creative spark that once animated them?

His work explores these questions from five different perspectives:

- The city as a cultural crucible;
- The city as an innovative milieu;
- The marriage of art and technology;
- The establishment of the urban order; and
- The union of art, technology, and organisation.

In doing so, Hall explores some 20 cities, from Athens in 500 BC to London in the late twentieth century.

One of my take-home learnings is that while the golden age of an individual city appears to suddenly blossom, there is always a build-up of events that created the opportunity. Furthermore, some outcomes that appear to have been foundational for the golden age relate to aspirations that planners can influence. They are:

- cosmopolitan cities;
- leveraging growth, and economic and social transformation;
- open global cities;
- innovation and knowledge networks, with innovation either being market driven, or state supported, or a mix of both with long-term commitments;
- state-supported industry;
- state-supported research and development;
- facilitating high-quality science parks, to attract inward investment;
- project champions; and
- regulations to support start-ups at home.

Thus, if we seek to influence the potential for 'great' cities of the future, there are lessons to be learnt from the past.

2.3.2 Great Streets

Kostof (1992, p. 190) emphasises that the street was an invention and suggests the first possible location of a consciously developed (paved) street was in Khirokitia (Cyprus) in the 6th millennium BC. The first sidewalks are known to have appeared in Kültepe (Türkiye) around 2000–1900 BC.

Furthermore, Kostof (1992, p. 189) contends that every street has an economic function and social significance and that "The purposes of the street traditionally have been traffic, the exchange of goods, and social exchange and communication."

This book instead examines 'great' streets and the requirements for such, with a focus on Allan B. Jacobs' work *Great Streets* (1993). We should explore the qualities of streets as they take up a significant part of the urban area. Jacobs (1993, p. 6) indicates that between 25 to 35 per cent of the land area in American cities is devoted to streets.

Jacobs (1993) puts forward a range of considerations as to why understanding streets is important when planning cities:

- "In a very elemental way, streets allow people to be outside" p. 4.
- "Everyone can use the street" p. 4.
- "Sociability is a large part of why cities exist and streets are a major if not the only *public* place for that sociability to develop" p. 4.
- "If you cannot walk along a street or go from one side to the other, then you aren't likely to meet anyone on it" p. 270.

- "What is more, streets change. They are tinkered with constantly: ... Every change brings with it the opportunity for improvement" p. 6.
- Whether streets are about physical, social or economic outcomes "they still have to be laid out designed" p. 6.

Jacobs (1993, pp. 8–9) outlines his criteria for great streets:

- "First and foremost, a great street should help make community: should facilitate people acting and interacting to achieve in concert what they might not achieve alone."
- "A great street is physically comfortable and safe."
- "The best streets encourage participation ... Participation in the life of a street involves the ability of people who occupy buildings (including houses and stores) to add something to the street, individually or collectively, to be part of it."
- "The best streets are those that can be remembered."
- "Finally, the truly great street is one that is representative: it is the epitome of a type: it can stand for others: it is the best."

> **For the More curious reader**
> Jacobs (1993, p. 270) also contends that:
>
> > Certain physical qualities are required for a great street. All are required, not one or two. ... Most are directly related to social and economic criteria having to do with building good cities: accessibility, bringing people together, publicness, livability, safety, comfort, participation, and responsibility.
>
> The requirements are detailed with a focus on assisting the practitioner in designing great streets (Jacobs 1993, pp. 271–291). They are as follows:
>
> - Place for people to walk with some leisure;
> - Physical comfort;
> - Definition;
> - Qualities that engage the eye;
> - Transparency (at the street edge, where public space and private property meet);
> - Complementarity (where building on the street 'get along' with each other, not the same but they respect one another);
> - Maintenance (words like cleanliness, smooth, no potholes—it is more than keeping places clean, it involves using materials that are easy to maintain); and
> - Quality of construction and design (mostly to do with workmanship and how materials are used).
>
> I have some affinity for the requirement of maintenance:

> *While working at the City of Casey I engaged landscape architects to prepare a plan for landscaping of the public realm of a town centre. The plan included a design for rubbish bins in keeping with an overall design palette for the centre. However, the City's maintenance team advised that the bins had to also be functional in terms of ease of use and cleaning (emptying), hence we changed the design.*

In addition to the requirements for a great street, Jacobs (1993, pp. 293–310) outlines several qualities that contribute to great streets and again provides detail to assist the practitioner. The qualities include trees, beginnings and endings, many buildings rather than few and special design features: details, places, accessibility, density helps, diversity, length, slope, parking, contrast and time.

For those who wish to delve deeper into the work of Jacobs (1993), here is an overview of the content:

- Eighteen 'great' streets from around the world are examined across nine chapters, which describe the attributes and qualities of a variety of street types such as residential street, grand street, and medieval street, as well as trees and streets.
- The qualities of different types of great streets are outlined to act as a teaching guide for designers. This covers ancient streets, medieval main streets, post-medieval main streets, boulevards, central walkway streets, major central commercial streets, small town main streets, residential boulevards, residential streets, residential water streets, tree streets and one-sided streets.
- The context or setting for great streets are examined by comparing places at the same scale, with around 50 examples provided.

I finish this section with a powerful statement by Jacobs (1993, p. 202) about the implication of streets as a network, as it addresses what I feel is one of the most important outcomes that a city plan needs to address—**accessibility**. Jacobs states:

> If you were to walk all of the pathways and travel all the canals of one square mile in Venice, your task more than 1,500 separate intersections and circle at least 900 blocks. By contrast, in Brasília you would find fewer than 100 intersections in a square mile and less than 50 blocks. The numbers alone bespeak vast differences in the physical nature of cities: in city scale, in visual and spatial complexity, in the sheer numbers of things in one area versus another. In the amount and sizes of spaces, and in the numbers of individual choice points that are available to people. At every intersection in each city – where two different public paths meet – there is at least one choice that can be made, to go this way or that, to follow one street or another. In that sense, there are over 1,500 points of choice available in a square mile of Venice, and fewer than 100 in Brasília.

2.3.3 Public Spaces and Great Cities

Garvin's (2016) work *What makes a great city* overlaps with Jacobs in that it covers all aspects of the public realm, not just streets. Garvin contends that it is the collective public realm, and its qualities, that make for a great city. He states that his approach to understanding the importance of the public realm has been influenced by the thoughts and works of three people: Edmund Bacon in particular, with whom he had a long association; all the works of Fredrick Law Olmstead; and Pierre Pinon's works on the evolution of Paris. Specifically:

- From Bacon, that '… great cities develop around the public realm' (Garvin 2016, p. xxv).
- From Olmsted's works:

    First, … that any landscape will affect the lives of human beings who pass through it every bit as much as those human beings also will have an impact on the landscape. Therefore, the design, … must consider that interaction on an ongoing basis. Second, at all times, the public realm acts as the cradle for a civil society, and democracy, in particular (Garvin 2016, p. xxvi).

- From Pinon's work on the evolution of the city structure and urban form of Paris, is that cities are the product '… of the ongoing exploration of ideas by and the cumulative actions of generations of city dwellers' (Garvin 2016, p. xxvi).

Garvin makes additional points that are relevant here:

- His definition of the public realm includes street, squares and parks, and special places such as promenades. In addition, the whole transportation network is included, even though some parts are not always free (such as rail networks). Garvin (2016, pp. 3–4) also contends that "… it is a city's streets that contribute most to shaping its character".
- As with Jacobs (1993), Garvin (2016, p. 3) notes that the core function of streets is to transport people and goods from a to b, but they have many other functions.
- Garvin (2016, p. 9) makes the point that all public spaces started out as "underdeveloped public realm" and that it takes generations to transform the space into a place that is "convenient, vibrant, attractive, and nurturing"'.

The principal focus of Garvin's book is the exploration of the six characteristics of a great public realm. They are:

1. **Is open to anybody**. "… for the widest diversity of people to share the public realm it must be overwhelmingly identifiable, accessible, and easy to use. As important, when they get there, people must feel safe and comfortable enough to remain there" p. 13.

2. **Offers something for everybody**. There needs to be things for people to do and see. Also, importantly, authorities need to "… devote adequate resources to its maintenance and management" p. 14.
3. **Attracts and retains market demand**. Public spaces need to adapt to the changing character of a place. To emphasise this point Garvin uses four snapshots of Nicollet Avenue in Minneapolis across a 90-year period. It shows two versions of the street modelled for cars (1922 and 1947) then two later versions modelled for pedestrians (1979 and 2012). In terms of detail, interestingly, each version has differing streetlights pp. 14–15.
4. **Provides a framework for successful urbanisation**. Some locations are more likely than others to attract market demand, such as a waterfront. Therefore, targeted investment in the public realm can exploit market demand to the benefit of city dwellers p. 16.
5. **Sustains a habitable environment**. Where the natural features of an area and/or landscaping adds to the quality of the habitat environment, for city dwellers, from shade and flood management to natural flora and fauna habitats pp. 16–17.
6. **Nurtures and supports a civil society**. Public squares play a special role in this outcome. No single group should act in a way that impacts negatively on another. Also, the complex path of managing change within the public realm brings together a cross-section of society from which their interactions nurture civil society p. 18.

Garvin (2016, p. 249) concludes by exploring the question of creating a public realm of the twenty-first century. He emphasises his philosophy that the public realm of great cities must continually adapt. In doing so, he recognises that improvements bring disruption, cost and political tension. To minimise this disruption, he suggests:

- reconfiguring the public realm that already exists;
- inserting carefully conceived addition to the public realm that involve little or no impact to private property;
- converting obsolete property into an actively used public realm;
- retrofitting the public realm to accommodate further growth; and
- only when necessary, reconceiving entire cities, as was done in Bilbao at the end of the twentieth century.

Continuing the theme of the importance of the public realm, Mayor Joseph P. Riley (City of Charleston, South Carolina), the winner of the Urban Land Institutes JC Nichols annual award in 2000, made the following comment (ULI Americas website: americas.uli.org):

A city should be a place with such beauty and order that it is inspirational. A key component of urban design is a belief in the value of the public realm, which every citizen owns.

If we are a nation where all the nest zones are privately owned, then what we own together as citizens is not very much. The greatest cities are those with the most beautiful public places, …

2.3.4 Accessibility: At the Core of Great Cities

In planning for places, from whole metropolitan areas to town centres, I have found that accessibility to goods and services is one attribute of a city that often differs greatly from one place to the next. This view has also been informed by the many specialists I have engaged with over the years, including:

- Freight experts—minimising supply chains;
- Transport experts—connectivity and efficiency;
- Economists—productivity maximisation; and
- Open space and recreation experts—metrics for access to facilities.

Consequently, when viewed from the perspective of equity, differences across a city cannot be seen as a positive marker for labelling that city a great place—particularly when accessibility to say post-secondary school education can influence the economic outcomes for individuals and families. Likewise, longer commuting times to employment, recreation and leisure opportunities can influence the health and wellbeing of individuals, households and communities.

> **For the more curious reader**
>
> *In developing the 2018 plan for Greater Sydney we found that it was possible to identify a line, a diagonal line, across the city, as a demarcation between those above it, who had choice in access to a range of employment and services that enhanced productivity and liveability for the residents, and those living below the line who had less choice. Consequently, changing the accessibility opportunities across Greater Sydney, with the aim of removing this disparity is a fundamental underlying raison d'être of the plan.*
>
> How we define accessibility is also changing. A digital world and the Internet of Things is changing many of the dynamics of cities—how this plays out in terms of the spatial planning of cities is still unclear. What is already clear is that in parts of cities there is a digital divide reflecting socio-economic factors and/or differing infrastructure delivery technologies.
>
> Furthermore, on a specific aspect of accessibility, over the years I have also heard my peers and visiting international scholars or practitioners talk of walkability, a subset of accessibility, as the critical important factor for make great cities.
>
> Finally, transport networks (accessibility) not only provide a means of travel, they also have the potential to change the dynamics of cities by influencing land use activities. A 2012 report by SGS Economics & Planning, *Long run economic and land use impacts of major infrastructure projects*, outlines how three transport projects across Melbourne significantly influenced the economic geography of housing and employment outcomes over time. It

also shows that a major land use intervention did not have the same influence. Therefore, planning for transport is not just about serving the transport access needs of people and businesses, described as city-serving outcomes; transport networks can also shape cities—city-shaping outcomes—which are most effective when planned and integrated with land use outcomes.

I conclude this short discussion on accessibility by linking back to Kostof's (1991) analysis of urban forms. What distinguishes each urban form is the pattern created by the streets, as distinct from the land use patterns. Though land use patterns, as discussed by Kostof, do influence the arrangement of the street network.

2.3.5 City Leader Boards

In addition to seeking to define the elements of what makes a great city, there are several indexes which purport to identify the leading cities across the globe, such as Mercer's, *Cost of living ranking* (or liveability ranking), refer website links. Mercer's website states that:

- Cost of living is one of the key factors of city attractiveness for international talent, business and investments, …
- The survey is designed to help multinational companies and governments around the world determine compensation strategies for their expatriate employees.
- In addition to evaluating more than 200 goods and services, Mercer's Cost of Living Survey (Mercer 2022) highlights essential factors—such as currency fluctuations, cost inflation and accommodation price instability—in determining the cost of packages for internationally mobile employees.

In Australia, in 2017, the Committee for Sydney commissioned a cities benchmarking project that utilised just over 50 international city indexes to distil 14 city benchmarks to assess the performance of Sydney against 33 global cities (refer website links).

In the published report, the author, Professor Greg Clark, states:

It has never been more important to understand city performance. The ability of cities to attract investment, manage their growth and deliver quality of life will define the character and, ultimately, the success of the 'metropolitan' century'. One important resource to track city performance, perception and progress is the huge body of city indices, benchmarks and rankings.

2.3.6 Who Defines 'Great'?

Starting with a reflection:

> *I remember a project my first employer, Dr Wolinski, undertook for the City of Melbourne in the early 1990s to explore benchmarking for that city. To ensure a comprehensive approach, Dr Wolinski undertook a worldwide search of city benchmarks that he was to report to a city leaders panel established for the project.*
>
> *The panel acknowledged that it was a comprehensive list of benchmarks for cities across the world, but – did it reflect what residents of the City of Melbourne valued?*

This view of what is important for a city or place has remained a cornerstone for my approach to strategic planning. This starts with the premise that all places are different and thus you must always seek to understand the setting of a place, the people, the history and the characteristics of the place when commencing a plan.

Consequently, when preparing the metropolitan plan for Greater Sydney, an early piece of research sought to understand what the people of Greater Sydney saw as important (Newgate Research 2015). Moreover, the research was not limited to a simple view of the whole of Greater Sydney; it explored the separate views of the residents of the six districts we were seeking to plan for at the time (later the number was reduced to five).

That work demonstrated, at a statistically valid level, differences in how a range of characteristics of the city were viewed between the residents of the six districts. The six reports can be found on the Greater Cities Commission website under Background material (refer website links).

Therefore, in planning for great cities it is necessary to consider the task from two perspectives:

- Firstly, seek to learn from the findings of those who have sought to understand what makes a great place and how those learnings can be applied to your specific task; and
- Secondly, seek to understand what is important to your community, as what they value should be the starting point in developing a vision and plan for a city or place.

2.3.7 Insights for a Strategic Planning Framework

The attraction of cities for the good life is driven by the benefits of specialisation providing city dwellers with choice. Innovation has underpinned specialisation, with collaboration as the enabler. Planning for cities needs to retain the opportunities for innovation and collaboration. Cities should be neither too ordered, nor too chaotic if they are to be successful—they need to be complex.

From the multiple perspectives of what makes a great city, we can learn that:

- The opportunity for creating new public spaces occurs as cities expand. What is important at that point in time is considering the range of roles that public space can play and ensuring these can be accommodated as the need arises into the future.
- Understanding a community's perspective of what attributes of a city are important is a first step on the pathway to a great city.
- The seeds for the emergence of a world-leading city can be nurtured by the actions of governments that focus on supporting the building blocks which enable them.

I conclude this chapter with what is the salient point and the concluding paragraph to Kostof's work *The City Shaped*.

> If we believe that cities are the most complicated artifact we have created, if we believe further that they are cumulative, generational artifacts that harbor our values as a community and provide us with the setting where we can learn to live together, **then it is our collective responsibility to guide their design.** P. 335 [My emphasis]

2.4 Summary

This chapter provides a context for the subject of this book—cities. It provided an historical context to the emergence of cities, whereby specialisation and collaboration were at the heart of what drove their development. The discussion outlined that with the first cities, and the concentration of thousands of people into one location, came the need to plan for the basic necessities of life, specifically water and sanitation as well as the need for fortification and in many cases religious precincts.

The final piece for discussion on cities themselves is that of urban form, and how the variety of urban forms can be understood in terms of their drivers and that there are also common elements that are present in all urban forms.

As for great cities what was revealed is that there are several perspectives on what makes a great city and each can inform our approach to city planning. This includes:

- How we plan for and manage the public realm, specifically streets, which make up a significant proportion of a city's footprint;
- How we may foster the attributes which can enhance the potential for a city to be immensely creative or exceptionally innovative;
- The significance of accessibility on influencing equitable outcomes as to how residents can work, rest and play; and
- How the many qualities of cities can inform indexes used to rank cities, with the objective in some cases being to identify which cities would be most attractive to footloose knowledge workers.

A final concluding remark on great cities comes from Garvin (2016, p. 11):

> Remaining a great city depends on people continuing to want to be there to enjoy being there, and to remain there, and that depends on continuing to make improvements to the public realm – improvements that meet the needs of future generations.

References

Beveridge C E, et al (ed) *The Papers of Fredrick Law Olmsted, Volumes I-IX and Supplementary Series*, The John Hopkins Press, Baltimore US.
— As cited in Garvin (2016).
Crawford, H (ed.) (2013), *The Sumerian World*, Routledge, Milton Park, Abingdon, Oxon
Garvin, A (2016), *What Makes a Great City*, Island Press Washington DC.
Glaeser, E (2011), *Triumph of the City,* Pan Macmillan UK.
— A must read for anyone interested in urban economics.
Hall, P (1996), *Cities of Tomorrow: An Intellectual History of Urban Planning and Design in the Twentieth Century*, Blackwell Publishers Ltd UK
Hall, P (1998), *Cities in Civilisation: Culture, Innovation, and Urban Order*, Orion Books Ltd London.
—Extraordinary exposé on what makes a great city, with 20 case studies covering 2500 years of cities.
Jacobs, AB (1993), *Greet Streets,* MIT Press US.
—Provides a detailed exposé of what are great streets and why so.
Kirkpatrick, A (2015), *The Image of the City in Antiquity: Tracing the origins of Urban Planning, Hippodamian Theory, and the Orthogonal Grid in Classical Greece*, Thesis, University of Victoria, Unpublished
Kostof, S (1991), *The City Shaped, Urban Patterns and Meanings Through History*, Thames & Hudson, London, UK.
—A detailed exploration of urban form and what drove different structures.
Kostof, S (1992), *The City Assembled, The Elements of Urban Form Through History*, Thames & Hudson, London, UK.
—Kostof's second detailed analysis of urban form through history, with a focus on the elements of a city.
Mithen, S (2003), *After the Ice, A Global Human History 20,000–5000 BC.* Weidenfeld & Nicholson GB.
—A detailed journey through time, of life as a hunter gatherer.
Mumford, L (1961), *The City in History*, Penguin Books, Australia.
—The definitive book on the history of cities through the ages.

Website links

Committee for Sydney (2017) *Joining the Top Table? Benchmarking Sydney's Performance 2017* CfS-Issues-Paper-16-Joining-the-Top-Table-July-2017.pdf (sydney.org.au).

References

Mercer (2022) *Cost of living ranking* Cost of Living Index 2022 | Most Expensive Cities in the World List | Mercer.

Newgate Research (2015) *Research Report, Community research to support the implementation of A Plan for Growing Sydney*. Six reports North, South, Central, West Central, West, and South West Districts https://www.greater.sydney/background-material.

NSW *Movement and Place Guidelines* Movement and Place (nsw.gov.au).

United Nations Department of Economic and Social Affairs (2018) *Revision of World Urbanization Prospects* 2018 Revision of World Urbanization Prospects | Multimedia Library - United Nations Department of Economic and Social Affairs.

What is Planning About? 3

3.1 Introduction

Planning for cities, as we understand it today, emerged in the early 1880s and its evolution since then reflects the social, economic and environmental pressures of the time. Stein's statement (2017) that *'Planning' is essentially whatever planners do ...*, could be an apt description of the activities of the planning profession.

However, if we seek a practical framework to enhance our ability to undertake strategic planning then that definition is insufficient.

This chapter starts the journey of examining why and how we plan cities. It focuses on planning activities that have emerged since the 1880s when modern planning is seen to have begun.

This journey asks what planning is about, as I believe we need to clarify the scope for planning. For example, should planning be responsible for all the urban ills of a city?

I hope that by Chapter 5 you will see a robust and practical framework for strategic planning.

3.1.1 Warm-Up Exercise

Rather than jump straight in I suggest an exercise that gets to the heart of this chapter.

Imagine you are standing before a planning minister, a mayor or a business or community group, and you have been told to outline how you and your team are going to prepare a new city plan. Before you start your presentation, you are asked a quite different question:

> Why do we need to do the plan at all?

Your enquirer points out that a plan was done just five years ago and there are zoning controls in place that outline how decisions will be made for new developments. In addition, government departments already have their own plans, and they are building many infrastructure projects.

How will you respond to this question? Jot down a few points before you start reading and as you work your way through this chapter reflect on what is raised and how it may influence your thoughts. My experience suggests the better you can articulate why a specific plan is needed, the more likely you will be adequately resourced to prepare it.

3.2 The Emergence of Modern Planning

By the late nineteenth century, the appalling conditions of the inner urban slum, described as the 'urban ills' of the industrial revolution, became the catalyst for modern planning across Europe and North America (Hall 1996).

3.2.1 A Response to the Urban Ills

In the early 1880s, people from various quarters began to advocate for a response to the urban ills of the industrial age. In 1884, the United Kingdom commenced its Royal Commission of the Housing of the Working Class (Hall 1996, pp. 14–23), which is considered the birth of modern planning.

The planning response to the commission was not simply to build sewers or reduce pollution. Interventions included new planned cities (towns) as part of the garden city movement, which started in the late 1890s. It was as much about social reform as it was about city planning. For example, Ebenezer Howard's well-known publication, *Garden Cities of To-Morrow* (1902), was originally titled *To-Morrow, A Peaceful Path to Social Reform* (1898).

Christine Garnaut, in *Towards metropolitan organisation: town planning and the garden city idea* (eds. Hamnett and Freestone 2000, pp. 47–48) provides a useful synopsis of the intent of planning in England at that time:

- The early advocacy called for anticipatory and comprehensive planning which resulted in the *British Town Planning and Housing Act 1909*, which "embodied the goals of the town planning movement and became a benchmark for legislative efforts elsewhere" (p. 47).
- At the same time, Ebenezer Howard's Garden city idea was advanced as a model for city planning and organisation by the London-based Garden City Association. Howard is referred to as a 'social revolutionary'.

> Howard's vision of 'a healthy, natural and economic combination of town and country life' offered a means to control overcrowding and expansion, redress rural depopulation,

3.2 The Emergence of Modern Planning

improve residential and workplace environments, and affirm the role of the individual and the home in the urban landscape' (p. 47).

In his proposed model of urban reform—'Social City'—he demonstrated a means to check overpopulation and ill-regulated growth, reserve open space in order to shape and contain the city, and establish fully planned, self-contained communities (p. 47).

- Howard's ideas had contemporary and enduring influence on international planning.

    The renowned exemplars, Letchworth Garden City (1903) and Hampstead Garden Suburb (1907), represented an environmental ideal readily embraced by the town planning movement. (p. 48)

- A contemporary of Howard's was the architect-planner and leading garden city practitioner Raymond Unwin.

    ... Unwin played a central role in both translating the 'detailed' site planning aspects of garden city idea onto the ground and in marketing its 'larger' metropolitan aspects – decentralisation, satellite communities and reserved public land to keep the metropolis 'always within reasonable touch of open country'. (p. 48)

    Unwin's adaptation of Howard's idea also found favour in contemporary planning thought and, together with Letchworth and Hampstead, helped take the garden city idea to the world. (p. 48)

Hall (1996) also addresses the events of that time, across the globe, and made several observations:

- Hall asks why, if a problem was so universal, the responses were so different (p. 46). Even though the report of the initial Royal Commission in 1895 "abundantly confirmed the nature of the problem, it could reach no unanimous conclusion as to remedy" (p. 19).
- Change occurred at a time when the political and social histories of North America and Europe were different, which contributed to the divergence in responses. For example, North America rejected the concept of benevolent housing, a public intervention mechanism, and chose ordinances to control quality, a market mechanism (pp. 58–59).
- Also, where England's garden city movement evolved to garden suburbs, in Berlin it emerged as apartment garden suburbs (pp. 112–122).
- However, to say that all positive change to cities at this time can be attributed to the actions of the social reformers would be an overstatement. In London, changes to transport technology, new agencies (for example, building societies), and cheap labour and materials all contributed to the suburbanisation of the city and improved "the housing standards for a wide spectrum of the population" (p. 48).

- However, not all of those in poverty benefited from the changes. In London it was the 'mobile' working poor who could take advantage to get the best design. In New York in the 1920s it was the planning and zoning system that locked the poor out of the new suburbs being built along the streetcar tracks and subway lines (p. 61).

3.2.2 The Australian Experience

In examining planning history in Australia, as well as contemporary planning activities, we need to recognise the implications of the principle of federalism, on land use planning, as enshrined in the *Commonwealth of Australia Constitution Act 1900*.

Federalism divides political power between the Commonwealth Government and the governments of the states and territories. It limits the powers of the Commonwealth Government to a set of prescribed areas (Part V Powers of the Parliament, Section 5 Legislative powers of the Parliament); all other powers are a state responsibility. Land use planning is not a prescribed power; therefore, its responsibility falls to the states.

3.2.3 Evolving Planning Eras in Australia

Australia's history of planning since the late nineteenth century is documented in *The Australian Metropolis, A Planning History* (Hamnett and Freestone 2000). This comprehensive work provides commentary on 10 eras of planning in Australia (p. 6) (see Table 3.1). The book also offers a 40-page bibliography.

3.3 Reflections on Planning Eras in Australia

The detail behind Hamnett and Freestone's (2000) chronology of planning eras suggests there are some issues worthy of reflection.

3.3.1 Evolving Planning Eras in Australia

3.3.1.1 We have seen it all before
There is little in the way of events that have not been previously experienced, so there would appear to be much to learn from our past. Past issues include (Hamnett and Freestone 2000):

- Planning paradigms coming in and out of favour.

Table 3.1 Basic chronological framework of Australian metropolitan planning

Core period	Planning era	Major concerns	Major events
Nineteenth century	Colonial and town planning	Town founding and design Public infrastructure	Light's Adelaide Public health reforms
1900s	Emergence of planning concerns	City improvement City beautiful	1901 Melbourne Congress Federal capital
1910s	An organised planning movement	Garden city Planned suburbs	Town planning associations National planning conferences
1920-30s	Experimentation, institutionalisation and legislation	Regulation Comprehensive town planning	Melbourne and Perth town planning commissions Town planning acts in SA and WA
1940s	Idealism and reconstruction	Establishment of statutory planning systems Housing Emergence of regional planning	Commonwealth Housing Commission and state housing authorities Cumberland County Council
1950s	Mark One master plans	Town and country planning Professionalism	Sydney, Melbourne and Perth metropolitan planning schemes Land use zoning
1960s	Mark Two master plans	Structure planning Corridor cities Planned suburban development	Transport and land use strategies Canberra's Y Plan
1970s	Reorientation and conflict	Rise of environmental and heritage concerns Public participation	Federal urban policy Green bans and resident action
1980s	Revival of strategic planning	Urban management Ecological sustainability	Urban consolidation policies Joint ventures Better cities
1990s	Competitive versus sustainable cities	Compact cities Entrepreneurialism Cultural planning	Deregulation, privatisation and planning systems reform Whole-of-government approaches Urban design

Source The Australian Metropolis, A Planning History (ed. Hamnett and Freestone 2000, p. 6)

- At the end of the nineteenth century, healthy suburban life emerged as the desired model. Consequently, John Sulman, the chief advocate for town planning in Australia at the time, opposed the grid system (p. 26).
- In the 1950s, planning institutionalised the suburban mosaic.
- Corridor planning became a principal city-shaping outcome in the 1960s (p. 130).
- In 1970 the Sydney Planning Authority sought to introduce a betterment tax, but it was abandoned by 1973 along with the State Planning Authority (p 140). Note that the Victorian Government recently legislated for a windfall gains tax to commence in July 2023.
- High population growth.
  - After World War II, the world's 15 major cities grew by 2.0 million people from a base of 4.0 million. In the decade to the 1960s they grew by a further 2.0 million people (p. 113). Such growth rates are far beyond what has occurred in recent decades.
  - Debate on outward expansion of Sydney, where the Cumberland County Council argued that there was sufficient land, began in the 1950s. By 1959, 119 km^2 of greenbelt land was abolished, mainly in response to pro-development lobby groups (p. 110).
  - At the same time, Melbourne and Sydney urban expansion was in part a consequence of an underestimate of population growth (p. 111).
  - By around 1968, in Perth, the government released 6000 hectares of land to take heat out of escalating land prices (p. 127).
  - While growth rates fluctuate across Australia, in the main, capital cities outgrow the regions in percentage terms.
- Outward urban expansion.
  - If the dominant concern of the 1930s discourse on cities had been 'slums', in the 1940s it was 'sprawl', as housing spread to cheaper land in the outer suburbs (p. 91).
  - One of the most consistent and continuing trends is outward urban expansion. Even with the varying tools utilised across multiple state planning jurisdictions to create more compact cities and contain and better manage growth, there remains many decades of outward expansion in most capital cities.
- Changes in consumption patterns.
  - The 1960s were not just about population growth but the increase in consumption. Increased car ownership increased mobility for shopping, social activities and recreation, which increased kilometres travelled. The 1960s are a reference point in cities as changes in retail, manufacturing and warehouses are suburbanised (p. 113).
- The alignment of strategic planning with delivery.
  - In the 1910s and 1920s there were various attempts to have parkland as a major structural element in the design of Australia's capital cities. None succeeded (p. 55).

- The shift to the garden suburb in the 1920s, as distinct from the garden city, meant the economic objective was lost. Perth Endowment Lands (Floreat Park and City Beach) were such garden suburb examples that lacked an employment outcome (p. 55). A positive consequence was the emergence of planned suburbs as distinct from simple land subdivision.
- In 1943–44, the Commonwealth Government attempted to deliver a national plan for cities and regions. This was rejected by the states and a lack of understanding federally as to who had planning powers (pp. 92–83).
- In the 1940s, "it was eventually recognised that even if local government had undertaken the kind of planning made possible by the legislation, an assembly of local plans would not add up to an effective metropolitan plan. Within the metropolitan region it was necessary to have comprehensive plans" (p. 91).
- The 1970s saw a focus of aligning infrastructure with growth. In Adelaide, one response was to prepare projections and undertake modelling (p. 145).
- In the late 1970s in Sydney, a new Planning and Environment Commission and a Planning and Environment ministry were established together with a new planning act in 1979. All still failed to control the utility agencies (p. 141).
- The quality of cities and the amenity of places.
  - In 1899, Melbourne surveyor John Kelly proposed that each planned community have its own identity (p. 28).
  - In 1908, the *Royal Commission for the Improvement of the City of Sydney and Its Suburbs*, had as part of its terms of reference the task of considering 'ornamentation and improvements as will tend to add to the attractions and beauty of the City and adjoining Suburbs' (p. 36).
  - Around 1910, beautification actions were relatively easy to implement, and many were achieved. However, the age of 'city beautiful' failed to address practical issues such as better roads, improved subdivision and adequate housing (p. 45).

3.3.1.2 Each Historical Trend Has Brought New Ideas

As planning evolved, it created new ideas and ways of approaching urban challenges, such as (Hamnett and Freestone 2000):

- 1910s: "Town planning emerged as a tool for urban reform, and a set of clearly defined social, environmental and administrative goals was established. To make people 'cheerful, hopeful and healthy'" (p. 47).
- 1920s. Planning activities in Melbourne were influenced by the functional North American approach. "The concept of a city planning commission combining a local government, public utilities and (sometimes) business membership charged with preparing a comprehensive plan was at the core of North American practice" (p. 70).

In this context, while trends and shifts in cities can be identified in a particular decade, the slow nature of change in cities means the consequences of those changes typically plays out over decades. However, often a new trend is seen to raise the need for a new plan, as distinct from the need for an evolving implementation plan.

3.3.1.3 Further Notable Events, 1890–2000

In addition to the issues raised above, other notable events provide insight into why the urban landscape changed as it did and how the legacy of these events influences planning today. Such as (Hamnett and Freestone 2000):

- Circa 1910: "As cities were composed primarily of buildings, it followed logically for Sulman that city planning was essentially an architectural problem" (p. 33). More detail on Sulman's views can be found in his work *An Introduction to the Study of Town Planning in Australia* (1921).
- Circa 1920: By the late 1910s, planning increasingly moved to the American-inspired functional model. James Morell, architect of the Victorian Public Works Department, succinctly encapsulated this focus when he declared:

    > Town planning ... concern(s) the planning of a city ... the improvement and extension in such a manner as to provide for the free movement, safety and control of traffic and transportation, the segregation of buildings and activities, of specific types, to restricted areas ... together with a sufficient percentage of parks, and other open spaces for securing economic, convenient, healthful and pleasant conditions. (p. 63)

- 1920s and 1930s: Most planning legislation at this time allowed for public objections to draft policies, a forerunner to public participation processes (p. 78).
- 1940s: The emerging private sector created suburbs (p. 89).
- 1950s: Post war saw a shift from social reformers to technical professionals (p. 80).
- 1950s: Research in 1980 showed that the Cumberland Plan successfully brought jobs closer to homes in the suburbs; however, there was a gender-based disadvantage with women losing access to jobs. "The plans were largely written by men who accepted the dominant patriarchal paradigm. This placed 'men's business' (the world of work and strategic planning) before 'women's business' (the world of home and bringing up the kids)" (p. 106).
- 1950s: The network of major highways and freeways incorporated into metropolitan plans was more the result of the concepts of road construction authorities incorporated by naïve land use planners rather than integrated land use and transport plans (p. 108).
- 1950s: In Perth and Sydney trams were removed as an obstacle at a time when US traffic engineers dominated (p. 109).
- 1950s: The beginning of the car era, which dominated planning for the next 60 years (p. 110).

3.3 Reflections on Planning Eras in Australia

- 1960s: The beginning of Australia's research organisations such as the Australia Institute of Urban Studies (p. 119).
- 1970s: Margot Huxley contends that by the 1970s, planning brought into stark relief the tension between interventions to achieve collective goals and private property rights (p. 148).
- 1990s: South Australia's planning review was a major attempt in the beginning of the 1990s to bring together major elements of planning orthodoxy and provide a shared community vision. However, economic disaster in the early 1990s and the failure of the South Australian State Bank overtook these reforms (p. 164).
- 1990s: Political scientist Martin Painter suggests urban policy is too complicated to be successful (p. 182).
- 1990s: It was seen that the traditional planner needed a wider range of skills than just planning (p. 186).

3.3.2 Events From 2000 to 2020

The work of Hamnett and Freestone (2000) ends the narrative of planning eras with the decade of the 1990s. If I were to consider the events of the two decades since I would see their focus as follows.

3.3.2.1 2000s: Rail Revival and Sustainability is Embedded in City Planning

- The concept of sustainability, as a triple bottom line outcome, emerged into mainstream thinking in the late 1980s with the Brundtland Report (*Our Common Future*). The Melbourne metropolitan plan *Melbourne 2030* was released in 2002. While it had a range of implementation challenges, its legacy is that it made sustainability a mainstream and explicit element in metropolitan plans.
- The revival of rail patronage in the 2000s prompts significant planning in Melbourne and Sydney for the development of new metropolitan rail lines.
- The considerable challenges, changing objectives and the time required for planning and building new rail lines means that in both Melbourne and Sydney construction is still underway for the projects first mooted in the 2000s.
- New rail corridors were delivered in Perth and Brisbane.

3.3.2.2 2010s: Integrated Regional and Metropolitan Strategic Plans

- The focus of rail planning brought about a focus on the need for integrated land use and transport plans.
- Subsequently across all capital cities, except greater Hobart, new metropolitan plans were developed.

- Regional plans also become a major focus, with more than 50 regional plans prepared across Australia.

3.3.2.3 Post 2020

- The year 2020 saw the world impacted by the COVID-19 pandemic and its impact on communities will clearly continue to influence the activities and development of cities and regions across the globe for at least the next decade.
- The immediate planning response in Australia was to fast-track development that was already in the pipeline. The implications of planning in general are still unfolding, particularly given the shift to working from home, a change in housing preferences (including the shift to regional locations), and the role of CBDs. Additional emerging issues include:
  - *Climate change*. Various global political changes are bringing climate change back to the forefront of issues for society to address. The review of Australian capital city plans (refer Sect. 3.4.1) highlights that more work is required before there is a deep and consistent understanding of how city plans respond to the changing climate.
  - *First Nations heritage*. The review of the capital city plans also suggests that consideration of First Nations culture and heritage and a thorough understanding of Country is yet to be addressed other than reference to heritage protection controls, except for *Shaping SEQ, South East Queensland Regional Plan 2017* (2017). Increasingly, such a limited approach to this important issue is unacceptable.
  - After two decades of focusing on city-shaping infrastructure a gap in city infrastructure is emerging—local serving infrastructure. Whether it be to enable new development or enhance liveability, there appears to be a need to establish collaborative approaches from all levels of government to bring the quality of the local environment up to the standard set for city-shaping infrastructure. I potentially see this shift as an opportunity to reimagine the quality of our local communities just as we did our central CBDs and recognise that for them, their enhancement was a 30-year journey.

3.3.2.4 Emergence of a Suite of Delivery Levers

Today discussions of delivery levers for planning often quickly default to policy and regulations, the latter in the context of planning legislation and planning controls, specifically zoning. However, the levers developed to achieve desired societal benefits are varied and most are still the focus of how we manage growth and change in cities today.

In fact, most levers were developed within a relatively short period of time, 20 years, at the start of the modern era of planning as outlined in Table 3.2.

3.3 Reflections on Planning Eras in Australia

Table 3.2 The emergence of planning interventions since the 1880s across the globe

Intervention	Comment
Advocacy	Modern planning began with significant advocacy around 1880 seeking Parliament to act on the urban ills of the city (England)
Policy	Detailed urban design principles, such as by Raymond Unwin, *Town Planning practice: An Introduction to the Art of Designing Cities and Suburbs.* (1909) Master plans such as for the new garden cities, late 1890s and early 1900s in England
Regulation	The *Housing and Town Planning Act 1909* came into force in England Zoning was introduced in the City of Los Angeles (part only) in 1904 to protect residential areas and in New York in 1916. George McAneny, the borough president of Manhattan in 1913, stated (Dunlap 2016): … to arrest the seriously increasing evil of the shutting off of light and air from other buildings and from the public streets, to prevent unwholesome and dangerous congestion both in living conditions and in street and transit traffic, and to reduce the hazards of fire and peril to life
Funding (taxation)	The use of bonds to fund Hausmann's urban renewal development in Paris in the 1860s Funding mechanisms for garden cities started in 1900 in England
Public works	Underground rail systems • Paris Metro 1900, population of Greater Paris approx. 4.0 million in 1900 • London Metro significant delivery 1863–1906, population of Greater London in 1900, 6.2 million • New York City Subway 1904, population of New York City in 1900, 3.4 million Australia's rail network • Melbourne 1870s and 1880s, population in 1899, 477,800 • Sydney's first rail line opened in 1855 and by 1894 there was an extensive rail network, population in1900, 481,000
Governance	Melbourne Metropolitan Board of Works 1891 English delivery authorities such as the First Garden City, Limited and the Garden City Pioneer Company (1900 and 1902) in England
Business and community development	Formation of planning associations • England, Town Planning Institute, now the Royal Town Planning Institute (1914) • Royal Australian Planning Institute, now the Planning Institute of Australia (1951)

3.3.3 Insights for a Strategic Planning Framework

What can we discern from the activities to manage growth and change in cities since the emergence of modern planning? In terms of developing a strategic planning framework there are several insights:

- **Evolving scope of planning**. A defining aspect of modern planning has been the broadening scope of issues that are the focus of city planning activities. It is also evident that the issues of the day have varied with the circumstances of the time.
    - A strategic planning framework should provide clarity for the scope of activities.
- **Relevance of ongoing land use segregation**. An early outcome of modern planning was the separation of land uses in response to a range of health, amenity and urban efficiency pressures. While transport congestion remains a challenge, many of the negative aspects of land uses of that time are no longer relevant, due to regulations influenced by community expectations regarding health and safety. However, the philosophy of land use segregation remains.
    - A strategic planning framework should include an investigation of the inter-relationships between land uses.
- **Same problem, different solution**. Hall's (1996, p. 46) insight that different jurisdictions arrive at different responses to the same problem due to differing cultural approaches to managing cities emphasises that one size does not fit all.
    - A strategic planning framework needs to ensure the political and cultural context for managing cities is understood, which requires interaction between decision-makers and the community.
- **Private sector delivery of cities**. The private sector incrementally builds cities and, in many cases, plans and builds whole parts of cities from new communities to major transport infrastructure.
    - A strategic planning framework needs to explicitly focus on delivery, including the delivery players and how they are to be involved.
- **Functionality versus liveability**. Transport projects have significant city-shaping impacts (SGS Economics and Planning, 2012) and transport economics has placed economic benefit as a major determinant for city planning since the 1950s. However, in the words of Aristotle (cited in Hall, 1998, p. 5), we stay in cities for the 'good life' and modern planning was born out of the response to enhance the quality of life for city workers and their families. Furthermore, the impacts of government requirements to manage the impact of the COVID-19 pandemic has seen community and individual wellbeing re-emerging as an important consideration for city planning.
    - A strategic planning framework needs to consider the scope of activities that should inform a plan as well as the assessment tools to determine responses.
- **From city beautiful to garden suburbs and local amenity**. At the outset of modern planning 'beauty' was an explicit objective for the planning of cities. Over time this holistic view evolved to one of localised amenity—the garden suburb, as distinct from the aesthetics of wider city design.
    - A strategic planning framework should include city design as an area for investigation to understand the community's sense of identity and imagery.
- **Time lag from issue identification to response**. Understandably there is usually a lag between the acknowledgement of an issue and the response. We need to recognise the timeline of change and that at each decision point, those

involved will potentially stamp their authority by adjusting their perspective. Thus, with each decision the response moves a little away from the original problem statement.

In England, at the turn of the nineteenth century, this meant that the garden city concept moved to a garden suburb, with the implication that the jobs element was lost.
- A strategic planning framework needs to ensure decision points reflect on the problem statement.
- **Environmental value**. Concerns for the environment have moved from an anthropocentric view to one that values the intrinsic values of nature independently of humans.
  - A strategic planning framework needs to consider the value of the environment as an ecosystem and that its value is the same in 100 years as it is today.
- **Delivery tools available to planners**. The range of delivery tools or intervention levers highlights the complex nature of how cities develop, and the levers required to influence change. This topic is discussed in Sect. 4.5.3.
  - A strategic planning framework should provide clarity on the tools available to effect change.
- **Planning delivery authorities**. The role of institutional authorities to drive planning outcomes has waxed and waned. For my undergraduate thesis, I studied the merger of Melbourne's planning delivery agency, the Melbourne Metropolitan Board of Works, with the Ministry for Planning, the policy agency. Approximately 30 years later a delivery agency was re-established.
  - A strategic planning framework needs to explicitly consider the governance arrangements for implementing the city plan, including the organisation with delivery responsibility.
- **Planning literature**. With the advent of town planning as a profession and the emergence of planning associations came many great works on city planning, which have shaped the thinking and actions of planners over the last 100 years. For those keen to further explore these writings, here are a few of the notable classics in chronological order (detailed citations at the end of this chapter):
  - 1909, Raymond Unwin, Town Planning Practice: An Introduction to the Art of Designing Cities and Suburbs
  - 1960, Kevin Lynch, The Image of the City
  - 1961, Jane Jacobs, The Death and Life of Great American Cities
  - 1961, Lewis Mumford, The City in History
  - 1962, Rachel Carson, Silent Spring
  - 1971, Ian L. McHarg, Design with Nature
  - 1977, Christopher Alexander, Sara Ishikawa, and Murray Silverstein, A Pattern Language: Towns, Buildings, Construction
  - 1995, Allan B. Jacobs, Great Streets
  - 1996, Peter Hall, Cities of Tomorrow: An Intellectual History of Urban Planning and Design in the Twentieth Century

Other writings I would recommend include:
- 1967, Edmund N. Bacon, The Design of Cities
- 1971, George F. Chadwick, A Systems View of Planning: Towards a Theory of the Urban and Regional Planning Process
- 1992, Mitchell E. Waldrop, Complexity
- 2005, Jared Diamond, Collapse
- 1998, Peter Hall, Cities in Civilisation: Culture, innovation, and urban order
- 2012, Edward Glaeser, Triumph of the City
- 2017, Geoffrey West, Scale.

Finally, for those looking to begin the journey of learning about First Nations culture, heritage and Country, I recommend the following:
- 2010, Libby Porter Unlearning the Colonial Cultures of Planning
- 2021, Alison Page and Paul Memmott Design: Building on Country.

3.4 Contemporary City Planning

Where planning literature can provide some direction on the issues that planning activities should consider, contemporary planning documents provide an indication of what today's governments deem to be important for the management of growth and change in cities.

3.4.1 Insights from Australian City Plans

Over the period 2015–2018 metropolitan plans were released for Australian Capital Territory (Canberra), Adelaide, Greater Darwin, Melbourne, Greater Sydney, Perth (Perth & Peel) and South East Queensland (SEQ).

I use these Australian capital city plans as case studies of contemporary planning in Australia and examine a range of insights in this book. The following insights focus on what planning is about:

- **The scope of planning**. While there are some areas of divergence, in general there is a high level of commonality in the scope of issues covered. The findings in this area are discussed in Sect. 3.6.2.
- **The structure of plans**. The structure of the plans takes either a traditional thematic approach with chapters covering themes such as housing, environment, economy, transport, or they take an integrated approach based on the principal outcomes sought. The findings in this area are discussed in Sect. 9.5.
- **Delivery**. Approaches as to how the plans will be delivered varies. Monitoring is the consistent theme. The findings in this area are discussed in Sect. 10.3.6. The variety of delivery tools is discussed in Sect. 4.5.3.

3.4 Contemporary City Planning

There are also some more general insights worthy of reflection:

- **Evolving policy considerations**. The greatest nuance of topics is in traditional areas such as housing and transport, which suggests approaches to newer policy areas such as the circular economy and wellbeing will become more complex in the future.
- **Diverse places**. While there are many common themes across the plans, there are equally many differences in the importance given to each—a hierarchy of objectives. That is, where for one plan an issue is a leading objective, for another it is a subservient point. This divergence of importance would appear to highlight the notion that every city is different.
- **Context creates meaning**. Continuing the point of diverse places, the context for similar objectives creates clarity of local intent. For example, all plans have policies relating to centres. For Melbourne, the policy to grow local centres sits under the wider policy objective of '20-minute neighbourhoods' (Plan Melbourne, Policy 5.1.2, p. 99). This context provides greater clarity as to the objectives of the plan.

  Conversely, sometimes there are isolated statements such as 'improve cycle ways' without any reference to the outcome sought, such as to provide access to centres, journey to work trips, or recreational paths in high amenity areas.

  Also, the word 'strengthen' is used in numerous cases. It is an interesting descriptor, as in reality it does not mean a lot. And yes, I am guilty of this.
- **Jurisdictional context**. There is no uniformity of planning language across the city plans. Interpreting the plans requires a level of understanding of the planning jargon for the city. For example, in Victoria the planning act has 'objectives', in NSW they are called 'objects', and in Melbourne the concept of 'liveability' has an innate meaning understood by the local planning profession. This is one of the small challenges for any attempt at formulating national planning principles or objectives.
- **Operational versus strategic**. It is often difficult to comment on the ins and outs of a plan unless you were in the room. That said, one area that is always a challenge is restating business-as-usual policy positions where such policy positions should be standard planning objectives for the whole state, not point in time objectives as part of a plan. An example is protecting the environment, where all states have an objective about protecting biodiversity. When operational objectives are instead part of a state policy framework, city plans can then focus on the actions required to achieve specific outcomes in relation to the higher order objective.
- A related issue is restating objectives from other portfolios. Heritage is one of these. All the plans address heritage and all jurisdictions have separate heritage legislation. The Perth and Peel @ 3.5 million plan (p. 51) takes the preferred approach. It directly addresses the issue, but rather than restating objectives it links to the relevant state planning policy.

3.4.2 Insights From International City Plans

I have reviewed four international metropolitan plans:

- *The London Plan*, The spatial development strategy for Greater London, 2021, The Mayor of London
  - London Plan
- OneNYC 2050 *Building a Strong and Fair City*, 2019, The City of New York, Mayor Bill De Blasio
  - OneNYC plan
- A Place to Grow, Growth Plan for the Greater Golden Horseshoe, 2020, Ministry of Municipal Affairs and Housing, Ontario
  - Greater Golden Horseshoe (Toronto) plan
- *Metro* Vancouver 2040, *Shaping Our Future*, 2011, Updated 2020, Greater Vancouver Regional District Board
  - Metro Vancouver plan

Some of the overarching issues identified in the review include (refer Table 3.3):

- **Scope**. The review revealed that, generally, the themes covered in the plans are similar to those in the Australian plans. See Sect. 3.6.3 for a detailed review.

  As with the Australian plans, differences are more about the depth of issues rather than the breadth of the issues, not discounting that OneNYC covers education and justice issues reflecting the responsibilities of local governments in the United States.
- **Structure**. There are differences in the structure of the plans from a range of perspectives:
  - The plans for Greater Toronto and London have limited to no contextual information, they simply outline the policies and actions.
  - The plan for London is very detailed with 106 policy areas with just under 1000 more detailed policy statements supported by many thousands of policy clarifications. That said, the document, while more than 500 pages long, is easy to navigate.
  - The London and Greater Toronto plans provide direction through policy, whereas the New York City and Metro Vancouver plans use policy to provide direction for their actions. The Australian plans have both approaches.
- **Delivery**. All the plans identify performance measures or commit to monitoring. Other implementation considerations in the plans include:
  - London Plan—Outlines funding considerations across a range of delivery areas and proposed monitoring activities, including intended performance measures.
  - Greater Golden Horseshoe (Toronto) plan—Outlines delivery issues including coordination responsibilities, the requirement for growth forecasts and targets, and monitoring and performance indicators activities.

- Metro Vancouver plan—Requires local governments to prepare Regional Context Statements to ensure local plans align with the regional plan, coordination with First Nations people, and coordination across other agencies.
- OneNYC plan—Focuses on actions with an indication of the responsible agency, and funding status.

3.5 The Rationale for Planning Cities

From the outset cities have been a crucible for specialisation, enabled by collaboration, which provided choice and became magnets for people. Retaining the ability for specialisation through innovation is therefore a fundamental pre-condition for planning cities.

The magnetic attraction of cities brings challenges, for more people increase the demands on the necessities of life—health, through sanitation, and water. Interventions are therefore required where the marketplace does not deliver on the needs of the city.

Since the industrial revolution, the community's expectations of what interventions are required **have expanded from the necessities of life to the good life.** With that expansion there has been increased clarity as to why we need intervention. The reasons can be categorised to reflect the drivers behind the desired benefit as follows:

- **Reduce or prevent negative externalities**. This is about failures of the market to manage the consequences of production/development, such as pollution, noise, odour and overshadowing.
- **Create opportunities or improvements for society**. These often reflect the implications of cumulative development and population growth, such as more local community services and more open space or improved urban tree canopy to improve local micro-climates. It could also mean improving economic outcomes and opportunities for business, such as improving supply chains and communications (ICT) infrastructure (for example, ports, airports, freight rail, telecommunications, 5G, etc.) and/or creating new opportunities for business activity linked to such infrastructure.
- **Protect natural systems**. These often have a cumulative impact and cover areas such as:
  - the need to sustain life, that is, the direct interplay between the environment and what is needed to sustain human life such as clean water and clean air;
  - the need to protect biodiversity values, in the context of the intrinsic value of natural eco-systems;
  - the tragedy of the commons, that is, the overexploitation of a shared resource, such as the harvesting of fish; and
  - the cumulative impact of negative externalities, such as impacts on the environment external to the source, for example, acid rain; sediment impacts

Table 3.3 Australian and international metropolitan plans: Variability in content

This table outlines the differences in several elements in plans for Australia's capital cities and a select number of international plans. This includes the depth of policy hierarchies from level one down to level four; whether the plans have actions and sub-actions; and how long each plan is, in pages.

Plan elements	ACT	Adelaide	Darwin	Greater Sydney	Melbourne	Perth & Peel	South East Queensland	London	Newyorkcity	Greater Toronto	Metro Vancouver
Level 1	5	15	14	10	7	5	5	10	8	3	5
Level 2	25	122	46	40	32	33	35	106	30	27	14
Level 3	–	–	–	62	–	–	144	Approx 950	–	140	–
Level 4	–	–	–	–	–	–	–	Many 1000s	–	–	–
Actions	60	68	–	15	–	–	52	Many 1000 s	114	–	111
Sub-actions	–	–	–	–	–	–	–	–	225	–	–
Pages	116	188	84	194	152	94	192	542	332	114	80

Note The number of policies and actions is a best estimate noting that in many cases there are clear discrete sub-actions as per the *OneNYC* plan whereas in other cases it is not so clear. As such, I have attempted to estimate discrete tasks to emphasise the approach taken as distinct from seeking to suggest an accurate assessment

from stormwater run-off; and weed and pest invasion at the interface between development and natural habitat.
- **Achieve orderly and coordinated development**. Doing so prevents a disconnect between development and the infrastructure required to support it (both timing and location of delivery) for whatever reason, such as insufficient funds to support its timely delivery.
- **Meet societal norms**. Besides cities being places where we live, work and play, they are cultural places that reflect collective values, beliefs and aspirations. Consequently, within cities and regions some built form elements and places reflect intangible values that the community has codified, such as local character (for example, many Australians' long connection to a suburban built form) and heritage values. Societal norms change over time, requiring planning to continually adjust.
- **Support community and individual wellbeing**. Wellbeing reflects the level of social capital, social cohesion and the delivery of socially sustainable cities. It includes addressing the negative impacts arising from the structure of cities including urban alienation, loneliness, and obesity or enhancing the value of public spaces by creating spaces for informal social interaction.
- **Achieve social equity**. This includes improving accessibility, in its widest sense, to achieve equitable access to education, jobs and public transport.
- **Address housing affordability**. The great Australian dream of owning your own home is no longer an option for all. Housing affordability remains as a central challenge for planning better cities.

This view that intervention is required to deliver a range of societal benefits is emphasised by Gurran (2011). Chapter 1 of her book *Australian urban land use planning: principles, systems and practice*, explores a definition of spatial land use planning and focuses on the notion of intervention as the rationale for planning. Gurran suggests that the urban ills or challenges of cities and regions are the primary justification for public intervention into the land use planning system, with the intent to achieve strategic policy objectives.

However, there are those whose definition of planning would be far less interventionist. They argue that it is the interventions themselves that create some of the urban ills, such as housing affordability, and that we should not constrain housing supply artificially through regulations such as heritage controls, height controls, or density controls. Instead, decisions on housing outcomes should generally be left to the market.

Bertaud (2018) covers this issue in his book *Order Without Design, How Markets Shape Cities*. Bertaud argues that urban planners need to heed the advice of urban economists and let markets play out and resolve issues such as housing supply.

There are many arguments on both sides, but while a particularly important topic, it is beyond the scope of this book. Instead, I would stress that cities are not created simply by economic rules. Cities are also shaped by decisions arising from social norms, some of which are codified to become planning regulations, such as overlooking, overshadowing and minimum requirements for open space in a new residential subdivision. Moreover, these social norms continually evolve.

It may well be possible to develop market mechanisms for some social norms, However,

> *I have been involved in formal blue sky thinking with treasury colleagues who suggested a way for the market to manage overshadowing. Without going into the detail, an important aspect of strategic planning is the legacy element; that is, to the best of our ability handing over to the next generation a place which is better than the one we inherited, rather than one where sunlight is now precluded from someone's backyard, which can never be replaced.*

Thus, I would emphasise that planning's challenge is that it is not an exact science. Planning is:

- a social science and thus can be described from various viewpoints
- a discipline which directly impacts on most people's everyday life as they work, rest and play
- a discipline which many people directly or indirectly become involved in, often because of development proposals near where they live
- invariably highly contested, as it is influenced by social norms and the protection of an individual's private property rights
- often seen to be a panacea for all the problems of the city, due to all the above.

I would agree with Bertaud (2018) that planners should seek the advice of urban economists. At the same time, they are not the only experts who need to provide advice on the journey of planning cities. Furthermore, Forester (1999, p. 240) emphasises:

> Although economic analysis often assumes the commensurability of values, that assumption can be unwarranted, or worse: a recipe for producing resentment (for example, when a citizen's deeply felt values are treated as purely financial matters).

Therefore, planning processes must incorporate efforts to bring the community to the table, as it is the community that influences many of the social norms embedded in planning. Forester (1999) details of the role of planners as the bridge between planning decisions and the community in his work *The Deliberative Practitioner*.

3.6 The Scope of City Planning

A challenge for city planning is the risk that it will become an omnibus for all the ills of a city. This has been my experience. Often, other agencies or peak bodies seek a city plan that can resolve their sectoral challenges. The consequence is that the government of the day feels overloaded with policy issues—and some fall to the cutting floor (and not necessarily the right ones).

3.6 The Scope of City Planning

In this context, city planning processes need to recognise the many government agencies that have direct responsibility to provide guidance on a range of sectoral issues, such as health services, education outcomes, justice matters or transport needs. The underlying raison d'être of strategic planning is to determine how these sectors interconnect from a spatial perspective—it is not to write the sectoral policies per se.

Therefore, in setting out to prepare a city plan we need clarity as to what is 'its scope'.

3.6.1 Legislation Requirements

The objectives for planning as outlined in contemporary planning legislation provide some insights as to the scope of planning. To highlight this point, the objectives stated in the NSW and Victorian planning legislation are outlined in Table 3.4.

In addition, the NSW *Environmental Planning and Assessment Act 1979 No 203* also provides high level guidance in *Division 3.1 Strategic Planning, Section 3.3, Clause (2)*, where it states:

> A draft regional strategic plan must include or identify the following—
> (a) the basis for strategic planning in the region, having regard to economic, social and environmental matters,

These objectives provide some clarity for what governments deem to be important, yet they fall short of clarifying the domain of planners. They therefore do not provide a holistic framework for understanding what is important to people, their lives, and the places they live in, now and in the future.

However, the objectives emphasise that planning is about the community and managing various outcomes such as development, heritage and the environment as they relate to the 'land' (place).

3.6.2 Common Issues from Australian Contemporary Plans

The breadth of topics covered by the plans for Australia's capital cities provides some indication of what the scope of city planning should be. I assessed the seven plans (identified earlier in Sect. 3.4.1) in terms of explicit statements in either objectives, policies, or strategies, refer Table 3.5. In some cases, it is apparent that the objectives or policy directions are embedded in the general text of the plan.

The assessment sought to reveal whether there is commonality in the issues that are the focus of each plan. To provide structure to the assessment I have grouped the individual policy areas under a set of common headings. The headings utilised were those from *The London Plan* (2021), refer Table 3.6.

Table 3.4 Planning objectives as outlined in NSW and Victorian legislation (As of 6 November 2022)

Victorian Planning and Environment Act 1987, Part 1, Section 4 Objectives	*NSW Environmental Planning and Assessment Act 1979 No 203, Part 1, Section 1.3 Objects of Act*
4 Objectives (1) The objectives of planning in Victoria are— 　(a) to provide for the fair, orderly, economic and sustainable use, and development of land; 　(b) to provide for the protection of natural and man-made resources and the maintenance of ecological processes and genetic diversity; 　(c) to secure a pleasant, efficient and safe working, living and recreational environment for all Victorians and visitors to Victoria; 　(d) to conserve and enhance those buildings, areas or other places which are of scientific, aesthetic, architectural or historical interest, or otherwise of special cultural value; 　(e) to protect public utilities and other assets and enable the orderly provision and co-ordination of public utilities and other facilities for the benefit of the community; 　(f) to facilitate development in accordance with the objectives set out in paragraphs (a), (b), (c), (d) and (e); (fa) to facilitate the provision of affordable housing in Victoria; 　(g) to balance the present and future interests of all Victorians (2) The objectives of the planning framework established by this Act are— 　(a) to ensure sound, strategic planning and co-ordinated action at State, regional and municipal levels; 　(b) to establish a system of planning schemes based on municipal districts to be the principal way of setting out objectives, policies and controls for the use, development and protection of land; 　(c) to enable land use and development planning and policy to be easily integrated with environmental, social, economic, conservation and resource management policies at State, regional and municipal levels; 　(d) to ensure that the effects on the environment are considered and provide for explicit consideration of social and economic effects when decisions are made about the use and development of land;	**1.3 Objects of Act** (cf previous s 5) The objects of this Act are as follows— 　(a) to promote the social and economic welfare of the community and a better environment by the proper management, development and conservation of the State's natural and other resources, 　(b) to facilitate ecologically sustainable development by integrating relevant economic, environmental and social considerations in decision-making about environmental planning and assessment, 　(c) to promote the orderly and economic use and development of land, 　(d) to promote the delivery and maintenance of affordable housing, 　(e) to protect the environment, including the conservation of threatened and other species of native animals and plants, ecological communities and their habitats, 　(f) to promote the sustainable management of built and cultural heritage (including Aboriginal cultural heritage), 　(g) to promote good design and amenity of the built environment, 　(h) to promote the proper construction and maintenance of buildings, including the protection of the health and safety of their occupants, 　(i) to promote the sharing of the responsibility for environmental planning and assessment between the different levels of government in the State, 　(j) to provide increased opportunity for community participation in environmental planning and assessment

(continued)

Table 3.4 (continued)

Victorian Planning and Environment Act 1987, Part 1, Section 4 Objectives	NSW Environmental Planning and Assessment Act 1979 No 203, Part 1, Section 1.3 Objects of Act

(e) to facilitate development which achieves the objectives of planning in Victoria and planning objectives set up in planning schemes;
 (f) to provide for a single authority to issue permits for land use or development and related matters, and to co-ordinate the issue of permits with related approvals;
 (g) to encourage the achievement of planning objectives through positive actions by responsible authorities and planning authorities;
 (h) to establish a clear procedure for amending planning schemes, with appropriate public participation in decision making;
   (i) to ensure that those affected by proposals for the use, development or protection of land or changes in planning policy or requirements receive appropriate notice;
 (j) to provide an accessible process for just and timely review of decisions without unnecessary formality;
 (k) to provide for effective enforcement procedures to achieve compliance with planning schemes, permits and agreements;
   (l) to provide for compensation when land is set aside for public purposes and in other circumstances	

The assessment suggests a reasonable level of consistency across the plans as to the breadth of issues relevant to contemporary plans. In most cases the outlier issues reflect the depth to which issues are addressed as distinct from the breadth of issues.

International examples highlight one challenge in comparing plans—portfolio accountability. For example, for New York City, the city council has responsibility for overseeing the delivery of education and law and order, thus these issues are directly addressed in the city plan.

The assessment in Table 3.5 shows that the plans generally focus on issues that affect the management of land, including transport networks, emphasising that land use and transport planning are two sides of the same coin. Transport planning is also shown to be multi-faceted.

This inter-relationship, I believe, is fundamental to strategic planning and I have, for some time, sought to emphasise this point conceptually in a collection of vignettes as shown in Fig. 3.1.

Consequently, I feel this point cannot be overemphasised. As far as practical city planning activities should be joint land use and transport activities, and therefore require the direct involvement of transport planners in all strategic planning projects.

Table 3.5 Common policy issues across contemporary Australian capital city plans

A high level of commonality, within six or all seven plans	A medium level of commonality, within three to five plans		Outlier issues, within one or two plans
Spatial development patterns	**Spatial development patterns**		**Spatial development patterns**
Supported urban renewal linked to public transport	Housing around centres		Develop a new city structure (excluding the concept of a general network of centres)
Manage place (local) outcomes	Targeted urban renewal		Accessibility benchmarks, Greater Sydney's 30-minute city and Melbourne's 20-minute neighbourhoods
Centres as a focus for urban development	Integrated land use and transport planning		Protecting border interfaces
Hierarchy of centres	Urban containment		
Design	Targeted land use/transport initiatives		**Design**
None	Manage the values of hinterlands (peri-urban areas)		None
Housing	**Design**		**Housing**
Diversity of housing	Good design		None
Social infrastructure	Manage local character		**Social infrastructure**
None	**Housing**		Land set aside for social infrastructure
Economy	Housing supply		Planning for cemeteries and crematoria
Managing industrial land	Affordable housing		Diverse communities
Centres policies	**Social infrastructure**		Social needs of First Nations people
Support agricultural activities	Healthy communities		**Economy**
Support mining activities from stone resources and sand to mineral deposits such as coal	Social inclusion/wellbeing		Protect the operations of industry and freight
Heritage and culture	Support the arts and cultural activities		Economic needs of First Nations people
Post contact heritage,	**Economy**		**Heritage and culture**
First Nations heritage and culture	Support economic clusters		None
Green infrastructure and natural environment	Support the CBD		**Green infrastructure and natural environment**
Protect biodiversity	Protect industrial land		Encourage green infrastructure
Develop an open space network	Support health and education precincts		Safeguarding high priority groundwater resources
Water efficiency	Target economic initiatives		Open space within walking distance of homes
Sustainable infrastructure	Support tourism activities		**Sustainable infrastructure**
Align growth with infrastructure, including statements on sequencing	**Heritage and culture**		Digital infrastructure
Infrastructure meets the needs of the community	None		Adaptive infrastructure
Optimise existing infrastructure	**Green infrastructure and natural environment**		**Transport**
Transport	Healthy waterways and coasts		Regional transport connections
Walkability	Protect water catchments		
	Protect landscape values		
	Expand the urban tree canopy		
	Respond to natural hazards		

(continued)

3.6 The Scope of City Planning   67

Table 3.5 (continued)

A high level of commonality, within six or all seven plans	A medium level of commonality, within three to five plans	Outlier issues, within one or two plans
	Respond to urban hazards Manage heat waves/cooling cities **Sustainable infrastructure** Energy efficiency Improved waste management Low carbon cities Climate change adaptation activities **Transport** Public transport initiatives Support cycling Protect future transport corridors Freight initiative Protect and enhance trade gateways **Other** Collaboration and community participation	

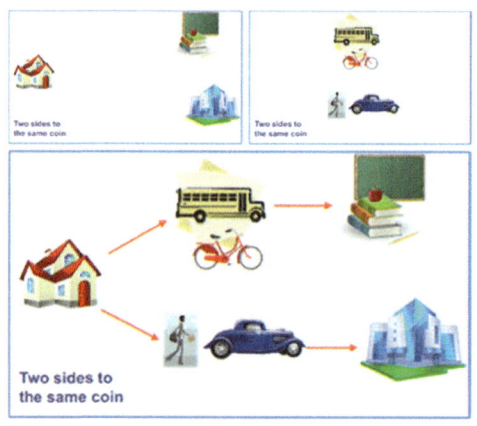

Fig. 3.1 Land use and transport, two sides of one coin

3.6.3 Common Themes from Contemporary International Plans

There is a divergence of themes and an emphasis of underlying issues across the international plans and the following insights are highlighted (refer Table 3.6):

- The different emphasis of issues covered reflect the maturity, location and growth management issues for a city. For example:
  - *The London Plan*, Metro Vancouver, and Greater Golden Horseshoe (Toronto) plans all include a range of policies to manage spatial outcomes.
  - The Metro Vancouver and Greater Golden Horseshoe (Toronto) plans address managing outward growth and rural areas.
  - *OneNYC* and *The London Plan* emphasise equity outcomes such as a sustainable economy for all, inclusive communities, efficiency and resilience.
- *OneNYC* takes the issue of equity a lot further than the other plans and addresses issues such as poverty, democracy, justice, equal rights and fair wages.
- *The London Plan* has an extraordinary level of policy detail with policy considerations covering four levels. For example:
  - **Level 1 – Chapter theme**: such as Chapter 4: Housing.
  - **Level 2 – Policy area**: such as policy H4 Increasing housing supply.
  - **Level 3 – Policy detail**: such as 10-year housing targets.
  - **Level 4 – Supporting policy qualification statements**: such as '… the Mayor's aim to ensure that Londoners have an opportunity to purchase new homes before they are marketed overseas …'.

3.6 The Scope of City Planning   69

Table 3.6 Policy themes across four international metropolitan plans

The London Plan	OneNYC	Greater Golden Horseshoe (Toronto)	Metro Vancouver
Chapter 1 Planning London's Future – Good Growth	**A vibrant democracy**	**Where and How to Grow**	**Create a Compact Urban Area**
	Empower all New Yorkers to participate in our democracy	Managing Growth	Contain urban development within the Urban Containment Boundary
	Welcome new New Yorkers from around the world and involve them fully in civic life	Delineated Built-up Areas	Focus growth in Urban Centres and Frequent Transit Development Areas
Chapter 2 Spatial Development Patterns	Promote justice and equal rights, and build trust between New Yorkers and government	Urban Growth Centres	Protect Rural areas from urban development
Chapter 3 Design	Promote democracy and civic innovation on the global stage	Transit Corridors and Station Areas	
Chapter 4 Housing	**An inclusive economy**	Employment	**Support a Sustainable Economy**
Chapter 5 Social Infrastructure	Grow the economy with good-paying jobs and prepare New Yorkers to fill them	Housing	Promote land development patterns that support a diverse regional economy and employment close to where people live
Chapter 6 Economy	Provide economic security for all through fair wages and expanded benefits	Designated Greenfield Areas	Protect the supply of industrial land
Chapter 7 Heritage and Culture	Expand the voice, ownership, and decision-making power of workers and communities	Settlement Area Boundary Expansions	Protect the supply of agricultural land and promote agricultural viability with an emphasis on food production
		Rural Areas	
Chapter 8 Green Infrastructure and Natural Environment	Strengthen the City's fiscal health to meet current and future needs	**Infrastructure to Support Growth**	**Protect the Environment and Respond to Climate Change Impacts**
	Thriving neighbourhoods	Integrated Planning	Protect Conservation and Recreation lands
Chapter 9 Sustainable Infrastructure	Ensure all New Yorkers have access to safe, secure, and affordable housing	Transportation – General	Protect and enhance natural features and their connectivity
Chapter 10 Transport	Ensure all New Yorkers have access to neighborhood open spaces and cultural resources	Moving People	Encourage land use and transportation infrastructure that reduce energy consumption and greenhouse gas emissions, and improve air quality
Note: Within these 10 chapters are 106 policy areas supported by around 950 more detailed policies issues		Moving Goods	
		Infrastructure Corridors	
		Water and Wastewater Systems	
		Stormwater Management	
		Public Service Facilities	
		Protecting What is Valuable	
		Water Resource Systems	

(continued)

Table 3.6 (continued)

Advance shared responsibility for community safety and promote neighborhood policing Promote place-based community planning and strategies **Healthy lives** Guarantee high-quality, affordable, and accessible health care for all New Yorkers Advance equity by addressing the health and mental health needs of all communities Make healthy lifestyles easier in all neighborhoods Design a physical environment that creates the conditions for health and well-being **Equity and excellence in education** Make New York City a leading national model for early childhood education Advance equity in K-12 opportunity and achievement Increase integration, diversity, and inclusion in New York City schools **A liveable climate** Achieve carbon neutrality and 100 percent clean electricity Strengthen communities, buildings, infrastructure, and the waterfront to be more resilient Create economic opportunities for all New Yorkers through climate action Fight for climate accountability and justice **Efficient mobility** Modernize New York City's mass transit networks Ensure New York City's streets are safe and accessible Reduce congestion and emissions Strengthen connections to the region and the world **Modern infrastructure** Make forward-thinking investments in core physical infrastructure and hazard mitigation Improve digital infrastructure to meet the needs of the twenty-first century Implement best practices for asset maintenance and capital project delivery	Natural Heritage System Key Hydrologic Features, Key Hydrologic Areas and Key Natural Heritage Features Lands Adjacent to Key Hydrologic Features and Key Natural Heritage Features Public Open Space Agricultural System Cultural Heritage Resources Mineral Aggregate Resources A Culture of Conservation Climate Change	Encourage land use and transportation infrastructure that improve the ability to withstand climate change impacts and natural hazard risks **Develop Complete Communities** Provide diverse and affordable housing choices Develop healthy and complete communities with access to a range of services and amenities **Support Sustainable Transportation Choices** Coordinate land use and transportation to encourage transit, multiple-occupancy vehicles, cycling and walking Coordinate land use and transportation to support the safe and efficient movement of vehicles for passengers, goods and services

3.6.4 Drivers of Change in the Twenty-First Century

In recent decades some new drivers of change have emerged as central considerations for planning. These include climate change, digital accessibility (the Internet of Things), new technologies that continue to disrupt) and most recently the COVID-19 pandemic.

3.6.4.1 Climate Change

Climate change is one of the most significant issues impacting cities and regions across the world. In February 2022 the Intergovernmental Panel on Climate Change (IPCC), the United Nations body for assessing the science related to climate change, released the *Climate Change 2022: Impacts, Adaptation and Vulnerability* report. One finding is that:

> … there is at least a greater than 50% likelihood that global warming will reach or exceed 1.5°C in the near-term, even for the very low greenhouse gas emissions scenario. (IPCC 2022, p. 8)

In the context of climate-resilient development for natural and human systems the report states:

> Interactions between changing urban form, exposure and vulnerability can create climate change-induced risks and losses for cities and settlements. However, the global trend of urbanisation also offers a critical opportunity in the near-term, to advance climate resilient development (high confidence). Integrated, inclusive planning and investment in everyday decision-making about urban infrastructure, including social, ecological and grey/physical infrastructures, can significantly increase the adaptive capacity of urban and rural settlements. (IPCC 2022, p. 31)

The issue of climate change and its impact on cities is discussed in Sect. 15.3.6 where, among other things, the variability in the approach to climate change in Australia's capital city plans is highlighted.

Common policy issues need common metrics if all governments across Australia are going to respond consistently to the challenges of climate change. The transport sector does this well, as all treasury departments have a consistent understanding of transport economics.

We need to address climate change issues in a more integrated way and promote the climate change benefits of the many core planning objectives inherent in city planning. A common framework would connect planning agencies to analysis techniques that could be adapted for local conditions, while detailing the levers available and their benefits.

3.6.4.2 Digital Accessibility

Since the turn of the century, digital technologies have increasingly influenced how we live, work and play. They challenge historical views of physical accessibility and the consequential impacts on urban form and settlement patterns.

- **The gig economy** has transformed several sectors, such as the taxi industry, courier services for food, and short-term accommodation, by connecting customers through an online service. Customers are attracted to a service more adaptable to the needs of the moment, combined with the demand for flexible lifestyles.

    Some changes in cities include the emergence of new activities such as dark restaurants, and a decline in rental accommodation due to supply servicing the short-term accommodation market—this has resulted in planning and related laws to manage the impacts of this new accommodation sector (Gurran et al. 2020).

- **Online retailing** has been around for some time; however, the COVID-19 pandemic accelerated its growth. The demand by consumers has seen the emergence of retail outlets found only online. The influence of these changes across cities is evident in supply chains, given the need to satisfy same-day service demands of customers. The consequence has been more complex distribution systems where goods are distributed across the city to consumers as small parcels rather than on pallets to retail outlets. A report prepared for Australia Post provided statistics on their activities for April 2020, which:

    > … saw large increases in the number of parcel deliveries for items such as Food and Liquor (159.5 per cent increase from the previous year). Homewares and Appliances parcel deliveries increased by 93.5 per cent from the previous year.

    As a result, we have seen a proliferation of small delivery vehicles to service last-mile distribution requirements.

    In addition, some logistics companies are exploring options for multi-level facilities in established areas due to land rents. My own discussions with logistics companies reveal they are also exploring drone services and robots to manage the last-mile needs of consumers.

    The traditional retail sector has responded, by both providing online services and adapting its approach and offerings to customers.

    The implication of these changes on the long-term structure of centres and transport supply chains and networks is difficult to predict. What is evident is the importance of retaining industrial lands right across the city so that these sectors can adapt. Activity in centres was impacted (more online sales) by the stay-at-home restrictions required to manage the impacts of the COVID-19 pandemic. The extent to which that change remains is yet to be revealed.

- **Work from home**. The work-from-home requirement for many industry sectors during the COVID-19 pandemic had a range of impacts:
    - Technology improvements for a range of business functions (such as secure document transfers and virtual meetings) cemented what was flexible working arrangements to become a real alternative working model.

- There are pros and cons for the work-from-home model, and businesses and organisation are continuing to experiment and determine the best outcomes for their own business needs.
- Edward Glaeser, in a podcast for the Committee for Sydney, discussed the issue of cities and the COVID-19 pandemic, drawing from his book *Survival of the City: Living and Thriving in an Age of Isolation*, co-written with David Cutler. Among a range of issues, he emphasised that while working from home has allowed flexibility, it is an inhibitor to learning.
- The implications for cities and city dynamics included a significant exodus of workers from CBDs, consequently, the focus as workers return, is occupancy rates, as distinct from vacancy rates. Support services such as the hospitality sector were impacted with many workplaces having to close. At the same time, workers benefited by avoiding the daily commute, and local centres experienced the benefits of people staying in their community. In Australia at least, numerous state governments looked to provide incentives for people to return to the CBDs to work.
- The scale of the work-from-home choice impacted transport demand, including public transport where perceived and real risks of catching COVID-19 influenced patronage.
- With workers returning to CBDs, what becomes the new normal, in terms of working arrangements, is unclear. There appears to be extremes. In Australia, the company Atlassian announced that its workers only need be in the office four times a year (Waters 2021), while at the other end Elon Musk, in the United States, announced that his staff should be in the office every day (Mac 2022). What becomes the norm is yet to be seen, but history suggests you rarely travel back to the past.
- What may well emerge is not some simple hybrid model of working from home some days and in the office the rest, but one where the pros and cons are carefully considered resulting in a completely new working model.
- **Virtual reality activities**. A few global technology companies are exploring enhanced virtual reality experiences. While they have existed for online gaming for some time, current research is considering experiences such as virtual holidays where you can visit far-off places from the comfort of your own home. A recent article suggests this could have an impact on traditional forms of travel (Templeman 2022).
- **Escape to the regions**. A combination of the stay-at-home restrictions and work-from-home options during the COVID-19 pandemic led many households to relocate to regional areas.

  Data from the Australian 2021 Census has shown that the population of regional Australia grew by 11 per cent for the period 2011–2021, still below that for the population growth in capital cities (17 per cent for the same period).

  The Australian Government's Centre for Population's *Migration between cities and regions: A quick guide to COVID-19*, released before the 2021 Census, found:

- A projection of a net shift in migration away from capital cities in favour of regional areas in 2020–21, before gradually returning towards the long-term average.
- Underscoring the uncertainty surrounding this topic, surveyed experts were split on the impact of COVID-19. Approximately half expect it to have no impact on migration patterns between cities and regions, with the other half expecting a slight shift in favour of migration from capital cities to regional areas.
- Early PRIME data indicates a net shift in migration towards regional areas. The impact of the lockdown in Melbourne and Victoria is clear, with Melbourne experiencing its largest net migration loss on record.

The extent to which these pre-Census findings and the actual changes as revealed will require continued monitoring and analysis.

While the benefits for some households are clear, negative impacts reported in media outlets include increased house prices in regional communities (Bell and Reading 2022) and reductions in rental housing supply (Smyrk 2022).

Throughout my career, I have consistently sought to understand how cities change—for example, how the knowledge economy and agglomeration economics influence the core of cities. Now I see a combination of digitally enabled drivers that may influence the overall structure of cities and settlements. Exactly how these new forces will play out is still revealing itself; it is a space to be watched and reflected and acted on.

3.6.4.3 Technology

The influence of new technology on cities is not new. Technologies such as aqueducts and sewer systems addressed the challenges of co-locating many people in small spaces. The steam engine facilitated the industrial age, from which modern planning emerged to manage the consequential impact on the health of the communities in cities. From this came new models for how to plan and structure cities.

New technologies continue to influence the dynamics of how cities function. In addition to the technology that has made working from home more feasible for many employees, there are other emerging technologies that will continue to create the need for cities and the people within them to adapt. These technologies include:

- **3D printing**, which has the potential to disrupt the manufacturing and construction sectors through on-site production of inputs for a range of needs and may be improving just in time logistics challenges for on-demand services.
- **Autonomous vehicles**, which are still in their infancy. A paper by Kersten Heineke, Ruth Heuss, Ani Kelkar and Martin Kellner of McKinsey & Company (2021), based on a survey of 75 executives from automotive, transportation and software companies working on autonomous driving worldwide, focused on:

- Regulation as one bottleneck for adoption of autonomous driving;
- Investment levels to enable highway driving;
- Benefit to companies from investing in software and hardware; and
- The need for new monetisation models to activate private autonomous vehicle usage.

In trying to determine when autonomous vehicles will hit the road, the survey findings revealed a range anywhere from 2024 to 2032. This highlights the uncertainties in what will potentially be a paradigm shift in how transport systems operate.

- **Safety and privacy** are two aspects of city life that are intertwined with new technologies. Digital technologies allow the monitoring of work-from-home employees, provide enhanced security for electronic devices through face and fingerprint recognition, and cameras allow surveillance of public places to enhance community safety. However, as with any technological change, the impact on the community needs to be examined and debated, particularly the issue of privacy.

3.6.4.4 COVID-19 Pandemic

Numerous city commentators, such as Richard Florida (Committee for Sydney podcast) emphasise that the COVID-19 pandemic has not changed how we behave; it has accelerated what was already occurring. Some behaviours are new, such as reduced patronage of public transport due to perceived and real risks of infection from the COVID-19 virus.

The more significant consideration is whether the accelerated changes created by the COVID-19 pandemic will change the trajectory of how we plan and manage cities, and whether the new normal requires a different approach, or the need to muddle through and learn as we go, or something in between.

Concluding Reflections

Dealing with change is a core requirement of strategic planning. These twenty-first-century drivers of change could potentially change current assumptions about cities as settlements and the behaviour of people and businesses within them. For example:

> In 2022 I worked in Western Sydney, a major greenfield growth area for Greater Sydney. The challenge is how to plan for new communities knowing that projections predict at least a 40-year supply of land for housing and industry. Considering that when the last estates will be completed, these emerging drivers will likely become mainstream practices. How then do we test the robustness of our current planning and delivery approaches against the influences of these new drivers of change? I feel this will be a focus for the next generation of planners.

3.6.4.5 A Definition of the Scope of Planning

Since the emergence of modern planning, the focus of activities appears to be influenced more by the major events of the day (from urban slums to climate change), as distinct from a change to the general themes being addressed, such as housing, jobs and transport. The evolving emphasis appears to influence the depth of issues more so than the breadth.

This overarching conclusion is invaluable in informing the scope of city planning, a necessary first step in establishing a framework for strategic planning. Defining the scope of city planning assists in identifying the areas for investigation and in defining the parameters for intervention.

A definition of the scope of city planning is proposed as follows:

- City planning should cover what is important to people, to their lives, and the places they live in, now and in the future
  and how these impact on
- land use and transport outcomes, including urban form and natural systems.

Effectively, city planning is responsible for the spatial outcomes of the three dimensions of a city (height, length and width) in the context of the needs of the community.

To emphasise the implications of this definition I provide the following examples:

- What transport networks are required to support population and jobs growth? As distinct from focusing on transport operational matters.
- What land management and development considerations are important for healthy waterways? As distinct from the management of the waterways themselves.
- What urban design outcomes will encourage social interaction? As distinct from managing community services programs.
- What are the benefits of co-locating health and education facilities in town centres? As distinct from considerations of the operational activities of those facilities.
- What development regulations or infrastructure investments are required to attract commercial activities (retail, office, etc.)? As distinct from directing businesses to make certain decisions.

My experience is that ultimately it is a balancing act of all these considerations.

Finally, the definition includes a temporal reference, in that the interventions we make today usually take time to come to fruition. Delivery by itself implies that city planning is about benefits to a future community.

3.7 Summary

This chapter outlines the case for why we need to plan. It has sought to articulate what looks like a simple question by considering the question from a range of perspectives including from the evolution of planning through the ages to the scope of contemporary city plans.

I argue that cities provide choice through specialisation, and that this is achieved through collaboration. It is the choices that cities offer that make them attractive, however, it has always been necessary to intervene in to sustain and protect life (health and safety) through sanitation, access to clean water and fortification.

Since the industrial revolution, and more particularly since the late nineteenth century, the focus for intervention has expanded to cover what Aristotle calls the 'good life', that which keeps us in cities. Interventions covered quality of life elements such as the protection of amenity through the separation of land uses to the provision of open space. In the late twentieth century, the value attributed to the environment shifted from protecting natural resources that help sustain life to recognising the intrinsic value of the environment itself for both now and the future—the concept of sustainability.

Contemporary planning has continued to expand on aspects of the good life by considering issues such as social equity, such as, the provision of affordable housing through planning mechanisms.

Therefore, the principal conclusion is that **planning is about intervention**, which reflects a need to achieve a societal benefit that would not be achieved by the market.

The reasons for interventions to improve the efficiency and quality of cities have evolved and continue to evolve. City planning must be evolutionary in nature to encompass what people expect of governments so cities can continue to provide the 'good life'. Thus, strategic planning processes need to articulate to the community why a plan is needed and what challenges need to be overcome—in other words, what is driving the need for intervention.

With many interventions responding to social norms where benefits are sometimes difficult to quantify, it is incumbent on city planners to best identify the trade-offs when looking to deliver interventions that address social norms.

As this could lead to a range of issues, I have considered scope for planning by assessing the objectives for planning defined in planning legislation and the breadth of issues covered in contemporary city plans for Australia's capital cities. From this, I believe city planning should cover what is important to people—to their lives, and the places they live in, now and in the future and how these **impact on** land use and transport outcomes, including urban form and natural systems.

Even with this definition of scope the potential issues for investigation are large. Chapter 4 unpacks what you need to investigate, as well as the importance of understanding delivery as part of expanding the discussion of what planning is about and the process of strategic planning.

References

Alexander, C, Ishikawa, S, & Silverstein, M (1977), *A Pattern Language: Towns, Buildings, Construction*, Oxford University Press New York
—Covers all the elements that make places, from cities to bedrooms, and their inter-relationships, including that every element should be an experience including a bus stop.
Bacon, EN (1967), *The Design of Cities*, Penguin Books, Ringwood, Australia
—From my university days and where I learnt about the power of city design (structure) and the art of communication.
Bertaud, A (2018), *Order Without Design, How Markets Shape Cities*, The MIT Press, USA
—An alternative view on the role of plannes and the marketplace.
Carson, R (1962), *Silent Spring*, Penguin Books Australia Ltd, Ringwood
—Seminal book on the impact of human activities on ecosystems.
Chadwick, GF (1971), *A Systems View of Planning: Towards a Theory of the Urban and Regional Planning Process*, Pergamon Press, Oxford, New York
—From my university days and still influences how I see cities.
Crawford, H (ed.) (2013), *The Sumerian World*, Routledge, Milton Park, Abingdon, Oxon
Diamond, J (2005), *Collapse*, Penguin Group (Australia)
—An interesting perspective on the why some civilisations collapse.
Dunlap, DW (2016), 'Zoning Arrived 100 Years Ago. It Changed New York City Forever'. *The New York Times*, 25 July, viewed 22 December 2020
Forester, J (1999), *The Deliberative Practitioner, Encouraging Participatory Planning Processes*, The MIT Press, USA
—The case study approach brings the issue of community engagement to life.
Glaeser, E (2012), *Triumph of the City*, Pan Macmillan UK
—A must read for anyone interested in urban economics.
Glaeser, E, & Cutler, D (2021), *Survival of the City: Living and Thriving in an Age of Isolation*, Basic Books, London, UK
Gurran, N (2011), *Australian urban land use planning. Principles, systems and practice. Second Edition*, Sydney University Press, Australia
—Provides the framework to understand Australia's planning systems.
Gurran N, Zhang Y, & Shrestha P (2020), 'Pop-up' tourism or 'invasion'? Airbnb in coastal Australia, *Annals of Tourism Research*, vol. 81, 102845
Gwilt, J (1874), *The Architecture of Marcus Vitruvius Pollio in Ten Books*, Lockwood & Co. Ludgate Hill UK
Hall, P (1996), *Cities of Tomorrow: An Intellectual History of Urban Planning and Design in the Twentieth Century*, Blackwell Publishers Ltd UK
—Completes the narrative of the history of cities.
Hall, P (1998), *Cities in Civilisation: Culture, innovation, and urban order*, Orion Books Ltd London
—Extraordinary exposé on what makes a great city, with 20 case studies covering 2500 years of cities.
Hamnett, S, & Freestone, R (ed.) (2000), *The Australian Metropolis, A Planning History*, Allen & Unwin, Australia
—The definitive text on the history of planning and Australian cities.
Howard, E (1898), *Garden Cities of To-Morrow*, Publisher
—The seminal text of the garden city movement.
Jacobs, AB (1995), *Great Streets*, MIT Press US
—Assists the reader you appreciate why some streets are better than others and that design matters.
Jacobs, J (1961), *The Death and Life of Great American Cities*, Random House, New York, US
—Seminal ground-breaking view of cities from the perspective of the people in them.

References

Kirkpatrick, A (2015), *The Image of the City in Antiquity: Tracing the origins of Urban Planning, Hippodamian Theory, and the Orthogonal Grid in Classical Greece*, Thesis, University of Victoria, Unpublished
—A master's thesis on the first use of the grid layout.
Lynch, K (1960), *The Image of the City*, The MIT Press
—Breaks down the complexities of how we perceive the city into a simple construct.
McHarg, IL (1971), *Design with Nature*, Doubleday/Natural History Press
—From my university days and helps you see the land before you see the city.
Mithen, S (2003), *After the Ice, A Global Human History 20,000–5000 BC*, Weidenfeld & Nicholson GB
—A detailed journey through time of life as a hunter gatherer.
Mumford, L (1961), *The City in History*, Penguin Books, Australia
—The definitive book on the history of cities through the ages.
Page, A, & Memmott, P (2021), *Design: Building on Country*, Thames & Hudson Australia Pty Limited
Porter, L (2010), *Unlearning the Colonial Cultures of Planning* Ashgate Publishing Ltd
SGS Economics and Planning (2012), *Long run economic and land use impacts of major infrastructure projects*, Unpublished
—Outlines the findings of four case studies on the economic impacts of transport and land use projects.
Stein, LA (2017), *Comparative Urban Land Use Planning, Best Practice*, Sydney University Press
—A detailed assessment of international urban land use planning practices.
Sulman, J (1921), *An Introduction to the Study of Town Planning in Australia*
—One of the earliest perspectives on planning cities in Australia
Unwin, R (1909), *Town Planning practice: An Introduction to the Art of Designing Cities and Suburbs.*, T. Fisher Unwin London
—One of the original texts for modern planning.
Waldrop, ME (1992), *Complexity*, Simon & Schuster Paperbacks US
—Changed how I understand the dynamics of cities, which are not linear.
Waters, C (2021), Four times a year in the office: Atlassian goes all in on WFH, *Sydney Morning Herald*, 29 April 2021.
West, G (2018), *Scale, The Universal Laws of Life and Death in Organisms, Cities and Companies*, Hachette, Australia
—Based on the research of hundreds of cities, this book outlines that there are relationships between the scale of cities and various attributes of cities.
World Commission on Environment and Development (1987), *Our Common Future*, Oxford University Press, GB
—Seminal work on sustainability.

Website Links

Australian Bureau of Statistics, *2016 Census Households Australian Bureau of Statistics*. https://www.abs.gov.au/websitedbs/D3310114.nsf/Home/Census
Australian Government, Centre for Population, *Migration between cities and regions: A quick guide to COVID-19 impacts*. PowerPoint Presentation (population.gov.au)
ACT Planning Strategy 2018 (2018), Australian Capital Territory. https://www.planning.act.gov.au/act-planning-strategy
A Metropolis of Three Cities (2018), State of New South Wales. https://www.greater.sydney/metropolis-of-three-cities
A Place to Grow, Growth Plan for the Greater Golden Horseshoe, 2020, Ministry of Municipal Affairs and Housing, Ontario. A Place to Grow: Growth plan for the Greater Golden Horseshoe | Ontario.ca

Australia Post, n.d., Economic Assessment of Australia Post's activities during COVID-19. Economic assessment of Australia Post's activities during COVID-19 (auspost.com.au)

Bell, P, & Reading, K (2022), Regional housing markets approaching peak, but still growing faster than capital cities, *ABC News*, 29 April 2022. Regional housing markets approaching peak, but still growing faster than capital cities - ABC News

Commonwealth of Australia Constitution Act (The Constitution) viewed 8 July 2020. https://www.legislation.gov.au/Details/C2013Q00005

Darwin Regional Land Use Plan 2015 (2015), Northern Territory Government, Department of lands, Planning and the Environment. https://planningcommission.nt.gov.au/projects/drlup

Edward Glaeser, October 2021, Committee for Sydney Podcast: *Survival of the City: living and thriving in the age of isolation*. Edward Glaeser on survival of the city - CFS (sydney.org.au)

Heineke, K, Heuss, R, Kelkar, A & Kellner, M (2021), What's next for autonomous vehicles? *McKinsey Centre for Future Mobility*. What's next for autonomous vehicles? | McKinsey

Mac, R 2022, Elon Musk to Workers: Spend 40 Hours in the Office, or Else, *New York Times*, 1 June 2022. Elon Musk Tells Tesla and SpaceX Workers to Return to Office 40 Hours a Week - The New York Times (nytimes.com)

Intergovernmental Panel on Climate Change 2022 Climate Change 2022: Impacts, Adaptation and Vulnerability, Working Group II Contribution to the Sixth Assessment Report of the Intergovernmental Panel on Climate Change Climate Change 2022: Impacts, Adaptation and Vulnerability | Climate Change 2022: Impacts, Adaptation and Vulnerability (ipcc.ch)

Melbourne 2030 (2002), State of Victoria. https://www.planning.vic.gov.au/__data/assets/pdf_file/0022/107419/Melbourne-2030-Full-Report.pdf

Metro Vancouver 2040, Shaping Our Future, 2011, Updated 2020, Greater Vancouver Regional District Board. Regional Planning Services (metrovancouver.org)

OneNYC 2050 Building a Strong and Fair City (2019), The City of New York, Mayor Bill De Blasio. OneNYC 2050: New York City's Strategic Plan - OneNYC 2050 (cityofnewyork.us)

Perth and Peel @ 3.5 million (2018), Government of Western Australia, Department of Planning, Lands and Heritage. https://www.dplh.wa.gov.au/perth-and-peel-@-3-5-million

Plan Melbourne 2017–2050 (2017), The State of Victoria Department of Environment, Land, Water and Planning. https://www.planmelbourne.vic.gov.au/

Richard Florida, October 2021, Committee for Sydney podcast: *1 year of COVID, what have we learned & where next?* Watch: Richard Florida - 1 year of COVID, what have we learned & where next? - CFS (sydney.org.au)

Revision of World Urbanization Prospects (2018). https://www.un.org/development/desa/publications/2018h-revision-of-world-urbanization-prospects.html

Shaping SEQ, South East Queensland Regional Plan 2017 (2017), The State of Queensland, Department of Infrastructure, Local Government and Planning. https://planning.dsdmip.qld.gov.au/planning/better-planning/state-planning/regional-plans/seqrp

Smyrk, K (2022), Rental housing squeeze hits regional hospitality workforce as tourist towns struggle to find staff, *ABC News*, 13 April 2022. Rental housing squeeze hits regional hospitality workforce as tourist towns struggle to find staff - ABC News

Templeman, VB (2022), Metaverse to disrupt transportation sector: Gartner Maverick Research, *Digital Nation*, 2 August 2022. Metaverse to disrupt transportation sector: Gartner Maverick Research - Metaverse - Digital Nation (digitalnationaus.com.au)

The 30-Year Plan for Greater Adelaide, 2017 Update (2017), Government of South Australia, Department of Planning, Transport and Infrastructure. https://livingadelaide.sa.gov.au/the_plan

The London Plan, The spatial development strategy for Greater London (2021), The Mayor of London. The London Plan | London City Hall

References

Waters, C (2021), Four times a year in the office: Atlassian goes all in on WFH, *Sydney Morning Herald*, 29 April 2021. Atlassian goes all in on working from home for employees (smh.com.au)

The Purpose of Strategic Planning 4

4.1 Introduction

Chapter 3 explored why we plan cities and arrived at two conclusions.

Firstly, planning is about intervention to deliver a public good that would otherwise not be achieved by the marketplace. What is regarded as a public benefit has evolved and broadened since the emergence of modern planning in the 1880s. Today the public benefits sought through intervention seek to:

- **address negative externalities**, such as pollution or overshadowing
- **create opportunities or improvements for society**, such as improving the efficiency of industrial activities by better connecting industry to logistics infrastructure (for example, ports)
- **protect natural systems and Country**, such as managing the cumulative impacts of sediment run-off into wetlands
- **deliver orderly and coordinated development** (including responding to cumulative negative externalities), such as expanding the capacity of utilities infrastructure to serve new housing estates
- **address societal norms**, such as the protection of places and objects of cultural significance
- **support the wellbeing of individuals and the community**, such as addressing the negative impacts of city structure including urban alienation, loneliness and obesity or enhancing the value of public spaces by creating spaces for informal social interaction
- **achieve social equity outcomes**, such as access to education, jobs and public transport
- **address housing affordability**, such as for essential workers—police, nurses and childcare

Secondly, the scope of city planning emphasises that planning is not seeking to resolve all the urban ills of a city. Instead, I propose parameters for the activities that city planning, specifically that city planning should cover:

- what is important to people, to their lives and the places they live in **and how these impact on**
- land use outcomes, including transport, urban form and natural systems.

This chapter seeks to explore the pathway to intervention. Since the emergence of modern planning, governments have moved away from ad hoc interventions and sought to base the interventions on a rational planning approach. However, in the absence of a pattern book, the strategic planning process for developing a pathway from problem to intervention is developed afresh each time.

This chapter lays the foundation for developing such a pattern book—the 7-Step Strategic Planning Process, which will hopefully provide meaning to the purpose of strategic planning. Specifically, we will explore some of the basic questions that underpin the journey, from why we need to intervene to why we need specific interventions.

4.1.1 Warm-Up Exercise

Here is another exercise that gets to the heart of this chapter. Imagine you are still standing before a planning minister, mayor, or business or community group.

You have just answered the question—Why do we need to do the plan at all?

In the ensuing discussion you also hear that there are lots of problems that need to be solved and you're asked how you will work out what to investigate because we can't wait all year for an answer. Furthermore, you hear that it's the planning controls that are the problem, and if you fix them all will be okay.

How will you respond to these questions? Jot down a few points before you start reading and as you work your way through this chapter look to see how what is raised may influence your thoughts. My experience suggests the better you can articulate what needs to be investigated and why, the more likely you are to both deliver the project on time and be adequately resourced.

4.2 The Purpose of Strategic Planning

Originally, I considered that the purpose of strategic planning was to ask five questions:

1. Where have we come from?
2. Where are we now?
3. Where would we like to go?
4. How do we get there?

4.2 The Purpose of Strategic Planning

5. How do we stay on track?

My work on metropolitan plans over the last decade started to challenge this approach, even though in a general sense it is still reasonably sound. The more I thought about it, the more I found that while it covers the temporal and broad considerations for the purpose of strategic planning, it does not provide an adequate basis from which to develop the detail that is required—specifically, what to research. This section provides a more deliberate perspective on the purpose of strategic planning.

4.2.1 Is Business As Usual Acceptable?

If planning is about intervention, then the underlying purpose of a strategic planning process is to determine whether a future based on business-as-usual activities (existing planning regulations and government commitments) is acceptable to the community, now and in the future.

If the answer is no, then you need to determine whether an alternative future is acceptable and whether that future can be delivered.

These simple questions raise several issues.

Firstly, we need to understand what is acceptable to people, their lives, and the places they live in, now and in the future, which requires an understanding of:

- What is meant by need, within the scope of city planning?
- What is meant by 'now and in the future'?
- How do we create and deliver place outcomes, as city planning is about communities defined by a place descriptor, such as a city, a suburb, or a centre.

Secondly, we need to recognise that the identification of an alternative future implies an understanding of the benefits and costs of the interventions required as well as confidence that the interventions can be achieved.

The strategic plan, therefore, must address these questions. The remainder of this chapter explores the implications of these questions as stepping stones towards a 7-Step Strategic Planning Process.

4.2.2 Needs of the Community—A Research Framework

Ultimately cities are about people, their needs, and the places where they live, work and play Glaeser (2011, p. 15) suggests that "the real city is made of flesh, not concrete". He emphasises this point when he says that "public policy should help poor people, not poor places" (Glaeser 2011, p. 9).

Furthermore, if we subscribe to Aristotle's notion that we continue to reside in cities for the 'good life' then cities must provide more than shelter and sustenance. Cities must include culture, the arts and the varied benefits of specialisation that do more than provide for the bare necessities of life.

We must therefore look behind the bricks and mortar and dissect the city from the perspective of the people who occupy it: the residents, the workers, the business owners, the visitors and, of course, the natural environment.

Drawing from the earlier definition of the scope of city planning, refer Sect. 3.6, the dynamics of the city that are relevant are those that influence spatial outcomes.

Firstly, the characteristics of the people and the place of the current community—essentially the context or setting for the plan. Specifically:

- How many people are living in an area (the demographic characteristics) and what are the household types?
- What are the socio-economic characteristics of people and households that may influence their needs, as well as the needs of businesses?
- What are the characteristics of places that may influence the ability to provide for the needs of people, households, and businesses and the environment?
- Who are the Traditional Custodians of this place and how did they interact with this area prior to colonisation?
- How and when these three characteristics come together, do they provide clarity on the setting for the plan?

Secondly, the needs of the community. Specifically:

- What do people and households need to fulfil their daily lives (work, rest and play)?
- What do businesses need to allow their establishment, growth and prosperity?
- What qualities of life enable people to experience the 'good life'?
- What are the anticipated levels of growth and change of people and activities in a city that need to be accommodated—the growth and change equation?

Thirdly, the qualities and performance of the place under investigation. Specifically:

- What level of accessibility is provided by transport and digital networks and how are they performing?
- What qualities of places influence people's experiences of the 'good life', including the natural environment?
- What issues require consideration in the planning and managing of places, such as infrastructure services and natural hazards?
- How do these elements come together in three dimensions and meet the needs of the community through city design?

This approach is outlined in Fig. 4.1. Behind the 12 research areas for consideration are many more detailed research topics (42 in total), outlined in Section 4.3. These form the basis of the Strategic Planning Research Framework used to develop the approach to research and analysis, as discussed in Chapter 6 and Part 3.

4.2 The Purpose of Strategic Planning

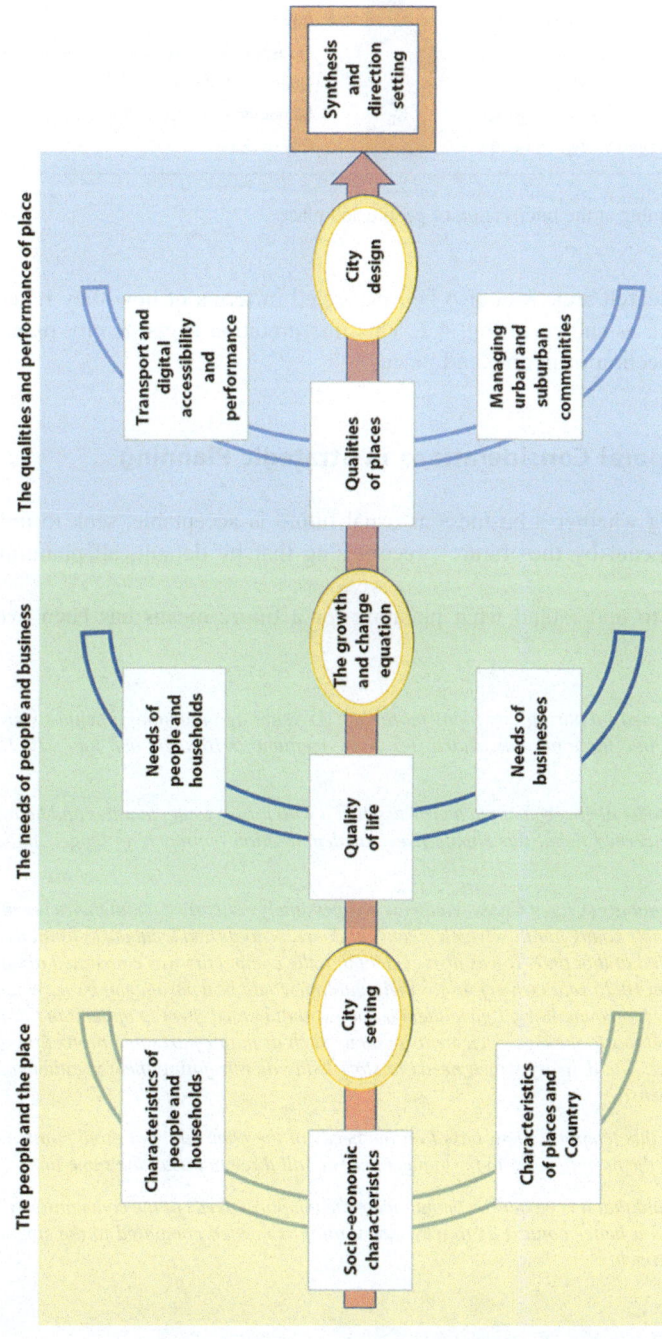

Fig. 4.1 The three-part strategic planning research framework

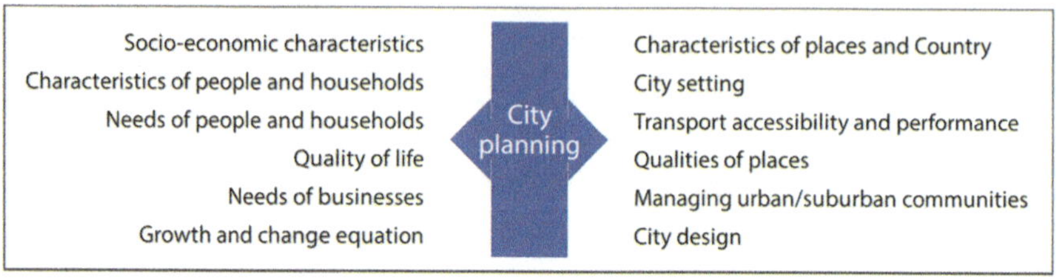

```
┌─────────────────────────────────────────────────────────────────────────┐
│     Socio-economic characteristics    │    Characteristics of places and Country │
│  Characteristics of people and households │    City setting                      │
│     Needs of people and households  ┌─────┐   Transport accessibility and performance │
│                    Quality of life  │ City│   Qualities of places                │
│                                     │plan-│                                      │
│                                     │ning │                                      │
│                 Needs of businesses └─────┘   Managing urban/suburban communities │
│            Growth and change equation         City design                        │
└─────────────────────────────────────────────────────────────────────────┘
```

Fig. 4.2 City planning at the intersection of people and place

These 12 research areas can also be interpreted in terms of how they relate to people and place as shown in Fig. 4.2. This interpretation suggests city planning sits at the intersection of people and place.

4.2.3 Temporal Considerations in Strategic Planning

In understanding whether a business-as-usual future is acceptable, seek to understand what is meant by the 'future', recognising that by default, all planning is about the future.

My journey to understand what planning for a future means has been evolutionary.

> *When I first started preparing city plans more than 35 years ago planning timelines were usually broken into three periods, short: 0-5 years, medium: 5-10 years and long: 10-15 years.*
>
> *When I moved to local government in a growth council with lots of young families and heard about what concerned them, this simple five-year demarcation approach no longer made sense.*
>
> *Firstly, the community (City of Casey, Victoria) was genuinely concerned about their current needs, particularly young families which meant childcare, schools and local parks for active sports, all needed at that time. It was also evident that the community was concerned about the medium term 10-15 years when jobs for their children would be a paramount issue. When I put these views to councillors, I gave them a context that helped them to understand that the long term relates to the legacy elements of a city such as major parks and protection of the environment. The delivery which needs to start today as retrofitting them is either not possible or expensive*
>
> *In considering this temporal view, based on the needs of the community at three points in time, I realised the need to work to try to meet needs of all three points at the same time.*
>
> *Moreover, I found that it is easier to communicate the temporal needs of the community this way. It provides a better context as to why intervention is needed compared to the simple time scale approach.*

Therefore, from this approach a plan needs to provide for:

- **today's community**, the needs of those living in, working in and visiting the city, suburb or centre
- **the next generation**, children today need jobs and other opportunities in the future
- **future generations**, our children's grandchildren need to be able to appreciate natural habitats and city parks – these cannot lose their value over time.

What we mean by planning for future generations has also evolved from simply providing tangible benefits, such as sanitation, to preserving wider environmental values. The notion of whether the next generation will inherit a world with equal or better choices than we have today is the concept of sustainability.

4.3 What is Important to People's Lives and Places?

Section 4.2.2 introduced the Strategic Planning Research Framework as the foundation for understanding what is important to people, to their lives and the places where they live, now and in the future. This section outlines 42 research topics in the context of the 12 research areas that underpin the Research Framework. I provide detail of each in Part 3 in Chapters 13, 14 and 15.

4.3.1 People and Households

Understanding the demographics of the community and the characteristics of the dwellings they live in is a starting point for all city planning.

The Census, conducted in Australia every five years by the Australian Bureau of Statistics (ABS), provides the principal data for understanding population and dwelling trends. The ABS also provides annual estimates of the population between Census periods. Many jurisdictions also have monitoring programs for new dwellings.

You need to understand two areas:

- **Demographic profiles**. This is the base data for many other assessments and includes total population numbers and age-specific data. Ideally, data is collected at a small spatial geography, depending on the place being investigated. For metropolitan planning, data at the ABS's Statistical Area 2 (SA2) scale is usually sufficient. You should also analyse historic trends.
- **Household characteristics**. Different household types are often attracted to different areas, such as students near tertiary institutions or young families in new greenfield development, where single detached dwellings are more affordable. Understanding trends in household characteristics can inform areas such as social planning.

4.3.2 Socio-Economic Characteristics

The needs of people and businesses are influenced by the characteristics of households such as income, age structure, and mode of travel. Importantly, similar-sized communities can have differing socio-economic attributes and thus differing needs.

These characteristics are generally referred to as **socio-economic indicators** and cover educational attainment, income, language, occupation, journey to work data, mode of travel to work, volunteering, Aboriginal and/or Torres Strait Islander identity, ethnicity, migration patterns and employment status. The ABS Census sources most of this data.

These socio-economic characteristics can inform:

- housing needs
- the financial and economic independence of households
- individual and household mobility (access to goods, services and jobs)
- the provision of social and community facilities
- cultural diversity.

4.3.3 Characteristics of Places and Country

Cities develop slowly. The population growth rate of Australia's capital cities in 2018–19 varied between 1.0 and 2.3 per cent (one outlier at −0.8) and averages 1.8 per cent (ABS Catalogue 3218.0). This infers that much of a city remains the same for long periods.

> *To remind myself of this, when I can, I visit the suburb and local shopping strip where I grew up as a teenager in suburban Melbourne. After 45 years it is still much the same.*

The attributes of places to investigate include:

- **The characteristics and evolution of land use systems and transport networks** to identify patterns, typologies (such as housing, industrial, commercial, centres, open space and trade gateways) and inter-relationships. This ranges from the positive such as jobs around public transport hubs, to the negative, such as housing crowding in on trade gateways or industrial development. The intent of this task is the same no matter the geography; what changes is the level of detail and method of collection.
- **The characteristics of the physiography and climatic conditions**. To understand how city planning responds to these attributes which typically cannot be modified.
- **The characteristics of places and Country**, to understand how city planning responds to the values First Nations peoples ascribe to Country.

4.3.4 City Setting

Most city plans have an opening section that describes the context for a city or place. These sections should bring together the principal attributes as outlined above, for the people and the place.

The collated information should be a deliberative task and not simply a last-minute addition. You should clearly set out the visible attributes of the city that can be recognised.

4.3.5 Needs of People and Households

We need to recognise that the needs of people and households can differ. For example, one household of four people typically needs one fridge, whereas two households of two people in each, will likely require two fridges. The areas for investigation are:

- **The level of housing choice**. This reflects price, type, and tenure by location, including culturally responsive housing.
- **The financial and economic independence of households**. This determines whether households with similar opportunities can advance their lives through access to quality educational opportunities (therefore maximising educational attainment) and access to jobs (maximising the depth and breadth of jobs available). Thus, the task is seeking data that can inform differences across a city.

  The recognition of spatial inequality across a city (such as areas of socio-economic disadvantage) is not a recent phenomenon. Plato raised the issue 2500 years ago when he noted "any city, however small, is in fact divided into two, one the city of the poor, the other of the rich", (cited in Glaeser 2011, p. 69). Mumford (1961, p. 61) also states that "on the negative side, the citadel introduced class segregation …".
- **The economic self-determination of First Nation communities**. Planning for a metropolitan area in Australia will likely cover the Country of numerous First Nations communities and include many off-Country First Nations people that live in the area. Plans should not only respond to cultural heritage issues, but they should also enable the economic independence of First Nations communities.
- **Urban amenity: the level of access to goods, jobs, and services**. We need some understanding of universal benchmarks of accessibility and or thresholds for provision of urban amenities such as housing, educational institutions (childcare to university), retail, leisure, recreation (including open space) and entertainment, health services (from health practitioners to hospitals), culture and the arts, social services (such as community facilities, cemeteries, and libraries) and employment.

- **The health of individuals and communities**. Health includes physical, social, spiritual, cognitive, cultural and emotional (although the latter is outside the influence of planning activities) and covers both private and public services.
- **The cost of living**. Most cost-of-living factors are outside the influence of city planning, but there are areas where a contribution to reducing the cost of living can be made such as the spatial relationship between goods, services, and jobs (travel costs).

4.3.6 Quality of Life

The areas for investigation relate to the more intangible qualities of people's preferences and are often governed by codified social norms. The areas for investigation are:

- **Individual and community wellbeing**. Wellbeing reflects the level of social capital, social cohesion, and socially sustainable cities. It includes providing for the spiritual, cultural and lifestyle needs of the community and contributes to a sense of welcome and belonging—social opportunity.
- **Cultural and artistic expression, participation, and appreciation**. Cultural and artistic activities include visiting festivals (ranging from music to surfing), galleries, museums, and heritage towns/places; attending entertainment (ranging from cinemas to bowling); undertaking cultural experiences such as First Nations cultural tours or eco-tourism; and sporting/recreational pursuits. Cultural safety for activities of First Nations communities requires consideration. These also contribute a sense of welcome and belonging.
- **Access to Country or natural and developed public places**. Country and natural public spaces include bushland, foreshores including beaches and waterways, and developed public spaces like parklands, town squares, and streets. For developed public spaces, design must ensure the places or spaces are fit for purpose and provide for inclusive accessibility.
- **The physical amenity of homes**. Physical amenity addresses safety, noise, privacy, odour, access to sunlight, microclimate (urban heat island effect) and covers both dwellings and private open space. These elements contribute to a sense of care (good design and built form).

4.3.7 Needs of Businesses

People and businesses are connected through demand and supply forces for goods and services.

We must recognise that city planning cannot 'make' jobs, yet they can influence the conditions to grow and attract businesses, from which jobs will follow. The role

4.3 What is Important to People's Lives and Places?

of planning is therefore to facilitate business activities by identifying the inhibitors and enablers and managing any unintended consequences such as pollution. A strong economy is critical to a successful city as it allows for many social and environmental outcomes.

The areas for investigation are:

- **Enabling businesses to grow, flourish and innovate**. We need to understand the spatial implications of business growth, barriers and opportunities to enhance business growth and competitiveness, and the locational preferences of businesses. Businesses include office, industry, retail, tourism, educational, residential, leisure, recreation, entertainment, health, culture, the arts, warehousing and logistics and agriculture.
- **The economy and spatial economic structure**. Understanding the economic context for the plan and the spatial structure of economic activity will determine the types of business, their location and how they are changing.
- **The operational needs of businesses**. The incursion of sensitive uses (such as residential) into industrial precincts and trade gateways can constrain the operational activities of many businesses. We need to protect the operational activities of businesses, particularly those that may have a need for 24/7 operational hours, create noise or odours, or cast light.
- **Transport and telecommunication access to support business activities**. Considerations include accessibility for aspects of business operations such as supply chains and business to business (B2B) interactions as well as access to freight networks including trade gateways. Telecommunications coverage and quality of service (for example, internet speed) influence accessibility.
- **Protecting natural resources**. Natural resources include minerals, energy and agricultural land. The value of agricultural land is influenced by a variety of factors, such as soil, topography and climatic conditions.

4.3.8 Growth and Change Equation

A plan for a place is about the people who live and work there. Understanding how many people there are and whether that number will change is a core input to a plan.

People and households create demand for various activities from housing to a range of goods and services. Changes to populations or households will influence the demand of these activities and how they are supplied.

That the economy of a city is also influenced by the number of people emphasises the need to understand the growth and change. For example, various retail business and/or developments have minimum population thresholds before they will locate in a community. Hence, until that threshold is reached residents must commute out of their community to gain access to those goods or services—we refer to this as 'escape expenditure'.

Our understanding of the scale of growth and change collectively can be described as a 'growth and change equation'.

The various elements to this are:

- **Population and demographic change across a city**. Firstly, understand the characteristics of the population, such as age, household make up, fertility rates, death rates, as well as the spatial differences. Secondly, understand projections of change by age cohort and down to the ABS geography of a Statistical Area Level 2 (SA2).
- **Housing demand across a city**. Understand demand and supply projections and preferences and the reasons for those preferences. Changes in population and dwelling trends do not necessarily correlate, as we found was the case when examining historic trends for Greater Sydney in 2017.
- **Commercial business activities**. These include retail, industrial, standalone office development, tourism and a range of specialised sectors. Understand the current and projected scale of activities, including their spatial distribution. Consider locational preferences, which differ from population-serving activities such as shops that we see right across metropolitan areas. This includes 'foot-loose' activities such as office development where locational decisions are more nuanced and activities can be linked to infrastructure, such as trade gateways and freight systems.
- **Agricultural and mining activities**. These tend to locate in a city's hinterland, though raw materials for construction, such as stone, sand and clay resources, can be found across the landscape of a city. The task is to understand changes in output and potential changes in activities.

4.3.9 Transport and Digital Accessibility and Performance

Accessibility influences many aspects of cities from quality of life to financial and economic independence or the productivity of businesses. Enhancing the quality of a city's transport networks remains a central objective in improving accessibility.

In the last decade, accessibility is no longer a two-dimensional spatial problem. Digital technologies have created a third dimension—a virtual dimension where people are able to undertake (access) many tasks (work, shop, leisure, fitness) from virtually any location.

Consider the following attributes of transport and digital accessibility.

- **Network performance**. We need to assess all transport modes, initially separately, but increasingly in an integrated way as the performance of one mode can be improved by the actions within another. The sky rail in Melbourne has improved network services for both public transport and road users by removing at-grade rail crossings that impacted on the performance of both.

- **Service provision**. This generally relates to public transport and addresses coverage, frequency and travel time. Increasingly, frequency is seen as a positive for users. Coverage also supports equity.
- **Digital coverage and performance.** The challenge here is that coverage and performance changes are controlled, in the main, by the market (in Australia) and heavily influenced by demand. This results in differing levels of service across a city in part influenced by differing infrastructure options, such as optic fibre versus fixed wireless. In the future an absence of intervention may result in a digital divide.
- **City structure—spatial equity—mode choice**. The availability of mode choices, as distinct from levels of accessibility, are central to equity across a city and city structure.
- **The city in its region**. Cities are not islands. We need to understand how accessibility influences wider economic links, and/or larger communities of interest. For example, good motorway access from the Latrobe Valley, in Victoria, directly to Chadstone shopping centre has historically meant that those regional areas are part of the shopping centre's wider trade catchment, even though the towns of the valley are between 120 and 150 kilometres away.

4.3.10 Qualities of Places

For cities and towns, the attributes of a place extend well beyond the physical elements. City planning must also consider:

- **A sense of place and community**. The focus here is the spatial element of individual and community wellbeing that covers a sense of place and community at various spatial scales and covers various groups from the school community to a First Nations community's sense of Country. Design quality is essential, for example, in creating spaces that facilitate impromptu social interaction.
- **First Nations Country, community and culture**. In addition to heritage values and the importance of Country, we need to think beyond physical places and consider cultural values and oral histories connected to that place.
- **Post-European contact heritage and history**. Heritage assessments need to cover scenic and cultural landscapes and consider histories in addition to tangible elements. It is important to consider truth-telling in the history of place.
- **The quality, aesthetics, and amenity of the urban fabric of a city and its hinterland**. Aesthetics and amenity include built form, visual landscapes (viewsheds or view corridors), urban structure (including topography), boulevards, open space networks (natural and developed), the concept of local character, the relationships between activities and their relationship with visual landscapes, the interface between the public and private realm, and the design of buildings, (individually and collectively) where the combined impact of buildings and space is a consideration from both an aesthetic and functional perspective.

- **Natural ecosystems, biodiversity and resilience**. This covers the needs of the environment, where the focus is protection, enhancement and management of natural systems, which can be terrestrial or aquatic. An interesting piece to read on the inter-relationships between flora and fauna and people and places is *The Sand County Almanac*, by Aldo Leopold, (1949).
- **Responding to climate change**. Climate change influences the natural qualities of places including a rise in the sea level, higher temperatures (bushfires), and changes in the variability of rainfall (flooding). These impacts have adverse effects on biodiversity as well as on many aspects of cities, including exacerbating urban heat island effects, increasing coastal inundations, and the management of urban infrastructure (for example drainage outfalls). Responses need to explore how cities can be better planned to both mitigate (a low carbon future) and adapt to climate change.
- **The values of the hinterlands of cities**. The values include activities such as agriculture, mining, national and state parks, historic townships, local communities (villages and towns) and biodiversity, which usually support and/or are an attraction for the city they frame.

4.3.11 Urban and Suburban Communities

Many aspects of cities are planned or managed in terms of communities (neighbourhoods). How this occurs requires us to consider the following issues.

- **How urban infrastructure aligns with growth**. Urban infrastructure includes water, sewerage, drainage, energy, waste management, telecommunications and green infrastructure. Efficiency is influenced by capacity levels or thresholds (triggers for augmentation); the timeliness of delivery (development ready); adaptability; the impacts of climate change and natural hazards; responding to ecologically sustainable development; and the long-term capacity vis-à-vis long-term development projections.
- **Managing risks associated with natural hazards**. Natural hazards include bushfire, flood, wind (for example, cyclones), heat (such as urban heat islands), coastal inundation and acid sulphate soils. Risk management practices can avoid, mitigate, adapt to and manage these risks.
- **Enabling choice**. New communities or large urban renewal projects should be designed to facilitate a choice in what is accessible. Enabling choice is a combination of land use considerations and transport network planning—city structure.
- **The influence of adaptation, emerging technological change, behavioural change, innovation and optimising efficiency**. The needs of the community and business can be accommodated without the need for traditional infrastructure interventions through actions such as smart motorway signalling, differential public transport pricing, and facilitating car sharing markets.

4.3.12 City Design

City design is about understanding and then representing a range of design values at the scale that is the focus of a plan. For example, for a metropolitan area it is about the broad interplay with land use and transport systems and its natural setting, whereas for a town centre the focus is on precincts, transport networks (especially walking), topography and the setting within the wider urban area.

In all cases there are at least four considerations:

- **Mass—activity—space**. Activity becomes the central consideration connecting and informing the relationship between mass and space.
- **Quality of life**. City design thinking extends well beyond the physical dimensions of a city. It must consider the elements which contribute to the quality of life, as discussed in Sect. 14.3.
- **Scale**. The scope of strategic planning changes with the scale of the place to which the plan applies; this equally applies for city design.
- **Structure**. Much of the spatial assessments of a city as part of a planning process are about structure. For city design as compared to urban design, the focus is structure and understanding what elements need to be either enhanced, created or ameliorated to inform detailed urban design.

The foundation of city design is understanding the 'place' and an appreciation of urban form and the elements of urban form It requires an in-depth analysis of design and related issues, an understanding of community values, a framework for analysing the city, such as that provided by Lynch (1960), and an understanding of the image of the city (principally when viewed from the public realm), the structure of the city (land use, transport and natural environment relationships) refer Kostof (1991 and 1992). Also clarify the scope of issues to be investigated such as the characteristics of places, quality of life, and qualities of places.

4.4 Planning for Places

Your planning needs to result in much more than statements of rules and regulations. Creating places needs deliberative, systematic and integrated actions. My approach in this area is a mixture of experience and learning from my readings over time specifically through the works of Alexander et al. (1977), Bacon (1967), Hall (1998), Lynch (1960), and McHarg (1971), and more recently Garvin (2016), Jacobs (1995) and two works of Kostof (1991 and 1992).

I categorise considerations in this area into two areas: the defining and the creating of places. Understanding places also requires an understanding of how the community perceives their place.

4.4.1 Defining Places

City planning focuses on the spatial implications arising from the collective needs of the people and businesses of a place. Therefore, for each plan, a definition of the place to which the community relates, such as a city or suburb, is required. This should consider the cultural landscape and how place fits into a broader understanding of Country.

Often, the notion of a single community for a single place is blurred, and in defining a place we need to consider several issues.

Firstly, most cities or town centres have a hinterland with which there is direct day-to-day interaction. A challenge is how to define it. From a policy perspective, in Australia, it is often simply the boundary created by the area covered by the local governments that straddle the urban fringe.

Secondly, when working below the metropolitan scale there are usually multiple communities that have differing relationships with a place. For example, for a town centre, people's behaviour shows that it is possible to define a walkable catchment and thus an area where greater housing could be provided with a lower demand for private car use. At the same time, people will come from considerable distances for specific purposes and they can be categorised (such as weekly versus comparison goods shopping). In each case there is a separate community that needs to be considered for the same place.

Thirdly, research shows that when the spatial attributes of a city are mapped in terms of sectoral considerations such as housing markets, journey to work patterns, and shopping centre trade catchments, the boundaries for each differ. This can be a challenge when planning for a suburb or local government area as intended outcomes may not materialise due to actions outside the area. For example, households may locate elsewhere in the same housing catchment but outside a local government boundary, due to say price point reasons. A new shopping centre close to the boundary of a local government area may impact the shopping behaviour of residents in the adjacent local government area. On this latter point, there are numerous historical examples where councils have allowed a shopping centre to locate to take advantage of such a circumstance resulting in jobs and rates.

4.4.2 Creating Places

With city planning directed at creating better places, we need to consider a range of place issues distinct from the needs of the community or values of the environment. In planning a place, a plan should demonstrate how it responds to:

- designing with Country and nature
- creating depth, choice and diversity, through layers of opportunity and experience, such as in activities, built form, transport, choice and landscapes
- redundancy, that is allowing space for growth and change which assists in adaptability

- wellbeing
- diversity in a place and between places, including as guided by an understanding of Country
- the ability to allow, facilitate and provide for innovation and complexity
- a positive experience, from sitting at a bus stop to the experience of shopping
- a safe experience for all
- an accessible (inclusive) experience for all.

One of the principal outcomes of creating places is the experience people have in the public domain, which generally is our experience of walking along a street, whether that be a residential, shopping, commercial, or industrial street as well as when walking in parks and open space areas. Garvin (2016) contends that it is the quality of the public realm that has the potential to create great cities, as discussed earlier in Sect. 2.3.3.

Figure 4.3 outlines, through a photo montage, examples of positive and negative experiences for the user in the public realm.

4.4.3 Responding to Community Values

Thirty-five years of planning has taught me that those who know most about a place are the people who live, work and play there. The 7-Step Strategic Planning Process draws on understanding community values and seeking community input as the most fundamental task for any city planning.

When looking to understand community perceptions of place, seek to understand the values of the whole community, not just specific individuals or groups, through appropriate statistical sampling methods. The community includes peak industry, environment and social bodies, community groups, sporting groups and the general community.

A survey of community values undertaken as input for the metropolitan plan for Greater Sydney—*A Metropolis of Three Cities* (2018) revealed interesting perceptions. We heard that "The look and design of buildings, streetscapes and public spaces" was the least important factor in making a good place to live, in the context of 18 other factors (Newgate Research 2015). Interestingly, this perception does not appear to correlate when change to existing buildings, streetscapes and public spaces occurs within a person's own neighbourhood.

4.4.4 Integrated Place Planning

Place-based planning is a phraseology that has gained traction in Australia in recent years. I believe it is often used out of context, particularly, when it refers to city (strategic) planning, which to the best of my knowledge has always been place-based.

Fig. 4.3 Positive and negative experiences when walking in the public domain

4.4 Planning for Places

Fig. 4.3 (continued)

Fig. 4.3 (continued)

Integrated planning and delivery, which seeks to coordinate infrastructure planning with city planning, is what I believe the concept of place-based planning is truly about, and its importance cannot be overstated.

Integrated planning and delivery requires:

- A commitment from infrastructure agencies to be actively involved in strategic planning projects (thus place-based), with their involvement including outlining their strategic infrastructure planning goals and short, medium and long-term infrastructure requirements.
- An understanding of the infrastructure needs of both local and state government, given that, in Australia:
  - This approach is not necessarily the norm.
  - It is a significant challenge when local government leads the strategic planning process.

- An understanding of the tension between planning for a long-term vision, and the reality of short-term budgetary commitments.

  A learning from the 2018 Greater Sydney Region Plan was the beneficial shift in thinking from 'predict and provide' to 'vision and validate', with the latter starting with an infrastructure vision (specifically the transport elements) based on a long-term understanding of the implications of growth on land use patterns.

The benefits of moving to an integrated planning and delivery approach is the opportunity to step away from piecemeal infrastructure assessments, which are generally based on a single project, to a whole of community planning and delivery approach. Moreover, such an approach provides the opportunity for the coordinated delivery of a range of infrastructure projects, such as schools, parks, roads, community facilities, and public transport. This results in the sequencing of development (due to its attraction power) and/or outcomes such as transport mode shifts or enhanced development density—which no single infrastructure project can do.

4.5 It's About Delivery

A bigger challenge is the ability to implement the vision for the future.

4.5.1 The Issues

Just as there is a range of considerations for investigating whether a business-as-usual future is acceptable, there are issues to consider regarding implementation, starting with the following questions:

- Is there clarity around why the proposed intervention is required?
- Is there an understanding of what the cause-and-effect issues are, in the context of the identified problem and the proposed intervention?
- Can social, economic and environmental benefits be clearly identified and are the costs required for implementation clear, including the ongoing operational costs?
- Is there an understanding of the resources and activities required to facilitate change?
- Is there a willingness to introduce the required change? Sometimes there may not be the political will to do so.
- Who will lead the change (both political and administrative champions) and what governance is required (typically delivery in a partnership) between multiple agencies and levels of government?
- How will the private sector respond to proposed interventions, from infrastructure to regulatory changes and are the drivers for investment clear?
- How will the change be communicated?

Several implementation issues are worthy of further consideration including:

- the diversity of intervention mechanisms (tools) available to the planner
- articulating the public benefit and costs of intervention
- the concept of selective strategic intervention, in that if there are not sufficient resources to change everything, interventions need to be a catalyst or have wide systemic impacts
- the importance of recognising that plans will not result in all parts of a city changing.

Recognise that not all alternate futures can be delivered. For example, when undertaking greenfield planning a reasonable amount of effort goes into establishing how much open space is required. However, for urban renewal areas that will see increases in population, usually per capita rates of open space provisions cannot be maintained—the cost is too prohibitive even when the aspiration is there.

4.5.2 Selected Strategic Intervention

Interventions by their very nature are targeted, whether that be a specific infrastructure project, or a regulation aimed to manage a specific outcome(s). This targeted approach to intervention was conceptualised as 'selected strategic intervention', by Dr. Jeff Wolinski, a Victorian economic and strategic planner, in the early 1990s. It starts with two premises:

1. The community has limited resources to implement a city plan.
2. The private sector, in the main, builds cities.

Therefore, selected strategic intervention emphasises that city plans must have, as a major focus, an understanding that interventions need to deliver a catalytic effect on market activities, such as a new rail corridor combined with changes to planning controls stimulating urban renewal.

This approach requires an understanding of cause and effect and not simply how a transport project improves accessibility. We need to understand the influence of a project on multiple systems—for example, how a road or rail project may influence business location decisions and the demand for new housing, or whether the development opportunities created by the new regulations are feasible or desirable for the market.

Selective strategic intervention therefore requires us to understand:

- critical deficiencies in the existing infrastructure/urban systems, including key industries; national/metropolitan transport links; business activity (employment distribution); housing and population trends etc.
- critical inter-relationships between the sub-systems that make up the urban environment

- cause and effect of actions within and between systems
- outcomes desired and why and what levers will meet those outcomes
- how the interventions can lock in a pathway toward the desired outcome(s)
- costs, resources, and benefits from proposed actions.

As cities change slowly, the selective strategic intervention will be most effective when it focuses on packages of projects that can catalyse multiple land uses and transport systems. The temporal nature of implementing the project within a package is also likely to achieve greater change.

When well implemented, selected strategic interventions are about simple concepts (for example, creating a new rail corridor linked to urban renewal initiatives) that achieve complex outcomes—increased housing supply and business investment, improved mode share or improved place-making (due to attracted development).

4.5.3 Intervention Levers

In thinking about what kind of interventions affect change, I have learnt to move well beyond the core levers of planners—that is, policies and regulations. As I see it there are 11 levers we can utilise to influence change (see Fig. 4.4).

Eight are hands-on interventions levers, while three are guiding levers. As discussed in Sect. 3.2.3, most of these levers were developed soon after the emergence of modern planning in the 1880s.

Policy. Providing guidance on expected outcomes should be the starting point for most planning activities. Policies can vary in status from legislated positions, and the objectives of legislation, to guidance statements on applying a policy.

Governance. Coordinating activities, decision-making and sharing information requires collaboration. Formalising these connections through governance arrangements ensures expectations and commitments are clearly understood, acknowledged and acted on. These formal governance arrangements must be complemented by informal arrangements. There needs to be a culture of collaboration. Glaeser (2011, p. 15) suggests that collaboration has driven the success of cities in providing choice.

Advocacy. State and local governments do not necessarily hold or control all the levers which can influence a specific outcome. Thus, one level of government will seek to influence the decision or policies of a higher level by advocating for a particular outcome. This is also a principal lever for community groups and peak bodies. It also includes governments promoting outcomes that they wish the market to adopt.

Public works. Public works were the first interventions undertaken in cities, such as fortifications, roads, water supply, sanitation, and civic and religious buildings. Today public works continue to be the most influential tool for influencing the shape, management and growth of cities, particularly, transport projects (SGS Economics and Planning, 2012).

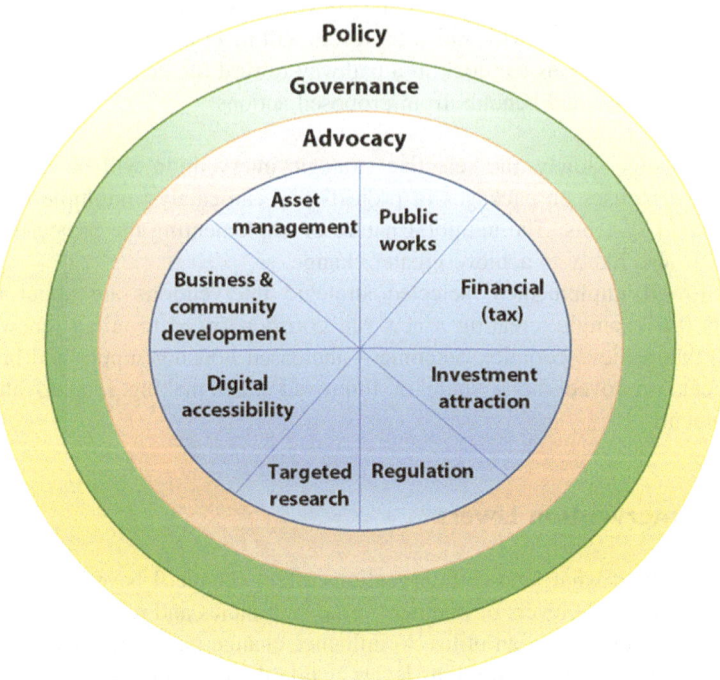

Fig. 4.4 Eleven intervention levers for city planning

Financial. Financial or taxing arrangements are targeted to a specific outcome, as distinct from the use of consolidated revenue. Development contributions are used in most jurisdictions in Australia. Funding mechanisms have been around for some time. Georges-Eugene Haussmann was one of the first to develop innovative financial levers for urban renewal for his work in Paris (1853–1870).

Investment attraction. Attracting economic activity to specific locations is often an objective in city planning. Usually, zoning land for a purpose is not enough to attract investment and businesses; more deliberative actions can vary from tax-free investment zones to direct investor/business attraction schemes.

Regulation. This is the staple lever for planners, with examples varying from land use zones to heritage controls. The regulatory framework that underpins the management of land uses is discussed in Sect. 5.3.1.

Targeted research. From time to time, we need further research to understand how the outcome is to be achieved.

Digital accessibility. In the last decade, it is clear that accessibility is no longer just a spatial challenge. Accessibility is also about virtual accessibility. The influence of the COVID-19 pandemic on how we work, shop and interact has emphasised both the opportunities provided by virtual interactions as well as the implications of a digital divide. Moreover, the challenge for planners is that the actions that create virtual accessibility are generally in the hands of the market, and in Australia regulations are at the Commonwealth level and thus out of the hands of state governments that are responsible for city planning.

Business and community development. Developing skills in the community can empower people to achieve the outcomes that directly affect their business or community such as programs to support chambers of commerce to improve the outcomes for their centre or programs in the community such as those that support community-based childcare.

Asset management. All levels of government have assets, particularly land, which in some cases could be repurposed for an alternative use such as an at-grade car park being converted into development (commercial or residential) to achieve a different public benefit.

4.5.4 Funding the Delivery of City Plans

Identifying how the initiatives of a plan will be funded is critical. Failure to consider this issue will potentially assign the plan to being '*The plan had some great concepts but was impractical in terms of delivery*'. How funding of projects is approached can vary from direct commitment to a project's delivery or a commitment to investigate delivery later.

> *For the Greater Sydney Region Plan, we (the then Greater Sydney Commission) worked closely with officers from Transport for NSW on this issue. They concluded that there were some projects that could be directly committed to, whereas for others the commitment was to investigate them in a 0 to 10-year time horizon and 10 to 20-year time horizon. This gives the community some clarity as to when a project would likely be considered for delivery.*

Behind the issue of funding is the blunt but important question from every treasury department—why should the project be funded? This issue is discussed in more detail in Sect. 8.4.6.

Let's now examine a few of the issues pertaining to the delivery and funding of projects.

4.5.4.1 Value Capture
Value capture has been considered for a long time. In Victoria:

> ... the Town and Country Planning Act (1961) which was repealed in 1985 to make way for the current Planning and Environment Act included a specific head of power for taxation of value uplift brought about by planning scheme changes. (Spiller et al. 2017, p. 2)

Spiller et al. (2017, p. 3), in their definition of value capture, emphasise that:

> Land value increase reflecting additional development rights. This value is not created by the landowner or developer. It is appropriate that a share is captured for the community.

That is, it does not reflect developer costs or profits, but relates to the change in value created by a change in land zoning—value uplift.

There have been several examples of value capture across Australia. One example, a 'windfall gains tax' to be levied across Victoria and the Victorian State Revenue Office website indicates that:

> From 1 July 2023, a windfall gains tax (WGT) will apply to land that is subject to a government rezoning resulting in a value uplift to the land of more than $100,000.

In terms of the value payable, on the Victorian State Revenue Office website it states:

> For a rezoning of land that results in a taxable value uplift:
>
> - more than $100,000 but less than $500,000: the tax will apply at a marginal rate of 62.5% on the uplift above $100,000
> - $500,000 or more: a tax rate of 50% will apply to the total uplift.

The Victorian State Revenue Office website also provides information on exemptions, who pays, when funds are payable, and who administers the tax.

4.5.4.2 Development Contributions

As a principle, the concept of development contributions is generally easily explained and supported. When a development proposal or multiple proposals are seen to trigger the need for specific infrastructure, the costs of that infrastructure should be funded, in part or full, by the beneficiaries of that development.

However, when it comes to applying the concept, the devil is in the detail. In Australia, most states have requirements and guidelines for how development contributions are determined. This space is continually evolving as updated processes are developed to deal with perceived and real challenges of application. The book *Funding Urban Services: Options for Physical Infrastructure* by Max Neutze (1997) is a useful place to start understanding the issues related to funding infrastructure.

From my experience in establishing a range of development contribution plans, four principles should underpin the application of the concept. The principles arose from a well-known Victorian legal case commonly referred to as the 'Eddie Barron case'. A 2012 report by the Standard Development Contributions Advisory Committee (Mitchell, et al. 2012), a report well worth reading, made the following comments regarding the case (page 15):

> The Eddie Barron decision was a landmark case for the understanding of the legal principles which underpin development contributions within the framework of the Victorian Planning System.
>
> In particular, the Tribunal identified four criteria that must be met before a levy could be validly imposed as a planning permit condition, namely (on page 25):

1) Need

> The need created by the development and the measures to satisfy the need must be adequately identified.

2) Equity

> The payment or levy must be a fair and reasonable apportionment of the cost of implementing the need satisfaction measures.

3) Accountability

> The responsible authority should implement procedures to ensure that the money collected cannot be used for any purpose other than that for which it was levied and which clearly show how, when and where the money collected is spent.

4) Nexus

> There must be a reasonable nexus between the development and the need satisfaction measures.
>
> In relation to the 'nexus' principle and the nature of the nexus that must be established, the Tribunal rejected any narrow approach which only examined whether facilities would be physically used by the occupants of new development. Rather it raised the question of whether the development formed part of a wider 'planning unit' that would ultimately need the infrastructure. In making these findings, the Tribunal commented on the distinction in nexus which existed between 'community infrastructure' as opposed to 'local infrastructure' and the level of justification required.'

Understanding how development contributions are approached within the jurisdiction of a city plan is an important background task. This determines if this funding delivery tool can be applied and/or modified to fund the initiatives arising from the plan.

As a last point on this issue, from time to time I have heard planners describe the concept as a 'developer' contribution, with a negative tone towards the developer. This is unfortunate, as developers build cities and thus are an integral part of the city planning and delivery environment. It is the impact of the development that is in question, not the developer.

4.5.4.3 Aligning Infrastructure with Growth

The implications of differing urban forms on the efficiency (costs) of developing cities was raised in the late 1990s in various papers including by Professor Peter Newman and Professor Jeff Kenworth, both of the Curtin University Sustainability Institute. There have been many studies since. One study I am familiar with is a 2010 report by the Centre for International Economics—*Economics Costs and benefits of alternative growth paths for Sydney* (refer website links).

All of Australia's capital city plans raise the issue of developing efficient cities, in terms of cost, in some way.

- *ACT Planning Strategy 2018*: Action 1.3.1 Continue to align land use planning and infrastructure planning to support the growth of the city (p. 46).
- *The 30-Year Plan for Greater Adelaide*: Policy P82 Coordinate and link strategic infrastructure across Greater Adelaide to ensure it meets the needs of a growing population with a changing demographic profile and supports a more productive economy (p. 94).
- *Darwin Regional Land Use Plan 2015*: Infrastructure objective: Integrate land use with transport planning (p. 30).
- *Plan Melbourne*: Principle 8: Infrastructure investment that supports balanced city growth (p. 11).
- *Perth and Peel @3.5 million*: Develop a consolidated urban form that limits the identification of new greenfield areas to where they provide a logical extension to the urban form, and that places a greater emphasis on urban infill and increased residential density (p. 21).
- Greater Sydney *A Metropolis of Three Cities:* Strategy 2.1 Align forecast growth with infrastructure (p. 39).
- *ShapingSEQ, South East Queensland Regional Plan 2017*: Element 4: Prioritised infrastructure investment: Investment in the regional infrastructure network is prioritised to service social and economic needs in a way that integrates with the desired growth pattern.

However, it should also be noted that, from time to time, when a housing pipeline is perceived to be in short supply governments are attracted to releasing land for development before the required infrastructure has been planned.

4.5.4.4 Recognising the Things that Do not Change

While city planning is fundamentally directed at managing change, when thinking about the future of cities, you need to recognise that many parts will not change. Plans need to be for the whole community; be clear about where change will and will not occur. For example, some things that rarely change include:

- subdivision patterns, both lots and streets
- the location of open space and its relationship to the subdivision pattern
- the general location of centres and their relationship to the street pattern and potentially the rail network
- the landform, and thus the opportunities and challenges it creates
- ideally regionally significant biodiversity
- transport gateways (port and airport) and the rail network.

Therefore, in greenfield areas, we need to recognise what shapes and drives these elements and how they will influence the needs of the community in generations to come.

4.6 Summary

This chapter together with Chapter 3 explores what cities are about so we may better plan them. The central finding is that for cities to meet the needs of people, their lives and the places they live, now and in the future, they require a level of intervention.

How that intervention is identified becomes the central focus of city planning and is the focus of this chapter.

This chapter starts with the proposition that strategic planning determines what interventions are required and that we need to determine whether a business-as-usual future is acceptable—and if not, whether there is an alternative future that is acceptable and deliverable.

I emphasise that cities are about people, thus a response needs to determine what is important to people, their lives, and the places they live in now and in the future. I developed a framework to structure the task of investigating the answer to this question. The framework outlines three areas that should be the focus of investigations to understand people and places as follows:

- What are the characteristics of the people and the place of the current community?—essentially the context for a plan.
- What are the needs of the community, both households and businesses?
- What are the qualities and performance of the place under investigation?

Also emphasised as implicit in strategic planning is a need to understand the notion of planning for places—how they are defined and created.

Finally, and potentially most importantly, intervention implies an understanding of implementation. Since the emergence of modern planning in the 1880s planners have many delivery levers to choose from.

References

Alexander, C, Ishikawa, S, & Silverstein, M (1977), *A Pattern Language: Towns, Buildings, Construction*, Oxford University Press New York
—Details all the elements that make up places, from cities to bedrooms, and their inter-relationships, including that every element should be an experience including a bus stop.
Bacon, EN (1967) *Design of Cities*, Penguin Books, Ringwood, Australia
—From my university days and where I learnt about the power of city design (structure) and the art of communication.
Garvin, A (2016), *What Makes a Great City*. Island Press.
Glaeser, E (2011), *Triumph of the City*, Pan Macmillan UK
—A must read for any interested in urban economics.
Hall, P (1998), *Cities in Civilisation: Culture, Innovation, and Urban Order*, Phoenix
—Extraordinary exposé on what makes a great city, with 20 case studies covering 2,500 years of cities.
Jacobs, A B (1995), *Great Streets*, MIT Press

Kostof, S (1991), *The City Shaped, Urban Patterns and Meanings Through History* Thames & Hudson, London, UK
Kostof, S (1992), *The City Assembled, The Elements of Urban Form Through History* Thames & Hudson, London, UK
Leopold, A (1949), *A Sand County Almanac and Sketches Here and There*, Oxford University Press
—A different style of writing on the environment and its inter-relationships with people and places.
Lynch, K (1960), *The Image of the City*, The MIT Press
—The complexities of how we perceive the city explained in breathtaking simplicity.
McHarg, IL (1971), *Design with Nature*, Doubleday/Natural History Press
—The why of designing with nature.
Mumford, L (1961), *The City in History Penguin Books*, Australia
—The definitive book on the history of cities through the ages.
Neutze, M (1997), *Funding Urban Services: Options for Physical Infrastructure* Allen & Unwin
—A useful introduction to the options for funding infrastructure.
SGS Economics and Planning (2012), *Long run economic and land use impacts of major infrastructure projects*, Unpublished
—Outlines the findings of four case studies on the economic impacts of transport and land use projects.

Website links

Australian Bureau of Statistics (2020), *3218.0—Regional Population Growth, Australia, 2018–19*. https://www.abs.gov.au/ausstats/abs@.nsf/mf/3218.0
Centre for International (2010), *Economics Costs and benefits of alternative growth paths for Sydney*. Costs and benefits of alternative growth paths for Sydney — The CIE — Boutique Economic Consultancy | The Centre for International Economics
Greater Sydney Commission, Background reports. https://www.greater.sydney/background-material
Mitchell, K, McCullough, T, Eade, R, De Silva, C, & Moore, B (2012), Standard Development Contributions Advisory Committee, Report 1, 'Setting the Framework' *Planning Panels Victoria*. Report-1-Setting-the-Framework.doc (live.com)
Newgate Research (2015), *Research Report, Community research to support the implementation of A Plan for Growing Sydney*. Six reports North, South, Central, West Central, West, and South West Districts https://www.greater.sydney/background-material
Spiller, M, Spencer, A, & Fensham, P (2017), *Value Capture through development licenses*. SGS-Economics-and-Planning-Value_capture_through_development_licence_fees.pdf (sgsep.com.au)
State Revenue Office, *Windfall gains tax*. Windfall Gains Tax | State Revenue Office (sro.vic.gov.au)

Australian capital city plans website links

A Metropolis of Three Cities (2018), State of New South Wales. https://www.greater.sydney/metropolis-of-three-cities
ACT Planning Strategy 2018 (2018), Australian Capital Territory. https://www.planning.act.gov.au/act-planning-strategy
Darwin Regional Land Use Plan 2015 (2015), Northern Territory Government, Department of lands, Planning and the Environment. https://planningcommission.nt.gov.au/projects/drlup
Perth and Peel @ 3.5 million (2018), Government of Western Australia, Department of Planning, Lands and Heritage. https://www.dplh.wa.gov.au/perth-and-peel-@-3-5-million

References

Plan Melbourne 2017–2050 (2017), The State of Victoria Department of Environment, Land, Water and Planning. https://www.planmelbourne.vic.gov.au/

Shaping SEQ, South East Queensland Regional Plan 2017 (2017), The State of Queensland, Department of Infrastructure, Local Government and Planning. https://planning.dsdmip.qld.gov.au/planning/better-planning/state-planning/regional-plans/seqrp

The 30-Year Plan for Greater Adelaide, 2017 Update (2017), Government of South Australia, Department of Planning, Transport and Infrastructure. https://livingadelaide.sa.gov.au/the_plan

A Strategic Planning Process 5

5.1 Introduction

I direct the first part of this chapter to the rationale for the 7-Step Strategic Planning Process. We bring together the findings of Chapter 3, which provided a rationale for planning and a scope for planning. These insights raise fundamental questions as to the purpose of strategic planning, which was the focus of Chapter 4. The questions and responses create a conceptual structure that provides the rationale and building blocks for the 7-Step Strategic Planning Process—the conclusion of the journey towards preparing a framework for strategic planning when developing a city plan.

The second part of the chapter outlines some of the common threads or considerations that permeate all aspects of the 7-Step Strategic Planning Process. They include planning systems, community and stakeholder engagement, politics and planning, planning and decision-making, confidentiality and project management, First Nations culture, heritage and Country, sustainability, complexity and a systems view of planning, and the challenge of planning for change.

5.1.1 Warm-Up Exercise

Before you jump in and read this chapter, here's another exercise that gets to the heart of this chapter.

Imagine you work for a consultancy, and you have submitted a proposal for a contract to prepare a strategic plan for a city. You have been asked to come in for an interview to explain your approach, so you have put together a presentation to explain your methodology.

- However, the interview committee asks several more philosophical questions: Can you explain the rationale behind your approach?

- What is the purpose of the investigations?
- Why can't we just let business-as-usual activities continue?
- Why will your plan not simply become another report that sits on the shelf?

How will you respond to these questions? Jot down a few points before you start reading and as you work your way through this chapter look at how the points raised may influence your thoughts.

5.2 A 7-Step Strategic Planning Process

5.2.1 Rationale for a Framework

The examination of planning since the emergence of modern planning in the 1880s together with contemporary planning activities reveals insights that inform my 7-Step Strategic Planning Process.

The principal insights in Fig. 5.1, as set out in the preceding chapters, inform the framework.

They reveal the importance of understanding what is meant by the public good, how planning scope influences intervention types and delivery pathways and the importance of identifying strategic, not operational issues.

The insight that planning is about intervention for the public good raises fundamental questions that reflect the purpose of strategic planning, starting with the question of whether a business-as-usual future will meet the aspirations of the community. This was the focus of Chapter 4.

The inter-connections between the questions examined in Chapter 4 are outlined in a conceptual framework shown in Fig. 5.2. This framework is presented as a logic diagram that seeks to draw out the implications of the questions, as a set of requirements informing seven building blocks or fundamental elements for a strategic planning framework:

- **Provide clarity as to why intervention is required.** Explain why a plan is needed—ask yourself whether it can be easily communicated in terms of the problem or issue to be addressed and the geography of the place to be investigated.
- **Provide evidence.** Outline how the evidence informs the basis of the vision and the interventions to achieve it. This also implies evidence based on sound research methods.
- **Ensure community participation.** Those who will ultimately own the plan should be involved in its preparation.
- **Use a deliberative and transparent process.** Provide clarity on the project scope, methodology, timing, approval processes and how people or organisations can participate.
- **Require an approvals process.** Include a governance framework that identifies the decision-makers responsible for implementing and resourcing the plan.

5.2 A 7-Step Strategic Planning Process

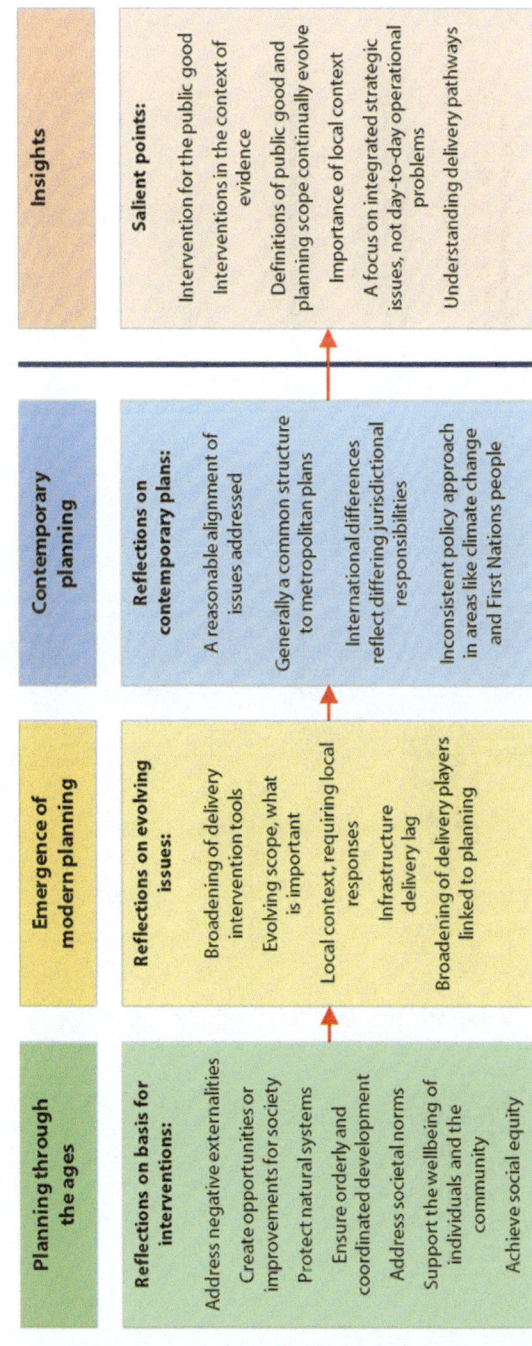

Fig. 5.1 Principal insights

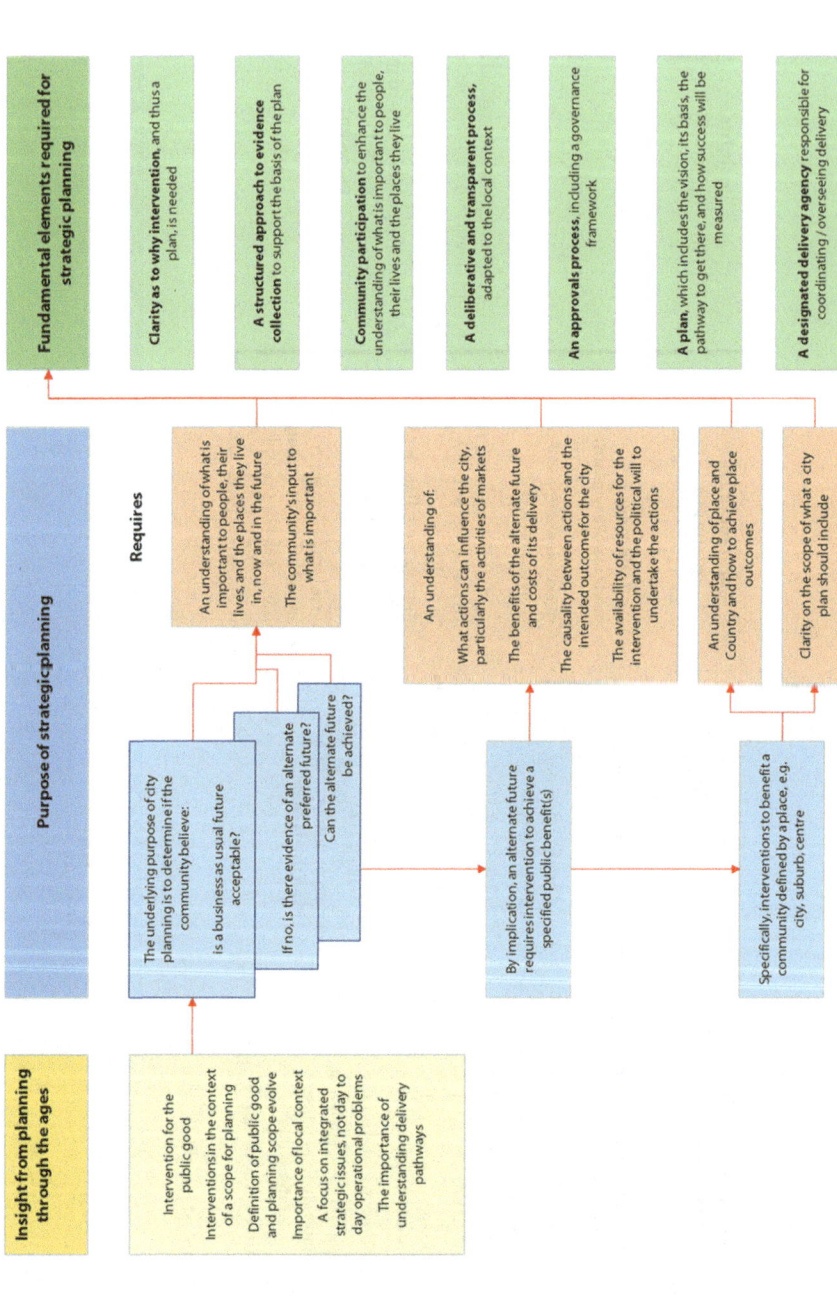

Fig. 5.2 A conceptual framework for a 7-step strategic planning process.
This diagram outlines the flow of logic that connects what planning is about (intervention) and insights from planning through the ages from Chapter 3, with the purpose of strategic planning from Chapter 4, to set up a rationale as to the fundamental elements required for strategic planning.

- **Deliver a plan** (as an output). Deliver a plan that gives the community an understanding of a vision for the city (place) and the pathway to get there.
- **Designate a delivery agency.** Identify the agency responsible for coordinating and overseeing the plan, including monitoring and reporting, and clarify which agency is responsible for each intervention.

5.2.2 The Model

In developing a 7-Step Strategic Planning Process, I have transposed the building blocks into a model, as outlined in Fig. 5.3.

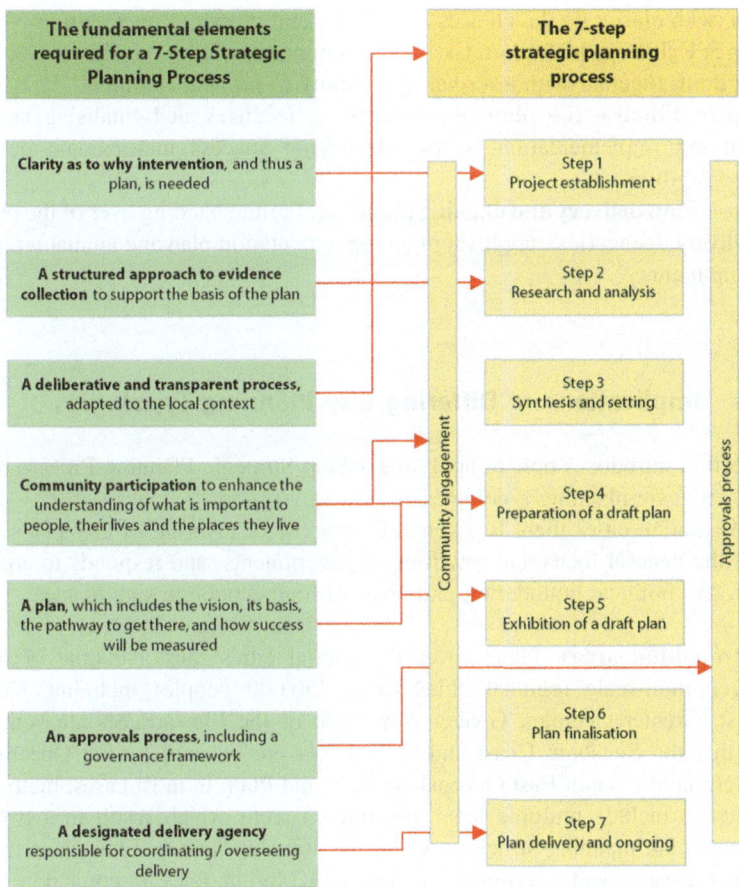

Fig. 5.3 The relationship between the fundamental elements and the 7-Step Strategic Planning Process

The process provides a disciplined 7-step structure to the task of strategic planning that can be adapted to the specific nature of the task at hand. The seven steps are:

- **Step 1: Project establishment**. Outlining the objectives and scope of the project, clarifying expectations with decision-makers and stakeholders and adapting the framework to suit the specific needs of the project.
- **Step 2: Research and analysis**. Gaining a detailed understanding of the dynamics of the city in the context of the project objectives and answering the simple question of whether a business-as-usual future is acceptable. Research activities include community engagement.
- **Step 3: Synthesis and direction setting**. Synthesising the principal conclusions of the research and identifying the direction and parameters of a vision.
- **Step 4: Prepare a draft plan**. Expanding the vision and directions into a draft plan, with clarity on the choices considered and proposed interventions.
- **Step 5: Exhibit a draft plan**. Giving the community clarity on what is proposed, as a draft, together with a formal opportunity to provide comment.
- **Step 6: Finalise the plan**. Responding to feedback and finalising content, clarifying implementation issues, identifying success metrics and delivery responsibilities.
- **Step 7: Plan delivery and ongoing planning**. Formal handing over of the plan to a delivery agency(ies), approval of an implementation plan and annual reporting requirements.

5.2.3 Implications of Differing City Planning Typologies

This section introduces how to apply the 7-Step Strategic Planning Process to the various strategic planning typologies.

In Australian cities there is a general hierarchy or layering of city plans. This reflects the general focus and activities of governments, and responds to areas of change, geo-political boundaries, and areas of high economic significance.

- **Metropolitan areas**. Plans cover the capital cities plus a couple of larger metropolitan-scale regional cities (over 250,000 people) including Central Coast, Greater Geelong, Greater Newcastle or the Illawarra/Shoalhaven, noting that the Sunshine Coast and Gold Coast are covered by the Queensland Government's South East Queensland Regional Plan. In most cases, metropolitan cities include multiple local government areas which result in a two-tier metropolitan planning structure where the state-led metropolitan plans inform plans for each local government area prepared by the relevant council.
- **Regional cities**. These plans vary in size yet have the unique position that they are, in the main, single-council cities. Consequently, some have ownership of local airports or get directly involved in residential land release to ensure

competition. Thus, regional councils usually have greater potential to influence city planning outcomes.
- **Town centres**. In Australia, town centres have been a focus for planning policy since the first plans were prepared for the capital cities 70 years ago. Their importance, in part, reflects a focus on the activities that make up the life of cities, from shops and entertainment to places of employment and as centres for administration, justice, health and education. Hence our interest in town centres usually reflects:
  - a desire to improve amenity, efficiency and accessibility
  - a desire to attract additional activity to expand the diversity of offerings available to the local community
  - a recognition of the increasing economic role in a knowledge economy—for example, in Greater Sydney's 1350 centres, the top 43 contain 50 per cent of the city's jobs (*A Metropolis of Three Cities*, 2018, p. 80)
  - a desire, particularly from state governments, to maximise the land use benefits for infrastructure delivery.
- **New greenfield communities**. All of Australia's metropolitan cities have expanded outward, even with urban renewal policies being a common aspiration. Consequently, the planning of new greenfield communities remains a major element of managing growth. State governments have often led planning in these locations due to the high need for state-funded infrastructure.
- **Community or neighbourhood planning**. These plans fuse community development activities with local land use planning and present themselves when there is a clear need to drive community development and improve socio-economic outcomes for local people. The approach centres around community development processes and is the most complex city planning tasks as it requires a different mindset—the community comes first. Importantly it needs a time frame of many years, not months.
- **Urban renewal**. Urban renewal is a major part of managing growth and change in major cities. Much of it occurs through market forces on a site-by-site basis, although there are numerous examples of larger planned precincts driven by tailored government development authorities and/or private consortia, such as Barangaroo in Sydney, Fishermans Bend in Melbourne and Subiaco in Perth. This specialised area of precinct-based city planning is not covered in this book, primarily because it has not been a major focus of my experience. However, given my knowledge of town centre plans and my time in state government, I expect the principles of the 7-Step Strategic Planning Process are applicable.

In addition, regional plans are developed across all states in Australia. For example, NSW is covered by 10 regional plans. In most cases the capital city of each state is identified as one of the regions.

The application of the 7-Step Strategic Planning Process for these differing typologies starts with the premise that, in general, all seven steps are relevant. Chapter 12 details how the purpose and spatial scale of the differing typologies influences the application of the 7-Step Strategic Planning Process. A brief outline of the process for each typology and how each differs is also provided at the end of the discussion for each step in Chapters 6 to 11.

5.2.4 From Plans to Planning

In the 7-Step Strategic Planning Process, Step 7: Plan delivery deliberately occurs after the finalisation of the plan and its launch. It recognises that cities are dynamic—there is no end state. The detailed discussion of Step 7 in Chapter 11 outlines how the preparation of a city *plan* should be part of an ongoing city *planning* process.

This view recognises that strategic planning seeks to set cities on a course that will achieve different outcomes, rather than achieve a specific vision or end state.

There are also unforeseen events, such as the impact of technology (the Internet of Things) or most recently the COVID-19 pandemic, which will potentially influence the delivery of a plan and maybe the vision.

Thus, the process of planning cities needs to be ongoing. Yes, we still need to regularly undertake a deliberative process to consider the future of a city; however, we also need to plan between the plans. We need to move from the staccato approach of intermittently preparing point-in-time city plans, to city planning as an ongoing deliberative process.

This deliberative and transparent ongoing process delivers what I call 'flexible certainty' for how we manage cities and meet the needs of the community and the environment.

5.3 Common Threads and Considerations

Sitting behind the seven steps are considerations that either underpin or provide a common thread to city planning:

- planning systems
- community and stakeholder engagement
- First Nations Country, community and culture
- politics and planning
- planning and decision-making
- confidentiality
- project management
- sustainability
- complexity and a systems view of planning
- the challenge of change.

These considerations must form part of the deliberations for each step of the 7-Step Strategic Planning Process. They are outlined in more detail below.

5.3.1 Planning Systems

For many of us, planning controls are the foundation for managing growth and change across cities, as planning regulations assign controls over what land use activities can occur on private property together with many other development considerations from height controls to the management of heritage values. However, not all cities have planning controls, such as Houston, Texas, in the United States. Also, as emphasised in Sect. 4.5, planners can utilise many other levers to affect change in cities.

Interestingly the City of Houston's 2015 strategic plan—*Plan Houston: Opportunity, Diversity, Community, Home* is not directed at establishing land use controls; rather, its focus is providing consensus on goals and policies.

5.3.1.1 Australian Context

In Australia, as outlined in Sect. 3.2.2, we need to recognise that responsibility for planning sits with state governments (not the Commonwealth Government), hence the differing technical approaches across the states.

Understanding the principles of the planning systems that govern land use is, however, a fundamental skill set for strategic planners, especially as a strategic planning process will potentially identify the need to change planning regulations to meet the vision of the plan. In this context, I would always use a specialist statutory planner to advise on how to modify planning controls—you need someone who not only knows the controls, but also understands how they are interpreted and the history of how they evolved.

With many books and short courses on planning systems, as well as it being a core subject area in most planning degrees, it is only lightly covered here. For those who wish to explore this topic more, I recommend:

- Gurran, N 2011, Australian urban land use planning. Principles, systems and practice. Second Edition. Sydney University Press, Australia
  – Provides a comprehensive outline of Australia's planning systems.
- Stein, LA. 2017, *Comparative Urban Land Use Planning, Best Practice*. Sydney University Press, Australia
  – Assesses international urban land use planning practices.

The principal elements of the planning system are:

- planning legislation that outlines objectives for planning, specific requirements for managing planning activities (such as development approvals), and areas for which regulations can be made (such as development contributions)
- state-wide policy frameworks to provide consistent direction in detailed planning matters, such as housing diversity or biodiversity protection, as outlined in Clauses 10 to 19 of the *Victoria Planning Provisions*
- development controls created under planning legislation

- policies and guidelines to support regulatory controls, with some given status under planning legislation and therefore must be addressed, while others developed to guide how to apply a control, especially when new regulations are released.

The NSW Government introduced a new division into the *NSW Environmental Planning and Assessment Act 1979 No 203* to support strategic planning activities. Among other things, Division 3.1 Strategic Planning requires the alignment between state and local strategic plans (and in turn local planning controls), where the local plan must "give effect" to the regional plan (noting there is a single regional plan covering Greater Sydney).

In all states, the administration of planning systems is managed by a state agency that may be a standalone department or part of a departmental cluster. Therefore, in one sense planning systems across Australia are the same—they are about the regulation of the use of land. What differs is how they work, what they seek to manage, and who is responsible for preparing or managing the controls. Their difference is in part explained by planning to be a state responsibility, so coordination and consistency across states is not mandatory.

5.3.1.2 International Context—Strategic Planning

In the United States, comprehensive (strategic) plans have guided the development of the application of planning controls since 1926 when the Standard State Zoning Enabling Act (SZEA) was put in place. "The SZEA called for zoning regulations to be 'made in accordance with a comprehensive plan' to, among other purposes, 'facilitate the adequate provision of transportation, water, sewerage, parks, and other public requirements.'" (Rouse and Piro 2022, p. 5).

Application of the Standard State Zoning Enabling Act has been supported by guiding documents since 1964 with the publication of *The Urban General Plan* by T.J. Kent and most recently in 2022 with *The Comprehensive Plan, Sustainable, Resilient, and Equitable Communities for the 21st Century* by David Rouse and Rocky Piro.

In the United Kingdom, the *Plain English guide to the planning system*, on the government website GOV.UK (refer website links) states:

> In London the Mayor remains responsible for producing a strategic plan for the capital. Local Plans in London need to be in line with (in 'general conformity' with) the London Plan, which will continue to guide decisions on planning applications by London borough councils and the Mayor. (Paragraph 25)

> Outside London: Local Plans are the key documents through which local planning authorities can set out a vision and framework for the future development of the area, engaging with their communities in doing so. Local Plans address needs and opportunities in relation to housing, the local economy, community facilities and infrastructure. They should safeguard the environment, enable adaptation to climate change and help secure high quality accessible design. The Local Plan provides a degree of certainty for communities, businesses and investors, and a framework for guiding decisions on individual planning applications. (Paragraph 27)

5.3.2 *Community and Stakeholder Engagement*

Community engagement occurs throughout the 7-Step Strategic Planning Process, making the ability to lead community engagement activities a core skill for the strategic planner. Not only is this a practical skill, but it also puts you directly in touch with the community you are seeking to plan for, which can be rewarding.

As community engagement activities occur throughout the 7-Step Strategic Planning Process be aware of a range of issues:

- the purpose of community engagement
- the role of planners
- what is meant by 'community'
- engagement approaches
- the use of experts.

5.3.2.1 Purpose

With city plans developed to benefit the community, it stands to reason that we engage with the community.

In this context, community engagement should:

- **seek input** on what the community perceives as relevant issues, their views on the issues identified for investigation for the project (the research agenda), the project scope, the research framework and its principal findings, and the draft plan
- **seek formal feedback** on information, from findings to draft plans
- **create trust** in the process, the outcome, and the government (the latter is incredibly challenging)
- **participate directly (in some cases)** in the preparation and decision-making of the plan
- **build capacity and enhance the learnings** of the community and planners in both engaging and content.

On the last point Forester (1999, p. 1) states: "So when city planners deliberate with city residents, they shape public learning as well as public action." He also emphasises that planning officials must also "… inform, advise and even coach a range of public officials and appointed, elected and grass-roots decision makers too."

Undertaking community engagement is challenging. From the community's side there can never be enough, and timelines are always too short. Conversely, engagement overload is real, especially when governments are pursuing multiple agendas and engaging on all of them.

To meet the purpose of community engagement, prepare a community engagement plan from the outset of the project to establish and communicate the role of the community in the strategic planning process and how they will participate. The community needs to be aware of what to expect. There is nothing wrong with some activities directed to information only; what is important is to let people know what you are doing, so they do not get frustrated when they cannot participate directly at that point in time.

5.3.2.2 The Role of Planners

Forester (1999) emphasises that planners have several roles when undertaking community engagement:

- as a go between, as they liaise separately and often continually with decision-makers and the community
- as a facilitator, moving between the various stakeholders for any project or policy proposal:

> They work to encourage practical public deliberation—public listening, learning and beginning to act on innovative agreements too—as they move project and policy proposals forward via viable implementation or decisive rejection (the 'no-build' option) (p. 3)

- as a navigator of political, ethical and rational considerations in day-to-day actions, observations, confrontations, negotiations and reporting (p. 3)
- as a consensus negotiator, bringing together technical information and community observations/values, often between conflicting groups, requiring some efforts in terms of how you convey information how stories are listened to; in this context, information is power and, as a related aside, acronyms are only understood by those who invent them, they are another source of power (pp. 1–15)
- as a "civic friend", in that you heed the advice of a friend due to the understanding of the relationship (p. 3)

Public servants tend to have clear guidance as to their role. For example, the NSW Public Service Commission website under the heading of 'The Westminster system' states:

Public servants work under the direction of their departmental secretary or agency head. Within this context they support ministers' efforts to:

- develop and advise on policy options and draft legislation,
- implement the Government's decisions, policies and programs,
- deliver services to the community.
- manage the state's resources, assets, and finances.

Furthermore, guidelines are provided under which public servants must act on a day-to-day basis. The NSW Public Service Commission also publish a Code of Ethics (2022, p. 8) which states:
How do I act in the public interest?

You should treat all people with whom you have contact in the course of your work:

- Equally without prejudice or favour
- With honesty, consistency and impartiality.

You should also, in the course of your work:

- Place the public interest over your personal interest
- Uphold the law, institutions of government and democratic principles
- Provide apolitical and non-partisan advice
- Provide transparency to enable public scrutiny
- Be fiscally responsible and focus on efficient, effective and prudent use of resources.

5.3.2.3 What is Meant by 'the Community'?

We often use the word 'community' with different meanings varying from a spatially defined group of people, such as a neighbourhood for a specific community group.

With no set rules, consider the following:

- **peak industry bodies**—formal organisations that act on behalf of members
- **peak environmental and social bodies**—formal member organisations usually focused on a specific issue, from the environment to people with a disability
- **community groups**—both formal and informal which act on behalf of the public and are usually focused on an issue(s) and/or a place
- **sporting, leisure or recreational groups**—both formal and informal, usually with a membership reflecting the activity, from tennis to skydiving
- **the general public**—people who are not linked to any group, but who usually make up the majority of people covered by a city plan. They often do not engage in any of the engagement activities, yet they are the people we are planning for.

> *I have never forgotten the advice of one of my university lectures, Trevor Tyson. He asked the class to stand in a row based on whether you like bananas. Our distribution resembled a normal distribution curve. Once we were in line, with some of us mumbling as to why we stood where we did—particularly those at either end of the line, Trevor made a key point: when you engage on most issues, it is only those who are strongly for or against an issue (do you like bananas?) that will make a noise, but you are planning for the people in the middle, the majority of the population.*

Planners also use the word 'stakeholders' and I use it in this book. Stakeholders is planning jargon for those known people, peak bodies or groups likely to have a direct interest in a project or planning issue. When time is short, engaging with these people is seen as a litmus test for wider community views. There is always a risk of overusing only stakeholders and thus getting a narrow or biased perspective on an issue.

5.3.2.4 Engagement Approach

Different engagement approaches are required for each step in the process. Many methodologies are available; there is extensive material on methods and many experts to seek advice from.

Chapters 6–11 detail the purpose of community engagement activities for each step in preparing a plan.

In recent years, the opportunities of social media have been pursued, as have opportunities from the 'big data' that sits behind social media. There are emerging specialists in this area. Most recently, government restrictions on movement due to the COVID-19 pandemic created innovative ways to utilise digital technologies.

I outline a range of approaches below.

Working directly with groups

- Direct engagement with individual peak bodies, who are generally well equipped to engage in this way, should consider transparency in dealings; clarity in purpose (why engaging); and clarity in the independence of both sides.
- Joint sessions between peak bodies can identify common ground on common issues. This was undertaken during social and environmental planning for the Greater Sydney Region Plan (refer background reports on the Greater Cities Commission website).
- During a direct engagement with community groups, the question of trust is paramount. Be aware that most people involved are doing so voluntarily, unlike most peak bodies that have a small number of paid staff. Thus, when you engage, think about the right time and place.

Working with the Public

- **Social media and digital technology** have created opportunities such as online forums, chat rooms, live feeds, submitting pictures and direct submissions.

    Importantly, social media has expanded the depth and breadth of people who can learn about and/or participate in city planning. Specialist advice is usually required and often available in-house for government agencies and larger local governments.

    Digital technology enables opportunities not traditionally available, such as online feedback forms that allow for structured feedback, which assists in the submissions review process. At the same time, social media needs ongoing moderation, which requires protocols on how responses will be managed.

    It is only a decade since I led the Victorian Government's first use of social media for a metropolitan strategy. We had many hurdles to navigate. One colleague felt we would lose control of the project; the Privacy Commission had to be convinced we met its

5.3 Common Threads and Considerations

requirements; and the head of the planning portfolio needed to know they were not going to be able to authorise every response that we would need to post on social media outlets.

In this context, social media has more to offer, particularly as a new generation of planners, who have grown up in a digital age, identify new ways of working with social media. On the output side, it makes it possible to move from hard copy thinking in terms of reports to more interactive web-based information—to allow people to access more readily what they feel is important.

- **Traditional engagement methods** in the community include 'town hall' meetings and pop-up stands in shopping centres. This requires us to manage vocal individuals who can negatively influence the level of participation of others, but at the same time you have a visible presence in the community.
- **Targeted engagement** such as forums targeted at young people, the elderly, people with a disability, and where language or ethnic considerations require specific engagement methods including the use of language translation services.
- **Have your say days** are an innovation I first utilised after seeking expert advice from Wendy Sarkissian, a renowned social planner (refer Sect. 11.5.3). The have your say day is a version of a drop-in session that the community can attend at any time, over a specified period (at least four hours). The objective is to both provide information and seek feedback in a variety of ways.

I have now utilised this method many times even for a compulsory acquisition engagement process. In this instance it was particularly beneficial as we provided the affected landowners with a range of information and engagement options when they arrived, such as project rationale, project details, their rights and the process of acquisition. We felt the process worked well for an emotionally challenging task. Most who attended thanked us and the activities were not reported in mainstream media.

- **Deliberative engagement methods** seek to target the silent majority through techniques from focus groups to community panels and deliberative workshops. The latter can involve 100 or more people and include community representatives and randomly selected people from the public.
- **Surveys** aim to connect with the silent majority and ideally with a sample size that is statistically valid, where findings are more likely to represent the views of the public.
- **Opportunities for informal input** should be considered to maximise the potential of social media tools. Issues of bias will need consideration when social media tools provide a stream of thinking which potentially takes the discussion along a specific path.
- **Innovative ways to gain community input** such as a travelling bus. On the Internet of Things side, people are exploring how to use the big data that sits behind social media tools, such as apps.

My most successful innovative community engagement approach was 'a camera for a day'. for a project in the City of Casey—the 'Casey Foothills' study. We provided 40 community members with a camera, with instructions on how to report on their photos. This clarified what aspects of the foothills they valued, which allowed us to brief a specialist visual consultant.

5.3.2.5 Engaging with First Nations Communities

When engaging with First Nations communities, in Australia, we need to look beyond simple engagement methods and think of partnerships. For First Nations people, the concept of reciprocity is important; this is about two-way sharing.

It is important to work closely with First Nations communities early in the strategic planning process to ensure their Knowledges, values and aspirations are embedded. Considering First Nations communities as partners and on a similar level with other government agencies will ensure you achieve mutually beneficial outcomes.

Given the long ancestral connection to Country and the lack of treaty in Australia, it is important to consider how you can increase First Nations authority in the decision-making process. Input shouldn't only be considered on an advisory level but as genuine.

Humility is also important; we need to recognise that we all come from our own cultural backgrounds and that includes a feeling about the right way of doing things. Acknowledge that there are two systems in play, one based on a history of planning systems and another founded on cultural knowledge.

Meaningful engagement requires deep listening, where you listen to understand and not to respond. The NSW guideline *Recognise Country* provides advice on how to achieve meaningful engagement (NSW Government, 2022, pp. 27–29). It outlines some engagement principles to consider (p. 29):

- **Relationships**—First Nations culture is firmly founded in relationships. Investing time in getting to know the community and building relationships will increase the success of project outcomes.
- **Respectful and informed**—ensure the team has conducted some desktop research to better understand the context of Country, community and culture in the area.
- **Flexible and local**—there is a wide range of community groups and organisations, it is important to align with their availability and location preference for meeting.
- **Visual and informal**—the use of visual tools and jargon free language will help to aid informed discussion.

The guideline emphasises the range of First Nations stakeholders to engage with and the need to consider their priority, role and relevance to the project. The priority order of stakeholders outlined includes (p. 28):

- Traditional Custodians

- knowledge-holders
- Local Aboriginal Land Councils
- the broader Aboriginal and Torres Strait Islander community
- Aboriginal service providers or businesses
- Registered Aboriginal Party (RAP).

For many planners, working with First Nations communities is a new community engagement experience where you can, liaise with Aboriginal Planning Officers in the relevant planning authority and/or a specialist First Nations planning consultant.

5.3.2.6 Using Experts

As for all areas in strategic planning, specialists (experts) can add significant value and there are many reasons for engaging them:

- independence, a community trust issue
- complexity of the task and/or specialised engagement techniques required (for example, a deliberative panel process)
- managing an emotionally/politically charged community issue
- capacity building, of your team
- straight out resourcing issues.

Clarify the purpose and task for the specialist and that the work is owned by your team to avoid the work ending up as an appendix.

Bring specialist community engagement consultants in at the start, so they can support the whole process rather than coming at the end to solve a problem.

When working at a council, community engagement is not just a deliberative task for a project, it is an ongoing day-to-day task for the planners who meet and talk with all members of the community from the resident to the developer. In this context, Forester's (1999) case study approach to examining participatory processes provides a clear working context to understanding the challenges.

> *It was the very nature of working at the coalface with the community that led me to observe, when I shifted to state government, that something did not seem right and after a month I realised—the phones (the community) did not constantly ring.*

5.3.2.7 General Considerations

Other issues to consider:

- Decision-makers may have expectations about what methods need to be included. Often town hall meetings are seen to be a required method as you are visibly in the community.

- Community engagement is likely to require many activities utilising a range of team members. Consistency of messaging is essential and requires scripted talking points.
- Community engagement is resource intensive; thus, consider your whole of project community engagement plan. If you work in an organisation with its own communications department, make sure you know who is paying the bill.
- If using external specialists or an internal communications department, make sure you as the planner lead and others understand the scope of the planning project. This is about ownership of the output. On the communication side 'comms' messaging may be different to what you see the project messaging as—this is always a challenging area where unambiguous language is important.
- Trust needs to be earned and takes time. It is not achieved just through one project. Furthermore, the more you use specialists, the less the community sees your organisation engaging, therefore the trust created is with the specialists and not with you. Hence, all strategic planners need to be adept at community and stakeholder engagement. It is about creating a culture of engagement. Ideally, strategic planning should include ongoing conversations with the community to build trust.

> More than 30 years ago I heard Eva Cox, a well renowned social planner, speaking at a conference. She made the point that you have not achieved the trust of the community until you can have a proper debate with them and both sides feel that they are listened to and respected. These words have always resonated with me.
>
> More recently I listened to Professor Nancy Odendaal, of the School of Architecture, Planning & Geomatics at the University of Cape Town in South Africa talk about engaging with communities in the slums of the major cities in South Africa. She raised an engagement philosophy that resonated powerfully and clearly, I feel it will stay with me for a very long time. It was:
>
> **"Moving at the speed of trust"**

- The opportunity to gain the community's trust can be enhanced through your approach to engagement. I have been fortunate enough to be involved in two processes where the engagement approach was tailored to enhance both trust and an understanding of local issues.

> The first was when I was at the City of Casey where, as part of a partnership with state government, our council had one officer included as a team of three working out of a community facility in a local community to deliver a long-term community development and housing initiative.
>
> The second example was at the then Greater Sydney Commission where we included local government secondees in our teams. We not only gained local intelligence, we also earned local champions.

- Active listening requires making changes. On this point, Habermas (as cited in Forester 1999 p. 201) states that:

   > Practical discourse is not a procedure for generating justified norms but a procedure for testing the validity of norms that are being proposed and hypothetically considered for adoption.

- The activities of community engagement can be confronting and emotionally charged which can put pressure on the attitude and behaviour of planners. Forester (1999 p. 57) contends that "Planners' day-to-day telling of stories of what they have seen, heard, and done shapes their practical, political, and ethical behaviour".

5.3.3 First Nations Country, Community and Culture

All Australia's jurisdictions have legislation that protects the First Nations heritage of tangible items, such as rock art, tools and burial remains. However, recognition and response to issues of culture and Country has limited traction in capital city plans across Australia. The NSW draft framework *Connecting with Country* provides advice on their meaning.

Country

   Country (capital C) has a specific and significant meaning for Aboriginal peoples. In the Aboriginal sense of the word, Country relates to the nation or cultural group and land that we belong to, yearn for, find healing from and will return to. However, Country means much more than land, it is our place of origin in cultural, spiritual and literal terms. It includes not only land but also skies and waters. Country incorporates both the tangible and the intangible, for instance, all the knowledges and cultural practices associated with land. People are part of Country, and our identity is derived in a large way in relation to Country. Dr Danièle Hromek, Budawang/Yuin, (p. 14)

Culture

   The many interpretations of Country are expressed through cultural practice. Culture includes knowledge, belief, art, morals, law and customs acquired by membership in a social group. Knowledge, habits and capabilities all make up culture. (p. 16)

   Cultural identity is the sense of belonging to a distinct group. First Peoples' identities are deeply linked to culture, community and the land, and this is a key factor to health and wellbeing.—Dr Danièle Hromek (p. 16)

NSW offers one example of the positive shift in how governments are addressing First Nations Country, community and culture. Resources developed by the Government Architect NSW address the wider issues of culture and Country for planning and design:

- Draft Connecting with Country (2020)
- Designing with Country (2020)

Place-specific guidelines have also been prepared such as *Recognise Country, Guidelines for development in the Aerotropolis*.

Furthermore, in 2022 the Greater Cities Commission released, the *Six Cities Region* discussion paper, in which the vision is framed around six city shapers, the first—*An embedded First Nations voice*.

5.3.3.1 Considerations

The draft framework *Connecting with Country* outlines the strategies planners need to consider to genuinely connect with Country.

- **Pathways for connecting**, is about recognising that cultural awareness must come first. This includes:
  - cultural expression, specifically engaging with First Nations' languages and the meaning of first placenames to learn more about Country (p. 21)
  - relationships with Country, which require time, sharing emotions and experiences to ensure decisions not only benefit people but also the needs of Country (p. 22)
  - learning from Country, by walking Country with First Nations knowledge-holders and Traditional Custodians using all senses to more deeply understand places (p. 23)
  - knowledge-sharing, explained as follows: "Within Aboriginal communities intergeneration teaching and learning is an important cultural value shared two ways between Elders and younger groups." Knowledge sharing can overcome barriers, help to find common ground and allow us to be guided by First Nations' knowledge systems that may be challenging within confirms of Western systems and processes. (p. 24)
- **Considering project life cycles with an Aboriginal perspective**, is about creating the opportunity for built environment projects (city planning) to connect with the Country. It requires you to "think differently through new words that reflect physical experiences of Country."
  - Sensing—Start with Country is about actively seeking the sense of Country and should be a focus of activities in the project formation phase. (p. 27)
  - Imagining—Listen to Country requires the guidance of Aboriginal knowledge-holders and should focus on helping Aboriginal people feel comfortable when speaking about Country. This occurs during project design and conceptualisation. (p. 27)
  - Shaping—Design with Country recognises the inter-relationships between all living and non-living elements with Country and thus how "making from and on Country respects and allows this relationship to continue." It is a project delivery consideration. (p. 28)
  - Caring for Country recognises that "Once built on Country, all projects belong to and are in a relationship with Country including buildings,

roads and parks." They should therefore be cared for as a system—project maintenance. (p. 28)

The draft framework addresses implementation by outlining seven statements of commitment each with principles for action and related considerations and challenges. A framework for measuring success and learning from failure is also included.

Recognise Country, Guidelines for development in the Aerotropolis provides a worked example of how the framework can be applied to a place.

5.3.3.2 Strategic Planning Response

We need to respond to First Nations culture and heritage, and how we care for and connect with Country, throughout the 7-Step Strategic Planning Process, including as part of several research topics within the Strategic Planning Research Framework.

Considerations include:

- Step 1: Committing to ongoing engagement, ideally a partnership, with local First Nations communities, refer Sects. 1.3.2.5 and 6.4.4.
- Step 2: Undertaking targeted research activities including First Nations perspectives, as outlined in the Strategic Planning Research Framework.
- Step 3: Directly referencing cultural landscapes as part of the SWOT analysis and inclusion of First Nations considerations within the vision, refer to Sects. 8.3.1 and 8.6.2.
- Step 4: Seeking specialist advice to ensure the findings from research into First Nations Country, community and culture are appropriately incorporated into the draft plan, directly involving First Nations communities in that activity as part of a partnership approach, and involving representatives of First Nations people as part of the peer review process, refer Sects. 9.3.1 and 9.3.4.
- Step 5: Directly engaging with First Nations communities, refer Sect. 10.2.3.3.
- Step 6: Monitoring outcomes, refer Sect. 10.3.5.
- Step 7: Maintaining an ongoing relationship with the local First Nations communities, refer Sect. 11.5.3.1.

Within the Strategic Planning Research Framework, as outlined in Sect. 4.3, multiple research topics which require use to consider the needs to First Nations communities:

- Section 14.2.1: Improving the level of housing choice
- Section 14.2.3: Enabling the economic self-determination of First Nations communities
- Section 14.3.2: Enabling cultural and artistic expression, participation and appreciation
- Section 15.3.2: Responding to First Nations Country, community and culture.

5.3.4 Politics and Planning

Hamnett and Freestone (2000, p. 2) argue that planning is a social product where its origins, agenda, evolution, forms and impacts are best appreciated within a broader societal context.

Planning needs to be seen in the context of political activities and this should not be seen as a negative. What is required is an appreciation of how planning is influenced by political processes. I outline the nature of these political processes here.

- **Contested decisions**. As planning is a social science, most issues are not clearly defined; rather they are about interpretation.
- **Codified societal norms**. The challenge from the outset is where to draw the line; for example, for overshadowing, how many hours of sunlight and at what time and day of the year are relevant? Recognising where the line is drawn influences the development potential of a site with an economic consequence.
- **Planning is very often reactive**. Leonie Sandercock, cited in Hamnett and Freestone (2000, p. 2), suggests that a challenge for planning is that its activities (based on why we plan) are invariably responses "about failure".
- **Participatory processes**. Developing strategic plans or making changes to regulatory systems generally utilise participatory processes as they create opportunities for advocacy or lobbying.
- **Deliberative agendas of governments**. Governments will often have clear stated agendas. For example, I recall that in December 2010, the incoming government in Victoria campaigned with a clear planning agenda that included a 10-point plan for a new metropolitan strategy.
- **Stakeholder groups have clear agendas**. Agendas are either overtly political and seek to influence government policy positions, or they are seen by the stakeholders as statements of their community's values (equally political).
- **Planning is about regulating development markets**. Australia's political parties are seen to have differing political positions in regard to regulating markets.
- **Property rights**. In the context of the point above, planning can directly impact the economic value of private property via planning controls. Additionally, landowners have social and/or emotional values about their property which may not align with the realisable economic value.
- **Positives for the government**. Governments usually like to see that there is a purpose for what they are doing, either a clear positive benefit or a policy solution they believe in. They are conscious that when they stand up in front of the public and look to sell a policy or plan, they need to be clear about how to explain the narrative. I have witnessed firsthand projects that stall, due to an inability to explain the benefits to the government.

For the planner involved in city planning, there are two critical issues:

5.3 Common Threads and Considerations

- recognise that planning activities occur within political processes
- **do not** participate in the political process.

Facilitate activities, enquire, assess and mediate, but don't be a player. That said, Forester (1999) talks of the role of planners as intermediaries in participatory processes.

Finally, the guiding principle for public sector planners is the dictum of providing frank and fearless advice untinged by politics. However, when working in government, your task is to provide advice to meet the objectives of the government. Yes, you outline the risks (the frank and fearless advice) but you are focused on the government's agenda. Thus, as I have said many a time to my teams, if this does not sit well with you, then work in the private sector.

5.3.5 Planning and Decision-Making

Planning is recognised as a discipline where contested decisions are the norm. Even in an area such as retailing, several peak bodies have differing views on how planning controls should be managed. Consequently, a minister making a decision that is seen to reflect the views of one peak body will potentially be at odds with others. For this reason, transparency in decision-making is critical.

Other considerations regarding decision-making are briefly described here.

- **Decision-making within government**. Every day in government there is a need to make decisions of state significance. This can create a tendency to focus a lot of effort and attention on major milestones. Strategic planning, however, often requires many decisions, as the development of a plan is a series of small decisions on interrelated building blocks, such as approaches to funding, the scope of investigations, new policy positions, and connecting land use actions to transport (or vice-versa). Try to foreshadow the implications of the interdependencies and manage the consequences of changes occurring at any given milestone.
- **The challenge of multiple portfolios**. City plans affect multiple disciplines which means multiple ministers are involved. Building a coalition of support requires both departmental and political relationships. Getting a plan across the line and approved is not sufficient. If some ministries are not truly on board, it will impact implementation and risk appropriately located infrastructure, for example, a hospital, or support for where investment should go.

> *I once had responsibility to achieve a specific outcome from a plan adopted by not just the planning minister but had been signed off by the whole of government. Yet the action required active support by one government agency, which was not forthcoming. Eventually I needed to advise that the initiative could not be delivered.*

- **The community and decision-making**. Community engagement must clarify the role of the community in decision-making. The International Association for Public Participation's *Spectrum for Public Participation* conceptualises a spectrum for increasing the influence of the community on decision-making starting with inform and moving to consult, involve and collaborate to empower. While there is often a good collaboration between levels of government and government agencies in strategic planning processes; with the community the focus can be anywhere between inform and involve.

> When I was working at the City of Casey (Victoria) the council allowed the community to determine how their local parks would be developed within a fixed funding limit.

When engaging with the community, clarify where the engagement sits in terms of this spectrum and thus their involvement in decision-making.
- **Negotiation and decisions**. Learning how to negotiate is important and getting training, including in mediation, is an advantage. A good place to start is Herb Cohen's *You can negotiate anything* (1984).

5.3.6 Confidentiality

Understanding the importance of confidentiality and what it means for day-to-day activities is essential for anyone working in government. Transparency in the activities of government underpins good governance and creates trust within the community.

In balancing the needs of transparency with confidentiality, consider the areas that must remain private:

- Protect the details of contracts or advice that may be commercial-in-confidence, such as the value of a property to be acquired or contract details that may advantage competitors or potential suppliers (when governments seek to get the best value for money for the cost of a project).
- Consider whether the exploration of an issue that is contentious needs to be public, such as a congestion tax that is then not proceeded with, to avoid unnecessary concern in the community.
- Note the confidentiality required around the assessment of planning controls that can impact the value of land, such as Melbourne's Urban Growth Boundary (a planning control where change requires the approval of both houses of parliament, within 10 sitting days). To minimise speculation on land values, the information is not released until it has been signed off by the government and is ready for whole of community comment.

> I managed the last major change to the Urban Growth Boundary in Melbourne in 2010. The process required many protocols in file management, email management, a clean

5.3 Common Threads and Considerations

desk policy, report distribution (such as numbered of reports), and even special paper for photocopying.

- Clarify the status of documents when preparing a plan. Up to the time of the final document, all documents should be marked as working drafts. Some agencies have clear protocols, particularly for documents to be used in a formal state government cabinet process.
- Determine what information should be kept confidential and what should be released. As far as I am aware, most jurisdictions have a formal (legislated) process to deal with this issue, often referred to as freedom of information.

5.3.7 Project Management

Project management and strategic planning are similar activities in terms of process. Both seek to manage a range of interconnected tasks to achieve a common goal. Thus, good project management skills are a core requisite for the strategic planner.

There is a significant amount of literature, short courses, and postgraduate qualifications in this area. A starting point in the literature is the PMBOK or *Project Management Book of Knowledge (PMBOK Guide) Seventh Edition* (2021). This highly regarded industry text outlines the issues pertaining to project management.

Utilising project management tools for strategic planning is straightforward, in that the more sophisticated elements of project management are generally not required for a typical city planning project. The principal areas where a good understanding of the issues is required include those often referred to as the project management triangle, refer Fig. 5.4.

The triangle covers the areas of time management, cost (resourcing) management and quality management. It shows that at any point there is a tension between resolving these three issues. For example, the time and/or cost available for a

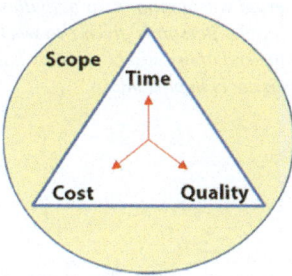

Fig. 5.4 Project management triangle

project may be fixed, thus quality comes under pressure. However, all three elements need to be considered in the context of the project scope. Hence, quality may not be impacted if the scope is changed.

In the literature on project management there are a few variations of this diagram. What is shown, in Fig. 5.4, is how I best understand the challenge, namely that the scope of the project sets the frame for understanding the other three.

Other areas for consideration include:

- **Project risks** in delivering the project, such as cost over-runs, political risks and losing the support of partner agencies.
- **Procurement**, especially for government agencies, noting there are usually teams with direct responsibility in this area, and value for money is an important guiding principle.
- **Stakeholders**, and planning to engage with them (in a community engagement sense) while also being prepared for the consequences of the independent actions of stakeholders.
- **Value management**, which is about some form of peer review. Transport agencies usually have deliberative processes in this area, especially for the staged review of progress when developing business cases for major infrastructure projects. The Greater Sydney Region Plan (2018, p. 183) includes an action where the Greater Sydney Commission (now Greater Cities Commission) has a peer review role for land use and infrastructure plans prepared by the NSW Department of Planning and Environment.

A final point on project management, in government, the funds available for projects are usually fixed through annual budget processes. Project flexibility is therefore directed to n the time and quality management areas, and clearly scope at the beginning of a project. Time management becomes a skill that the strategic planner needs to acquire. On this issue, the following lesson from my past.

> Most people draw a simple Gantt chart for their project showing how long each step will take, and over time these can become quite sophisticated. During my masters, Paul Steinfort, one of our lecturers, provided me with a rule that still holds true: "Your control is only as good as the length of the time period you monitor your activities." That is, if you monitor the status of tasks every two weeks and a person is given two weeks to do a task, the potential delay is two weeks, because at the end of two weeks you may find they have not started. How you approach and manage this issue is important.

5.3.8 Sustainability

Since cities began, rulers and governments have recognised the need to manage natural systems to sustain life such as clean water. This is now evolving into considerations of Country in a much more holistic way. The 'tragedy of the commons'

5.3 Common Threads and Considerations

has also been long recognised as an issue to retain the benefits of access to natural resources.

It is only more recently that the intrinsic value of the environment in its own right has become mainstream in city planning, particularly the contemporary notion of sustainability that recognises the need to balance present and future needs to ensure future generations have the same opportunities as we do today.

This concept of sustainability was elevated to mainstream debate when, in 1987, the World Commission on Environment and Development released the Brundtland Report *Our Common Future,* which discussed the notion of sustainable development through a triple bottom line (environment, social and economic). The report emphasised the entwined nature of the environment and development (World Commission on Environment and Development 1987, p. 6):

> ... the 'environment' is where we all live; and 'development' is what we all do in attempting to improve our lot with that abode. The two are inseparable.

Stein (2017, pp. 24–47) covers the issue of sustainability extensively in the context of city planning and makes several practical points including:

- the danger of only talking about sustainable development, as it implies primacy of economic development
- the importance of having legislative definitions that list the specific matters which decision-makers must consider
- the preference for setting out a government's intention for sustainability in a policy where it can be fully explained, to remove speculation as to what a simple definition means
- if incorporating sustainability principles in all the activities of preparing a plan and including sustainability indices, removing the need for specific reference to consider sustainability in decision-making as it is embedded in the details of the plan and becomes business-as-usual.

Stein (2017) also emphasises that how we approach sustainability varies from place to place and over time.

In terms of city planning in NSW, sustainability is identified in the *Environmental Planning and Assessment Act 1979 No 203* under Section 1.3 *Objects of the Act* as:

> To facilitate ecologically sustainable development by integrating relevant economic, environmental and social considerations in decision-making about environmental planning and assessment.

The concept of 'environmentally sustainable development' is separately defined in the *NSW Protection of the Environment Administration Act 1991 No 60*, Part 3, Section 6.

It is not surprising that it can be challenging for the lay person working their way through our planning systems.

5.3.9 Complexity, Cities and A Systems View of Planning

My view of cities dramatically transformed when I read a book on complexity while undertaking my postgraduate qualification. I see complexity theory as providing clear guidance for how cities operate as dynamic places and from some perspectives as complex organisms. For those interested in this topic I recommend:

- *Complexity* by Mitchell E. Waldrop (1992)
- How Nature Works: The Science of Self-Organised Criticality by Per Bak (1996)
- *Scale* by Geoffrey West (2018)
- The New Science of Cities by Mike Batty (2013).

Three specific issues are worthy of note:

- **Complexity theory and its relevance to city planning**. Cities can lock into futures that are not optimal due to increasing returns. General economic theory does not allow for this as it focuses on the concept of diminishing returns. Path dependency and the impact of the predict and provide approach to transport infrastructure can be seen as examples of this (Waldrop 1992).
  Bak (1996, pp. 183–198) covers complexity in economics and emphasises how economic systems are not fluid, rather decisions are incremental and large fluctuations can be explained by complexity theory. He also shows how complexity theory can be used to explain the dynamics of traffic jams.
- **Complexity and laws for cities**. In the main, city planning is a social science. West (2017) and Batty (2013) outline observations that suggest that there are 'laws' that can explain some of the attributes of cities. West (2018) demonstrates that when cities double in size, changes in a range of attributes reflect consistent power laws. The research shows that for hard infrastructure, such as utility services, there are constant efficiencies, whereas for soft outcomes (for example, economic output) there are positive dividends.
- **Systems thinking, a foundation for understanding the dynamics of cities**. When I was at university, the focus of thinking in this area was the work of Chadwick (1971) and McLoughlin (1969) and for my first decade in planning the practical application of a systems view of the dynamics of a city was core to understanding cities. Most important was learning how different systems interact with each other and how the dynamics of individual systems evolve over time.

The work on complexity and cities raises the question of a city as an organism as put forward by Francesco di Giorgio (late 1400s) in his *Trattato* (cited in Kostof

1991, p. 52) where he states that "The relation of the city to its parts is similar to that of the human body to its parts; the streets are the veins."

However, Kostof (1991, p. 53) and Lynch and Weiss, as cited in Kostof (1991, p. 53), all dispute the notion of the city as an organism, emphasising that "There is no evidence of any such lawful regularity at work in 'organic' cities." However, the work of West (2018) and Batty (2013) shows that there are laws for cities.

From the work of West and Batty, and my observations from working across many cities, it is the people, acting as the cells of an organism, that collectively work as the self-organising actors that influence where change in cities occurs and how they evolve—including what is good and bad and which parts grow or decline.

5.3.10 The Challenge of Planning for Change

The title of this book has a subtext—*Cities are in a permanent state of flux, there is no end state.* Incremental change is constantly occurring throughout the city, whether it is individuals changing jobs, buying new homes or renovating existing homes, businesses relocating, or major public works, the city is never standing still. Significant change occurs in localised areas whether that be new greenfield development or major urban renewal sites. Though for many it is the constants in our neighbourhood, perceived or real, that allow us to cope in this everchanging world.

Managing change is addressed throughout this book. At this point three issues will be examined:

- the community's perception of change
- observations of the nature of change in cities
- delivering change, from idea to mainstream, takes 10 years.

5.3.10.1 For Communities, Perception is Reality

The concept that planning is about change is well understood; however, from the perspective of the community, this is not necessarily the case, hence why we have the contested nature of planning and its influence in the local, state and Commonwealth political arenas.

In thinking about the community and change, think about perceptions of change. There are places where change occurs very slowly, for example, in most suburban areas, where second-storey extensions may be the biggest change. I witnessed this in the suburb of Glen Waverley (Victoria) when I was working for the local government in the early 1990s. In such places, a proposal for a simple multi-unit development, bring of a different character to a detached dwelling, can be seen as a major change for the neighbours adjacent to the proposal.

In some places where significant change occurs, what previously existed is often forgotten as we all move on in some way.

The younger members of my team, when I was working for the Victorian Government around 2010, had no recollection that Southbank (in Melbourne), a vibrant entertainment, arts and leisure precinct, had a generation earlier been a collection of industrial activities and car yards. Potentially this differing view of change reflected that there was something in it for the community.

However, we must recognise that perception is reality.

5.3.10.2 The Nature of Change in Cities
Some observations of change:

- The whole focus of developers is towards building or creating; their actions are about change.
- Businesses strive to provide consumers with products, and consumers continually change tastes which impacts the products people buy and how they are presented, created and delivered. Thus, businesses are continually pursuing two paths—addressing the certainty and opportunities of current markets, and responding to future markets, leading to a dual certainty/change environment.
- Families and individuals seek comfort and certainty within the confines of their home and local community (schools, shops, park, etc.) yet equally seek out new products, lifestyle choices and holidays, all which require change.
- Interestingly, the ABS Census shows that in Melbourne, 25% of existing residents move to a different home every five years.

As people seek the certainty and comfort of family, friends and the home and neighbourhood they live in, they forget or don't consider how the differing perspectives of change are part of everyday life. We forget that the house we live in, the car we drive, the shops we go to only exist because at some time a developer, investor or business sought to change something. As planners, we generally forget that this story is one we need to communicate, and equally develop processes to manage.

The last couple of points raise the issue of stable communities and the potential need for change, highlighting why community engagement is a central tool for planning. But this point also raises the vexed issue of when to intervene: if a community is maturing and the values of the past still dominate, when is it appropriate to act? History shows that at some point changing demographics will tip that community towards change. Typically, planning is reactive and when a certain point is reached the community seeks change. Maybe this calls for a better form of ongoing dialogue.

Consequentially, it is often the case in planning that we plan for the future while building for the past.

5.3.10.3 Delivering Change—From Idea to Mainstream Takes 10 Years
The need for a plan, no matter the scale, is usually because there is a belief that without intervention the most likely future is not the desired future. This notion is discussed in Chapters 3 and 4.

However, what is not always understood is the time required to see the effects of the interventions advocated in a plan. It is usually 10 years before the desired outcomes are measurable for land use planning, for several reasons.

At any point in time the private sector, particularly the development sector, is building part of the city, whether that be new streets, houses, shops or offices. Depending on the scale of these projects they may take several years to complete.

The same developers or investors usually have their next project in train based on current planning laws and market circumstances. These committed projects potentially provide another two to three years of development. Therefore, when regulations or other interventions are made, the development or investment sector's response is in the context of their current pipeline of projects.

To respond to any change the development sector needs to understand the market conditions created by the intervention, and it is not just about the development sector. There is also a need for the banks to understand the financial implications of interventions, as well as the full range of advisors who support the development sector.

The development sector can then identify its next project based on the new interventions. The new projects will also require a range of responses including land purchase, planning approval, building approval, construction and sales. Each of these steps takes time.

It is also not so much about when the first development occurs, but when there is a pipeline of development that reflects the vision facilitated by the intervention.

When considering major structural changes to a city, the time lag can be significantly longer. For example, in 1968 the *Sydney Region Outline Plan* proposed that planning and redevelopment be initiated to achieve a higher order role for the Parramatta centre. However, it is only in the last decade (2010 to 2020) that this role has been realised.

There is also a public policy element. Depending on the type of intervention, the policy implications may have to cascade down into a range of plans and policies. That is, an intervention by a state government or the Commonwealth Government may require further changes at the next local level before the development sector can respond to any new controls.

5.4 Summary

So far, this book has explored what planning cities is about in order to better plan them. The central finding is that for cities to meet the needs of people, their lives and the places they live in, they require a level of intervention. How that intervention is identified becomes the central focus of city planning.

The first part of this chapter identified the requirements of a strategic planning framework. This drew together all the findings from Chapters 3 and 4 into a conceptual framework including the identification of the fundamental elements or building blocks required for a planning framework, which include clarity in why intervention is required, evidence, community participation, a deliberative and transparent process, a plan, an approvals process and a designated delivery agency.

From these building blocks a 7-Step Strategic Planning Process was outlined:

- Step 1: Project establishment
- Step 2: Research and analysis
- Step 3: Synthesis and setting direction
- Step 4: Draft plan preparation
- Step 5: Exhibition
- Step 6: Plan finalisation
- Step 7: Plan delivery.

Part 2 of this book, Chapters 6 to 11, outlines the detailed tasks and considerations for each of the seven steps.

The second part of this chapter outlined common threads and considerations that underpin all planning activities and cover the areas of planning systems, community and stakeholder engagement, politics and planning, planning and decision-making, confidentiality, project management, sustainability, complexity and a systems view of planning, and the challenge of change.

5.4 Summary

5.4.1 Insights

Insight: Project management
It's more than a cost, quality and time triangle
There is a lot written on project management and there are plenty of good courses on project management from introductory lectures to masters' degrees. There will be real benefits if, at some point, you undertake some formal training in project management as it is critical to both preparing and implementing city plans
On budget and on time, but does the client want it?
On a day-to-day basis project management is about the management of time, cost and quality issues. However, sitting above all this are the needs of the client. Before you start these must be articulated and understood, thus scoping a project is critical. Re-visiting the project scope throughout the process, in a formal way, is also important
Squeezing time—you will never have enough
As a former client said to me—*if left to your own devices, you planners will just keep on planning, just one more issue to research*. He emphasised the 80–20 rule—in his case he was after a good (80%) answer not the exact answer (100%). That said, for most projects you undertake there will be a perceived, if not real, notion that there is not enough time to undertake the task that has been set. Hence, there is always a need to squeeze time. Undertaking tasks concurrently is the best way to save time, but it does need some project management. For example, while you are completing a draft document for exhibition, all the tasks required to set up the exhibition can be occurring at the same time. This does potentially require additional staffing or resources to allow such overlaps. I have found when you are given short time frames, it is often possible to put an argument for more resources (staffing) to meet the time frame
It can be rocket science
Some project management techniques are quite sophisticated such as the Monte Carlo risk management technique, and value management. The key point is that project management can make a difference and it can be much more than a simple bar chart (Gantt chart)

Sign-off takes time
Too often work programs include plenty of detail on how to do the work but no allowances for the briefings and meetings and then the report dissemination required to gain sign-off at each milestone. Often work programs show a single day for a milestone whereas, in reality, you will most likely need a month if you are working within a public sector environment
Nothing is impossible
As your experience grows you will learn how to achieve outcomes more effectively and efficiently. Your understanding of how to undertake tasks concurrently, when to bring in experts, how to negotiate for additional resources at pinch points, and when to determine a task is unnecessary; all these learnings will enable you to do things you previously thought were impossible
For me, the classic example was the need to process 1000 submissions in 19 working days when preparing the Greater Sydney Region Plan. This task required, among other things: significant pre-planning (over a three-month period); a lot more resourcing, essentially hourly project management; and importantly, support from the decision-makers. It occurred over the Christmas break, which required further negotiation. The result was, I believe, one of the best submissions assessments I have been involved in, and the achievement of something that earlier in my career I would not have thought possible

References

Bak, P (1996), *How Nature Works: The Science of Self-Organised Criticality*, Oxford University Press, Oxford, UK.
– The last chapter discusses complexity and traffic management
Batty, M (2013), *The New Science of Cities*, MIT.
– Cities and complexity, including the mathematics
Chadwick, GF (1971), *A Systems View of Planning: Towards a Theory of the Urban and Regional Planning Process* …
– From my university days and still influences how I see cities.
Cohen, H (1984) *You Can Negotiate Anything*. Bantam Doubleday Dell Publishing Group Inc., US
– A great introduction to the art of negotiation
Forester, J (1999), *The Deliberative Practitioner, Encouraging Participatory Planning Processes*. The MIT Press, USA
– The case study approach brings the issue of community engagement to life.
Garvin, A (2016), *What Makes a Great City*. Island Press.
– The public realm as a quality that makes great cities.
Gurran, N (2011), *Australian Urban Land Use Planning. Principles, Systems and Practice. Second Edition*. Sydney University Press, Australia
– Provides the frame to understand Australia's planning systems.
Hall, P (1998), *Cities in Civilisation: Culture, Innovation, and Urban Order*. Phoenix
– Extraordinary exposé on what makes a great city, with 20 case studies covering 2,500 years of cities.
Hamnett, S & Freestone, R (ed.) (2000), *The Australian Metropolis, A Planning History*. Allen & Unwin, Australia
– The definitive text on the history of planning and Australian cities.
Kostof, S (1991), *The City Shaped, Urban Patterns and Meanings Through History* Thames & Hudson London UK
– A detailed exploration of urban form and what drove different structures.
McLoughlin, BJ (1969), *Urban and Regional Planning, A systems Approach*, Faber and Faber, London
– From my university days, and still resonates for me today.
Project Management Institute, Inc (2021), *Project Management Book of Knowledge (PMBOK Guide). Seventh Edition*. Project Management Institute, Inc. USA.
– All you need to know about project management.
Sarkissian W and Bunjamin-Mau W (2009) *Speak Out,* Taylor and Francis Ltd, UK
– Hard to find a better place to start when heading out and engaging with people.
State Planning Authority of New South Wales (1968) *Sydney Region Outline Plan*
Stein, LA (2017), *Comparative Urban Land Use Planning, Best Practice*. Sydney University Press
– A detailed assessment of international urban land use planning practices.
Waldrop, EM (1992), *Complexity*, Penguin Books, Ringwood, Australia,
– An introduction to a different way of looking at the world, the science of complexity.
West, G (2018), Scale, The Universal Laws of Life and Death in Organisms, Cities and Companies. Hachette, Australia.
– Based on the research of hundreds of cities, this book outlines that there are relationships between the scale of cities and various attributes of cities.
World Commission on Environment and Development 1987, *Our Common Future*, Oxford University Press, GB,
– Seminal work on sustainability.

Website Links

2016 Census Households Australian Bureau of Statistics. https://www.abs.gov.au/websitedbs/D33 10114.nsf/Home/Census.

ABS Historical population of Australia since 1788. 3105.0.65.001—Australian Historical Population Statistics, 2006. http://abs.gov.au/

City of Houston, 2015 *Plan Houston: Opportunity, Diversity, Community, Home.* http://planhouston.org; Houston General Plan. http://houstontx.gov/.

Environmental Planning and Assessment Act 1979 No 203 (NSW), viewed 16 June 2020 https://www.legislation.nsw.gov.au/~/view/act/1979/203.

Government Architect NSW 2020 *Draft Connecting with Country.* http://nsw.gov.au.

Government Architect NSW 2020 *Designing with Country.* http://nsw.gov.au.

Greater Sydney Commission, Social Panel Advisory Paper (2016) and Environment Panel Advisory Paper (2106), background reports to inform the Greater Sydney Region Plan. Background material I Greater Sydney Commission.

International Association for Public Participation (IAP^2). https://www.iap2.org/mpage/Home.

New South Wales Public Service Commission, *Westminster System.* https://www.nsw.gov.au.

New South Wales Public Service Commission, *Code of Ethics and Conflict.*

NSW Government 2022 *Recognise Country, Guidelines for development in the Aerotropolis.* https://aws.amazon.com/.

Plain English guide to the planning system. https://www.gov.uk.

Protection of the Environment Administration Act 1991 No 60 (NSW) viewed 16 June 2020. https://legislation.nsw.gov.au/~/view/act/1991/60/full.

State of New South Wales 2018, A Metropolis of Three Cities. https://www.greater.sydney/metropolis-of-three-cities.

State of NSW 2022 Six Cities Region. The Six Cities Region: Discussion Paper, September 2022. https://aws.amazon.com/.

Victoria Planning Provisions, viewed 4 October 2021 https://www.planning.vic.gov.au/schemes-and-amendments/browse-planning-scheme/planning-scheme?f.Scheme%7CplanningSchemeName=vpps.

Part II
The 7-Step Strategic Planning Process

Part I explored the context for city planning. It concluded that we need to prepare and deliver on city plans as a response to the question—is a business-as-usual future acceptable?

In answering this question, we must think about what is important to people, their lives and the places they live in now and in the future.

Part I determined the fundamental elements that underpin a strategic planning process and ended by introducing my 7-Step Strategic Planning Process.

Part II gives you the 'how to' for the 7-Step Strategic Planning Process, which is the core of this book.

It outlines the detail for each of the seven steps:

- Step 1: Project establishment
- Step 2: Research and analysis
- Step 3: Synthesis and direction setting
- Step 4: Draft plan preparation
- Step 5: Exhibition
- Step 6: Plan finalisation
- Step 7: Plan delivery and ongoing planning

While we know there are several types of city planning activities, Part 2 is written in the context of preparing a metropolitan plan.

The seven steps are presented across six chapters.

- Chapter 6: Getting started
- Chapter 7: Gathering the evidence
- Chapter 8: Synthesis and direction setting
- Chapter 9: Preparation of a draft plan
- Chapter 10: Exhibition and a final plan
- Chapter 11: Plan delivery and ongoing planning

The purpose, principal tasks and activities for each step are outlined in these chapters and provide a more detailed discussion of the differing issues we need to consider when undertaking each step.

Part II concludes with Chapter 12: City planning typologies. It provides a discussion on how the 7-step Strategic Planning Process can be adapted to respond to the purpose and spatial scale of differing city planning typologies, such as town centre plans.

Part II: Summary

Part II outlines the details of each step in the 7-Step Strategic Planning Process. My objective has been to provide you with an understanding of the how-to tasks required to prepare a plan, from start to finish. The information was provided in six chapters.

Chapter 6: Getting started (Step 1) is detailed and deliberately so. It addresses all the issues required to get a project started, emphasising that the more thoroughly the task is undertaken the more likely the project will meet the expectations of decision-makers, which in the case of a metropolitan plan will be a minister or cabinet. Gaining clarity on the project objectives and scope together with an understanding of the expectations of what to research will maximise time and resources. Commence the engagement process in Step 1, with the initial focus on the principal stakeholder groups.

Chapter 7: Gathering the evidence (Step 2) is about collecting and analysing the evidence that will form the basis of the plan. A challenge is determining what to investigate. To support this task I introduce the Strategic Planning Research Framework, covering 42 research topics. I also emphasise the importance of turning findings into narratives to enhance the ability to communicate issues to decision-makers and the community.

Chapter 8: Synthesis and direction setting (Step 3) covers the crux of the whole process—moving from evidence to directions and a vision. This is also one of the hardest tasks to master and much of what is needed must be learnt on the job, including the need for lateral thinking to reveal opportunities. It is in this step that scenarios are developed and tested.

Chapter 9: Preparation of a draft plan (Step 4) deals with the main task at hand, preparing the plan. Collaboration is key as invariably the plan will include directions and actions that either impact the activities of other agencies or must be delivered by them. The draft plan should not be seen as a preliminary document to be finalised at a later stage; it should be a fully developed plan so the community and stakeholders can comment on all the issues intended to make up the vision. In the latter stages of Step 4, you need to undertake all the tasks required to deliver on the exhibition of the plan.

Chapter 10: Exhibition and a final plan (Steps 5 and 6) addresses two interconnected steps. First is the exhibition of the plan, a short, sharp and intensive process that has the twin aims of informing people of the content of the plan and eliciting feedback. The output of Step 5, the submissions, is the principal input and focus of Step 6. An assessment of the submissions informs the finalisation of the content of the plan. Providing early advice to decision-makers on the content of submissions is critical. One of the last tasks is confirming delivery responsibilities including governance arrangements and lead delivery agency post final approval.

Chapter 11: Delivery and ongoing planning (Step 7) covers interrelated activities. First is the bedding down of the delivery of the plan, where the focus is the finalisation of an implementation plan. Secondly, we focus on an underlying message of this book: the need to change how we approach the planning of cities. The planning of cities should move from the singular preparation of plans to an ongoing planning process, reflecting the dynamic nature of cities, with an emphasis on the targeted update of the plan based on the findings of monitoring processes and ongoing research. I call this 'flexible certainty'.

Chapter 12: City planning typologies examines the question of differing city planning typologies and how the 7-Step Strategic Planning Process needs to be adapted to respond to the purpose and spatial scale of the different typologies. It focuses on four typologies: local government area planning, town centre planning, new greenfield communities and neighbourhood community planning. For each typology, I cover the purpose, spatial planning and research framework considerations as well as specific issues as relevant.

Finally, Chapters 4 and 5 only provided an overview of issues as to how to approach research and analysis. Part 3, which follows, provides detail on the approach for each of the research topics.

Getting Started

6

6.1 Introduction

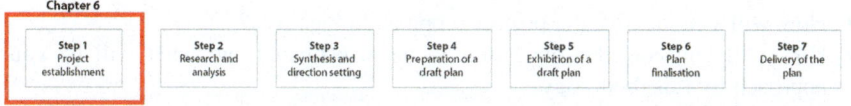

How well you plan at the start of your project

will influence how well you finish at the end

This chapter is about getting started, which for most projects is about jumping into some research. This is the fun part as you learn about the city you are seeking to plan.

However. before you start you need a project brief, which sets out how you are going to go about preparing the plan from start to finish.

This is the focus of Step 1: Project establishment—potentially the most important step in the 7-Step Strategic Planning Process.

This is where we formalise an agreed direction for the whole project, including project scope, objectives, methodology, resourcing needs, governance structure and timing. The project's direction should not be seen as fixed; you may need to revisit it against the research findings to determine if there is a need to change the project scope and objectives.

Considering the importance of Step 1 to the project's success, we cover a lot of material in this chapter. This task is more than simply the writing of a short brief before you get going. In addition to outlining the principal activities, including preparing a project brief, this chapter provides detail on:

- establishing working relationships
- auditing the planning context
- establishing the project objectives and scope
- developing the project methodology
- establishing project governance, sign-off and initiation.

6.1.1 Warm-Up Exercise

You have been asked to prepare a quick outline of a project brief for an upcoming metropolitan plan. Your paper will be the basis of a discussion with the Minister for Planning. What are the principal considerations? Jot down a few points for the following questions.

- How will you identify the project scope and objectives?
- How will you consider the issues to be investigated and what will be your approach to a methodology?
- How will the community be involved?
- What approach will you take when moving from research findings to a proposed vision and the actions to get there?
- What will be the scope of information to be included for exhibition for community comment?
- What actions will you take to ensure the final plan is implemented?
- What is the approach for signing off milestones and the final plan?

6.2 Purpose of Step 1: Project Establishment

The purpose of Step 1 is to establish a project brief. The project brief outlines the project objectives, project scope, study area, project methodology (including quality control and risks), timelines (milestones/decision points), resourcing requirements, and governance arrangements. Ideally there will be a public-facing project brief that includes:

- a short statement on why the project is being undertaken
- an outline of project objectives and principal milestones
- information that explains the scope of the project
- a map of the study area, and any other areas important to the project
- an outline of how the community will be engaged through the course of the project.

The project brief helps to manage expectations in terms of what the project is seeking to do in the time available, and the resources required. As many colleagues have said during my working career, whether as a consultant or as a public servant, it is better to finish on time and under budget than ask for more time and more resources. To manage the issue of expectations you must obtain authority to proceed, with the approval of the project brief by the decision-maker—such as the planning minister or government.

A project brief should also save time. Project managers will always talk about the diminishing returns of influence you have on the outcome (cost and quality) of a project the further down the path you have travelled.

When undertaking my postgraduate qualification in project management, those in the course working in the information and technology sector indicated that a third of their project time was developing the project brief.

6.3 Principal Activities

6.3.1 The Tasks

There is no standard approach to Step 1; moreover, often the team to do the work does not exist when the need for the project brief arises, which can make the task even more challenging. That said, there are several tasks essential for the preparation and approval of a project brief.

- **Confirming the requirement for the plan**. Whether there is a regulatory requirement (for example, planning legislation for NSW requires a review of the metropolitan plan every five years) or a direction from the government to prepare a new plan (for example in Victoria in 2010, the newly elected government took office with a policy commitment to prepare a metropolitan planning strategy).
- **Understanding the context and need for the plan**. Rarely does the preparation of a plan start with a blank canvas, and your stakeholders will be aware of this. The task here is a desktop audit of existing documents including any plan and related progress (monitoring) reports, related government policies that may influence the content of the new plan (such as transport plans, environmental policies or state planning policies), and any background reports that directly informed any previous plan.

  The audit should identify the **problem statement**, a concise outline of the need for the project, such as:
  - changed planning assumptions, for example the COVID-19 pandemic impact on overseas migration and thus population projections
  - new challenges and/or opportunities
  - new policy positions

- the findings of monitoring programs that indicate that anticipated outcomes are not occurring.

The problem statement informs the development of the project objectives, scope and methodology, the latter especially through the audit of existing relevant studies and the identification of data gaps.

The planning context can be formalised as a state of play report.

- **Engaging with decision-maker(s)**. What are their aspirations for the plan or important issues? The emphasis on *decision-makers* (plural) is deliberate; it is likely, for example, that at a minimum the transport minister will be actively engaged and potentially be a decision-maker. These discussions will reveal the expectations and scope for the plan and, therefore, what background reports need review and what areas require research.
- **Establishing working relationships**. Your initial focus is to identify people across government agencies and within the planning portfolio who should form part of working groups and governance arrangements, and who could provide initial advice on project objectives and scope. Also, prioritise connecting with the principal stakeholders (including local government) who can provide context for the project. Use this as an opportunity to establish ongoing working relationships.
- **Establishing relationships with local First Nations communities.** This will include connecting with a range of groups, such as Traditional Custodians, knowledge-holders, Local Aboriginal Land Councils/or Registered Aboriginal Party (RAP) to establish common aspirations and build partnerships.
- **Establishing the project objectives, project scope and what constitutes success**. These need to be informed by the expectations of the decision-makers and stakeholders, an understanding of the planning context, an understanding of the need for the plan and any specific issues to be addressed—the problem statement.

The objectives and scope provide the platform to develop the methodology and governance arrangements, including which agencies need to be at the table.

The project objectives and scope should be supported by the identification of a study area.

What constitutes success needs to be understood from the perspective of the client—the decision-makers. Their definition may not be simply to meet project objectives—there may be other political outcomes.

- **Preparing the project methodology**. This is the central task for Step 1. You should identify what activities need to be undertaken over the course of the whole project, from Step 2 through to Step 7, including consideration of timing, milestones and resourcing.

  In addition, from the methodology should come both a risk register and quality management procedures. Both are discussed in Sect. 1.7.5.
- **Preparing a preliminary community engagement plan**. The engagement plan identifies the target groups for direct engagement, opportunities for the wider community to participate, and anticipated engagement methods. This includes

a communication strategy that guides how any launch of the project will occur. More detailed plans will need to be prepared as the project progresses.
- **Establishing a governance structure.** A governance structure needs to show how day-to-day activities will be managed (project management), such as the establishment of a project control group, and how decisions will be made. The latter usually involves a steering committee, at a minimum, with its composition reflecting the project scope and reporting to a minister, though more likely through the minister to a cabinet committee or full cabinet process, reflecting the whole-of-government nature of city plans.
- **Liaising with the minister's office.** A project's success is influenced by the confidence a minister—as a decision-maker—has in the process and outcomes, which requires regular and concise briefings to the minister and the minister's office, and when required, briefings to other ministers affected by the plan.
- **Formally obtaining project brief sign-off and initiating the project.** Project sign-off is critical to ensure activities reflect the expectations of the decision-maker; sometimes this helps to open doors. The commencement of the project should be a deliberative task, where the details of the project plan are outlined with all members of the project team, as often the project team will be a new grouping of officers who will only stay together for the life of the project.

Before formal sign-off, consider targeted engagement with the principal stakeholders on the project objectives, project scope, engagement plans and a state of play report. This strengthens the relationship with peak bodies and community groups and potentially helps to build trust as it emphasises that the process of preparing the plan is not simply a *fait accompli*.

6.3.2 An Iterative Process

The previous section outlined the essential tasks required for the preparation of a project brief. The reality is an iterative and often compressed (timeframe) process. The iterative nature reflects the need to gain input across multiple areas within the planning portfolio as well as multiple government agencies and principal stakeholders, while focused on the preparation of an ever-evolving document.

Building relationships is the glue that brings people together and therefore binds the tasks together. It sets the stage for a collaborative working arrangement for the whole project and ultimately influences the quality of the plan and how well it will be delivered. Figure 6.1 outlines how the establishment of working relationships relates to all the required tasks in the preparation of the project brief.

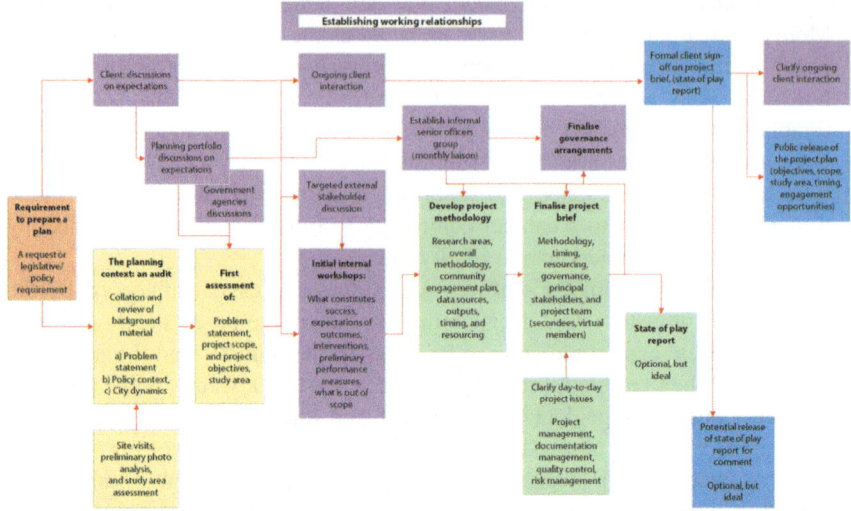

Fig. 6.1 Project establishment: A highly iterative process
(This figure outlines the relationships between the principal task areas required to set up a project plan (brief), including why the plan is needed; collating background information to inform the plan and identify the problem statement; liaising with the client, other parts of government(s) and stakeholders to confirm the issues to investigate and the problem statement; and finally gaining sign-off for the project)

In the context of the identified essential tasks (activities) and the reality of a highly iterative process, the more that Step 1 can be a structured process, the more likely the project brief can both satisfy the expectations of the decision-makers and foster ownership of the project.

6.3.3 The Project Brief

Some organisations have templates for project briefs. Their layout is often formulaic and the principal task of working out how to do the project is lost as the critical task becomes the filling out of a form, not how to approach the task.

In bringing all the tasks together into a single project brief there are several considerations:

- determine the time available for preparing and approving the project brief
- establish if there is a fixed time for project completion
- define what success looks like
- clarify which ministers are core to the project and ensure they are briefed
- identify if there is a project champion(s) driving the process
- understand the team and the organisational experience in preparing a city plan (noting they occur infrequently and thus are not a mainstream skill area), which

6.3 Principal Activities

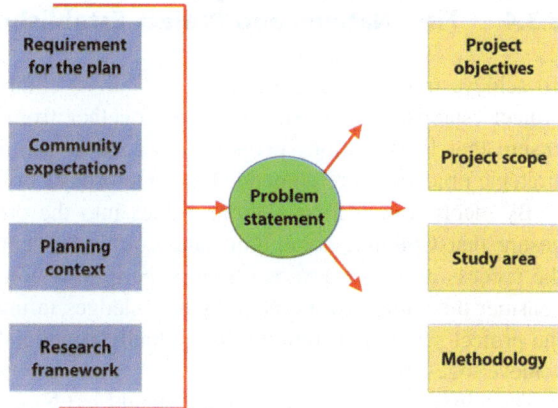

Fig. 6.2 The project brief: inputs and outputs pivot off the problem statement

may influence expectations (for example, striving for a 7/10 and preparing a polished plan or aiming for a 10/10 and risk failure), remembering plans evolve and elements are progressively enhanced
- establish the availability of background data that will influence the time required for research and analysis
- understand the need for the plan (whether it is a legislative requirement or not necessarily a priority of the decision-makers) to determine if more time may be required to understand decision-maker expectations
- identify the degree to which the issues driving the need for the plan are already actively discussed in the community (thus already of political interest) and whether requiring initial stakeholder engagement will clarify expectations.

In terms of the content of the project brief, develop it around the problem statement. Figure 6.2 highlights the drivers that inform the problem statement and principal outputs informed by the problem statement.

The project brief should include:

- purpose and scope, including principal inputs
- intended outcomes/outputs
- principal tasks
- timeline
- governance
- project management
- community engagement
- principal partners
- risks.

6.3.4 First Nations and Project Establishment

To achieve true partnership with First Nations communities' engagement during project establishment is key. Working together from the start of the project will ensure that First Nations people are valued as partners in the project and their strategic objectives are embedded into the project brief.

By incorporating First Nations values into the project establishment you will ensure that Country, community and culture are considered front and centre in the process rather than an addition or peripheral consideration. It is important to consider the value of First Nations Knowledges in understanding Country, setting the project scope and framing the mutually beneficial outcomes that you want to achieve together.

Deep listening is required to understand First Nations perspectives and potential apprehensions regarding the proposed change. First Nations peoples have custodial obligations for Country and a generational mindset when it comes to planning. Generally, this means that they will be advocating for the protection of Country including the sites that contribute to the overarching cultural landscape.

Working together early can help to establish a project scope that considers the most respectful approach to caring for Country and incorporates a generational lens. Political leaders, government officers, community members and industry professionals will all cycle in and out of project. First Nations people will carry the legacy of decisions made beyond any other stakeholder.

6.4 Establishing Working Relationships

6.4.1 Why It Is Important?

The whole-of-government nature of city planning makes collaboration an integral part of the strategic planning process; relevant agencies will ultimately own the plan and implement it. Many agencies recognise the importance of collaboration and invest significant effort into fostering a collaborative working culture as part of the day-to-day operations.

Successful collaboration requires other agencies to make their involvement part of the day-to-day business priorities as distinct from simply attending a monthly meeting.

Therefore, the task of establishing working relationships needs to be directed to developing collaborative processes by:

- identifying and engaging project partners across government
- identifying and engaging with groups outside government
- establishing informal working relationships across government.

6.4.2 Identifying Your Project Partners Across Government

The initial focus of this task is to understand the issues and expectations of agencies across the government, including within the planning portfolio, which have (or should have) a direct interest in the plan. An underlying goal is fostering a sense of ownership, reflected by their direct influence on the project brief.

Delivery agencies, especially transport departments, can use the city plan to identify new infrastructure projects during the preparation of the plan.

> *I once was involved in the development of a metropolitan plan where we were clearly advised, by the minister, that the proposed land use outcomes needed to directly reflect the aspirations of the existing transport plan.*

Remember—when liaising with colleagues from other agencies on the scope of a project they not only represent an agency, but most likely a minister whose input may be required.

A more significant task is to understand the desired level of ongoing involvement, including governance arrangements.

The agencies likely to have a direct interest in the plan are the portfolios of transport, health, education, treasury and environment and, depending on the natural resource values of the hinterland, primary industries and mining. Considering the whole-of-government nature of the engagement, the premier's department will generally want to be informed about the activities.

Depending on the emerging project scope, other organisations will include specialised planning commissions (in NSW the Greater Cities Commission has legislative responsibility to lead metropolitan planning), Aboriginal affairs, the environment protection authority (or equivalent), and industry, water and energy agencies.

Most planning departments already have contact lists for key personnel across the government, therefore ideally these people are already known.

Don't forget to liaise with the various areas across the planning portfolio. Organisational structures across state planning jurisdictions differ, but areas could include planning assessments, planning systems, major projects, heritage or research.

6.4.3 Establishing Informal Working Relationships

As a whole-of-government activity, city planning requires ownership by all parties. Ownership does not emerge from formal structures; rather, it arises as part of a journey where colleagues move from participants to advocates. Informal working relationships are the best mechanism to facilitate this journey.

Of all the things I am seeking to impart to you on city planning, informal relationships is one of the most important concepts. I have seen solid objectives fail because delivery agencies do not believe in the outcome.

Establishing informal working relationships starts by asking colleagues how to help them and whether an informal forum for sharing information on projects would assist. In my experience, the answer to this question is yes, and for 10 years across two jurisdictions, I facilitated such a group. Some considerations when looking to establish informal working relationships are outlined here.

- Membership and operations
    - Attendees should, at a minimum, reflect the agencies represented in the governance arrangements, plus a representative of the premier's and treasury departments.
    - Importantly, attendance must be voluntary with no constraints as to how many people attend.
    - It is not a decision-making group.
    - The specific focus of the group evolves as the activities of city planning evolve.
    - In line with the voluntary nature of the group, so long as the group is focusing on what is important at any point in time, you do not need a terms-of-reference statement.
    - Attendees should be at the executive director and director level, or those who can speak on behalf of agencies and can influence the allocation of resources. Again, it is not a decision-making group.
    - Agendas and notes (not minutes) of meetings are needed, but the focus is sharing and discussing working drafts and ensuring people respect the confidentiality of the information.
- The aims of collaboration
    - As far as practical, ensure there are no surprises when plans get to the cabinet process stage, allowing your colleagues to be well placed to give detailed briefings of all issues to their ministers. This is about creating trust.
    - Technical issues are best resolved by those responsible for technical detail. Aim for no issue to go above the working group for resolution (you lose control of the technical details). In the rare cases where there is no agreement, you agree to disagree; importantly there can be no surprises and ministers can be briefed accordingly.
    - Focus on the working drafts that your colleagues can influence.
    - Create an environment where colleagues can raise their issues that need wider understanding and support.

I have always called this working group the Senior Officers Group (affectionately known as the SOG).

A last point on collaboration and the importance of fostering two-way partnerships comes from a study tour I undertook of research parks, in a few places including Japan in 2002.

The manager at the Kyoto Research Park when we spoke about how to get a research precinct to work said: "You will need those around you to love you".

6.4.4 Engaging Outside Government

To best understand wider community attitudes when seeking to resolve the project objectives and project scope, undertake targeted engagement with stakeholder organisations including peak bodies representing the development sector and social and environment groups. At this project establishment stage, it is more about connections with executive officers with a focus on major concerns, expectations and suggestions for detailed research.

These people represent those on the ground. Gaining their perceptions potentially provides a different view to the policy makers and regulators. As representatives of people who will build and/or influence the plan's implementation, they can provide early warning of critical issue that may create a significant impasse later in the project.

There is also potential to start exploring ongoing engagement arrangements with these groups. Understand which segments of the planning portfolio already engage with these groups to avoid scheduling back-to-back meetings with the same group and causing unnecessary angst.

Engagement with local First Nations communities should commence at the start of the project. Ideally the connections should already exist, refer Sect. 5.3.2.5.

When working with external groups, transparency is critical, as is the explicit management of any conflict-of-interest issue. You will need to understand probity responsibilities. Most organisations have this covered with formal protocols. One worthwhile reference in this area is the 'Kaldas report', *Review of Governance in the NSW Planning System* (2018), where an underlying theme is ethics.

6.5 Auditing the Planning Context

6.5.1 What Are We Seeking to Achieve?

Projects do not start in isolation. There is always some contextual information that informs the planning for the project. Look at the background information to:

- understand the context in which your project starts, from existing policy positions to the findings of previous and recent related research and monitoring programs
- identify whether there have been changes in assumptions or policy positions since the approval of any previous plan
- document the problem statement which importantly is about both challenges and opportunities

- utilise contextual information, particularly the problem statement, with the project objectives to inform the research agenda, and to make sure the work of existing studies is not repeated.

6.5.2 Reviewing Existing Background Material

Reviewing background material can be a challenging task in the absence of a single point of information for all previous plans, background reports, assumptions (projections) or data. While many planning departments in Australia have shut down their in-house physical libraries, more recently many are investing in digital libraries including the utilisation of government-sponsored tools such as the 'digital twin'.

This therefore requires a desktop researching exercise. As an audit of existing material, this is distinct from new research into specific areas. The audit needs to help you:

- understand the status and success of existing plans and policies that relate to the study area
- critique background reports to ascertain their relevance and currency of evidence, including available data and data gaps
- assess the implications of outputs from any existing monitoring programs that cover relevant economic, social and environmental indicators, particularly to see if there are any changed assumptions compared to when earlier plans were developed
- gain a high-level overview of the current dynamics of the city, such as size, growth rates and the most relevant population and housing projections.

Ideally, you should complement this desktop research with site visits relating to the major issues.

The preparation of a problem statement is an important task when assessing the planning context for a project. The problem statement should:

- clarify why there is a need for the project (for example, is it based on an explicit challenge, such as a significant lack of housing supply)
- reflect the principal concerns of stakeholders and the areas they have suggested for investigation
- support the process of identifying the areas for investigation and help clarify expectations of success, likely interventions, and where any discretionary resources are directed.

In addition, you need to establish whether there are any related cross-agency working groups, such as research groups, examining projections for population and employment.

Reviewing the success of a previous plan can be a significant task by itself. You need a clear and transparent evaluation process. Often there is a desire to write and release a new plan rather than determine whether the existing plan is still valid. In that context, the NSW planning legislation relating to Greater Sydney requires a review of the previous plan, as distinct from requiring a new plan. Thus, a new plan may or may not follow; where it does the review is essentially the problem statement.

The work to inform the Greater Sydney Region Plan included a critique of the existing plan at the time—*A Plan for Growing Sydney*. The report on the review is on the website of the Greater Cities Commission.

6.5.3 The Outputs for the Project Brief

Document what is known before you start, as this will usually emphasise that there is already a significant body of knowledge available and may highlight data gaps. Such a document is your state of play report.

Not only does this create a bridging piece linking past planning with the new, it also turns the task of context setting into a more deliberative process and will demonstrate why investigations in certain areas are needed.

If time permits, a short, targeted engagement on the report with principal stakeholders would help to clarify the task at hand, test the veracity of any of the starting assumptions, and enhance stakeholder buy-in. This would allow a more focused scoping of the project and potentially save on resources and/or allow more time for other tasks.

6.6 Establishing the Project Objectives and Scope

6.6.1 Be Clear on the Objectives

City planning activities often become a magnet for all the ills of a city and this is very much the case when undertaking metropolitan plans. To manage this challenge, clarify the objectives and scope of the project to:

- explain why the project is being undertaken
- identify the specific project objectives, as distinct from the plan's objectives, which in effect should define success for the output of plan
- outline the spatial area to be directly covered by the plan (the study area) and any wider areas for the investigation to inform the plan
- outline, at a high level, the principal issues (scope) to be investigated
- understand early if there are any limitations to the types of actions (interventions) that may arise in the final plan.

6.6.2 Approach

Developing the project objectives and scope needs to:

- **Identify the principal issues to be addressed in the plan** from the investigations undertaken for both the planning context and project methodology. Broadly, this is the project scope. Identifying the issues to investigate implies that there will be a response to each issue in the final plan. Therefore, aim to define the breadth and depth of investigations and the intent of the investigation as part of the project methodology.
- **Establish an understanding of success**, in the context of the expectations of the client (decision-makers). The political view may be different from the technical view, which is perfectly fine as city planning is just as much about understanding and codifying social norms as it is about assessing quantifiable technical data.
- **Understand the expectations as to the type of actions**. Ultimately the *raison d'être* of any city plan is to identify interventions to achieve a stated societal benefit. Thus, it is important to understand how a plan will be implemented and to consider:
  - Are changes to regulations under consideration?
  - Is it about identifying a list of potential infrastructure projects or sweating existing assets?
  - Are all policy areas on the table?

It is *seldom* the case that all interventions are on the table. Again, this is okay as there are many good reasons why, such as constrained budgetary circumstances or clear historic policy positions.

- **Identify the study area**. Here clarity is important:
  - The geographic spatial area or Country that the plan must provide directions on is the core study area.
  - All cities have a hinterland which is an integral part of day-to-day activity dynamics, which should normally be included as part of the study area.

    In capital cities, the geo-political boundary created by fringe local government areas is generally used as a surrogate boundary, though this can create challenges in terms of consistency of the extent of the hinterland to be included. The boundary of the Shire of Yarra Ranges (in Melbourne) comes to mind.
  - You need to identify the economic, social and environmental communities of interest (catchments) that need to be considered. They may extend well beyond the core study area.

One toolkit that can be used to formalise the process is the *Investment Logic Mapping* process developed by the Victorian Treasury. It is useful for clarifying the problem and identifying causal links to strategies and actions, as well as assisting in developing key performance indicators. At this early stage, its use is not to obtain a definitive answer but to assist in clarifying what is potentially in and out of scope.

6.6.3 Outputs for the Project Brief

The outputs from this task form the central part of the project brief and any public-facing outputs from Step 1. They include:

- a short statement on why the project is being undertaken
- a clear outline of the project objectives
- information that will explain the scope of the project
- a map that shows the study area, and any other areas important to the undertaking of the project.

6.7 Developing the Project Methodology

6.7.1 What Are We Seeking to Achieve?

The project methodology seeks to achieve several outcomes:

- the identification of research areas to be investigated in Step 2
- the identification of the principal activities to be undertaken in Steps 3 to 7
- the preparation of an outline community engagement plan
- the establishment of a project timeline and required resources (team members and other costs).

At this early stage, the development of the project methodology must clarify the general approach. Once sign-off for the project has been received, detailed research methodologies can be resolved in Step 2: Research and analysis.

Understanding the timing, costs and inter-relationships between tasks is essential, as you will normally only get one chance to put forward your case for how much time you need and the total project costs.

6.7.2 Approach

Development of the project methodology requires you to:

- identify specific areas for research
- develop an outline community engagement plan
- hold workshops with agencies and stakeholders
- establish the overall project methodology

- assess project timing and costs.

Other issues to consider include:

- risk management and quality control
- the impacts on the timing of procurement
- the need for good filing and documentation procedures
- back of house administrative issues.

6.7.2.1 Research Areas for Step 2

At this project establishment stage, the focus is to identify what research areas are to be investigated in Step 2, including community engagement activities and the general research methodology for each research area. This is a challenging task; seek advice on general approaches and timing from experts from specialist fields.

The project scope should provide guidance in determining which areas to investigate by outlining the principal issues to be investigated and any considerations arising from discussions with decision-makers, agencies and stakeholders. In addition, a broad understanding of the total project time will influence the potential methods of investigation, from desktop to detailed fieldwork and surveys.

The three-part Strategic Planning Research Framework, outlined in Sect. 4.2.2, should be the principal guide for investigating what areas of research may be required. It will help you identify a broad approach for time and resourcing requirements, and any sequencing with other activities.

The breadth of research topics highlights the complexity of resolving an overall project methodology. Therefore, Chapters 13, 14 and 15 detail the research considerations, objectives and approaches for each research area, to assist the project planning task.

Several good textbooks detail the overarching issues that the Strategic Planning Research Framework seeks to identify. They include:

- Rogers, D, Keane, A, Alizadeh, T, & Nelson, J (2020) *Understanding Urbanism* Palgrave Macmillan, Singapore
- Sipe, N & Vella, K Eds (2017) The Routledge Handbook of Australian Urban and Regional Planning Routledge Oxfordshire, UK
- Thomson, s & Maginn, PJ Eds (2012) *Planning Australia, An Overview of Urban and Regional Planning, 2nd Edition* Cambridge University Press Port Melbourne, Australia

How to approach the research and analysis stage, in terms of purpose, principal tasks and considerations is outlined next in Chapter 7.

For some projects you may not know where to start, partly because there is no clarity in the problem statement. One way to cut through the fog is to get an external person to do a first order answer.

I did this for a plan for a well-established town centre that was performing poorly, but it was unclear what the issue was. In that circumstance a quick first order solution provided clarity as to the poor integration between activities and car parking and allowed a project methodology to focus on the opportunity for an incremental restructure to create street frontages.

6.7.2.2 Overall Methodology

Regarding Steps 2 to 7, at this early stage, the key is to broadly identify the principal areas of activity, the general method of investigation, the resources and time required, any dependencies with other tasks and any engagement requirements, from agencies to the wider community, for each task. The detailed approach for each can be developed later as the project progresses as discussed in Chapters 7 to 11.

Discussions with government agencies should reveal if there are any specific milestones or tasks, such as detailed transport or economic modelling, that require you to share the project methodology with other agencies to gain their input and ownership.

6.7.2.3 Agency Workshops

Evaluating what issues need to be researched and how the plan will be developed should not be limited to a desktop exercise. It is important to gain input from the wider planning portfolio, other government agencies, and potentially local government and some stakeholders. Time constraints may prevent you from talking to all stakeholders.

Ideally this input, especially from within government, should come from structured workshops. Interactions with external stakeholders are more likely to occur as one-on-one meetings.

For all groups, aim to understand their definition of success, their perceptions on scope and issues to be investigated, their principal issues of concern and potentially how they may wish to be engaged going forward.

6.7.3 Timing

The most critical element is to understand the total time available to undertake the project. This will determine the level of detail that can be investigated for each research area and the other steps in the process.

Preparing a project timeline requires you to identify milestones, decision points, the sequencing and inter-relationships between tasks, and community engagement activities. We often allocate insufficient time to gaining sign-off at each milestone, to procure research and bringing together a project team.

Considerations in developing a project timeline include:

- **Understanding project flexibility**. That is, in terms of the project management triangle—time, cost and quality. For example, are any of these elements fixed or

constrained? Answering this question gives clarity to your project contingency and how you can manage emerging issues that may then be declared out of scope.
- **How much time**? This is unfortunately determined by experience. But if you logically and methodically outline the tasks, noting many can occur concurrently, a first order time frame usually reveals itself; the decision-makers will always see that to be too long.
- **Overlapping activities**. In terms of available time, each step should not be seen as a fixed period. Many tasks, including research, can overlap. What is important is that there is sufficient information at each decision point for the next task to be commenced. Final documentation can often come later.
- **Ideal project timeline**. Ideally, you need six months post exhibition until the release of the final plan. I would also suggest that in total an ideal time for undertaking the entire project is 18 months. Such a timeframe is sufficient for research and a two-month exhibition period. It also has the option of, hopefully, having a finish date in the calendar year after the commencement of the project.

    Recognise that through the course of the project some interest groups will advocate to decision-makers that the project is taking too long, while others will say the whole project is rushed. Managing these expectations requires direct attention; it is challenging.
- **Establishing the project team**. Ideally, this needs to occur before the launch of the project, as once started there is not only an expectation that activity will occur, but stakeholders will start to make contact and there needs to be people ready to respond.
- **Time requirement for formal approval**. In allocating time for each task, remember that gaining formal approval from the government for a milestone takes at least a month. Most projects need three to four approval points after the formal sign-off on the project brief, as follows:
    - report on principal findings, early advice on the direction of the plan
    - approval to release a draft plan for public exhibition
    - report on submissions, identifying potential issues requiring changes to the plan
    - approval to release the final plan and agreement on delivery responsibilities.

This adds up to three to four months of the total project time, noting of course other activities can occur during the approval stage.

- **Contingency planning**. When preparing a project brief, do some contingency planning to address time slippage; cost overrun; the need for additional activities that have cost and/or time implications; and general project risk issues.

6.7.4 Resourcing

In developing the project methodology, the resource requirements should become apparent. Begin working out who is required for the project team.

A lesson from my time at the then Greater Sydney Commission was the value of using local government secondees. City plans require a large team for a short (18-month) period; at the same time, local government usually has significant responsibilities post completion of a plan for delivery. Therefore, if team members can be seconded from local government you gain someone who can highlight delivery issues, understands the local context, and, when they return to their home council, are positive advocates.

In assessing costs and resourcing requirements (internal and external), in addition to the obvious staffing and contractor costs, consider engagement, communications and production. Be clear on who is responsible for communications and engagement costs.

Resourcing the First Nations community to be involved in the process is vital. Consider the value of First Nations Knowledges on par, if not beyond technical professionals that will assist in the process. Appropriately remunerating First Nations stakeholders for their contribution is imperative for success.

The cost of research is insignificant compared to the costs of delivering change. It is, more significantly, infinitesimal compared to the value of the investment the private sector makes each year based on the direction and requirements of the planning system. The annual capital value of residential, commercial and industrial development in Melbourne and Sydney is in the order of $20 to $25 billion (ABS Building approvals Jan to June 2019, Catalogue. 8731). Planning has a real influence on where this development occurs and in what form. Planners, however, have yet to link the benefits of this investment to the analysis that underpins their decision-making, unlike transport planners. Thus, planners do not receive comparable resources (compared to transport planners) to support the planning of the significant daily investment in cities.

6.7.5 Other Considerations

6.7.5.1 Risk Management and Quality Control

The focus for risk management, at a minimum, needs to be on issues that will influence the delivery of the project, not the content, such as:

- procurement delays and delays to research and other activities by external consultants
- loss of support by other core ministers/agencies to the project or the timeline
- existing or emerging contentious issues that can divert the resources of the team and/or require additional research/community engagement outside the project timeline.

Quality control needs to cover the core issues that affect people's perceptions of the quality of the plan, such as:

- the accuracy and robustness of commissioned research
- the presentation of the content of the draft and final reports, including typos, consistent nomenclature, consistency between graphics and text, and version control.

6.7.5.2 Procurement

If activities require external advice from consultants, procurement processes can take considerable time.

As many strategic planning projects are limited to a timeframe of around a year, open tender processes will unlikely be pursued as they can take months to complete. Consequently, large and costly research initiatives are usually only undertaken when it is critical, which is not ideal in terms of the best possible plan. Hence, time is the underlying challenge for all city planning projects.

Considering this challenge, many jurisdictions have procurement processes in place where some consultancies are pre-qualified to provide advice in specific areas, with costs limited to a set amount, to ensure governments get value for money. Procuring under these circumstances is reasonably quick, but it is not overnight. Usually some sort of request for tender needs to be prepared by the government agency followed up by a response and contract. If the task required has a value above a set amount, then either a limited tender process or full public tender process is required—this takes time (no change out of a month).

Procurement processes are, however, essential. There is a perception that it takes too long, but as procurement managers say time and time again, if it goes wrong, it will be the quality of the documentation, in line with their procedures, that will be seen as time well spent.

6.7.5.3 Document the Journey

Documenting the journey, through a clear records management process, can:

- let decision-makers know how the final recommendations were arrived at, through a comprehensive record of what has been investigated
- provide those who may review the plan in the future with the context of the issues that informed the preparation
- respond to external requests to substantiate specific issues.

Those who have previously worked in government will know the request will arrive first thing in the morning and an answer will be assumed by lunchtime, if not earlier. Thus, there is a benefit in starting with comprehensive processes rather than seeking to file everything at the end.

Filing should include the retention of drafts and comments on drafts to allow the evolution of documents to be explained. Today, electronic filing makes this an easier task.

6.7.5.4 Back of House Activities

Consider a range of back of house issues early:

- The look and feel of the report such as layout (landscape or portrait) is often influenced by the shape of the study area; whether the document will be hard copy or purely digital; and the need to design for accessibility (for example, whether maps comply with requirements for colour-blind readers). Increasingly layout is less of an issue as plans go digital, though it is still surprising how often a hard copy version is also desired.
- Determining whether a digital rather than hard copy plan will be produced.
- Nomenclature, such as common phrases (names), capitalisation, use of hyphens, and acronyms (my preference is not). All these specifications should be put in a style guide.
- Records management protocols.
- Designation of a person responsible for all maps and graphics.
- Designation of a person responsible for quality and consistency checking and version control.

One challenge when preparing the Greater Sydney district plans was to get five teams to use common text. We found that each team sought to add value to their plan by improving the language of common policy positions and statements. Generally adding value is naturally supported, but in some cases, we need to retain a consistent and approved policy statement. Colour coding the text can clarify the content that has to be consistent.

6.7.6 Outputs for the Project Brief

The principal outputs include:

- the project methodology, including a community engagement plan
- a project timeline, including milestones and decision points
- a resources' plan
- a project risk assessment, which should include the areas of governance and project management
- quality control procedures.

6.8 Governance, Sign-Off and Project Initiation

6.8.1 What Are We Seeking to Achieve?

Preparing the project brief is an iterative process, though a last step is typically the resolution of governance arrangements. Principally, who needs to be at the table is informed by most of the earlier activities, particularly the project scope.

As noted earlier in the chapter, governance arrangements need to address decision-making needs and project management requirements. It is then through the governance arrangements that the last task of gaining sign-off on the project brief from the decision-maker(s) can occur. Formal sign-off will typically, generate the need for some type of launch activity. Ideally, the launch should have an initial narrative that seeks to create interest in the project as a first step in creating wider community engagement and participation.

Potentially, in this last stage of finalising the project brief, you may want to undertake a short and targeted engagement with the principal stakeholders to refine the project objectives and project scope.

Also consider including a formal project induction task for what is most likely a new project team. Think about outlining the task at hand and growing the teams as one team. This is particularly relevant if there are formal cross-agency working arrangements and local government secondees.

Project induction will be an ongoing task as new members arrive, such as editors and a graphics team during the finalisation of the draft and final plans.

The implication of failing to obtain sign-off for a project can be disheartening for a project team.

> *I once took over the management of a team that had been doing some interesting work on a good idea for around six months. However, the project had never been signed off by the relevant decision-maker – the Minister. Thus, when the team found out that the Minister did not see the project as a priority (six months before an election), there were a lot of disappointed people.*

6.8.2 Governance Arrangements

Governance arrangements should be seen as a hierarchy of decision-making, reflecting the management considerations required to deliver a project, including project management and technical sign-off.

Decision-making (Fig. 6.3) outlines this hierarchy, which includes:

- **The client(s)—decision-maker**, is usually the planning minister, but decision-making can also require government approval from either full cabinet or a committee, or one or two designated ministers. As soon as the client is more than the minister, then the time required for decisions increases by four to six weeks.
- **A formal steering committee**, with senior representatives from principal agencies responsible for delivering the plan, particularly for the signing off on the content which goes to the client, usually at deputy secretary level depending on department structures. Agencies likely to be part of this committee include planning, transport, health, education, environment and treasury. The project director would also attend.
- **A formal executive working group**, chaired by the project director, with membership at a minimum reflecting the steering committee, but at an executive director/director level.
- **Informal working group (the SOG)**, an informal senior officers' group established instead of the formal working group. This concept was outlined in Sect. 1.4.3.
- **A designated project director**, who is responsible for delivering the plan. The person's day-to-day title could well be different, such as Executive Director Strategy.
- **A designated project manager**, responsible for coordinating all the activities of the project.
- **A formal project control group**, responsible for coordinating day-to-day activities. Representatives need to include the lead for any working group, a representative from communications, and potentially a representative from the transport portfolio.
- **Working groups** (as required), charged with specific tasks, such as managing the submissions process or a specific research area.

6.8.3 Outputs for the Project Brief

In addition to the finalisation of a project brief, you need to finalise the governance arrangements for the project.

It is critical that the project brief is approved by the decision-makers, including those most likely to be responsible for the delivery of the plan. On approval it

Fig. 6.3 Governance layers

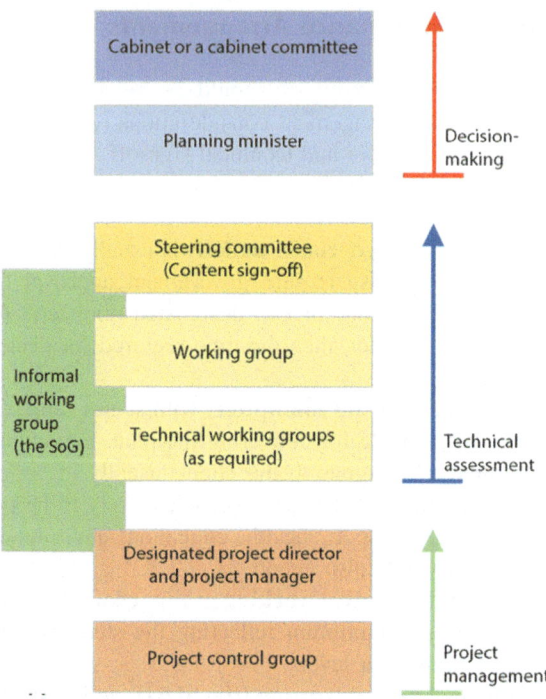

is also important to have a publicly available document that, at a minimum, outlines the study objectives, study area, project scope, timing, and opportunities for community involvement.

The public release of such a document should be supported by a communications plan.

6.9 Implications for Other Planning Typologies

You need to consider several other issues when applying the approach outlined in this chapter to the other planning typologies.

These are outlined in Table 6.1 and considered in detail in Chapter 12.

6.9 Implications for Other Planning Typologies

Table 6.1 Applying Step 1 to other planning typologies

Planning activity	Local government area plan	Town centre and regional centre plan	Greenfield community plan	Neighbourhood community plan
Project brief; purpose of the plan	n/a	The preparation of town centre plans often has support of state governments through funding initiatives for either plan preparation or project delivery. Potentially there will be several local stakeholders who can be utilised to inform the issues to be investigated. Defining the study areas needs to consider the extent to which adjacent residential and/or industrial areas are included	Central to the process is integrating the spatial planning with infrastructure planning. Plans need to show the intended long-term structure of land uses and transport networks to guide delivery as distinct from recommending actions for delivery. Many outcomes need to be understood at a cadastre level to ensure an understanding of the implication of the plan on individual properties. This will influence the level of detail to be investigated	These projects should have time frames of five to ten years. The preparation of a plan is not a core short-term output; more importantly, the project is working on several stated goals, which the community will have helped to define
Project scope	Greater specificity of detail will be required, including a consideration of wider land use and transport networks outside the local government area	A significant difference in the level of detail will be required in many areas and expectations from the community as to delivery, hence a requirement for a first order testing of the feasibility and costs for delivery. You will need to consider the influence of wider land use and transport networks outside the centre boundary. Understanding land ownership could be significant from an asset management perspective	The subject land is often defined in a higher order growth management plan but could also be defined by the land holdings of an individual developer(s). Understanding demand, particularly for residential development, is core to the task. Detailed advice is needed on natural hazards and hydrological characteristics. Research usually needs to consider how the area will be integrated with existing urban systems and potentially future communities and/or hinterlands which will remain rural or protected natural areas	The project is a combination of community development activities with strategic planning resulting in neighbourhood community planning. The spatial scope is typically a suburb, where links to adjoining areas are generally only important from the perspective of accessibility. The community will have a major say in what activities are the focus of the project at any point in time. All research topics may be relevant. It is critical to gain community support for investigating them. Hence, research becomes a learning journey

(continued)

Table 6.1 (continued)

Planning activity	Local government area plan	Town centre and regional centre plan	Greenfield community plan	Neighbourhood community plan
Project methodology: research areas	Unlikely that all land uses typologies and transport systems will be present, thus several research topics will not be relevant Research methodologies for population projections will differ, as data for the cohort survival' methodology are unavailable	A range of detailed surveys and demand assessments are required in the areas of land use, transport networks, urban design qualities, retail and commercial activities Investigations are likely to cover areas not included in other planning typologies, such as access and disability audits and safety audits	n/a	The project seeks to bring together the strategic planning research activities with the community development activities
Governance	There is greater opportunity for cross organisation interaction—all staff generally in one location The challenge is gaining involvement of state government agencies. It is ideal to have research methods approved by government agencies Engaging with neighbouring councils where activities can impact is essential There is a need to engage with all councillors, as distinct from a single minister	Invariably a town centre will have a chamber of commerce and/or a centre manager (for internalised malls) who need to be part of any governance arrangements As applicable, consider how ward councillors are involved The biggest challenge is gaining state government involvement in the project, considering the likelihood of actions arising requiring their funding In some cases, centres straddle council boundaries. In such cases, input from state agencies can bring the parties together and broker common outcomes	Critical to delivery is the timely delivery of infrastructure, hence relevant agencies need to be involved In Australia, depending on the state, the agencies could be state run or private, which will influence governance arrangements	It is critical that the community is a major participant in the governance for the project In addition, the project should have direct involvement of state and local government and potentially peak bodies from the community sector Moreover, governance arrangements will evolve over time, hence induction processes for new community and team members and records of the journey are important activities

This table outlines how the planning activity undertaken for a metropolitan planning project in Step 1: Project Establishment needs to be adapted for the other city planning typologies. Additional detail is provided in Chapter 12.

6.10 Summary

This chapter focuses on the activities required to develop the project brief, which sets the direction and approach for preparing a new city plan. The principal considerations are:

- the importance of providing clarity in the project objectives, as they will define how the project will be judged, and in the project scope as it will create the expectations for the content of the plan
- the importance of identifying project partners across government and gaining their input to the project brief, specifically from delivery agencies and establishing how ongoing collaboration will occur
- the challenge of developing the project methodology, specifically identifying the research areas, a general approach for each and the timing for the tasks
- the need to connect with principal stakeholders to gain their input to the project brief and to develop a community engagement plan
- gaining approval to commence, based on a project brief that outlines the project objectives and scope, the project methodology, including community engagement linked to a timeline and resource requirements, and governance arrangements.

The importance of a project brief is amplified when Step 2: Research and analysis commences, when there can be high levels of interconnected activity and resources allocated to what is essentially the basis of the plan. How this step is approached is the focus of the next chapter.

6.10.1 Insights

Insight: In the beginning
Where is my manual, and what am I supposed to do?
It's not about planning
Cities are about people, not roads, zones or planning processes. Furthermore, people see things, feel things and believe in things. Too often planning processes take a far too technical view of the physical attributes of the world and miss this point
Believing
Belief—a fundamental rule
Once when working on a town centre strategy for which the future did not look promising, I was reminded that as the project manager, if I did not believe in that city, who would?
The city as an organism
A city can be described in terms of a set of interconnected systems that are continually in a state of flux, with some systems evolving and growing and others fading. Thus, an understanding of systems thinking is a pre-requisite for strategic planning. Do not limit yourself to seeking to understand the social science, explore other disciplines with the objective of changing the way you see systems
Influencing change
Cities are always changing at the micro and macro level, but what do we really know about **why, how, where and when** cities change? By default, all city planning is focused on influencing futures that are different to what we have now. Yet, while much is written about what we may desire from 'new urbanism' to 'environmentally sensitive urban design', not much is written about understanding and influencing change
Knowing that you can't change everything
Change in cities requires energy (investment) and in most established cities energy is a limited resource (population growth, finance, capital, public works, etc.). Therefore, you only have two choices—use a little bit everywhere and most likely not much gets done, or direct it selectively. Selected strategic intervention is one of the fundamental tenets that underpins the philosophy of this book

Insight: Why do the plan?
Because we were told to do it, is not sufficient
Why are you preparing the plan?
You must understand why you are preparing a plan. Is it a vision to guide public works, a vision to articulate the aspirations of the community, or a vision to influence market failures? Whatever the reason, the success of a plan is going to depend, in part, on your ability to articulate to the community why you are doing what you are doing
A review means a review
Most reviews of existing plans do not include an assessment of the existing plan. It is rare to see a comprehensive assessment of how successful an existing plan has been, including why or why not its intentions were delivered. Too often we jump straight into preparing a new plan with no recognition of what has gone before
Insight: Implementation: the end at the beginning
You must think about where you're going before you get started
It is very unlikely you will deliver it
Cities are complex; consequently, the responsibility for change within a city rests with different organisations and individuals, remembering it is individuals who do things, not organisations. Therefore, the success of any project relies on the partnerships that are generated in its preparation
No funds, no plan
The most important outcome of all is ensuring that the implementation plan is resourced.
Repeat: From the outset it is critical to remember that the most important outcome of all is ensuring that the implementation plan is resourced

(continued)

6.10 Summary

(continued)

Insight: No such thing as a cookie cutter
Every starting point is different
Not only are all cities, centres, suburbs and precincts different, but they are also at different points in their evolutionary. The suburbs that were the fringe of a city 40 years ago, which then faced all the challenges of a new community, are today mature communities, potentially middle suburbs, where diversity and choice are their defining elements. Thus, any strategic planning process needs to recognise that when looking at the opportunities of where a place could go, the choices are, in part, shaped by the journey on which they have been travelling and a requirement to understand where they will be in 40 years and beyond

Insight: Use of advisory panels
They need support
Advisory panels provide enormous advantage to a project as they bring a wealth of knowledge
From my experience with advisory committees in two jurisdictions, panel members can work fast, and progressively reveal many opportunities, which will then require further investigation – the panel will not see the task of following up the detail as their responsibility
Consequently, advisory panels require a senior and experienced planner(s) to provide the required support

Insight: Resourcing
Who pays for what?
Production costs. I would not mind a dollar for each time I thought, 'comms will pay for that'
When to go over budget? You have two choices; do not finish and take the hit of a failed project or finish and be admonished later for marginally exceeding the budget. You will work out which is correct

Insight: Managing the client(s)
The 'book of truth'
On the journey of preparing a plan there will be lots of small milestones where decisions are made and agreed to by either senior executive officers or the people who will ultimately approve the plan. Sometimes approved points will be lost in edits, re-writes and updates. To counter this, have a separate 'book of truth' as a run sheet of what has been signed-off along the way

Insight: The process
A new plan —a new process
Too often I have been asked for a copy of a previous brief so it can be used as the basis of a new brief. If it were that easy, I would not be writing this book. However, there are five standard questions that every study seeks to answer:
- Where have we come from?
- Where are we now?
- Where would we like to go?
- How do we get there?
- How do we stay on track?

Determining the details for each is the principal task of the project establishment step

You are not the first
It is rare that there is no existing material on some or part of your project. It may or may not necessarily be correct, but it is important to critically review what has been done. Many plans are often expressed as though they started with a clean sheet of paper, as distinct from acknowledging the path dependency of many existing issues

You can't study everything
It is usually not possible, due to time and cost constraints, to study all aspects of an issue. This dilemma is usually resolved by defining a brief that includes both the problem statement and the process to address the problem

Re-evaluate
Just because you have signed off on a process does not mean you cannot change it. In fact, it should be a step in your process to re-check your study objectives and process, at various milestones. The findings from research can change both the objectives and process of a study

Insight: The team
Don't forget those who will deliver the plan and those who are the ultimate stakeholders, thus who is advising you on their behalf?

Who needs planners?
Most teams will have a combination of planners, transport engineers, urban designers/landscape architects. So, who in your team understands people, such as anthropologists or sociologists, and what type of questions should you ask them? Who are the people who will cover the decisions of the marketplace (investors, bankers, etc.), and the environment?

(continued)

(continued)

Insight: The brief
Cities are complex, and your brief should reflect this
And don't forget…
Despite what lawyers say, you can change your mind
Study objectives are not the vision
The study objectives are part of the problem statement. They are a statement of what the study process is directed at achieving or investigating. They should not be confused with the goals and objectives of the vision (the answer) that the study reveals
Those who work alone gets covered in dust
This relates to implementation and delivery. Resourcing is an opportunity to bring together the people who will deliver a project. Projects often fail for lack of a project champion. With most city planning being complex, there is an opportunity, in fact a need, to assign each task not only to an appropriate level of resources (experts) but to link the tasks to the people who will deliver it
Study purpose—be clear!
The brief needs to indicate what you want, for example, a plan that identifies the retail needs of a community over the next 30 years. The clearer you can express what you require the plan to achieve, the better chance you have of delivering it
Defining a flash of brilliance
Most briefs are quite explicit in how the analysis will be undertaken, such as noise assessments and floor space surveys. Generally, little is provided on how the synthesis, direction setting and design phase is to occur. It is possible to outline the steps that will occur at this phase, and not just those steps to do with community consultation

Insight: Project scoping
Scoping takes time
To varying degrees, we allocate time to develop a strategy, though we usually allow very little time to prepare the project brief. We often forget the scoping task itself takes time and resources need to be allocated to undertake this front-end task

Insight: Consultants
Who needs them? You do
Realise that consultants differ
It is not about the obvious differences, it's about the qualities and specialisations of experts in the same field that differ. The part that takes time, and starts with learning the differences between like consultants, is reviewing their stated experience, and understanding when these differences matter
Over the years I have worked with several landscape architects. Some are skilled in designing urban design treatments for a main street, where the will explains why a piece of street furniture will be in a specific spot. Others will describe the landscape qualities of a whole metropolitan area. Hence, I have learnt to be clear on the skill I require
Create relationships
Unfortunately, consultants are occasionally treated as the scapegoat when things go wrong. As a result, this may impact the relationship between project teams and a consultant. Consultants should be seen as part of your team, especially since experience tells us that when you have a good team, you can have robust discussions. Also, I was a consultant once, and we are not bad people
They're experts, not mind readers
Consultants have expert knowledge in a range of fields. You have the information for your community, and it is critical that you share it with them. Maximise the use of their technical skills, don't put obstacles in their path or have them do what you or your team have the skills to do
One new thought
Expectations of the role of a consultant are often misunderstood. Yes, they have a task to do, and most will do it well, and yes, we engage consultants to undertake tasks that we either don't have the skills to do or do not have the time to do. The real value when utilising consultants is the 'one new thought', the one bright idea that is the real kernel of the question at hand, and one such thought is plenty for any project

(continued)

6.10 Summary

(continued)

Insights: Fact or fiction
Research, as a matter of fact
Gantt (1916, p. 88) stated that:
First: we have no right, morally, to decide as a matter of opinion that which can be determined as a matter of fact
Second: if we allow ourselves to be governed by opinion where it is possible to obtain facts, we shall lose in our competition with those who base their actions on facts
His statement is as true today as it was then. Sometimes city planning is based on professional opinion or on theories that have not been tested for their validity as truisms for all places, or worse still stakeholder post-it notes workshops (lazy consultation). Strategic planning is not just about literature reviews and land use surveys, there are a whole range of research techniques that can be used. You need to get your hands dirty and do some primary research
Significant or 'significant'?
Most of us study statistics at some stage and we learn to say that there is a 'significant' difference between two numbers and this 'means something'. It is interesting how this disciplined approach to numbers is lost when we get out into the real world of town planning. It does not need to be this way and it should not be so. Significance matters
Insight: A city is more than the people who live in it
Don't forget the business community
City life is often perceived in the context of the residents, particularly in the context of how they live their lives. However, a big part of city life is business to business activity, which is often invisible and usually not understood
Take the image of bread, at the start of Chapter 2, and think of all the business activity that is required to get the 230 different types of bread into such a small area of the city—everything from the bread manufacture and distribution (which is visible) to the ordering and planning. At the other end of the CBD in the same city (Sydney) freight is invisible at Barangaroo; it has an entire underground network created so freight activities don't interfere with the street level pedestrian activities. Thus, a street level survey, at Barangaroo, is unlikely to pick up all the transport activity required to make that location function

Insights: What do I need to know?
You can't know everything
In my view there are at least 15 skill areas that relate to strategic planning. As a strategic planner you need to gain mastery of about a third of all the different fields of 'planning', understand the basics of at least another a third, and then you will have to rely on first principles to contemplate the rest
If you seek to lead the preparation of city plans (at any level or scale) the task of acquiring knowledge and experience is something you must undertake, and it takes time
Don't be afraid to ask questions
Questions allow you to move from first principles to new knowledge. This is particularly important when you come across answers you do not expect, and it is at this point you need to remember Professor Julius Sumner Miller's famous saying: "*Why is it so?*". In fact, it is much harder to ask questions than to answer them, and ask you must
Don't be afraid to say you are wrong
Our assumptions about different issues may need to be challenged from time to time as things change, new knowledge leads to new constructs and of course you may be wrong. Unfortunately, many of our planning processes utilise combative processes where we are forced to defend positions as distinct from collectively seeking solutions
I will never forget being in a room many years ago with one of Melbourne's most combative barristers and he surprised us all by saying we should stop these arguments in court, and all get in a room and work together to solve the problem
Search for the why
As planners we look at questions, such as 'How can we solve housing choice?' and conclude from examples of inner urban renewal or fringe greenfield development that housing choice is a function of housing itself and we need a housing policy and more housing codes. My experience, especially with housing, is that what is happening is the result of an interplay between a range of non-housing issues
For example, housing choice is influenced by other issues such as where schools are located, where a person's parents live, where a person used to live, where a person works and how they get there, the level of public transport, lifestyle opportunities, proximity to goods and services, and investment value. Thus, what is needed is a plan that understands and responds to these complex issues, not simply a plan about houses

References

Rogers, D, Keane, A, Alizadeh, T, & Nelson, J (ed.) (2020) *Understanding Urbanism* Palgrave Macmillan, Singapore

Sipe, N, & Vella, K, (ed.) (2017) *The Routledge Handbook of Australian Urban and Regional Planning* Routledge Oxfordshire, UK

Thomson, S & Maginn, PJ Eds (2012) *Planning Australia, An Overview of Urban and Regional Planning, 2nd Edition* Cambridge University Press Port Melbourne, Australia

Website links

Australian Bureau of Statistics Building approvals Jan to June 2019, Catalogue. 8731. https://www.abs.gov.au/ausstats/abs@.nsf/mf/8731.0

Greater Sydney Commission, 2017 *Review of A Plan for Growing Sydney.* https://www.greater.sydney/publications

Greater Sydney Commission Act 2015 No 57, Division 2 Objectives and functions of Commission viewed 13 August 2020. https://legislation.nsw.gov.au/#/view/act/2015/57/part2/div2

Investment Logic Mapping, toolkits. https://www.dtf.vic.gov.au/investment-management-standard/ims-workshops-and-examples

Kaldas, N 2018 *Review of Governance in the NSW Planning System.* https://www.planning.nsw.gov.au/Policy-and-Legislation/Under-review-and-new-Policy-and-Legislation/Kaldas-review-of-decision-making-in-the-planning-system

NSW Environmental Planning and Assessment Act 1979 No 203, Part 3, Division 3.1, Section 3.5 Making and review of regional strategic plans viewed 12 August 2020. https://www.legislation.nsw.gov.au/#/view/act/1979/203/part3/div3.1/sec3.5

The Victorian Liberal Nationals Coalition Plan for Planning (2010). http://images.theage.com.au/file/2010/11/18/2051811/VictorianLiberalNationalsCoalitionPlan_planning.pdf

Gathering the Evidence

7.1 Introduction

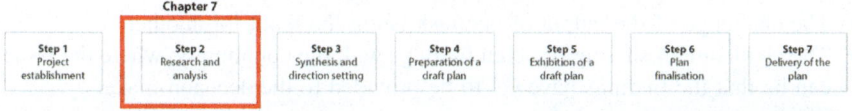

First: We have no right, morally, to decide as a matter of opinion that which can be determined as a matter of fact.

Second: If we allow ourselves to be governed by opinion where it is possible to obtain facts, we shall lose in our competition with those who base their actions on facts. The implications of differing city planning typologies on research activities

Gantt (1916, p. 88)

Step 2 focuses on gathering the evidence—the research and analysis stage. This is the make-or-break step, as it is the information gained that justifies and forms the basis of the plan. It is a resource-intensive step, where project management of multiple interconnected tasks undertaken simultaneously is vital and where the allocated time will always seem too short. Consequently, task completion invariably spills over to later steps.

It is during Step 2 that community engagement activities begin in earnest. The engagement activities are also part of awareness raising for the project.

An important task in Step 2 is critically evaluating the information to distil the principal findings, which will then guide the development and direction of the plan. As with any emphasis on learning, listening and understanding, it is easy to get caught up in the detail.

In reality, the detail behind the activities is considerable. Therefore, the general outline of activities in this chapter is supported by detailed discussions of research methods in Part 3: The 12 research areas.

7.1.1 Warm-Up Exercise

Another small exercise.
Now that the timeframe and budget is established, your boss would like to know exactly how and what evidence you are going to collect. When providing a response how will you juggle the myriad of tensions that influence this task? Jot down a few points as to how you may consider:

- The time it takes to procure consultants
- The benefits of relying on experts versus advice from a generalist planner
- The benefits of primary research versus using secondary data sources
- The challenge of the output of one task being the input for another
- The challenge of sharing research findings with the community, where the issue can be that the findings have yet to be provided to the decision-makers
- The need to recognise that the management of the tasks is a task that needs to be resourced
- The task of distilling findings to principal conclusions and emerging narratives needs resourcing.

7.2 Purpose of Step 2

The principal aim of Step 2 is to gain evidence to substantiate all aspects of the plan, from explaining the vision to the actions to achieve it. Specifically, you want to understand whether a business-as-usual future is acceptable. Research and analysis should be directed to understanding:

- Why, if relevant, a business-as-usual future is not acceptable
- The growth and change equation, as explained in Sect. 14.5, as the fundamental foundational input to the plan
- What is important to the people, their lives, and the places they live in now and in the future, specifically in the areas of:
  - Socio-economic characteristics
  - Characteristics of places and Country
  - Needs of people and households
  - Quality of life
  - Needs of businesses

- The growth and change equation
- Transport and digital accessibility and performance
- Qualities of places
- Managing urban/suburban communities
- The inter-relationships between differing themes which may highlight leverage points for intervention
- The choices (scenarios) to be considered
- The types of interventions required.

These considerations need to be in the context of the project objectives and scope, which is why the approach to each research area differs from project to project.

In addition, the purpose of Step 2 is to:

- Seek input from stakeholders and the community on their concerns and expectations for the future
- Enhance collaborative activities across government with the aim of building ownership for the delivery of the plan
- Develop an ongoing engagement role with stakeholders, beyond the preparation of the plan, aimed at growing trust with the community
- Create/enhance the awareness of the community of the issues and choices being considered and enhance the level of transparency, to grow trust with the community.

When undertaking the research, remember that the intent is to influence the content of the plan. Therefore, each principal finding should be addressed in the objectives of the plan and vice-versa; each objective should be able to be traced back to the research.

7.3 Principal Activities

Step 2 differs from other steps in the 7-Step Strategic Planning Process as is not simply a series of sequential tasks; it is more about the management of many interrelated activities (Fig. 7.1). The activities of Step 2 also draw on the project brief, particularly the project methodology. The principal activities are:

- **Finalising individual research briefs**. This should build on the proposed approach for each research area in the project methodology. You will now develop the detail of the research briefs—Chapters 13–15 provide detail on how to approach the research topics that form the Strategic Planning Research Framework.
- **Coordinating research activities**. This requires an effective project management system, as many tasks will occur concurrently, many potentially by external consultants. In addition, the output for some research areas is the

input for other areas, such as population projections for transport modelling, so coordination is critical.

Importantly, coordinating the research requires technical management in terms of content quality control, including consistency across research areas and the initial problem statement.

- **Engaging with the community**. This also requires detailed work plans. Timing and logistics are usually key challenges. Engagement activities need planners to be available to explain technical issues. This can impact timing as technical staff are likely to be involved in other research activities.
- **Undertaking procurement**. This is a standard activity that follows the research briefs and work plans. Be aware of the time required and give advance warning to the people who manage procurement.
- **Distilling the principal findings**. This is a deliberative task as ultimately it is the findings of the research that will be the basis of the plan. You need to ensure the findings, which may be quite technical, can be converted into clear and simple narratives. Also, consider quality control and the veracity of conclusions.
- **Reporting principal findings to decision-maker(s)**. This activity is about avoiding surprises and advising what findings might mean in terms of the final plan, and the intervention required. If findings differ to initial expectations, assess whether the project objectives and scope need to be reset. My experience is that governments are good at shifting the narrative if required. So, if assumptions change, the earlier there can be a deliberative shift in the project direction the better.

7.3.1 First Nations and Research and Analysis

First Nations people are considered among the most researched people in the world. It is almost guaranteed that some literature will exist relating to the First Nations community in the area and broader topics that relate to best practice. It is important to invest resources and time into understanding the different needs of First Nations people when it comes to housing, access to the Country, cultural design, open space planning, business operations, kinship structures, health and community services, education and many other topics relating to strategic planning.

Consultation fatigue is a real challenge when working with First Nations communities. Repetition of conversations, lack of detailed consultation outcomes and the siloed approach of government agencies leads to frustration. It is important to work with a range of government agencies and partners to understand any previous consultation undertaken with the community and to source any summary or outcome reports in the local area.

Local First Nations organisations such as Traditional Custodian corporations, native title groups and land councils/registered Aboriginal parties might have

7.3 Principal Activities

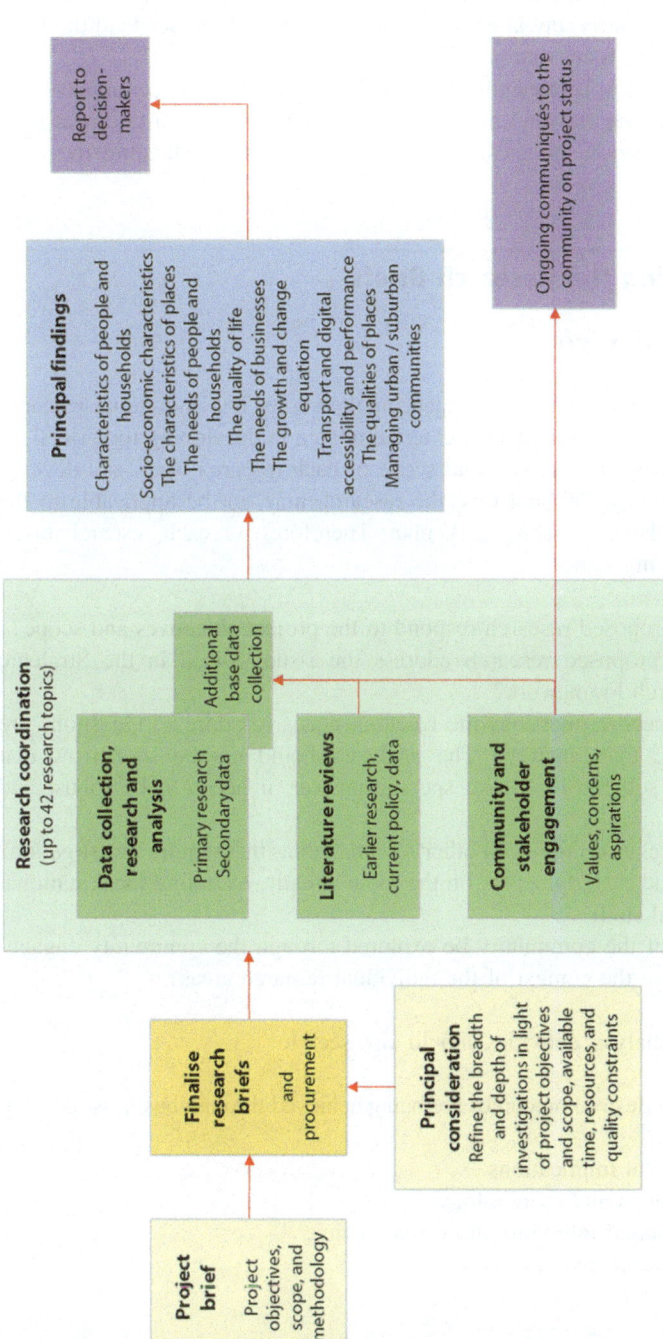

Fig. 7.1 Step 2: Research and analysis: principal activities
(This diagram outlines the principal activities required to undertake Step 2: Research and analysis. The activities include finalising the research briefs, undertaking and coordinating the range of research activities, bringing together the principal findings and communicating them to decision-makers, and ideally the community)

strategic planning documents that outline their goals and aspirations. These documents will help to identify any aligned outcomes and help to understand the local communities' areas of focus and need.

Utilising ABS data to better understand the local First Nations community will help to frame demographics and needs. Community profiles from the local government or other service agencies might also assist in understanding the local community.

7.4 Finalising the Research Briefs

7.4.1 Research Briefs

Step 2 requires you to convert the project methodology into individual research briefs. In some areas, you might seek external advice in developing the briefs.

You need to clarify the purpose and scope of each research brief, and develop a detailed methodology. Without this, the research may not be applicable to the specific needs of the overarching city plan. Therefore, for each research brief, consider the following issues:

- How does the proposed research respond to the project objectives and scope?
- How does the proposed research address the issues raised in the Strategic Planning Research Framework?
- What are the specific questions the research needs to address? Questions are harder to frame than answers. The analysis should not be so narrow that the research is self-fulfilling to a specific answer, it needs to be robust and replicable.
- Are there inter-relationships with other research areas that require investigation?
- What background material exists on the topic already, including local, national and international studies?
- Can the views of the community be explored through the community engagement activities, in the context of the individual research areas?

The research and analysis activities should also seek to:

- Identify whether desired outcomes are being achieved through business-as-usual activities
- Identify any spatial implications
- Clarify assumptions and terminology
- Identify enablers and inhibitors of desired change
- Identify performance criteria.

7.4.2 Research Activities

When developing research briefs, consider the type of research and analysis activity to be pursued, recognising that the time and resources available will be the principal constraint on what is proposed.

Typically, the types of activities utilised are:

- **Literature reviews** of previous plans, studies and policies. Ideally, most of this task is completed during Step 1: Project establishment. When undertaking literature reviews, understand why and what information is to be sourced. Consider using a template to focus the work of multiple officers—otherwise, there can be a lot of information, though little insight. Several software programs can be utilised for this task. Section 11.5 of Chapter 11 introduces the concept of a repository of all information relating to the strategic planning of a city (a book of knowledge) as part of the discussion of ongoing strategic planning processes.
- **Data collection** will range from new primary research (such as surveys) or secondary data sources (such as ABS Census data). Primary research takes time and is costly; often this activity is targeted to indispensable answers. Consequently, strategic planning research usually focuses on the analysis of secondary data. This can be a weakness when seeking to understand the full implications of an issue.

  Documentation can be time consuming and costly. Ensure the documentation is fit for purpose. I have often indicated that handwritten notes or sketch diagrams are perfectly okay for keeping a record. Nowadays they can be scanned and put on files. The objective here is to ensure a record that can be reviewed later, as required.

  The findings of some activities such as literature reviews and community engagement may also create the need for additional data collection.
- **Analysis**. The principal consideration here is how the data/information is analysed. You may use off-the-shelf models such as those available through the AURIN (Australian Urban Research Infrastructure Network) Workbench or bespoke models based on accepted standardised processes used in economic modelling. Ideally, all information is assessed in a deliberative and transparent way where the method used is articulated.

  At this point, the assessments usually relate to individual systems, though some may rely on inputs from multiple areas, such as transport modelling which, together with data on the performance of the current transport networks, requires population and jobs data.

7.4.3 Research Methods

Part of the purpose of this book is to emphasise that much of what is needed for a plan should be undertaken as part of a deliberative research methodology. In this context, the 7-Step Strategic Planning Process and Strategic Planning Research Framework provide structured platforms for strategic planning, whereby strategic planning is a discipline that can achieve positive outcomes rather than a collection of feel-good statements.

Strategic planning requires planners to think about research methods and what they mean. For example, when people say something is significant, are they saying so in the true sense of statistical significance, or just because there is a bigger number? Equally, when doing a survey, or when people have responded to an online exercise, is there confidence that the survey involved a true stratified representative sample, not just those who happened to log on, even if there were thousands of people? For those wishing to have a deeper understanding of research methods I would recommend reading Blaikie (1993).

7.4.3.1 Sticky Note Planning

There are a variety of engagement methods used when seeking input from the community; some involve sticky notes to catch ideas. This technique is creeping into more traditional research activities. I do not advocate it as an effective technique. If it is used, consider the following comments:

- The question of purpose is paramount. A sticky note workshop is like a focus group where you seek ideas to help frame a way forward. The role is not to arrive at an agreed position or agreed list of something.
- All such sessions should have pre-reading; there is rarely a topic that is new. A session should build on what has been learnt to date, even if it is only about determining the key areas for a study.
- Technology allows for electronic sticky notes with input via apps. The advantage here is responses in full sentences, not just three or four words that could have multiple meanings. In the absence of technology, use larger post-it notes to encourage people to write out in full what they mean.
- Remember that people need plenty of time to think, then discuss, and then write and post.
- Clarify the purpose of any feedback session and create opportunities for those at a table to add or disagree. Comments are often put up as a consensus view.
- Finally, any sticky note workshop should provide participants with the opportunity to comment on a summary of the day's activities to avoid over simplifying information.

7.4.4 Approach for Each Research Area

Chapter 4, specifically Sect. 4.3 outlined a framework for considering the research required to determine if a business-as-usual future is acceptable. This section lists the proposed research topics and provides an initial checklist of potential research activities. The information is presented as the Strategic Planning Research Framework:

- Part 1: Context, the people and the place
- Part 2: The needs of people and business
- Part 3: The qualities and performance of place.

In addition, I also outline the activities required as part of the wider issue of planning for places.

7.4.4.1 Context, the People and the Place

The focus for this area is to understand the characters of the people and the place. Comparisons to wider places, such as a suburb in the context of a district or local government area, is a central part of understanding the place and determining how it may be unique. In this context, focus on the basics; other areas in Part 2 and 3 focus on the detailed qualities of the people and the place.

Table 7.1 provides an overview of the principal research activities for the research areas of Part 1. Undertaking most of these activities is a core skill of the strategic planner.

7.4.4.2 The Needs of People and Business

The research for Part 2 focuses on the dynamics of each area, such as performance, adequacy, barriers and enablers. Most activities require specialist input, though over time it is likely you will gain a reasonable level of competency in a few of the areas. Understanding how they relate to each other is a core skill.

Table 7.2 provides an overview of the principal research activities for the Part 2 research areas.

7.4.4.3 The Qualities and Performance of Place

The assessments for Part 3 are similar to Part 2. They are about understanding dynamics, but in this case the dynamics of the place, including the performance of the transport network which provides accessibility across the place.

Table 7.3 provides an overview of the principal research activities. Undertaking most of these activities is a core skill of the strategic planner.

7.4.4.4 The Planning for Places

Several issues regarding the planning for places require deliberative attention—see Table 7.4.

Table 7.1 Part 1: Overview of research activities

Research area	Overview of research activities
Characteristics of people and households	
Demographic characteristics (profiles)	Assessment of total population and age cohorts, including past trends
Household characteristics	Assessment of household types, such as single person or family
Socio-economic characteristics	
Socio-economic characteristics such as educational attainment, household type, income, language, occupation, industry of employment, journey to work data, mode of travel to work, home ownership, volunteering, ethnicity, migration patterns, and employment status	Assessment of current socio-economic characteristics and past trends, by small area, with consideration of obtaining any crosstabulations of individual data sets from the ABS relevant to the purpose of a specific project
The characteristics of places and Country	
The characteristics and evolution of the land use systems and transport networks (including inter-relationships) of a city	Land use assessments, including land use by type including vacancies, multiple levels and use of ANZSIC (Australian and New Zealand Standard Industry Classification) codes, floor space and land ownership Built form assessment, including built form (3D), site coverage, public spaces, disability access, walkability, visual, and active frontage assessment Utilities, including water, drainage, sewerage, waste, energy and communications (including digital access) Transport networks by type, including road, public transport, freight, logistics, air, sea, cycle, walking, ports, airports, car parking and intermodal terminals Spatial land use (functional) characteristics and change over time by land use typologies (including natural ecosystems) and transport networks and their inter-relationships Major accessibility barriers, such as topographical (river) or constructed (rail line) Comparative accessibility assessment (transport connectivity patterns)
The cultural landscape which informs the local First Nations communities' perspective of Country	Cultural value including historical and contemporary values, oral stories and mapping and covers significant sites, traditional movement corridors, view lines, landscape, flora and fauna, waterways, cultural practice, caring for Country and narratives of Country Augment desktop reviews with an on-Country review with knowledge holders
The characteristic of the physiographic and climatic conditions	Physiography and natural systems assessment: topography (catchments and stream systems), waterways and wetlands, coasts and harbours, geology, air, water, urban tree canopy, natural hazards and native vegetation The climatic conditions across the city—rainfall, temperature and climatic events (such as cyclones)

(continued)

7.4 Finalising the Research Briefs

Table 7.1 (continued)

Research area	Overview of research activities
City setting	
The collective, overarching, quality(s) of a place	An integrated view of how the characteristics of people and households, their socio-economic characteristics, and the characteristics of the place define the setting or image of the place as a context for the plan

This table highlights the type of research that could be undertaken for each of the six research topics, which form Part 1 of the Strategic Planning Research Framework: The people and the place. I discuss the approach to research for all the research topics in Part 3 of this book

Table 7.2 Part 2: Overview of research activities

Research topic	Overview of research activities
The needs of people and households	
The level of housing choice	Housing opportunities by type, price, tenure, and location and choice preferences (housing markets) Housing supply and demand considerations by housing submarkets Affordable housing (demand and supply) for low and very low-income groups Social (public) housing demand and supply considerations Other housing areas such as student, retirement, nursing home and rural residential
The financial and economic independence of households	Individual educational attainment, skills, and occupations Relative accessibility to tertiary education facilities Primary and secondary school educational outcomes Relative accessibility to jobs— breadth and depth
Enabling the economic self-determination of First Nation communities	Engaging with First Nations communities Understanding of the planning controls of land held by First Nations communities
Urban amenity: level of access to goods, services and jobs	The distribution, size and role of centres Accessibility to goods and services, including retail, leisure, recreation, entertainment, cultural and the arts, and health Identification of major accessibility barriers, such as topographical (river) or constructed (rail line)
The health of individuals and the community	Quality of the urban structure, that is, walkability to goods, services, jobs, open spaces and public transport The extent and quality of the cycle network The extent and quality of the pedestrian network Accessibility to recreational/sporting facilities Accessibility to community gardens
The cost of living	Relative accessibility to jobs and goods and services—breadth and depth by private vehicle and public transport (therefore potential for only one or no car)

(continued)

Table 7.2 (continued)

Research topic	Overview of research activities
The quality of life	
Individual and community wellbeing	Social and community services needs Accessibility to social and community services Accessibility to informal meeting places Urban design quality of the public realm Quality of the urban structure—legibility and opportunity for impromptu social interaction Comparative accessibility assessment (transport connectivity patterns) Levels of volunteering (a proxy)
Cultural and artistic expression, participation and appreciation	Accessibility to cultural and arts facilities and dedicated public spaces Flexibility of planning systems to accommodate cultural and artistic activities
Access to natural and developed public places	Open space provision (distribution) by type (accessibility) Recreation and sporting facilities, activity and needs (demand and supply) Qualitative values of the open space network from pocket parks to national parks
The physical amenity of households	The amenity requirements for protecting residential land use interfaces Quality of the urban structure—assessing spatial land use relationships
The needs of businesses	
Enabling businesses to grow, flourish and innovate	The development, activity and spatial barriers to growth and innovation for retail, office, industrial and freight and logistics land uses including market assessments The development, activity and spatial barriers to growth and innovation for health and education precincts The development, activity and spatial barriers to growth and innovation for specialised areas as required, such as mining and agriculture
The economy and spatial economic structure	GDP, changing economic structure, economic drivers, macro-economic context, emerging sectors, productivity/competitiveness, business interactions Employment by type, employment density, effective employment density, location quotient analysis, sectorial structure, new business and start-up locations
The operational needs of businesses	The amenity requirements of differing businesses, such as the needs of town centre activities The operational needs of differing business typologies, including the freight sector and trade gateways (e.g. 24/7 operation)
Transport and telecommunication access to support business activities	Transport network performance, all modes, including trade gateways Operational constraints on freight activities Relative levels of telecommunications accessibility (e.g. download speeds)
Protecting natural resources	Identification of resource values and protection considerations

(continued)

7.4 Finalising the Research Briefs

Table 7.2 (continued)

Research topic	Overview of research activities
The growth and change equation	
Population and demographic change across a city	Population and demographic characteristics and trends Population and household projections
Housing demand across a city	Housing typologies, current and trends Housing markets, and demand and supply projections
Commercial business activities	Commercial sectors (retail, industrial, standalone offices and specialised areas as required) current characteristics (including requirements) and trends Demand and supply projections
Agricultural and mining activities	Mapping of land values and current activities

This table highlights the type of research that could be undertaken for the 19 research topics that form Part 2 of the Strategic Planning Research Framework: The needs of people and business. I discuss the approach to research for all the research topics in Part 3 of this book

Table 7.3 Part 3: Overview of research activities

Research area	Overview of research activities
Transport and digital accessibility and performance	
Network performance	Mapping network performance
Service provision	Mapping levels of accessibility by mode
Digital coverage and performance	Mapping coverage by service type and performance
City structure, special equity, and mode choice	Mapping city structure and transport networks (mode choice)
The city in its region	Mapping regional connections, levels of interaction, communities of interest and role vis-à-vis the city
The qualities of places	
A sense of place and community	The barriers to neighbourliness The diversity of communities (income, cultural) Quality of urban structure—legibility and opportunity for impromptu social interaction Identification of major accessibility barriers, such as topographical (river) or constructed (rail line) Comparative accessibility assessment (transport connectivity patterns)
First Nations Country, community and culture	Identifying the cultural landscape including culturally significant sites from a First Nations perspective Understanding the significance of Country, community and culture from a First Nations perspective
Post European contact heritage and history	Identifying culturally significant sites Understanding the history of people and places Identify opportunities for truth telling regarding colonial narratives and events

(continued)

Table 7.3 (continued)

Research area	Overview of research activities
The quality, aesthetics and amenity of urban area of a city and its hinterland. The characteristics and evolution of the urban parts of a city	Quality of the public realm Assessment of the image of the city Quality of urban structure—legibility Urban design quality of the urban structure and built form Design quality of the city design Major accessibility barriers, such as topographical (river) or constructed (rail line)
Natural ecosystems, biodiversity and resilience	Terrestrial and aquatic biodiversity values and management considerations of the ecosystems within the city and its hinterland
Responding to climate change	Understanding changing climatic conditions—temperature and rainfall Understanding the impacts of natural hazards, including flooding and coastal inundation
The values of hinterlands	Identifying their characteristics, values, roles and economic output
Managing urban/suburban communities	
The efficiency in providing urban infrastructure and its alignment with growth	Infrastructure capacity and threshold considerations and the demand for services
Managing risks associated with natural hazards	Spatial identification of the natural hazards and the risks/responses for differing urban typologies How risks associated with natural hazards are avoided, mitigated, adapted to and managed, including bushfire, flood, wind (e.g. cyclones), coastal inundation and acid sulphate soils
Enabling choice	Understanding the level of accessibility and barriers to accessibility at a community scale, particularly in new greenfield communities
The influence of adaptation, emerging technological change, behavioural change, innovation and optimising efficiency	Identifying current and emerging issues and their influence
City design	
Understanding and representing a range of 'strategic design values at the scale that is the focus of a plan	A strategic design assessment process that considers the inter-relations between mass, activity, and space; quality of life, in an experiential sense; design considerations at the scale of the place to which the plan applies; and the spatial structure of the city in terms of the elements that need to be enhanced, created or ameliorated to inform future more detailed urban design activities

This table highlights the type of research that could be undertaken for each of 17 research topics that form Part 3 of the Strategic Planning Research Framework: The qualities and performance of place. I discuss the approach to research for all the research topics in Part 3 of this book

Table 7.4 Planning for places: issues for consideration

Issue for consideration	Overview of research activities
The planning for places	
Defining of places	Communities of interest Transport network influences on defined communities
The creation of places, with consideration of designing with nature, creating depth, choice and diversity, redundancy, wellbeing, attention to detail, diversity in a place and of places, complexity, and a positive experience	Systematic assessment during the draft plan preparation phase of a project

7.5 Community Engagement Activities

7.5.1 Purpose of the Engagement Activities

Step 2 aims to maximise the opportunities for the community to input to the plan. This will create:

- awareness that the government is preparing a new city plan and there is an opportunity to be involved
- a variety of opportunities for the community to be engaged, with a focus on understanding what they value, what they would improve, and their comments on the main issues being considered
- opportunities for specific groups and hard to reach groups to be involved through targeted activities with peak bodies, community groups, culturally and linguistically diverse (CALD) people, First Nations communities, young people and the elderly
- a program for working with local government, not only for seeking input in the research and analysis step but for the duration of the project, leading to the establishment of a safe place where information and ideas that are not set policy can be shared.

I have used the word *program* here deliberately, as initially there should be separate working sessions on a range of research areas, then multiple sessions on plan preparation, exhibition sessions and finalisation discussions.

To enable true engagement, consider the size of working groups. In Melbourne and Sydney with more than 30 local government areas, regions/districts are an obvious starting point. The Greater Sydney Region Plan used a district grouping of local governments, as provided for through NSW planning legislation and defined by a ministerial order.

7.5.2 Approach and General Considerations

An important companion piece for considering the approach to planning and undertaking community engagement activities is outlined in Sect. 5.3.2.

Also consider the following points when preparing the community engagement plan:

- understand the existing material and who from the planning portfolio is engaging with the community – on what and when
- utilise existing processes and/or activities of local government, as local government is usually continually engaging with local communities
- integrate the community engagement plan with a wider communications plan for the project to avoid mixed messages
- use jargon free language so that people better understand the relevant policies, regulations and guidelines
- recognise that, in some jurisdictions (Victoria), the intention to create an engaging environment through simple complementary activities, such as having a barbeque, requires team members to obtain a formal food preparation certificate
- finally, listen to what the community is saying.

> *One experience brought this home to me. I was working at a council that resolved to prepare town centre beautification plans across major centres and villages. We proposed a range of different urban landscape treatments across about a dozen centres. At several meetings with traders and landowners, we talked about how the council was proposing to enhance the amenity of the centre and the council would go 50-50 in paying for the cost. It took several meetings before we finally heard what the traders and owners were saying, which was that they did not want trees and seats but wanted a new access point off the main road with some signage to show where the centre was. Fortunately, we did eventually listen, and the new access point was built.*

7.5.3 Coordinating the Activities

In coordinating the community engagement activities, consider:

- involving senior planners in the engagement activities, both their planning and undertaking, to ensure the activities and outputs are fit for purpose
- how engagement activities may be influenced by the findings from the research areas, such as output from housing analysis
- the provision of timely information to senior executives and decision-makers on concerns being raised and the number of people with whom you have engaged, potentially through formal weekly or daily processes
- having sufficient resources to evaluate the information provided, with an emphasis on using planners who can interpret the information in terms of what it means for a city plan.

7.6 Coordinating the Research Initiatives

The research and analysis step is one of the most challenging project management tasks, as activities can be internal and external, cross agency, interconnected, highly confidential, and vary from traditional planning research to online social media events. To address this complexity the coordination of activities should consider:

- **The reporting period**. The time interval between checking in on progress is the maximum time of potential absence of activity. This point was emphasised to me, when studying for my master's in project management, by one of Australia's foremost project managers, Dr. Paul Steinfort. I recommend the reporting period is two weeks or less.
- **The need for contingency planning**. The consequences of delays and/or unexpected findings is not just about time, but also about potential impacts on resourcing and quality. Hence, you need contingency planning.
- **Content control**. Coordinating monitoring activities is not simply a project management consideration. It is also about progressively keeping abreast of the content. Thus, you need to involve those who will lead the preparation of the plan, including any theme or topic leads. Their involvement should also cover feedback from engagement activities.
- **Independent advisory committees, commissioners or similar experts**. These individuals may be an integral part of the planning process and may be engaging with many people and organisations during the research and analysis stage. Aim to shadow their activities, and to action any opportunities or issues arising. I cannot over-emphasise the importance of these two resourcing tasks.
- **Pressure for early answers**. All senior officers and decision-makers are keen to get advanced information of preliminary findings. In this space, a word of caution—sometimes early findings can ultimately prove to be incorrect, and in those cases, they can create a lot of angst and unnecessary activity. The management of this point is a balancing act that will come from experience.

Table 7.5 Applying the Step 2 approach to other planning typologies

Planning activity	Local government area plan	Town centre and regional centre plan	Greenfield community plan	Neighbourhood community plan
Community engagement	Councils have existing engagement programs and greater experience, which allows more sophisticated and in-depth activities Stakeholder databases are more extensive	Engagement activities need to be more targeted, with opportunities for deeper levels of interaction. A recognition that the various communities who interact with the centre will provide an understanding of the issues and ideas for change Direct engagement with businesses and landowners is critical	As no community exists (other than existing rural landholders), gaining an understanding of expectations requires innovative approaches, including surveying residents of newly developed areas	Community engagement is core to every task and most importantly the community is part of the project team and the decision-making for how the project will be organised and what will be investigated
Research activities	n/a	n/a	n/a	The community needs to be actively involved in many of the research activities over the life of the project, including projects they identify The pathway for many projects may therefore be circuitous, but it is critical to gain trust

This table outlines how the planning activity undertaken for a metropolitan planning project in Step 2: Research and analysis can be adapted for other city planning typologies. Additional detail is provided in Chapter 12

7.7 Distilling the Research Findings into Narratives

A challenge for research and analysis is information overload. It is important not to get lost in the detail; focus on the bigger picture, specifically items of metropolitan or district significance. The NSW transport plan, prepared at the same time as the 2018 Greater Sydney Region Plan, *Future Transport 2056* (2018) illustrates a clear narrative on their approach to transport networks (both road and rail) for Greater Sydney. Rather than focusing on a specific mode or individual challenges, their narrative looks at the transport network as:

City-shaping corridors—major trunk road and public transport corridors providing higher speed and volume connections between our cities and centres that shape locational decisions of residents and businesses.
City-serving corridors—higher density corridors within 10 km of metropolitan centres providing high frequency access to metropolitan cities/centres with more frequent stopping patterns.
Centre-serving corridors—local corridors that support buses, walking and cycling, to connect people with their nearest centre and transport interchange (p. 35).

Less significant findings should be addressed in business-as-usual activities rather than being addressed in the plan and, if required, referenced that way.

When seeking to identify the principal findings, distil the findings to narratives as distinct from technical findings. As a plan needs to capture the attention and imagination of the community and decision-makers, it needs to be a call to arms. However, at the same time, we need the technical background documentation for the findings.

Developing the narratives is also the beginning of the synthesis and direction setting stage (Step 3), particularly the identification of inter-connections between research areas and integrating the findings into more complex narratives.

7.8 Implications for Other Planning Typologies

Several issues need to be considered when applying the approach in this chapter to the other planning typologies—see Table 7.5 and the detail in Chapter 12.

7.9 Summary

This chapter focuses on obtaining the evidence that forms the basis for the plan. It outlines the range of activities and considerations required for technical research, which seeks to determine if a business-as-usual future is acceptable; and for community engagement activities, which seek to understand the values and concerns of the community who are ultimately the recipients of the plan.

The principal considerations are:

- Projects do not form in isolation, there is a need to identify existing material.
- The focus of the research activities is the Strategic Planning Research Framework. It outlines, from a city planning perspective, what is important to people, their lives, and the places they live in, now and in the future. The task for Step 2 is to convert the research framework into individual research briefs in the context of the project objectives and scope.

- It is more than just technical research; it is especially important to engage with the community and seek input. This requires a variety of opportunities for people to participate, including hard to reach groups.
- In undertaking all the activities in Step 2, time is the main challenge. Clarify what research is important as well as effective project management skills to allow concurrent research efforts and the sequencing of research pieces as required, in a timely manner.
- Findings expressed as technical data on their own are often difficult to communicate; converting the data to a narrative will gain the attention of the community and decision-makers if intervention is required.
- Keep decision-makers abreast of early findings, especially if they raise new conclusions—no surprises should be the motto.

Ultimately Step 2: Research and analysis is about distilling the principal narratives that will inform the direction setting for the plan.

It is also the beginning of the process of integrating the findings across themes and identifying inter-dependencies that collectively reflect the more complex dynamic nature of cities and is the focus of the next chapter—Step 3: Synthesis and direction setting.

7.9.1 Insights

Insights: Research #1
As they say—GIGO—garbage in, garbage out.
If you have a choice, use experts
Strategic planning requires an understanding of a myriad of issues. In most cases, there are specialists who have highly developed skills, even within the same discipline. Sourcing the best advice is a big step in resolving the problem of garbage in, garbage out.
Don't guess
Planners sometimes hide behind professional opinion and the subjective interpretation of amenity impacts and call it planning. Why? Because research in new areas is hard and takes lots of effort. However, even when time is constrained there is usually an opportunity to undertake some investigative work. Go back to first principles to ensure your work is not biased by first impressions.

Insight: Research #2
Remember to ask, why is it so?
Sometimes the results of our research do not reflect our expectations of what the answer should be. Facing up to the findings and developing a response to the unexpected answer is a challenge.:
During my time at the City of Casey, council undertaken a regional project that sought to identify business clusters. The research, undertaken by SGS Economics & Planning, was some of the best hard-yards primary research by a consultant that I have seen. However, the client group dismissed the study as it did not meet the initial expectation of finding business clusters (the research showed they did not exist).
In that instance, the client group failed to consider consideration the favourite saying of Professor Julius Sumner Miller, "Why is it so?" I feel this shortcoming relates to our general disinclination to seek out new information (the evidence); thus, we are ill-equipped to assess the findings of such research.

7.9 Summary

I remember being asked by Dr Jeff Wolinski (then of Ratio Consultants, Melbourne) to examine the opportunities to develop an entertainment centre in the Latrobe Valley in the late 1980s. I started the task by thinking about demand; however, in the absence of an existing major facility, that was proving difficult. Jeff nudged me down a path that saw me undertake detailed telephone interviews with the existing half dozen entertainment centres across Australia. The information provided a framework to understand the parameters of what makes a viable centre.

Description is not analysis

Data collection without analysis is meaningless. Technical reports often include site-by-site land use assessments and reams of Census data, but with no assessment of what it means for the problem at hand.

You can never map too much

A lot of what happens in a city reveals itself in some spatial context. This is one area where I believe cities express themselves in similar ways to the natural sciences. One proposition of mine is that cities are 'lumpy'—they display clusters. When they become mono-dimensional, and particularly when no new activity is added, they decline and even decay. Thus, when our research reveals patterns, determine whether the answer should be similarly structured.

Time series, a research legacy

Usually, some good primary research is carried out while preparing a structure plan. However, it is often only for a point in time and no process is put in place to establish an ongoing data collection and analysis system. It is often suggested that this is due to limited resources for the delivery of the structure plan and further research does not come up high on the agenda. This is unfortunate as the next time the centre is evaluated new data needs to be collected and often the older data has been lost. There would be long-term benefits to use not just structure plan processes, but ongoing monitoring, review and refinement if a legacy of information systems could be established.

The costs of documentation

Documenting research can be one of the most expensive aspects of a planning project. There is always a need to ensure the information is fit for purpose, but that could simply mean prepared notes and a hand-drawn image.

It's okay to say we don't know

There is an assumption, I believe, created by the more legal aspects of development approval, that there is an answer to every question. Sometimes there is no answer, and this is important to acknowledge.

(continued)

(continued)

Insight: Research #3
The past matters
Two centres that may appear similar may have different futures, not because of the opportunities created by the surroundings, but because of the implications of their history. Understanding the past is a task often overlooked, which lessens our understanding of the decision-making framework of a community. This is an essential requirement when the end of the study is approached, and final decisions are required.
My direct experience in this was working with a council on a foreshore plan where the objective was to create more activity, yet we established, albeit a bit late, that part of the foreshore was out of bounds for activity, because of a long decision-making history which had continually identified it as open public place (and still does).

Insight: Existing systems
Don't judge a book by its cover.
Description is meaningless without a performance statement
While we might describe the elements of an existing system such as the road network including arterial roads, trunk collectors and streets, etc., this can often be a bit 'so what' and will not allow the delivery of a long-term plan unless the performance of the system is provided.
Again, using roads as the analogy, we usually give performance levels when it is easy, for example, traffic volumes versus capacity showing intersection delays (for example, SIDRA analysis). However, how often for the same centre do we include economic performance measures such as comparisons of rents or retail turnover densities, let alone provide measures over time? It is the performance assessments that indicate the need for intervention.

Insights: Activity analysis
What most planners focus on
Numbers are for mathematicians
A major part of city planning is examining demand for various activities such as retail, manufacturing, office, and technology. We are seeking to determine the collective implications of this analysis—and we need to look beyond the numbers.
Your research needs to go to the design stage to examine physical outcomes, including asking whether the activity relationships of the past are what we want for the future. At what depth this design analysis needs to occur will reflect the scale of the planning underway. The task could vary from understanding the building blocks of new growth area cells of around 10,000 dwellings to understanding if you can fit a supermarket into a centre including providing a loading bay. The classic example of the need for this is when demand assessments show the potential for major new retail activity, yet no work is undertaken to understand whether the desired centre for this activity can in fact accommodate it, from the market's perspective.

Planners, consider the marketplace
How much time is given to talking to the marketplace, by planners, with the objective of achieving the positive outcomes seen in other jurisdictions? We don't do this well when we continually suggest that a car park around shopping centres could be turned into multi-level activity. This response is short-sighted on many levels. It does not generally reflect the long-term planning for the centre (usually the need to keep expansion options flexible) and, more importantly, it may not stack up financially. This may seem a simplistic example, but making the multi-level development happen requires research and intervention.

(continued)

(continued)

	Trevor's insight—you can't have excitement everywhere There is not enough activity to ensure all streets in a town centre have active frontages. Even in dense CBD environments, for every quality frontage there is a quiet backstreet. The resolution of this issue needs careful consideration. Mega centres such as Chadstone in Melbourne result in the attraction of some activities that might not otherwise exist. A consequence is fewer centres overall. Here, my point is that if you have a higher concentration of activities than normal in one location (for example, restaurants in Lygon Street, the Italian food zone in Melbourne) you have a less than normal concentration somewhere else (Trevor's insight). Trevor Wakefield, former team leader in city planning at the City of Casey, Melbourne.
Insight: Access (transport) *It's not about buses or cars.* **Relative accessibility** We can map the bus service and count the cars, when what we really need to do is ask questions about the relative accessibility of the community by mode of transport, type of activity and socio-demographic group. For example: What proportion of people can walk to a park and a convenience shop? Is the bus service about equity or mode choice? What proportion of jobs are within 30 minutes by car or public transport? What are the maximum distances to a whole range of activities? **Don't forget to count the cars and the pedestrians**	**Insight: Community engagement #1** *Planning is about people.* I have learnt that local governments are the most experienced at community engagement. To me this is a reflection of their day-to-day activities, which require direct interaction with the community, from rubbish collection to providing Meals on Wheels services. I have always valued my career pathway of working in local government before state government. It made me more aware of what is required to implement government policy, particularly who must sell government policy to the community. *The consultation for the Casey Foothills project is the best example of a community engagement initiative that I have been involved in. It sought to understand the complex elements of a very divisive community issue. In the end we managed to have the community reference group present the findings to the council.*

(continued)

(continued)

Yes, examine the existing transport system and how it is performing, but do not forget to count the pedestrians. Some aspects of transport planning are quite sophisticated; however, we should remember that traffic modelling is an art, not a science, that seeks to show relative outcomes not fixed futures.

Access for all

In examining how the transport system operates, understand the level of accessibility for the entire community. Transport disadvantage ranges from limited to no access to various forms of transport for those with disabilities including vision impairment and ambulatory ability and those without disability.

I also learnt the importance of retaining the engagement of the community during the development and refinement of the options, even as they were initially only draft ideas before council. What we struggled with was talking to the council about perceived sensitive options for resolving a plan, not realising in the absence of engagement in this step parts of the community commenced their own engagement process. This resulted in an unfortunate fear campaign; we lost a new and ground-breaking approach to a problem.

It's a leap of faith

Community engagement is about letting go, because it is in part about providing the community with an opportunity to help steer the ship, an act that planners and decision-makers usually wish to keep to themselves. Thus, it is a leap of faith for yourself (the most critical step, to ensure you can provide confidence in those around you), for your team and for the decision-makers.

Think of a number and double it

A comprehensive engagement process will most likely utilise significantly more time and resources than simply a consultation process.

Take baby steps

Experience and formal learning are important here, not just for you, but for the whole team. The best way to start is slowly, or even better still with professional help where the process is seen as a real transfer of skills.

Insight: Community engagement #2
You can make rules

Consultation is not about handing over the responsibility for undertaking a project. Articulate to the community the rules of engagement for each project; this will range from providing information to direct involvement in preparing the plan.

Independent facilitators—when to use

Some projects are highly political.

Insight: Community engagement #3
The power of a few people

The ability to sway decision-makers, whether they be local or state political representatives, does not always require the overwhelming support of a community. Just a few can achieve the outcome.

Once at a council I witnessed the power of a few. The presenting issue focused on a piece of open space and how it should be utilised—remain as passive open space or be converted to an oval and become a place for active open space and organised activities. Around 20 members of the community turned up to the council meeting and were all well behaved; no person spoke out of turn. But they all wore plain red t-shirts to express their anger. The decision went in their favour.

(continued)

(continued)

Early in my career I was involved in a community workshop where parts of the community loudly demonstrated against what was being proposed at the back of the hall where it was being held.

When undertaking community engagement, be aware that this can happen. Work out how to manage the demonstration and the safety of the other participants and your team.

In the case above we had engaged an independent facilitator who, with great skill, managed the situation, including running a successful workshop that included the demonstrators.

Community engagement is a required activity in all strategic planning processes. Capacity building of your team in the art of community engagement is a necessary task.

Perception is reality

This is important to understand when talking to the community. It cannot be over emphasised, and as a concept it is self-explanatory. An earlier reflection emphasises this point "… remember what you call a slum I call my home". Good engagement will allow perceptions from both sides to be challenged.

Two examples:

Glenorchy, where it was clear that the community did not envisage street tree planting as part of the plan for the city, and wished to retain their outward views from their properties.

Central Coast, where research of community housing preferences revealed a desire for detached dwellings, either old or new.

References

Blaikie, N (1993), *Approaches to Social Enquiry*. Blackwell Publishers, UK.
— As per the title, outlines methods for social enquiry
Gantt, H (1916), *Industrial Leadership*. Yale University Press.
— The source of the quote on why evidence is important

Website links

AURIN Workbench. https://aurin.org.au/resources/workbench/
Declaration of Districts for Greater Sydney. https://www.legislation.nsw.gov.au/view/html/inforce/current/act-1979-203#sec.3.2
State of New South Wales (2018), A Metropolis of Three Cities. https://www.greater.sydney/metropolis-of-three-cities

Synthesis and Direction Setting

8.1 Introduction

The whole is greater than the sum of its parts

Attribution, Aristotle (circa 350 BC)

Step 3: Synthesis is often categorised as being about a SWOT (strengths, weaknesses, opportunities and threats) analysis, but it is much more. Synthesis should be a journey towards directions and a vision. It requires a deliberative approach that includes a search for interdependencies and the identification of choices.

It is often the most challenging task. While there is a benefit in utilising technical experts for targeted research and analysis, Step 3 is about connecting the dots and identifying pathways for the future; this is at the heart of strategic planning.

It also requires intuitive leaps of logic; traditional analytical thinking, while important, is not sufficient. Lateral thinking is required, so I would recommend reading some of the works of Edward De Bono (refer to the reference list).

I see the task of synthesis as a core skill area for the strategic planner, where watching and learning, with guidance, will set you on the right path.

Step 3 focuses on integrating the findings and identifying interdependencies; assessing scenarios as the basis for the spatial plan; and setting the direction, vision and principal objectives that will form the basis of the plan.

This chapter outlines the considerations for these areas with an emphasis on developing and evaluating scenarios.

8.1.1 Warm-Up Exercise

Another small exercise.

I've worked with design colleagues who tell me they go from analysis to answer through inspiration. For city planning, I find that while there may be the occasional flash of brilliance as the plans evolve—there will be a lot of perspiration.

Synthesis is the task where you as the strategic planner move to the front—where you sought input from technical experts in Step 2, in Step 3 you're working to understand the inter-relationships between the findings. You'll need to understand if the whole is greater than the sum of the parts.

In this context, think about a scenario where your boss has put that challenging task to you by suggesting that while it was great that you found a lot of interesting facts, what does it all mean? Specifically, what tasks will you undertake to move from findings to directions for a plan?

8.2 Purpose of Step 3

Cities operate like complex organisms with each part interacting with another. To understand how they work, you need to understand both the attributes of the individual parts (the systems) as well as the dynamics of the whole and how the systems interact with each other. Consequently, the full benefit of the research and analysis step is not realised until the findings are integrated, allowing a richer set of conclusions to reveal themselves—a simple collation of the research findings does not make for a plan.

The overarching purpose of the synthesis process is to identify how the principal findings from Step 2 will inform the setting of the plan's vision, directions and objectives, which in turn inform the development of the strategies and actions that make up a draft plan (Step 4).

You'll need a deliberative process to transition from data to planning directions.

Direction setting will invariably require scenario assessment, which is primarily an exploratory and evaluative activity. It requires you to understand the choices available to accommodate the growth and change equation and achieve the desired liveability, productivity and sustainability outcomes.

8.2.1 Principal Activities

Step 3 can be considered as three interconnected areas, refer Fig. 8.1.

8.2 Purpose of Step 3

1. **Synthesis** of the research findings identified in Step 2, with a focus on identifying issues of district and metropolitan importance and identifying interdependencies and opportunities.
2. **Scenario development and evaluation**, where you assess the acceptability of a business-as-usual future and, as required, develop and evaluate alternative scenarios for the future.
3. **Direction setting** by bringing these findings into an emerging vision and objectives.

8.2.1.1 Supporting Activities

Supporting activities and considerations that need to occur as part of Step 3 are:

- **Writing the plan**. This should commence during Step 2. Start by focusing on structure and consider how the research and analysis will be reported. Sections such as the introduction, the context for emerging directions, and a glossary can also be commenced. These simpler writing tasks assist in discussing the tone, level of content and general look and feel of the report or web-based format.
- **Developing the report structure** should move from a discussion about a thematic versus integrated structure to that of an emerging overarching narrative that will continue to evolve.
- **Collective understanding of the basis for the plan** requires not just a need to collaborate but the need for a collective understanding of the major findings and proposed responses. Discussion of these issues should occur through informal workshops between relevant senior officers across agencies and should cover the:
  - growth and change equation
  - proposed infrastructure investments
  - strategic land use principles to guide the plan
  - distribution of activity (housing and jobs).

  These may seem obvious, but if agreement is not achieved across all agencies a plan may be more of a land use statement than an integrated land use and infrastructure plan.
- **Championing the vision**. The plan's success can be enhanced when its principal elements become part of the wider narrative of a government. The potential for this to occur is enhanced when the preparation of a city plan is supported by a project champion.

  This was true for the Greater Sydney Region Plan where the Deputy Chief Commissioner, who was also the Economic Commissioner, relentlessly engaged with all levels of government (ministers and bureaucrats), stakeholders, and the wider community with a consistent and simple story. He said he had told the story more than 1,000 times. Consequently, when attending a meeting of senior transport officers, they told the story back to me – the biggest hurdle of a plan, ownership, was in this case achieved.

216 8 Synthesis and Direction Setting

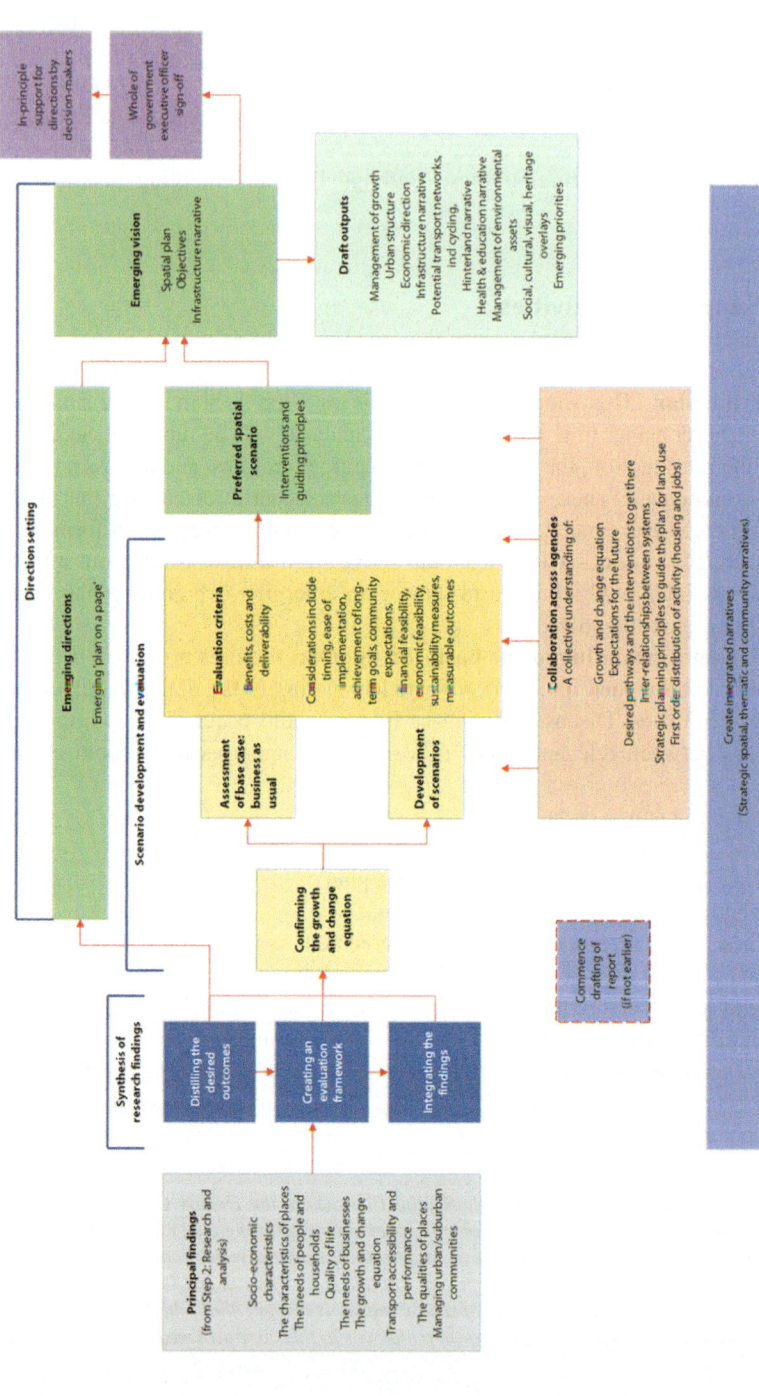

Fig. 8.1 Step 3: Integrating the findings and setting the direction: principal activities
(The principal activities to undertake the synthesis and direction setting occur in three principal areas: synthesis of the research findings, scenario development and evaluation, and direction setting. You must engage in the activities across all government(s) agencies to ensure buy-in. At the end of the process, seeking in-principle support for the proposed directions of the plan from decision-makers also ensures the resolution of a draft plan can occur with some confidence)

8.3 Synthesis of the Research Findings

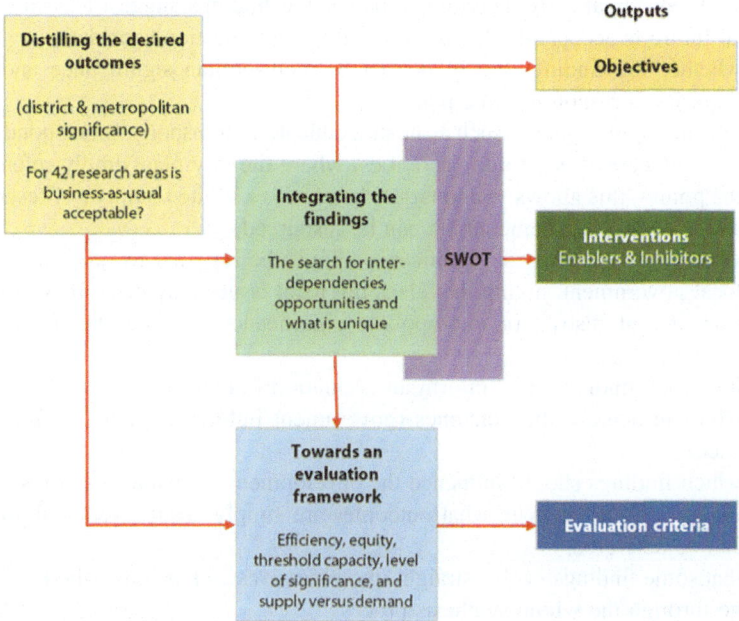

Fig. 8.2 Integrating the findings

A further lesson is that implementation is even further enhanced when the role of the champion continues well beyond the completion of the plan.

The boundaries between research and synthesis and direction setting are blurred. Those involved in the research and those responsible ultimately for the preparation of the plan should commence informal discussions as soon as findings start to emerge as this will evolve from informal discussions to deliberative processes.

8.3 Synthesis of the Research Findings

There are several interrelated activities required to synthesise the principal findings arising out of Step 2 (refer Fig. 8.2).

8.3.1 Principal Activities

The activities are as follows.

- **Distilling the desired outcomes**. The research and analysis step will potentially require the assessment of many individual research areas. Each assessment

needs to systematically determine whether the findings suggest a business-as-usual future is acceptable. In answering this core question consider:
- whether the findings are of district or metropolitan significance and thus requiring a response in the plan
- whether a line agency (such as health, education, transport) can respond to an issue as part of day-to-day activities, where the city plan simply references the point—this allows you to target the plan to a limited number of responses and ensure its implementation can be resourced
- whether issues of local significance should be reported to line agencies or local government, noting that elevating local issues may mean they are seen as being of district or metropolitan significance and thus be treated and resourced as such
- how each finding could inform an evaluation framework
- who can achieve the outcomes (government influence versus market influence)
- which findings should influence the development of spatial scenarios
- the distinction between what outcomes are simply desired versus those that can be delivered
- that some findings evolve straight into objectives and actions, whereas others go through the whole synthesis process.

The output from this activity is the emerging set of objectives that will guide the development of the plan and the evidence for why intervention is required.

- **Integrating the findings**. This task identifies the interdependencies and potential enablers and/or inhibitors to achieve integrated outcomes and should build on the learnings from the previous two tasks. The SWOT analysis technique is a principal tool.

  Aim to enhance and achieve significant opportunities and strengths and remove or unblock threats and constraints, leaving the more general issues to be addressed by line agencies. The focus is on metropolitan and district issues that directly reflect the project objectives and scope. As already noted, the wider the responsibilities of a plan, the more resources must be spread across many areas.

  The output will be the emerging spatial plan for the city and the interventions required to achieve it, including infrastructure investments and land use requirements.
- **The SWOT analysis**. A SWOT analysis is one tool that can assist in distilling the results of analysis into meaningful findings. Sometimes there is confusion in separating strengths from opportunities or weaknesses from threats. To simplify this task, it is useful to focus strengths and weaknesses on internal factors of a place and opportunities and threats to external issues. I also prefer to undertake an iterative process that examines issues thematically and then collectively. The collective SWOT is the most important to assist in direction setting and the identification of objectives. Thematic assessments are useful for confirming with external agencies the significance of specific issues.
- **Cultural landscapes**. The knowledge gained from learning about Country should be one of the thematic areas to inform a SWOT analysis. It should

address the findings from the research responding to First Nations Country, community and culture as outlined in Sects. 14.2.3, 14.3.2, and 15.3.2
- **Towards an evaluation framework**. To move from the research findings to a vision and direction needs an evaluation framework to underpin decisions on specific interventions and investments. Base the evaluation metrics on the assumptions underpinning the research findings.

  Across all the research areas there are likely to be diverse evaluation metrics from the levels of heritage significance, reflecting the principles of the Burra Charter (refer to the website link under further reading) to catchments (number of dwellings) for a school, which can inform an evaluation framework.

  These evaluation measures generally address one of the following issues: efficiency, equity, threshold capacity, levels of service, levels of health, levels of significance, and supply versus demand relationships.

  In establishing an evaluation framework, determine which evaluation metrics reflect:
  – the issues of metropolitan or district significance
  – the project objectives
  – the types of choices to be considered, such as expanding the urban footprint of the city or managing urban renewal and congestion
  – the degree to which community expectations (social norms) are considered. Most treasury departments would say the cost and implications of accepting the social norms should be explicitly stated.

  While the evaluation framework will evolve, it needs to be clear by the time you reach the scenario assessment and direction settings stages.

  From this task you will have an emerging set of performance metrics that guide the evaluation of scenarios and proposed directions and ultimately the ongoing measurement of the performance of the plan.

8.3.2 Integration and Interdependencies

In accordance with the words attributed to Aristotle—"the whole is greater than the sum of its parts"—synthesising the research findings is about integration and the search for interdependencies, opportunities and the unique. Where systems intersect, many opportunities to leverage outcomes occur. For example, where multiple rail lines intersect at an interchange, the enhanced accessibility of that location attracts activity and potentially makes it a place to focus specific land uses such as health and education facilities. This activity creates feedback that creates the opportunity for further transport investments and activity attraction.

Integrating the findings and searching for interdependencies starts with an understanding of the evaluation considerations such as efficiency, threshold capacity, levels of significance, and supply versus demand relationships. These in turn allow a distillation of what is important—specifically issues of district or metropolitan significance and thus issues that warrant consideration in a metropolitan plan.

With this knowledge, the process of integration becomes a multi-layered and iterative task through the assessment of like groupings of the systems that make up the city. Importantly the word 'like' here does not simply mean a thematic view, such as environmental considerations; instead, 'like' refers to systems that interact with each other. Once individual groups are evaluated then consideration can be given to all the attributes in a single assessment.

> *For me, clarity of the significance of integration occurred in a meeting when working on a project at the then City of Waverley in Melbourne. I drew a diagram to explain the importance of the linkages between different city systems (land use, environment, etc) showing each system and the links between them, the critical points of connection, and where interventions usually are focused, as distinct from the individual systems.*

The groupings to assess are:

- Country or blue-green grid (waterways and open space corridors), physiography, biodiversity, First Nations heritage (including trails), utilities, cycle and pedestrian desire lines, visual values, climatic conditions, government-owned land (all three levels) and natural hazards.
  - Focus on missing connections, dual use, amenity enhancements, protection, negative impacts.
  - Once the assessments are undertaken add two additional layers—housing and centres—to help you identify what is unique and any deficiencies.
- Arterial roads and motorway network, rail freight network, road freight network, intermodal terminals, industrial areas, industry sectors and major centres.
  - Focus on transport connectivity, efficiency of logistics and land use sequencing.
- Locations for knowledge economy jobs, health and education facilities, educational attainment, knowledge start-up businesses, areas of socio-economic disadvantage, and top performing primary and secondary schools.
  - Focus on the financial and economic independence of households.
- Housing, centres and public transport network.
  - Focus on land use and access barriers.
- Housing (labour market), employment concentrations, and public transport and road-based networks.
  - Focus on barriers to access.

> *This was a major issue for the Greater Sydney Region Plan, when considering opportunities to grow activity in Parramatta, where investigations showed limited catchments to labour markets by public transport, for what had been Greater Sydney's recognised second CBD for 50 years. The response was the proposal for potentially three new train links/mass transit corridors to serve the centre.*

- Socio-economic values, tertiary facilities, and public transport.
  - Focus on barriers to access.

- Urban tree canopy, climatic conditions, urban form, overhead utilities, remnant vegetation, biodiversity within the hinterland.
  – Focus on barriers to tree canopy, wildlife corridors and biodiversity enhancements and protection.
- Tourism attractions, transport networks, centres and natural amenity.
  – Focus on the amenity of the journey and opportunities for supporting activities such as hospitality and accommodation.

The issue of the quality of the journey has been emphasised by tourism agencies in the planning for the hinterland of Melbourne, to ensure visitors experience a rural setting as they travel to Ballarat (avoidance of ribbon development), so it is perceived to be a place separate from Melbourne, a journey through the countryside.

Groupings are not limited to those above; through experience you will learn to identify the groupings which best reflect the issues for the specific city or place. The groupings and issues change with the different planning typologies, though the logic and process remain the same).

In the preparation of the Greater Sydney Region Plan we undertook a spatial grouping of economic attributes. Data on educational outcome and economic precincts revealed one of the fundamental drivers for the spatial plan - a clear demarcation of economic opportunities for the residents of Greater Sydney. The analysis maps are shown in Fig. 8.3.

Reiterating here, the principal assessment tool—the SWOT analysis—needs to include both spatial and thematic assessments. In undertaking the analysis you need to identify what will enable the emerging desired outcomes; simply identifying strengths, weakness, opportunities and threats is insufficient. Again, issues in the SWOT should be of district or metropolitan significance. Furthermore, in terms of a response, consider whether the issue will be addressed through business-as-usual activities or whether intervention is required.

8.3.3 First Nations and Synthesis and Direction Setting

Many of the integrations and interdependencies outlined in Sect. 8.3.3 and associated groupings have a First Nations lens. Working with First Nations Country, community and culture at the direction setting stage is vital and can help to elevate perspectives:

- First Nations Knowledges relating to Country, her systems and values can help to inform spatial considerations and decisions
- Understanding the traditional movement corridors and pathways used by First Nations communities will give context about the best way to move through Country
- Spending time working with Traditional Custodians and knowledge holders can reveal pre-contact uses of Country and inform spatial decision-making.

Fig. 8.3 Overlay of economic data sets for Greater Sydney
(The map on the left highlights the spatial distribution of several attributes, as outlined in the legend. Collectively they reveal a distinct pattern, shown on the map on the right, where those residents north of the line have a higher level of access to institutions or specialised employment and thus higher levels of employment choice and opportunities) (*Source* Unpublished data, Greater Sydney Region Plan [2018] Published with permission from Greater Cities Commission)

For example, the University of Sydney is located in a place of learning and gathering
- First Nations housing and typologies that are culturally responsive are critical in strategic planning
- Access to employment and tertiary education is vital in achieving self-determination
- Protection of Country is central to First Nations cultural frameworks and should be integrated into strategic planning
- Accessing Country and sharing knowledge through tourism opportunities is a key aspiration for many First Nations people.

8.3.4 The Importance of Narratives

Presenting findings as narratives remains a core requirement, especially as you seek support from ministers and other agencies for the emerging vision and directions.

All findings do not need to be turned into emotive narratives. What is needed is a way to describe them, so they become more than just data. In the first instance, aim to develop narratives within each research area.

What is required is a deliberative approach to storytelling.

> When working on what was to become the metropolitan plan for Greater Sydney – 'A Plan for Growing Sydney', I was talking with the Director General about the significance of the change that was occurring in Western Sydney. The technical story was that in the long term the area would grow to have more than 350,000 dwellings. Such a statistic does not mean much, it is just a big number. However, when I switched to a narrative that emphasised that west of the M7 Motorway would, in the long term, be a city the size of Adelaide, I had the Director General's attention. I could then talk about the need for universities, hospitals, etc.
>
> The moral here is, often we are too close to our own analysis. There is a need to step back and change a story from one simply about facts and figures, to one that resonates with decision-makers.

For those interested there is literature on this topic which provides support for the importance of effective storytelling. For example, from an article by Hulst (2012, p. 312) in the journal *Planning Theory*:

> Researchers like Forester, Throgmorton and Sandercock have done an excellent job in 'translating' the concepts and ideas of story and storytelling into the planning domain and 'to render them accessible and useful for planning and its practices' (Friedmann, 2008: 248). They have taught us to see both the importance of storytelling in everyday planning and the possibilities of storytelling in future planning processes.

Conveying narratives, does not necessarily require a narrative to be told. How information is presented is an equally important skill. Here the task is more about showing a flow of thought or the logical connection between several findings which leads you to a clear conclusion.

The importance of storytelling for First Nations people aligns with the need to consider a narrative for the project. Positioning the need for change within storytelling will help to convey emotions and articulate the vision in a format that will help to connect with individuals. The oral traditions of First Nations Knowledges was key to passing down important information, repetition was generally used to ensure the integrity of the message.

Figure 8.4 shows an example of how connecting individual pieces of housing data can take us from the why to the emerging priorities. In this case, integrated assessments in six areas—housing data (as shown), housing in demographics, long-term housing supply, growth areas (greenfield), housing affordability and apartments—were then brought together in an overarching narrative (logic diagram), refer Fig. 8.5.

8.4 Scenario Development and Evaluation

The most important task for any plan is to understand the implications of projected growth and change for the city, with analysis directed to whether business-as-usual activities will be sufficient to accommodate the growth and change.

8.4.1 The Evaluation Process

The initial output of this assessment is typically called a base case. Scenarios are developed and evaluated in response to the base case being recognised as inadequate.

Briefly, the principal activities are:

- **Confirmation of the growth and change equation**. The vision for cities is influenced by expectations of the levels of growth and change, recognising that not all cities grow, nor is growth evenly spread. Furthermore, the implications of growth and change impact the infrastructure planning of most, if not all, agencies, service providers and utility organisations. Therefore, it is critical that there be some whole of government forum for the peer review of the assumptions and methodology underpinning the growth and change equation.
- **Assessment of business as usual**. Scenarios allow us to explore and understand the implications of alternative futures against an understanding of the business-as-usual future. Generally, the scenarios and the business-as-usual options focus on the spatial implications of growth and change, together with what infrastructure is needed to support them.

  The business-as-usual case also needs to consider if other social, economic and environmental aspects of the city will be impacted. Here, I emphasise that

8.4 Scenario Development and Evaluation

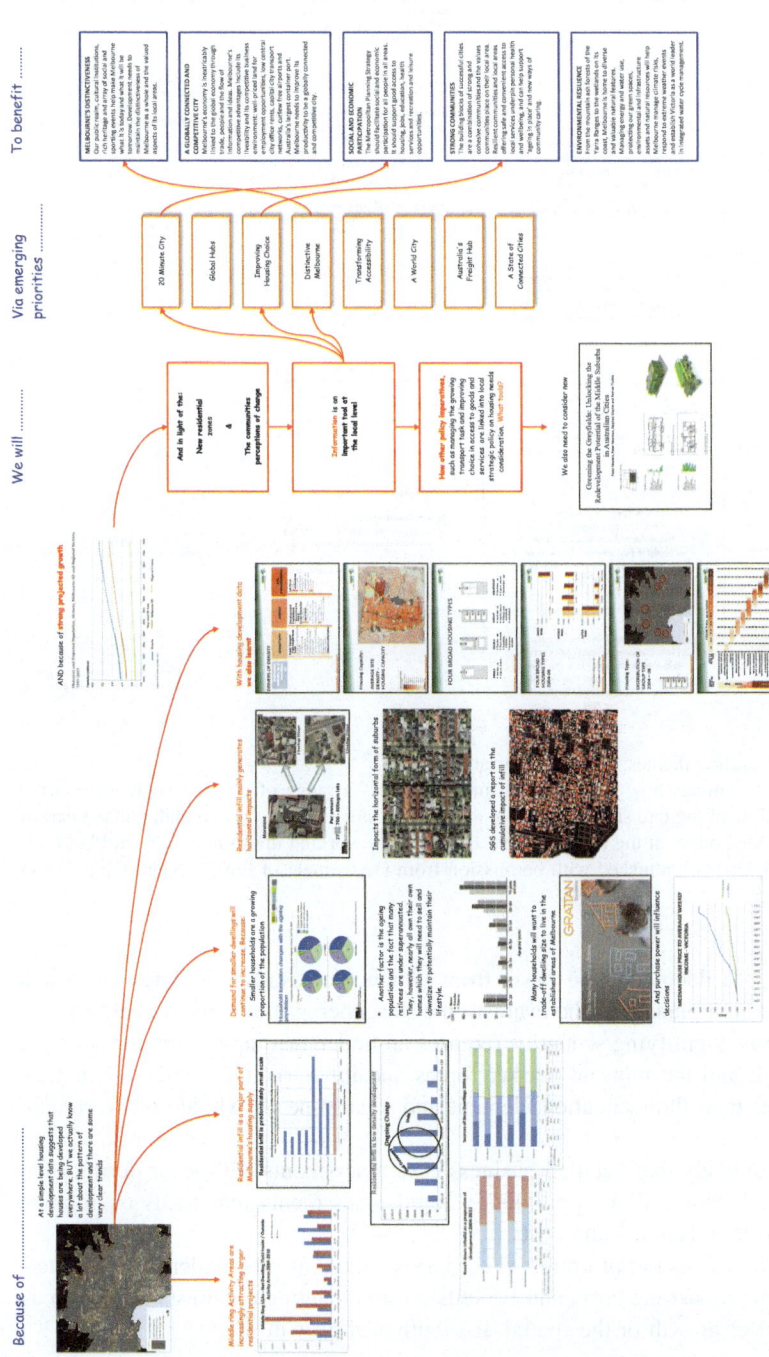

Fig. 8.4 Integrating themes - understanding housing #1 - housing development data (This diagram shows a flow of logic across different data sets (the principal findings) to inform a narrative as to how the housing analysis informed the emerging priorities of the plan) (*Source* Unpublished working draft material from Plan Melbourne, draft [2013]. Published with permission from Department of Environment, Land, Water and Planning)

Fig. 8.5 Integrating themes: a housing narrative
(This diagram outlines how the principal findings across a range of housing areas were structured into a flow of logic to simply structure the housing story (narrative) that underpinned part of the plan for Melbourne at the time) (*Source* Unpublished working draft material from Plan Melbourne, draft [2013], Published with permission from Department of Environment, Land, Water and Planning)

we need to document the basis from which the research findings suggest a response in a plan, with the evaluation criteria being the focus of decisions.

- **Scenarios**. Identifying scenarios requires an understanding of how they will be achieved, and the relevant market forces and infrastructure choices. This task is harder than the evaluation element and ideally needs whole-of-government input.

It is unlikely that detailed business case assessments will occur during Step 3; instead, they will be preliminary rapid assessments that focus on relative differences in benefits and costs.

Sensitivity testing of preferred scenarios should also be undertaken to determine how robust the costs and benefits are to changing circumstances, such as the level of growth or the spatial distribution of growth.

- **Evaluation**. Transparency is important here. There will not be much difficulty in economic assessments; the challenge is bringing in the social and environmental issues, which are not so easily monetised.

  To address this, multi-criteria assessments are often used. They bring all the evaluations together into a single framework. The type of assessments can vary in complexity from simple 'traffic light' tabulations of specified criteria against the individual scenarios to sophisticated assessments utilising complex methods for weighting each individual criterion. An article by Carli et al. (2018) provides a good introduction.

  Ultimately evaluation criteria must be traced back to the research findings and/or reflect recognised industry standards. For example, benefit-cost ratios are used in assessing transport infrastructure projects, where state treasury departments typically have guidelines, as is the case in NSW.

8.4.2 The Multi-Criteria Analysis Method

Infrastructure Australia released a report on multi-criteria analysis in July 2021—*Guide to multi-criteria analysis*. It provides a step-by-step guide on designing and applying the multi-criteria analysis method to infrastructure delivery.

The assessment criteria are structured in three layers (Infrastructure Australia, 2021, p. 21):

- Strategic Fit—Is there a clear rationale for the proposal?
  - Case for change
  - Alignment
  - Network and system integration
  - Solution justification
  - Stakeholder endorsement.
- Societal Impact—What is the value of the proposal to society and the economy?
  - Quality of life
  - Productivity
  - Environment
  - Sustainability
  - Resilience.
- Deliverability—Can the proposal be delivered successfully?
  - Ease of implementation
  - Capability and capacity
  - Project governance
  - Risk
  - Lessons learnt.

For those looking to explore this topic more, here is a list of a few articles as a starter (a full reference for each is provided at the end of the chapter):

- Awasthi, A, S.S. Chauhan, SS, Goyal, SK (2010) A multi-criteria decision-making approach for location planning for urban distribution centers under uncertainty
- Carli, R, Dotoli, M, Pellegrino, R, (2018) Multi-criteria decision-making for sustainable metropolitan cities assessment
- Egilmez, G, Gumus, S, Kucukvar, M, (2015) Environmental sustainability benchmarking of the U.S. and Canada metropoles: An expert judgment-based multi-criteria decision making approach
- Kiker, GA, Bridges, TS Varghese, A Seager, TP, and Linkovjj, I, (2005) Application of Multicriteria Decision Analysis in Environmental Decision Making
- Mosadeghi, R, Warnken, J, Tomlinson, R, Mirfenderesk, H, (2015) Comparison of Fuzzy-AHP and AHP in a spatial multi-criteria decision making model for urban land use planning
- Patel, MR, Vashi, MP, Bhatt, BV, (2017) SMART – Multi-criteria decision-making technique for use in planning activities
- Velasquez, M and Hester, PT, (2013) *An Analysis of Multi-Criteria Decision Making Methods*

8.4.3 The Base Case: Business as Usual

Chapter 4 covered the purpose of strategic planning. At the heart of the discussion was the question of whether business-as-usual activities will meet the needs of people, their lives and the places they live in now and into the future. It is in Step 3 that we must answer this question. The notion of a base case is the focus of consideration.

The task is to understand the capacity of the city to accommodate the findings of the growth and change equation and whether expectations as to a desired future, can be achieved.

This task traditionally starts with projections of the distribution of population, housing and jobs and an assessment of their distributions in terms of future transport patterns.

The singular challenge is to understand what is meant by a 'base' case. The base case for transport planning assumes:

- Existing and committed infrastructure (such as for transport, education, health, and open space)
- Development opportunities informed by existing land use zones and related policies.

Consequently, it is not surprising that an analysis of base cases of more than 20 years shows a failure of a city to accommodate change when reasonable levels of growth are predicted. Thus, scenarios with new infrastructure investments and activity will likely show a benefit. Yet we know that governments have always intervened to manage growth and they allocate funds annually for a base level of infrastructure investment. Therefore, assuming no additional investment is different from what actually happens.

Additionally, from a land use perspective, it is difficult to determine the location of growth in the medium to long term as it will be influenced by infrastructure decisions.

For example, for Western Sydney, Greater Sydney Region Plan shows the potential for four rail extensions/connections to the committed North South Rail Link Stage 1. All four options are identified for investigation (not delivery) in the 0–10 year period. Once investigations are completed it is unlikely that all will be delivered at once; rather, they will be prioritised.

The challenge for base case planning is where to allocate the growth for greenfield areas in the medium and long term, knowing that each of the four rail projects will influence growth distribution, yet nothing is committed. Thus, from one perspective, base case planning can be seen to be a bit of a *Catch 22* exercise.

This simple example is the challenge at the heart of all base case planning. Furthermore, distribution will influence the local planning for schools, roads and utility infrastructure.

As there appears to be no numerical solution to this base case dilemma, transparency is key. Even for a base case, there is potentially the need for scenarios to accommodate medium to long-term growth when there is an absence of evidence for its distribution. I recognise this view is challenging as infrastructure assessments require a base case against which benefits and costs can be assessed.

8.4.4 Importance of the Growth and Change Equation

Typically, discussion about the future of cities focuses on population 'growth'. Here the emphasis is on growth and **'change'** as population, housing and jobs growth across cities is not uniform—some areas can decline. Figure 8.6 shows how, for Melbourne, the population of some individual suburbs waxes and wanes even though at the metropolitan level there has essentially been continued growth for 100 years.

In addition, not all cities grow; some are stable, and some cities decline. Detroit is one example where its population has declined by more than a million people since its peak of 1.85 million in 1950 (refer to website link). Similarly, the population of London peaked at approximately 8.5 million around 1939 but declined to less than 7 million around the 1980s and 1990s and it was not until 2018 that the population grew back past 8.5 million (refer website link). Understanding growth and change for a city, therefore, needs both a temporal and spatial view to ensure metropolitan and local planning can best respond to the dynamics of cities.

Understanding levels of growth and change can also inform an understanding of the influence of growth on the dynamics of a city. West (2018) suggests that as the population of a city grows there are measurable relationships between the

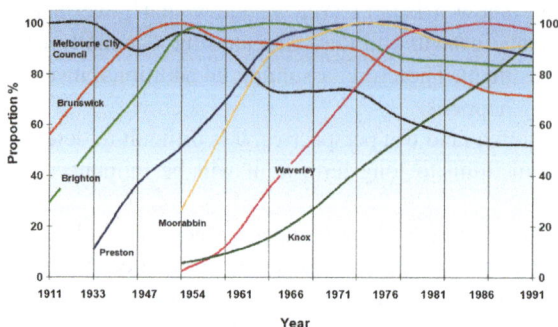

Fig. 8.6 Population changes over time for selected local government areas across Melbourne (This diagram highlights how the population of local government areas across Melbourne grow and decline over time) (*Source* Unpublished working draft material from Plan Melbourne, draft [2013] Published with permission from Department of Environment, Land, Water and Planning))

amount of growth and various aspects of city life. For example, population growth sees improved income and economic output yet an increase in the crime rate, where the rates of change are consistent across cities (that is, consistency in terms of the level of change in the context of the level of growth). West's conclusions suggest that the monitoring of change in cities should measure differences to those identified in research as distinct from just reporting on identified changes. Strategic planning should seek to reduce the negatives and enhance the positives.

8.4.5 An Evaluation Framework

The evaluation framework outlines the assumptions that will be used to evaluate the performance of business-as-usual activities. It supports decisions on both individual objectives and scenario evaluations.

Evaluation measures should cover issues of:

- **Performance** including financial feasibility, economic feasibility, sustainability measures and measurable outcomes
- **Delivery** including timing, sequencing, establishment requirements (such as enabling legislation, rezoning requirements), contribution to long-term goals, political risk due to impact (demolition of homes), or community expectations (political support).

When developing an evaluation framework consider:

- If performance metrics are readily available and based on the research findings - not all measures of performance can be monetised, but this does not mean that they are not influential—see the example of Fig. 8.7—this is highly effective in conveying the importance of an issue when engaging with decision-makers.

8.4 Scenario Development and Evaluation

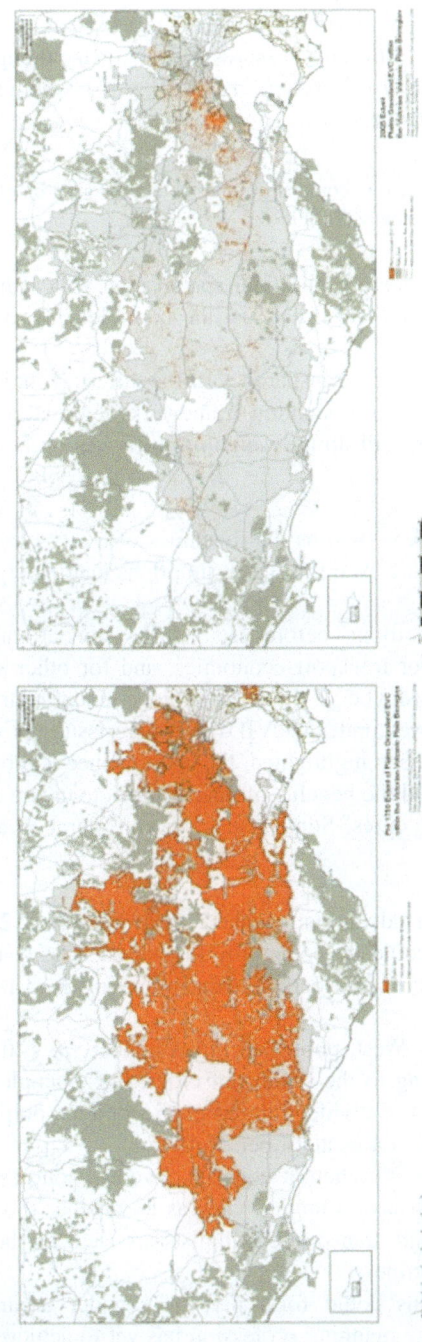

Fig. 8.7 The decline of the Victorian Plains Grasslands, pre 1780–2005 (This diagram highlights the extent of grasslands across western Victoria, pre-European occupation (the diagram to the left) compared to what remained in 2005 (the diagram to the right). Collectively these two diagrams set a visual context, significant at that, to the biodiversity assessments that informed the metropolitan planning at the time) (*Source* Unpublished working draft material from Delivering Melbourne's Newest Sustainable Communities [2010]. Published with permission from Department of Environment, Land, Water and Planning)

- How different types of performance measures can be brought into a common framework, such as the multi-criteria assessment tool.
- How the issue of relative importance of different measures can be addressed, and the concept of weighting different measures. A cautionary thought here is emphasised by Fainstein, in her book *A Just City* (2010, p.16), where she makes a point that reflects this challenge.

> If the content of justice is defined by community, and the city is made up of diverse communities, whose definition should prevail, …

- How the evaluation of scenarios and the final spatial plan will address wider issues that influence spatial outcomes, not just the core elements of housing, people, jobs and transport.
- Whether decision-makers will have transparency of the differing choices within the individual areas of a singular evaluation framework. Ultimately decision-makers, specifically ministers, will do the weighting of issues on behalf of the community.

The benefit of such a framework is that, as the dynamics of a city change, those assessing priorities in the future are aware of the assumptions that underpinned the earlier decisions.

Finally, there is still a way to go before establishing standard assessment methods, like those that exist for transport economics, and for other social and environmental aspects of cities. Maybe, in the wake of government restrictions on how we have had to live our lives under COVID-19, where issues of individual and community wellbeing have been highlighted, the consequence is more holistic assessment methods to understand the benefits of interventions to create more liveable, sustainable and productive cities. Some issues for consideration are briefly outlined here.

- The benefits of tertiary level education, touched on in Sect. 14.2.2 with the findings of Glaeser (2011), could be potentially monetised. The health sector is increasingly identifying economic benefits from pursuing land use related health initiatives.
- The recent work by Geoffrey West, published in his book *Scale* (2017), identifies a series of 'laws' relating to the scaling of cities. For example, if a city doubles in size there is a positive dividend in terms of economic outputs which appears to be consistent across cities at 14 per cent.
- There are constructs such as Marchetti's constant (average journey to work time). Again, planners do not have a unified view as to whether this principle is important. On the other hand, transport economists are clear on the value of a kilometre saved in journey time.
- These types of considerations could form part of a wider urban benefits assessment, something that the planning profession has yet to achieve.

8.4.6 Net Community Benefit

Planning interventions seek a public (societal) benefit. Ideally in the preparation of a city plan evidence will demonstrate that the vision will achieve public benefits not otherwise achieved through business-as-usual activities.

This is a significant issue, in that the more correct statement should be that the plan achieves a net community benefit—one where the total benefits derived exceed the total costs incurred. In this context McHarg (1967, p. 32) states "The best route is the one that provides the maximum societal benefit, at the least social cost."

The challenge for land use planning, as distinct from transport planning, is one of evaluation and measurement. For city planning in Australia, planners have yet to adopt a systematic method for evaluating net community benefit. In part, I believe, planners have not come to a consensus on how to measure social and environmental costs and benefits, as distinct from economic benefits, which are generally well understood.

Spiller (2022) argues that economist have developed methods to calculate most social and environmental costs and benefits as part of the application of the cost-–benefit analysis approach. More importantly, he argues that an advantage of the cost–benefit analysis method is its transparency, thus allowing third-party peer review and examination.

Spiller (2022) further emphasises that the cost–benefit analysis method is used by most agencies wishing to determine if a new public intervention should occur. However, the planning profession has not adopted such an approach and thus net community benefit is determined on a case-by-case basis.

There are a couple of reasons why city planning needs to resolve a structured approach to assessing net community benefit, such as via the cost–benefit analysis approach:

- Increasingly city planning is seen as a core area of public policy. In my experience it was not always so.
- Significant government resources are allocated to transport and health projects where cost–benefit analysis is utilised. This is not the case for 'planning' interventions, in Australia at least.
- In 2022 there are numerous global challenges such as climate change, supply chains and the continued impacts of the COVID-19 pandemic. Collectively these issues are creating significant demands on government resources. Those agencies which can best articulate the benefits, and cost, of proposed initiatives are likely to be best positioned to have their initiatives resourced.

8.5 Scenario Typologies

Scenarios assist in establish a spatial distribution of activities that best meet the needs of people, their lives, and the places to live in, now and into the future. There are two principal tasks, developing the scenarios and then evaluation of the scenarios. This section covers the scenario development task.

In undertaking this task, recognise that scenarios are just that—scenarios. They are only the best assessment of a possible future; they are not a statement of fact.

Scenarios are also often linked to conceptual urban growth models for a city such as containment or dispersed development, as these models often reflect well understood development processes and generic cost–benefit analysis techniques, which provide a context for understanding the potential impact of different scenarios.

There are different approaches for developing the different elements that make up a scenario (housing, employment, and transport), which I discuss further in the next sections.

Where possible, scenarios should be informed by related research findings, such as the need to enhance pedestrian networks, which could influence the location of houses or public transport when developing scenarios.

Sensitivity testing, another important task, tests the robustness of a scenario under different hypothetical conditions, such as higher or lower growth levels or more or less growth on the fringe of the city.

8.5.1 Housing Scenarios

Housing scenarios help you understand how to create additional supply where research indicates a deficiency and/or the need to achieve wider societal objectives, such as walkable communities, creating by planning for housing supply close to shops, open space, health and education precincts and employment nodes.

Housing scenarios are influenced by housing markets and demographic trends. Housing research reveals that people restrict their locational preferences to certain areas in a city; thus, scenarios need to consider supply in each housing sub-market. Demographic trends highlight a range of issues such as the location of household formations and whether older people are staying in their homes or downsizing.

At a macro level, housing scenarios typically identify choices in greenfield development (estate by estate), incremental infill (lot by lot), and planned urban renewal (precinct by precinct) as there are usually historic data sets for each of these. They also provide control for managing local distributions.

The details behind the drivers of demand as well as supply side issues are outlined in Sects. 14.2.1, 14.5.1, and 14.5.2.

8.5.2 Employment Scenarios

Employment scenarios are complex as they require an understanding of differing distribution patterns for a range of business typologies. Modelling needs to reflect business location decisions, not simply a single generalised employment model. I describe the principal employment distribution typologies below.

- **Retail**. The distribution of retail development generally reflects the distribution of the population. There is also a hierarchy of centres, though it is becoming increasingly blurred with the continued expansion of bulky goods (large format) retailing away from traditional shopping areas, together with increased online retailing.

    Within established areas the distribution of centres generally does not change, larger centres just tend to become larger. There are few examples of new centres, such as Victoria Gardens in Melbourne, together with the development of bulky goods retailing in industrial areas.
- **Industrial**. Development generally seeks cheap flat land with good vehicular access to one or motorways, airports, ports, freight rail or inland ports.

    Generally, governments plan and provide for a sufficient long-term supply of industrial land. In some cases, the issue is more about the timely delivery of infrastructure to support the release of land for subdivision and development.

    Projections for industrial activity relate to the 'take up' of vacant land for new development. Governments have data bases on this, such as the Victorian Government's Urban Development Program (refer website reference). The other more challenging task is estimating employment within industrial areas. Consider the ongoing evolution of industrial areas and their intensification, which requires assessments of historic trends and comparisons with similar areas.

    In more recent times a contested policy area has been whether the existing inner and middle suburb industrial areas should be retained.
- **Standalone office development**. Predicting the location of office development is difficult. In Australia's capital cities, central CBD locations dominate, and suburban locations do not reflect the distribution of the population. Furthermore, the pattern of suburban development differs between the capital cities but is generally limited to defined office precincts and/or inner-city locations.

    There is limited evidence of governments successfully creating new office precincts, which generally need to reach a scale of 100,000 m^2 of floor space before they are recognised by the market as attractive locations.

    A report prepared as an input for the Greater Sydney district plans outlines the locational issues for office development (refer website link).

Understanding the distribution of employment requires an understanding of demand and supply considerations for centres, which are influenced by the typologies outlined earlier. This is due to the high proportion of jobs in centres. For example, in Greater Sydney around 50 per cent of all employment is in the 40 identified metropolitan and strategic centres; if this list is expanded to the largest

200 centres for the whole of Greater Sydney the percentage grows to nearly 70 per cent (refer website link). Thus, to best prepare employment projections you should undertake background research on the growth potential of centres including the enablers and inhibitors for growth.

This concentration of employment in centres may be challenged in the near future as the implications of working from home and emerging flexible business operations play out. The result may be a greater proportion of jobs within suburban areas. This has been a long-term goal of planners and potentially would achieve wider benefits such as reduced travel demand and improved individual wellbeing. Consequently, actions may be taken to facilitate such an outcome.

One challenge for employment projections is the peculiarity of different models. Some models such as the computable general equilibrium (CGE) model have the ability for sensitivity testing of a range of economic impacts but are generally limited to whole of metropolitan area analysis. More bespoke models focus on small areas utilised for retail planning modelling, which focus on the catchment areas of individual centres. There are benefits in utilising both when you need to understand employment changes across a city.

When utilising models for small areas, dealing with the aspirations of the local community can be challenging. Often there is a desire for higher employment numbers; however, employment projections are linked to populations (the working age) and participation rates. Thus, at any one time, the total number of jobs for a metropolitan area is generally fixed, and if the numbers for one local area are increased then another area must go down. Otherwise, assumptions on total growth need to be re-examined.

8.5.3 Transport Scenarios

Transport models are developed through an iterative process that utilises metrics from the current performance of road and public transport networks together with projections of housing and jobs as inputs to well-developed transport models. With these inputs, the models are then used to test the influence of new transport proposals (scenarios) on network performance.

Therefore, the development of transport scenarios is influenced by assumptions on both the location of housing and employment as well as how transport investments may further influence their location.

Transport scenarios are also influenced by the assessment of costs and benefits of proposed infrastructure investments, as distinct from simply being based on network impacts.

The testing of transport options generally takes the 'predict and provide' path where capacity constraints drive the search for opportunities. The challenge in this pathway is that the model aims to identify options that improve the performance of the existing system, based on current usage patterns plus the impact of growth.

Thus, new infrastructure always builds on and benefits the existing transport networks (the status quo), in the context of growth, not necessarily a future vision based on the needs of the whole community.

Consequently, where there is high congestion and increasing demand, scenarios will likely come out favourably. That is, reflecting the principle of increasing returns, as outlined by Waldrop (1992), those who have, get more; or, more specifically, the current structure of the city potentially locks it into certain pathways. Conceptually this reflects the thinking behind complexity theory, which was briefly outlined in Sect. 5.3.8.

The specific challenge for city planning is to explore options based on wider outcomes such as equity in access, with a focus on a long-term view of the land use and transport structure of the city, as distinct from an incremental process focused on the here and now (which in one sense stays in the here and now).

The Greater Sydney Region Plan used such an alternative pathway by adopting a vision and validated methodology. The difference is that the methodology seeks to identify a network to support the needs of the city at the end of the planning horizon (such as 20–40 years) and then is identified by working backwards to the most efficient prioritisation of projects.

Therefore, scenario planning for transport networks ideally should be an integrated process with land use systems.

8.6 Direction Setting

The activities in Step 3 are not strictly sequential; rather, an iterative process is required to enable alternative choices to be considered and evaluated. In particular, the process of setting directions is both informed by and informs the development of scenarios. I outline the principal activities for directions setting below.

8.6.1 Directions (Objectives) Setting

You will aim to establish a set of directions or objectives that set the frame for the more detailed elements of the plan.

8.6.1.1 Varied Nomenclature

Tables 8.1 and 8.2 highlight the varied nomenclature used for describing the desired outcomes for Australia's capital cities and a select number of international cities.

My review of a cross-section of plans highlights that within planning there is not a standard approach to describing the outcomes which will deliver on the vision for a place.

In NSW, legislation specifies the use of the terminology—Objective (Part 3, Division 3.1, Sect. 3.3 of the Environmental Planning and Assessment Act 1979 *No 203* [NSW]).

Table 8.1 Nomenclature of capital city plans

Capital city	Nomenclature used in each plan
Australian Capital Territory	Strategic directions, directions, and actions
Adelaide	Principles, policy themes, policies, and actions
Darwin	Objectives
Greater Sydney	Directions, objectives, strategies, and actions
Melbourne	Principles, outcomes, directions, and policies
Perth	Principles and objectives
South East Queensland	Goals, elements, and strategies

Source My review of Australia's capital city plans as listed in the section at the end of this chapter on further reading

Table 8.2 Nomenclature of international plans

International city plan	Nomenclature used in each plan
The London Plan	Policy
One NYC	Initiatives
Greater Golden Horseshoe (Toronto)	Policies
Metro Vancouver	Goal, strategies, and actions

Source My review of a selection of international metropolitan plans as listed in the section at the end of this chapter on Further reading

My preference is to use the nomenclature of objectives, with any grouping of objectives included under overarching heading of Directions.

8.6.1.2 Developing the Objectives

During Step 3, before priorities are set, identify between 20 and 50 objectives. Then, as a greater understanding of the options, choices and priorities emerge, group and potentially prioritise the objectives to allow a simpler narrative. This is an important step to allow the holistic nature of the plan to be easily understood.

The goal is to present a plan on a page see *Plan Melbourne* (2017, pp. 12–13) and the Greater Sydney Region Plan, *A Metropolis of Three Cities* (2018, pp. 22–23) refer Fig. 8.8

When developing the objectives, make sure to:

- reflect the research findings and/or the conclusions of the integration stage, that is, they are based on evidence
- identify the intervention required to meet the objective
- clarify what is meant, using more words than less, with supporting context that provides the rationale
- note that the activities of direction setting overlap and intersect with the scenario development and evaluation activity.

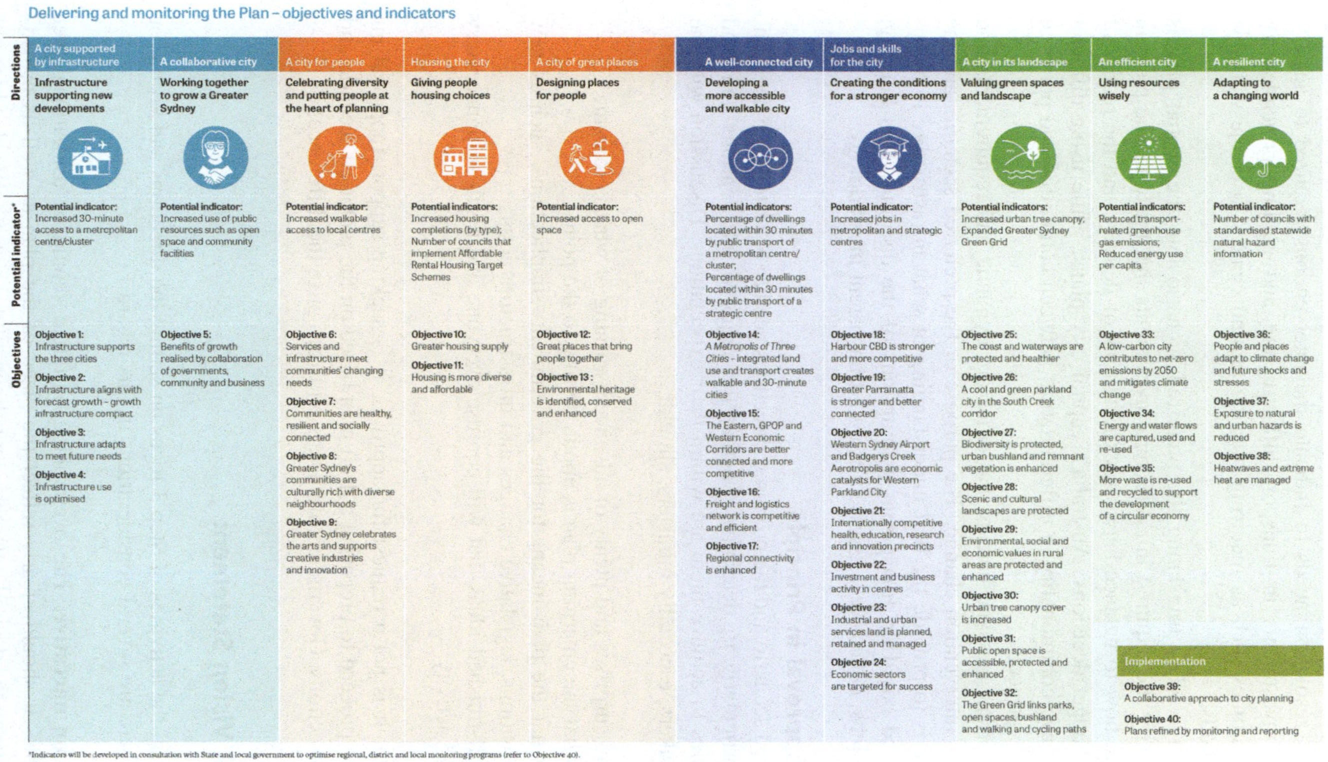

8.6 Direction Setting

Directions	A city supported by infrastructure	A collaborative city — Working together to grow a Greater Sydney	A city for people — Celebrating diversity and putting people at the heart of planning	Housing the city — Giving people housing choices	A city of great places — Designing places for people	A well-connected city — Developing a more accessible and walkable city	Jobs and skills for the city — Creating the conditions for a stronger economy	A city in its landscape — Valuing green spaces and landscape	An efficient city — Using resources wisely	A resilient city — Adapting to a changing world
Potential Indicator*	Potential indicator: Increased 30-minute access to a metropolitan centre/cluster	Potential indicator: Increased use of public resources such as open space and community facilities	Potential indicator: Increased walkable access to local centres	Potential indicators: Increased housing completions (by type); Number of councils that implement Affordable Rental Housing Target Schemes	Potential indicator: Increased access to open space	Potential indicators: Percentage of dwellings located within 30 minutes by public transport of a metropolitan centre/ cluster. Percentage of dwellings located within 30 minutes by public transport of a strategic centre	Potential indicator: Increased jobs in metropolitan and strategic centres	Potential indicators: Increased urban tree canopy; Expanded Greater Sydney Green Grid	Potential indicators: Reduced transport-related greenhouse gas emissions; Reduced energy use per capita	Potential indicator: Number of councils with standardised statewide natural hazard information
Objectives	Objective 1: Infrastructure supports the three cities. Objective 2: Infrastructure aligns with forecast growth – infrastructure compact. Objective 3: Infrastructure adapts to meet future needs. Objective 4: Infrastructure use is optimised	Objective 5: Benefits of growth realised by collaboration of governments, community and business	Objective 6: Services and infrastructure meet communities' changing needs. Objective 7: Communities are healthy, resilient and socially connected. Objective 8: Greater Sydney's communities are culturally rich with diverse neighbourhoods. Objective 9: Greater Sydney celebrates the arts and supports creative industries and innovation	Objective 10: Greater housing supply. Objective 11: Housing is more diverse and affordable	Objective 12: Great places that bring people together. Objective 13: Environmental heritage is identified, conserved and enhanced	Objective 14: A Metropolis of Three Cities – integrated land use and transport creates walkable and 30-minute cities. Objective 15: The Eastern, GPOP and Western Economic Corridors are better connected and more competitive. Objective 16: Freight and logistics network is competitive and efficient. Objective 17: Regional connectivity is enhanced	Objective 18: Harbour CBD is stronger and more competitive. Objective 19: Greater Parramatta is stronger and better connected. Objective 20: Western Sydney Airport and Badgerys Creek Aerotropolis are economic catalysts for Western Parkland City. Objective 21: Internationally competitive health, education, research and innovation precincts. Objective 22: Investment and business activity in centres. Objective 23: Industrial and urban services land is planned, retained and managed. Objective 24: Economic sectors are targeted for success	Objective 25: The coast and waterways are protected and healthier. Objective 26: A cool and green parkland city in the South Creek corridor. Objective 27: Biodiversity is protected, urban bushland and remnant vegetation is enhanced. Objective 28: Scenic and cultural landscapes are protected. Objective 29: Environmental, social and economic values in rural areas are protected and enhanced. Objective 30: Urban tree canopy cover is increased. Objective 31: Public open space is accessible, protected and enhanced. Objective 32: The Green Grid links parks, open spaces, bushland and walking and cycling paths	Objective 33: A low-carbon city contributes to net-zero emissions by 2050 and mitigates climate change. Objective 34: Energy and water flows are captured, used and re-used. Objective 35: More waste is re-used and recycled to support the development of a circular economy	Objective 36: People and places adapt to climate change and future shocks and stresses. Objective 37: Exposure to natural and urban hazards is reduced. Objective 38: Heatwaves and extreme heat are managed

*Indicators will be developed in consultation with State and local governments to optimise regional, district and local monitoring programs refer to Objective 40.

Implementation
Objective 39: A collaborative approach to city planning
Objective 40: Plans refined by monitoring and reporting

Fig. 8.8 Plan on a page: greater Sydney region plan
(This diagram is a copy of the plan on a page from the Greater Sydney Region Plan—*A Metropolis of Three Cities*. It outlines the 10 directions, objectives, and potential performance indicators of the plan) (Source *A Metropolis of Three Cities* [2018, pp. 22–23]. Published with permission from the Greater Cities Commission)

8.6.1.3 Preferred Scenario

The resolution of the preferred scenario is about identifying the preferred spatial plan. Its resolution needs to indicate the interventions required to achieve it, such as investments in transport infrastructure and guiding principles for land use outcomes such as requiring housing around centres to create walkable neighbourhoods.

A challenge when translating the preferred scenario into the spatial plan is how to classify the required infrastructure investments that make up the plan; in other words, how to balance between expectations of delivery and the reality of short-term budget decisions. Australia's capital city plans, while using different languages, have commonality in differentiating between committed and potential infrastructure projects.

The important message here is that cities are dynamic and requirements and priorities for intervention change. The purpose of the preferred scenario, and the spatial plan, is to provide the best understanding of what infrastructure is potentially required based on transparent assumptions of the distribution of housing, people and jobs, collectively assessed using a transparent methodology.

8.6.1.4 Approval in Principle

The preferred scenario and the proposed directions need to be tested with decision-makers, particularly to determine whether the required interventions and land use principles to achieve them are within their expectations. Discussion with the decision-makers, especially ministers, should:

- ensure no surprises and plenty of advanced warning of what is to come
- clarify what the emerging plan is about, getting to the point
- clarify what the plan means for the government—implications, such as new policy positions, legislative changes and infrastructure costs
- avoid half-finished ideas that will confuse everyone and result in unnecessary angst and activity.

At this point it is not a request for approval, it is seeking support (approval in-principle) to proceed to preparing a draft plan based on the preferred scenario and proposed directions. Government ministers will recognise the difference.

8.6.2 A Vision Statement

Ultimately all the activities of Step 3 focus on setting the directions and vision for the plan. There are several considerations in this regard:

- **The vision narrative**. The overarching narrative should be aspirational, yet achievable. It should clearly reflect the place of the plan as well as providing clarity on the desired outcomes—what constitutes success. We should avoid

high-level statements that could, on reflection, be for nearly any city. The vision should also reflect the expectations for change.
- **Imagery**. The vision can be more than words. Imagery that shows the desired outcomes can be powerful and after 20 years I still feel this example from the City of Casey's 2002 plan, *Casey C21: A vision for our future* is a good example of the use of imagery, refer Fig. 8.9.
- **More than just a paragraph**. Occasionally it is possible to encapsulate the vision for a place in a paragraph; however, my experience is to outline what is important and potentially why, including at least one map, takes more than a paragraph. At the other extreme, the Greater Sydney Region Plan (2018) vision covers 13 pages.
- **A pathway**. Some elements of a vision are seen to be big steps. In these cases, recognise that your plan is not the last. Thus, there can be benefit from providing a hook to allow for a project in the next version, or a delivery process to take up the detail and advance the issue.
- **Vision-led plans versus process-led visions**. Both pathways are equally valid. If the former pathway is pursued, it has more inherent risks for implementation as it will have been developed in the absence of an understanding of the interventions required to deliver it.
- **A First Nations response**. Where a process has included a partnership with the local First Nations community, the pathway for developing a vision will likely be different to traditional process. A more engaged and participatory process will likely see First Nations outcomes clearly embedded in the vision.

A final comment regarding the vision for a plan (Wolinski and Dalheim, circa 1995):

> *Strengths and resources will never show things of vision. By definition, things of vision require a quantum leap from existing conditions. Things of vision come out of a search for the 'unique' – which is also compatible with the culture of the region. A vision is not about a piece of land, it is about changing fundamental relationships and establishing new structures, systems, environments or ways of doing thing.*

By the end of Step 3, the emerging vision and direction of the plan should be supported by several preliminary outputs including a proposed urban structure (the spatial plan), potential transport networks, environmental assets to be managed, emerging narratives for the economy, infrastructure, the hinterland, health and education, and any emerging social, cultural, visual, and heritage priorities.

Fig. 8.9 Vision diagram from the City of Casey's 2002 strategy Casey C21: a vision for the future (This diagram, copied from the vision page of the City of Casey's 2002 city strategy *Casey C21: A vision for the future* highlights how imagery can be used to enhance the meaning of the printed words) (Source: *Casey C21: A vision for our Future*, City of Casey [2002] [Published with permission from City of Casey])

8.7 Implications for other planning typologies

Several issues need to be considered when applying the approach as outlined in this chapter to other planning typologies. These are outlined in Table 8.3 and considered in detail in Chapter 12.

Table 8.3 Applying the Step 3 approach to other planning typologies

Planning activity	Local government area plan	Town centre and regional centre plan	Greenfield community plan	Neighbourhood community plan
Evaluating options	n/a	Understanding the feasibility of potential projects (actions) including demand, design concepts, costs and benefits is critical to ensure expectations can be managed and that the final plan is deliverable	Changes in development assumptions can influence infrastructure (utilities) requirements and the need for activities linked to residential development, such as community facilities, schools and retailing. Therefore, scenarios need to test the impacts of changed development outcomes	In addition to examining land use options, you need to understand the implications of sequencing development on services delivery
Setting objectives	n/a	n/a	At the time of development, residentially development is typically the most profitable activity to undertake. Thus, consider the long-term needs of a community, and not just for the next 20 years	n/a

This table outlines how the planning activity undertaken for a metropolitan planning project in Step 3: synthesis and direction setting, needs to be adapted for the other city planning typologies. Additional detail is provided in Chapter 12

8.8 Summary

This chapter has outlined a critical step in the 7-Step Strategic Planning Process: the synthesis of the findings from Step 2 into the vision and directions (objectives) that will form the basis of the draft plan.

The pathway for achieving this occurs in three stages and is iterative in nature. The discussion outlined that the task occurs across three stages and emphasised the following issues:

- The importance of identifying the findings that are of district and metropolitan importance, as distinct from responding to every issue
- The need for an evaluation framework to guide the identification of objectives in the assessment of scenarios
- The importance of integrating the findings to identify interdependencies as these connections are likely to create the best opportunities for delivering the desired future
- The need to determine if a business-as-usual future is acceptable and, if not, the need to develop and evaluate scenarios which can accommodate the growth and change equation
- That not everything needs to be in the plan, some things should go to delivery agencies for business-as-usual management
- The importance of clarity when developing the objectives which will underpin the plan, specifically the need for each objective to be supported by a contextual statement
- The importance of engaging with other agencies in developing the directions and scenarios including seeking collective agreement on the major conclusions as the first step milestone in gaining ownership of the plan
- The importance of gaining in principle support from the decision-makers on the proposed direction before advancing on developing the detailed draft plan.

The outputs of Step 3 are the core of the draft plan and thus the activities will blur with the next step—the preparation of the draft plan.

8.8 Summary

8.8.1 Insights

Insight: Bringing it together
A hothouse only creates hot air.
Thinking takes time—John's law
Strategic thinking requires time for reflection and consideration.
I remember once at an interview for a project our team was asked whether we could undertake the project in a shorter time. John Stanley a member of our team responded by saying, yes, the actual tasks could be undertaken in a shorter time; however, it would be better if we had time to reflect on the analysis.
John Stanley is a highly regarded Australian advisor in the areas of sustainability and transport planning.
Synthesis is a step not just a word
Too often, lots of analysis is undertaken for a project then we jump into the design phase. However, the synthesis and direction setting step is when you bring all the analysis together and consider how it relates and interacts. It is at this point where you clearly define the problem. The final output from this step should be the strategic direction statements that indicate what your plan seeks to achieve. This last step may blur with design, so you need to refine the statements as you go forward, for it is this task that is the defining aspect of strategic planning.
Insight: Infrastructure projects
Make sure it's realistic
Over the years I have watched projects originally identified in a strategy many years earlier deemed unviable following more detailed cost benefit assessments. This is not necessarily new. The challenge for planners, and sometimes governments, is to openly abandon the project. The consequence is a project review every decade or so—typically with the same conclusion.

Insight: Where to find the answer?
Do not think about this place for what it is today, think about it for what it can be.
Brian Carter (circa 2002). Brian was the place maker in the team at the City of Casey, Melbourne.
Developing a plan is not a linear process, it is iterative
Sometimes pathways reveal themselves early which means they can be tested ahead of time. With this in mind, the strategic planning process is intended as a disciplined way of thinking and researching. Importantly, when ideas do emerge, still follow through on researching these ideas, as it will likely add depth and richness to the plan.
The future creates the future
Most of us recognise that we cannot change the world in a day; however, when things have changed, people in the future will see the world through different eyes than you do now. Thus, they will see new opportunities and therefore the need for change. You need to recognise this; thus, your plan (the answer) should not seek to solve all issues or resolve all details.
Part of the answer is not to resolve all things now. In most cases, city planning is about providing the community with a journey that has alternative choices, reflecting their aspirations. The key is to keep them on the path, but equally provide opportunities for the future community to determine how they will respond to a fork in the road.
It's not just about if you believe, but whether they believe
You need to get the faithful to believe in your plan. The more believers, the better chance you have of success. The faithful include politicians, public servants, agencies, developers and the general community. Related to this is understanding who coordinates the plan's implementation. State policies can fail because they neglect to understand who the project champion will be.

(continued)

(continued)

Insight: It is what differs that matters
It is not just centres that are different, suburbs differ, just as subregions, towns and whole cities differ. They differ not in what we see but also in their history, politics or economics. These elements collectively create a path dependency that influences the potential choices, and thus the future. It takes time to recognise that cities need different solutions, at different times, in different places. Hence the need to tailor your approach to different problems and places.

Insight: Start writing the plan
Start writing early
It is never too early to start writing the plan. While the strategic planning process is intended to be a stepped, iterative process, do not wait until the strategy stage to start writing. I have learnt this the hard way.
Once when we waited until the strategy stage to start the writing process, we found we never had the chance to sit back and review what we had written, as we were essentially writing the first draft right up to the approval stage.
So, start early. From day one you can write context sections.

When to bring in the editors
This can be a challenge for a team and one that needs consideration early. Firstly, there is a need to find good writers within the team. This should not be a spur of the moment task, but one where experience prevails, and is also about capacity building of the team. At a minimum you need consistency, clarity in language and plain English. The challenge is when you bring in editors too early you potentially lose the emotion and life that comes from the minds of those who have thought of the ideas or carried out the research.

Version control—Silvija's law
While writing a plan, particularly one that is written over a period of six months or more, archiving and version control are essential.
The head of a government department once told me of their experience of having to provide a decision-maker with an earlier version of a report, to clarify when a decision was made—you don't forget stories told to you by a Secretary, especially when you are in the process of writing a plan for that person.

A common driver of change may produce different outcomes across multiple cities
Urban renewal has been a major factor for accommodating growth in both Melbourne and Greater Sydney. However, in Melbourne, development has been predominantly centralised around the inner parts of the city, whereas in Greater Sydney it has been widely disbursed across the whole city. Consequently, it is not sufficient to simply identify a driver of change; deeper understandings are required.

Insight: quality control
Managing multiple authors—you need an editor
There is often a need for various parts of a plan to be written at the same time. It is also imperative that the future readers of the report do not experience many different voices talking to them, thus the critical need for a single editor to work with and provide guidance to the writers and review their work. Part of the role of the editor is to establish a range of grammatical rules up front, to ensure consistency of voice.

Checking the editing
Ultimately a single person on the team needs to be responsible for the content in the report, in my mind the project director. A challenge is the need to ensure meaning is not lost through final editing processes. A more critical issue is when key sentences or words are changed.
When preparing the plan for Greater Sydney we used different coloured fonts to distinguish between what text could not be altered and what was still in development.
You will need to work out your own process to manage this, including tracked changes. Employing an editor who has expertise in the planning field definitely helps.

It's a journey—the structure will change
People will want to see structure—provide it, then change it. That is, early on there will be requests from the senior executives for a first cut of the report structure, even an annotated version. Do not worry that it is not perfect. As narratives unfold during the course of the project, it will be relatively easy to modify the structure, as long as you are confident of the findings of your work.

(continued)

(continued)

In preparing the Greater Sydney Region Plan, we had our own need to reference back from time to time, fortunately we had Silvija on our team, who kept both soft and hard copies of edits and comments of the plan—a very large pile. The bottom line is, you need to keep copies, not just electronic copies, but hard copies of each version that has comments on it—you will need to refer to them!
Silvija Smits, a former principal planner at the then Greater Sydney Commission.

Insight: Options
Different options are based on different assumptions, reflect on what that means.
It's not about distinct options—it's about evaluating choices
Here is the logic. You state various assumptions, and these produce an answer, noting that different assumptions give different answers. However, these answers are not choices per se. The assumptions are the choices (options). Experience has told me that the community will reject a whole option due to the presence of a single element, even though after some discussion you establish that they like all other aspects of the option.
The harder task is to identify and communicate the different assumptions and seek comment on these. The trick is to learn how to isolate the assumptions, *and* to learn to sell elements of a strategy, not the whole. You need feedback on each piece. Workshops, open days and surveys are examples of the types of consultation required—the process must be some form of interactive discussion.
Options evaluation—defining success
Project briefs usually provide clarity as to the purpose of a project such as growing the economic opportunities of a town centre. What is not often provided is the definition of success—for example, the level of capital investment, the number of jobs created, increased rate revenue and/or related outcomes such as increased activity on the high street or an increased night-time economy. Gaining clarity from the decision-maker as to what is desired is therefore important when defining success criteria.

You need a style guide
As you progress through the writing of the report you need to ensure all working on various parts use similar writing rules, such as whether you capitalise titles and if you need a definitions page—my preference is no to the definitions page, it should be in plain English.
Delete the unnecessary
When writing a plan, one skill is learning to delete paragraphs, pages or even sections that have become obsolete, even though someone may have spent a lot of time crafting them.

Insight: Too little, too late
If the community is not on board and your delivery partners are not fully across the delivery tools, it could be back to the drawing board.
When to present the vision
One of the biggest challenges in engagement is when to present the vision. If it is presented before it has been fully developed, there is a chance that it may be accepted but in the end is not achievable, for a range of reasons. Conversely, if it is presented after it is fully developed there is a risk it will be challenged by the community, because the vision is seen as being a *fait accompli*, and their support will be lost.
Leadership in planning
The community planning process, if conducted effectively, is a useful tool for identifying the current and future needs of a community. However, the future, as seen by the community, is naturally from a personal perspective. It is unlikely to take into consideration a range of unseen elements that also influence or facilitate change.

(continued)

(continued)

Sometimes the research is only a benchmark against which you test the answer Never assume your research will necessarily provide the answer. Answers (visions) may appear to come out of left field. Many designers will suggest that they go straight to the answer. Whether this is the case or not is irrelevant here. Experience in planning cities demonstrates that the more researched conducted, to find the answer, the greater the longevity and robustness of the plan. The critical point is that if an answer does come out of left field it needs to be critically tested against the research findings. Analysis prepared after a vision has been found to be flawed.	A challenge is when the research and community views are at odds with each other. Such plans are often contentious as they are not always recognised by the community and are outside their view of the future. Thus, a researched plan may fail if the leadership element is not considered to ensure the community can walk the same path.

References

Awasthi, A, Chauhan, SS, & Goyal, SK (2010), 'A multi-criteria decision making approach for location planning for urban distribution centers under uncertainty', *Mathematical and Computer Modelling*, vol. 53, pp. 98–109.

Carli, R, Dotoli, M, & Pellegrino, R (2018), 'Multi-criteria decision-making for sustainable metropolitan cities assessment', *Journal of Environmental Management*, vol. 226, pp. 46–61.

City of Casey (2002), *Casey C21: A vision for our Future*. Unpublished.

De Bono, E (1967), *The Use of Lateral Thinking*, Penguin Books Australia, Limited, Ringwood, Australia.

— Outlines lateral thinking, a skill invaluable to strategic planners.

De Bono, E (1985), *Six Thinking Hats*, Penguin Books Australia, Limited, Ringwood, Australia.

— Moving beyond negative criticism.

Egilmez, G, Gumus, S, & Kucukvar, M (2015), 'Environmental sustainability benchmarking of the U.S. and Canada metropoles: an expert judgment-based multi-criteria decision making approach', *Cities*, vol. 42, pp. 31–41.

Fainstein, S (2010) *The Just City*, Cornell University Press, Ithaca, New York.

— Some clear principles to guide planning in a 'just' city.

Hulst (2012), 'Storytelling, a model of and a model for planning', *Planning Theory*, vol. 11, issue. 3, pp. 299–318.

— Brings together literature from a number of sources and connects them via a detailed case study.

Kiker, GA, Bridges, TS, Varghese, A, Seager, TP, & Linkovjj, I (2005), 'Application of multicriteria decision analysis in environmental decision making', *Integrated Environmental Assessment and Management*, vol. 1, issue 2, pp. 95–108.

Mosadeghi, R, Warnken, J, Tomlinson, R, & Mirfenderesk, H (2015), 'Comparison of Fuzzy-AHP and AHP in a spatial multi-criteria decision making model for urban land-use planning', *Computers, Environment and Urban Systems*, vol. 49, pp. 54–65.

Velasquez, M, & Hester, PT (2013), 'An analysis of multi-criteria decision making methods', *International Journal of Operations Research*, vol. 10, issue 2, pp. 56–66.

West, G (2018), *Scale, The Universal Laws of Life and Death in Organisms, Cities and Companies*, Hachette, Australia.
— Based on the research of hundreds of cities, this book outlines that there are relationships between the scale of cities and various attributes of cities.

Website Links

A Place to Grow, Growth Plan for the Greater Golden Horseshoe, 2020, Ministry of Municipal Affairs and Housing, Ontario. A Place to Grow: Growth plan for the Greater Golden Horseshoe | Ontario.ca.

BIS Shrapnel (2015), *Forecasting the Distribution of Stand Alone Office Development across Sydney to 2035* Unpublished. https://www.greater.sydney/background-material.

Burra Charter. https://australia.icomos.org/wp-content/uploads/The-Burra-Charter-2013-Adopted-31.10.2013.pdf.

Cost Benefit Analysis Guidelines, NSW Treasury. https://www.treasury.nsw.gov.au/finance-resource/guidelines-cost-benefit-analysis.

Department of Environment, Land, Water and Planning (2017), *Plan Melbourne*, The State of Victoria, Australia. https://www.planmelbourne.vic.gov.au/.

Detroit population decline. https://worldpopulationreview.com/us-cities/detroit-mi-population.

Environmental Planning and Assessment Act 1979 No 203 (NSW), viewed 16 June 2020. https://www.legislation.nsw.gov.au/~/view/act/1979/203.

Greater Sydney Commission (2018), A Metropolis of Three Cities, State of New South Wales, Australia. https://www.greater.sydney/metropolis-of-three-cities.

Infrastructure Australia (2021), *Guide to Multi-Criteria Analysis, Technical Guide of the Assessment Framework*. Assessment Framework 2021 Guide to multi-criteria analysis.pdf (infrastructureaustralia.gov.au).

Trust for London, *Population changes over the decades*, London. https://www.trustforlondon.org.uk/data/population-over-time/.

Patel, MR, Vashi, MP, & Bhatt, BV (2017), 'SMART – Multi-criteria decision-making technique for use in planning activities', *New Horizons in Civil Engineering*, Gujarat, India. (PDF) SMART-Multi-criteria decision-making technique for use in planning activities (researchgate.net).

Victorian Urban Development Program, Department of Environment, Land, Water and Planning. Urban Development Program (planning.vic.gov.au).

Australian Capital City and International Plans Website Links

A Metropolis of Three Cities (2018), State of New South Wales. https://www.greater.sydney/metropolis-of-three-cities.

ACT Planning Strategy 2018 (2018), Australian Capital Territory. https://www.planning.act.gov.au/act-planning-strategy.

Darwin Regional Land Use Plan 2015 (2015), Northern Territory Government, Department of lands, Planning and the Environment. https://planningcommission.nt.gov.au/projects/drlup.

Metro Vancouver 2040, Shaping Our Future, 2011, Updated 2020, Greater Vancouver Regional District Board. Regional Planning Services (metrovancouver.org).

OneNYC 2050 Building a Strong and Fair City (2019), The City of New York, Mayor Bill De Blasio. OneNYC 2050: New York City's Strategic Plan - OneNYC 2050 (cityofnewyork.us).

Perth and Peel @ 3.5 million (2018), Government of Western Australia, Department of Planning, Lands and Heritage. https://www.dplh.wa.gov.au/perth-and-peel-@-3-5-million.

Plan Melbourne 2017–2050 (2017), The State of Victoria Department of Environment, Land, Water and Planning. https://www.planmelbourne.vic.gov.au/.

Shaping SEQ, South East Queensland Regional Plan 2017 (2017), The State of Queensland, Department of Infrastructure, Local Government and Planning. https://planning.dsdmip.qld.gov.au/planning/better-planning/state-planning/regional-plans/seqrp.

The 30-Year Plan for Greater Adelaide, 2017 Update (2017), Government of South Australia, Department of Planning, Transport and Infrastructure. https://livingadelaide.sa.gov.au/the_plan.

The London Plan, The spatial development strategy for Greater London (2021), The Mayor of London. The London Plan | London City Hall.

Preparation of a Draft Plan   9

9.1   Introduction

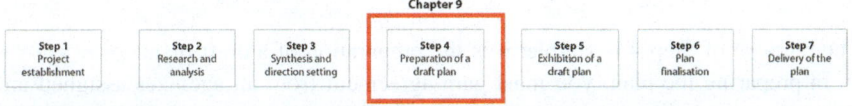

Collaboration:

The action of working with someone to produce something

Brevity:

"I have made this longer than usual because I have not had time to make it shorter."

Translation from "Lettres Provinciales" by the French mathematician and philosopher Blaise Pascal in 1657. First recorded use of the phrase.

The draft plan is the most significant milestone in the 7-Step Strategic Planning Process. It reflects the combination of all the research, collaboration and investigation of opportunities to meet the needs of people, their lives and the places they live in, now and in the future.

The preparation of the draft plan is the focus of this chapter. I emphasise here that what is to be developed should not be a preliminary document, to be finalised after the exhibition period. It should be seen as the final plan to give the community the best opportunity to comment on what will be the vision for their future.

The chapter outlines that the major areas of activity occur across three interconnected phases. I outline the core elements that make up the plan and emphasise the importance of refining the document to ensure clarity of intent.

9.1.1 Warm-Up Exercise

Again, a small exercise.

In one sense the preparation of a draft plan is simple: identify a vision then write up the objectives, strategies and actions required to achieve it. However, delivery is the critical point. Your boss recognises this and asks what other activities you intend to take to ensure delivery of the plan as you set about writing the content.

Jot down a few notes on how you would provide a response to the following issues:

- the whole-of-government nature of the plans
- the probable need for resources to undertake actions
- the information you will provide to the community, so they best understand what is proposed.

9.2 Purpose of Step 4

The purpose of Step 4 is simple: it is the preparation of a draft plan.

In preparing the plan, you must gain agreement from all agencies assigned an action that they will take responsibility for its delivery.

You also need to determine what background material will be released alongside the draft plan. This allows the community to see what has informed the plan and may include information on scenarios considered and the differences between them in terms of benefits and required interventions.

Finally, and importantly, the purpose of Step 4 is also one of a collaborative approach to prepare a plan, at a minimum between government agencies and potentially also with local government. This will make successful implementation more feasible.

9.3 Principal Activities

The activities of Step 4 occur within three interconnected phases (refer Fig. 9.1). The interconnected nature of the activities means the boundaries between each of the phases are blurred.

- **Phase 1: Plan development.** Here activities build on the output of Steps 2 and 3 and are directed to developing the major content elements of the plan—objectives, strategies and actions together with the spatial (structure) plan.
- **Phase 2: Plan refinement.** Refinement focuses on writing, editing and reviewing, together with gaining consensus on content across agencies. It is about getting clarity on the outcomes in terms of the precise wording and fine tuning the context elements required to enhance the understanding of the plan's intent.

9.3 Principal Activities

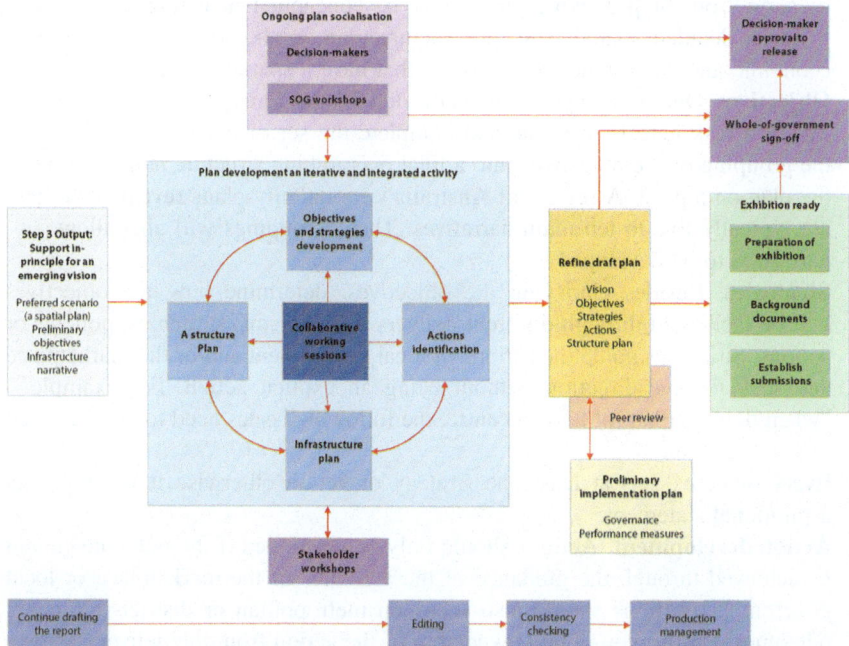

Fig. 9.1 Step 4: Preparing the draft plan: Principal activities
(This diagram outlines the flow of the principal activities required to prepare the draft plan, including an iterative and collaborative process (across government(s) agencies) of plan development focused on objectives, actions, a spatial (structure) plan and an infrastructure plan; ongoing engagement with decision-makers, government agencies and stakeholders; refinement; preparation of exhibition material; and seeking approval to exhibit from decision-maker(s).)

- **Phase 3: Sign-off and getting exhibition ready**. Decision-makers will generally assume you are ready to exhibit the plan when you seek sign-off. Getting ready for the exhibition of a draft occurs when the implementation chapter is written, outlining the purpose of the plan and monitoring and reporting arrangements. In addition, throughout Step 4 there are a few supporting tasks that need attention including editing, proofreading and version control.

9.3.1 Phase 1: Plan Development

There are several areas of activity linked by whole-of-government collaboration to ensure both the integration of opportunities and the ownership of the plan. The activities included are:

- **Resolution of the spatial (structure) plan**. This is a key element of the plan as it is the spatial representation of the vision. The task is to take the preferred scenario from Step 3, which may only be conceptual in nature, and convert it into a detailed spatial plan—a structure plan. It should include the social, economic and environmental outcomes that have a spatial dimension.

- **Objectives**. One of the main outputs of Step 3 is the emerging set of objectives. The first task here is to refine and complete the set of objectives and resolve the grouping of the objectives into a final overarching structure and narrative—the plan on a page. A review of Australia's capital city plans reveals that there are typically five to ten main narratives. These groupings will also allow sub-narratives to be developed.
- **Strategies**. Besides clarifying the objectives, determine how the objectives will be facilitated through different delivery mechanisms, strategies, policies or actions. Strategies guide the actions of local government and/or the marketplace and seek to give direction without being an explicit action. For example—"when doing a plan for a town centre, the following issues need to be addressed …".

Every objective has at least one strategy or action otherwise it is simply an aspirational statement.

- **Action development**. Actions should only be developed if the outcome cannot be achieved through the guidance of the activities of the marketplace or local government. Actions should also focus on metropolitan or district-significant outcomes. Ensure you obtain ownership of the action from the delivery agency responsible.
- **Infrastructure plan**. The infrastructure elements of city plans vary depending on the maturity of the city, in whole or parts, but generally always include transport initiatives. For areas such as health, justice or education, it is often the case of restating of existing commitments in other agency strategies. This reflects the city-shaping influence of transport infrastructure and thus the importance of its inclusion in a plan. Health, education and justice initiatives can be covered by principles such as the need to locate new facilities in major centres, therefore allowing new projects to be announced as needed and as funding is available.

When including new infrastructure projects, assess delivery issues—not just cost, but impacts, timing and sequencing to ensure decision-makers are aware of the requirements for delivery.

- **First Nations Country, community and culture**. Embedding First Nations considerations of Country, community and culture into city plans is only beginning to emerge as a required part of planning processes in Australia. To avoid misappropriation and tokenism there is benefit from obtaining guidance from specialised consultants in this field. As stated in the *Recognise Country* guideline:
  – It is important for practitioners to be conscious of not imposing design concepts from other contexts and be aware of Aboriginal cultural and social protocols associated with design. P24

Elements to be included in the draft plan will cover cultural landscapes; culturally responsive housing, design guidelines, social infrastructure and public art; and language and place naming, refer Sect. 15.3.2.

9.3 Principal Activities

- **Collaborative working arrangements.** Having a collaborative working arrangement at the heart of activities for Phase 1 is a pre-requisite for an integrated plan that covers all social, environmental and economic issues. These working arrangements need to include structured sessions that allow for a level of sign-off on technical issues to ensure no surprises arise when delivery starts, including expectations of responsibility and/or involvement.

  To deliver on the desired principle of a partnership these collaborative activities require engagement with the local First Nations people.

- **Stakeholder discussions.** Part of a collaborative approach requires engaging with stakeholders. If that includes local government, focus on testing principal concepts, especially if there is an expectation that local government will deliver them. Confidentiality is often raised as a concern; however, it is manageable, particularly as local government officers are also held accountable for the issue of confidentiality for their own work for councils.

  It is not appropriate to discuss the details of a plan with peak bodies before it has been made public. Discussions can focus on how issues they have raised (through earlier submissions) could be implemented, such as the need for changes to planning controls or infrastructure requirements.

- **Value management.** Peer review is not about seeking advice on an alternative plan; rather, it is about understanding robustness and fit for purpose considerations, such as:
  - Does the plan achieve what the vision says it will?
  - Does the plan cover all the principal findings?
  - Does the plan reflect contemporary planning issues?

9.3.2 Phase 2: Plan Refinement

The focus of plan refinement is the enhancement of the ever-evolving draft document. At this stage, development of the plan should cease, and focus now must be on refinement.

Refinement includes a tightening of the vision to ensure it covers all the principal narratives across the plan. This may be a single word such as "walkability" that provides a hook later for new but related actions to be pursued. As things change, delivery activities may need to be refocused; if there is a hook in the vision this is much easier to do.

Adding graphs and diagrams can also enhance what is intended, avoid misinterpretations of the objectives, and allow new strategies or actions to be pursued as the result of monitoring the performance of the plan.

It is often the case that right up to the end, the document is managed as separate individual chapters, where theme leads to manage the content. A theme could be either cover environmental, social and economic issues or be integrated in terms of specific outcomes. In these circumstances editing across all the documents becomes critical to ensure consistency in the tone, language and narrative.

When there is an overlap between objectives, it will be a judgement call as to whether they are merged or remain partly overlapping. No single plan structure allows a perfect fit for where each objective should be placed.

Finally, it is around the end of this phase that there should be an indication as to a date for pens down. This is a hard thing to enforce, and the benefit is not simply to be able to finish the document. It is when these final additions are made that errors and mistakes may creep in. Last minute changes are often just that, a last-minute idea that should not have been included.

> I was once involved in a strategy, and we were asked at the last minute to address an issue and the quick conclusion was that office development should be allowed within a specified distance of the centre with no basis as to why. Thereafter, developers were proposing developments where they had literally measured off the distance and quoted the sentence in their development application.

9.3.3 Phase 3: Sign-Off and Exhibition Ready

Towards the end of Step 4, the main task is gaining approval for the public release of the plan and getting ready for the exhibition of the plan. You also need to finalising expectations regarding implementation of the plan, which is often not documented until near the end of the process.

9.3.3.1 The Implementation Section

It is typically only towards the end of the preparation of a draft plan that the implementation section is drafted. As the release of the document is for public comment, it is not being endorsed from the perspective of adoption for delivery. Hence, it is often just a preliminary section even though this may not be specified.

At a minimum, the implementation section should outline the purpose of the plan, its legislative significance, the general governance arrangements and responsibilities going forward, and proposed monitoring and reporting arrangements, including at least a draft set of performance measures. This issue is discussed in Sect. 11.3.2 in the context of the final approval of the plan in Step 6.

9.3.3.2 Getting Exhibition Ready

The last major task for Step 4 is preparing for the exhibition of the plan, a major milestone and the turning point from researching, reflecting, creating and drafting, towards finalisation.

When a draft plan is completed the recommendation to the decision-makers is usually along the lines of "the attached draft plan be approved for exhibition purposes in line with the attached engagement plan". Therefore, there are a few tasks that must be completed by the time the draft is ready for exhibition, all are covered in detail in Sect. 10.2. In summary:

- prepare the collateral for the exhibition period, such as printed reports, summary documents, flyers or posters and web material

9.3 Principal Activities

- finalise the background material that informed the development of the plan for exhibition—depending on the number of documents, this can be a substantial task which requires senior officer involvement
- prepare a communication engagement plan that outlines how you will engage with stakeholders and the wider community
- develop a submissions review process, including ensuring sufficient staff resources are available.

The last task in Step 4 is gaining approval of the plan from decision-makers. This typically requires multiple briefings to ministers, due to the whole-of-government characteristics of city plans. Factoring in time for this is important. The approvals process should address the principal conclusions of the plan, the implications for the government (such as resourcing or new policy positions), the proposed engagement process, and the background material to be released. There may also be a need to brief the shadow planning minister.

9.3.3.3 Exhibition Material

There are several considerations when preparing the collateral for the exhibition period:

- Think about the time required to prepare web-based material once there are no longer changes to the document. The idea of pens down is usually only seen by the decision-makers and senior executives as a guide, not a rule -consequently this is always a challenge. Thus, changes can occur up to the day before the release of a document. This often means that on the day of the launch there is only a PDF version of the plan available instead of a fully interactive web-based copy.
- Make the material accessible to different groups. The planning profession has some inherent jargon, as planning activities include decisions made in courts where words and phrases have specific meanings, so plans for exhibitions must manage this challenge.
- Proofread the final documents. Ultimately the project director is responsible.

Regarding the draft plan and background material, I feel that soon there will no longer be hard copies. This will be a liberating opportunity as it will allow for new ways of presentation and providing access to plans. For example, the need for all plans to fit onto a single page will disappear and there will be opportunities to allow all information for a single topic to be shown, and this in turn should encourage integrated thinking.

9.3.4 First Nations and Preparation of a Draft Plan

By this stage it is expected that you have already partnered with key First Nations stakeholders in steps 1, 2 and 3. Therefore during the draft plan stage it is important to check back in with those already involved to ensure that their feedback is accurately captured in the draft plan and reflects their contributions.

9.3.5 Supporting Activities

Several other important activities and considerations need to occur as part of Step 4:

- Ongoing liaison with the transport agency will require attention to determine a final agreed package including commentary for the plan, as the transport elements are likely to be the most significant commitment by government.
- Informal briefings with the client, senior planning executives and agencies will avoid surprises and ensure the plan reflects the expectations of the decision-makers.
- Formal editing needs to be managed so as not to lose important meaning during attempts to enhance the quality of the writing. The timing of editing is also important. If it starts too early, when there is still a level of flux to the document, the editing is lost and makes for an unnecessary cost.
- Consider engaging a production manager during the closing stages of Step 4 and Step 6 to coordinate last-minute changes, any proofreading, finalising maps and web material and printing. Saving hours, not just days, matters at this point. From experience it is important that the production manager take control of the timing of all activities at this point.
- A final sense check or peer review of the plan is essential—after you and your team have expended considerable time and energy in creating the plan, all involved are often too close to the detail to be able to stand back and do one final sense check, including considering whether the plan will deliver on the expectations of the community. Bringing in a few highly experienced people, under clear confidentiality guidelines, is the best way to manage this and typically is a pro-bono exercise. This should include First Nations Traditional Custodians and knowledge-holders from the local communities.

9.4 Report Role, Structure and Content

Across Australia there are differing approaches to how metropolitan plans are structured and the nomenclature used.

9.4 Report Role, Structure and Content

Table 9.1 provides a high-level summary of the principal elements for capital city plans across Australian states and territories; Table 9.2 provides the same information for a selection of international plans.

As with the Australian plans there are differences in how the international plans are structured and the nomenclature used to describe the content. The London and New York City plans are also more detailed than any of the other international or Australian plans being between three and twice as many pages respectively.

It is also evident across all the plans that the question of an integrated versus thematic approach to structuring the content is clearly a local decision, with about a 50–50 split across the plans.

This overview reveals differing approaches to what is included in the plans and emphasises that there is not necessarily a correct way to structure a plan. In NSW, the *Environmental Planning and Assessment Act, 1979, No 203* specifies a minimum plan content (refer Part 4, Division 3.1, Sect. 3.3).

All the plans provide their objectives, or policies and actions, under a series of headings. The plan for Perth and Peel is an outlier—in addition to providing explicit headings for specific objectives many are included in the body text as part of the general narrative. In addition, some of the plans cover issues not mentioned in other plans, though it is more the issue of providing greater depth under a common theme, such as the plan for Melbourne that has detailed directions for housing and transport. These two examples emphasise that there is no set way to write a plan; it is more important to meet the needs of the community and place in question.

Stein (2017, pp. 47–51) addresses what should be included in the content of a plan. He emphasises the importance of a full narrative to convey the rationale for the plan as well as the benefit of adding photographs and descriptions of the character, architecture and impressions of the place to set a tone for the community to envisage the imagined future.

Discussions regarding the structure and role of the plan should start back in Step 1: Project establishment. This will be influenced by the scope of the plan and the breadth and depth of research to be pursued.

By Step 4 the task should be to clarify/confirm the role and purpose of the plan. When considering the role of the plan it is useful to define the audience, to:

- guide state government agencies that will deliver the infrastructure
- guide local government authorities that will oversee most of the day-to-day planning decisions (such as undertaking detailed local planning and approval of development)
- influence the decisions of the private sector, which will, by and large, deliver the plan.

In terms of structure, the principal issue is how to approach the narrative—thematic or integrated. If the integrated path is chosen, be aware that at some point decision-makers will indicate that they cannot see the narrative for a particular theme such as housing or transport, and you need to be ready with a response.

Table 9.1 Principal elements of capital city plans across Australia (Table 9.1 and Table 9.2 highlight the principal elements of metropolitan plans for Australia's capital cities and a select number of international cities.)

Capital city plan	Vision, and spatial plan	Theme versus integrated	Directions	Objectives	Strategies	Actions	Delivery	Pages
ACT	Yes	Integrated	Yes	Yes	Sort of, in text	Yes	Monitoring	116
Adelaide	An overarching narrative	Thematic	Yes, as five targets	As policies	No	Yes	Monitoring	188
Darwin	Yes	Thematic	No	Yes	No	No	–	84
Greater Sydney	Yes, multi pages	Thematic	Yes	Yes	Yes	Yes	Governance, monitoring	194
Melbourne	Yes, multi pages	Integrated	Yes, as outcomes	Yes, as directions & policies	Maybe their policies	No	Monitoring	152
Perth & Peel	Yes	Thematic	Yes, as series of principles	Yes	For economy and in text	No	Governance, monitoring of land supply	94
South East Queensland	Yes	Integrated	Yes	Yes	Yes	Yes	Governance	192

Source My review of Australia's capital city plans as listed in the section at the end of this chapter under Further reading

9.4 Report Role, Structure and Content

Table 9.2 Principal elements of four international metropolitan plans

Capital city plan	Vision, and spatial plan	Theme versus integrated	Directions	Objectives	Strategies	Actions	Delivery	Pages
London	Yes, as Chapter 1: Good Growth	Thematic	No	Yes	Yes, the focus of the plan	No	Funding, monitoring and performance indicators	542
New York City	Yes	Integrated	Yes, as goals	Yes	No	Yes	Delivery responsibility, indicators and funding status	332
Greater Toronto	Yes	Thematic	No	Yes, as principles	Yes, called policies and focus of plan	No	Approved under legislation, targets, performance monitoring, requirement to work with First Nations and Métis	114
Metro Vancouver	Yes	Thematic/integrated	Yes, as goals	No	Yes	Yes	Approved under legislation, governance, performance monitoring, requirement to work with First Nations people	80

Source My review of a select number of international metropolitan plans as listed in the section at the end of this chapter under further reading

Also, at some point the question will be raised—how many pages is the report? My answer is, as many as it needs, but as short as possible. From Table 4, it is evident that there is a range in lengths with the average at 145 pages. Do not forget, you will be asked by all the senior decision-makers towards the end of the process to make it shorter, but at the same time to add their little bit.

9.4.1 Core Plan Elements

At a minimum, a plan should include the following elements:

- **A vision**. This needs to be more than a single paragraph. It should articulate the focus of the plan by a limited number of directions or goals connected to the spatial plan(s). It should read as a narrative and potentially emphasise a hierarchy of important elements as not all things have the same importance.
- **A structure plan**. This demonstrates the integration of land use and transport systems and outlines any spatial directions, refer example from the Greater Sydney Region Plan (Fig. 9.2). It should cover the principal land use outcomes including priority change areas, transport networks, open space networks and natural systems, as relevant, cultural landscapes and hinterland relationships.
- **Objectives**. The objectives or similar (goals, aims, policies or directions) should provide the full scope of the plan and identify the hierarchy of objectives.
- **Strategies**. These are linked directly to objectives and there should be at least one strategy for each objective.
- **Actions**. There should be a limited number. Often plans are filled with actions that reflect the day-to-day business of governments. The actions in a city plan should be those required to shift the trajectory of a city towards the vision.
- **The basis of the plan**. To give their support, stakeholders need to see the logic of how the plan was derived. The logic should cover economic, social, cultural and environmental considerations, together with a statement on the growth equation covering population, housing, commercial development and jobs.
- **An implementation plan**. This identifies governance, priorities for action and how we will stay on track (monitoring and reporting), including the accountability and responsibility for implementation.
- **Infrastructure priorities and principles**, including expectations for delivery over time (sequencing), potentially with considerations of optimisation and adaptation of existing infrastructure assets.
- **International, national and regional connections**, covering transport, economy, open space and natural systems (including biodiversity).

9.4.2 Optional Plan Elements

A plan could also cover the following elements:

9.4 Report Role, Structure and Content

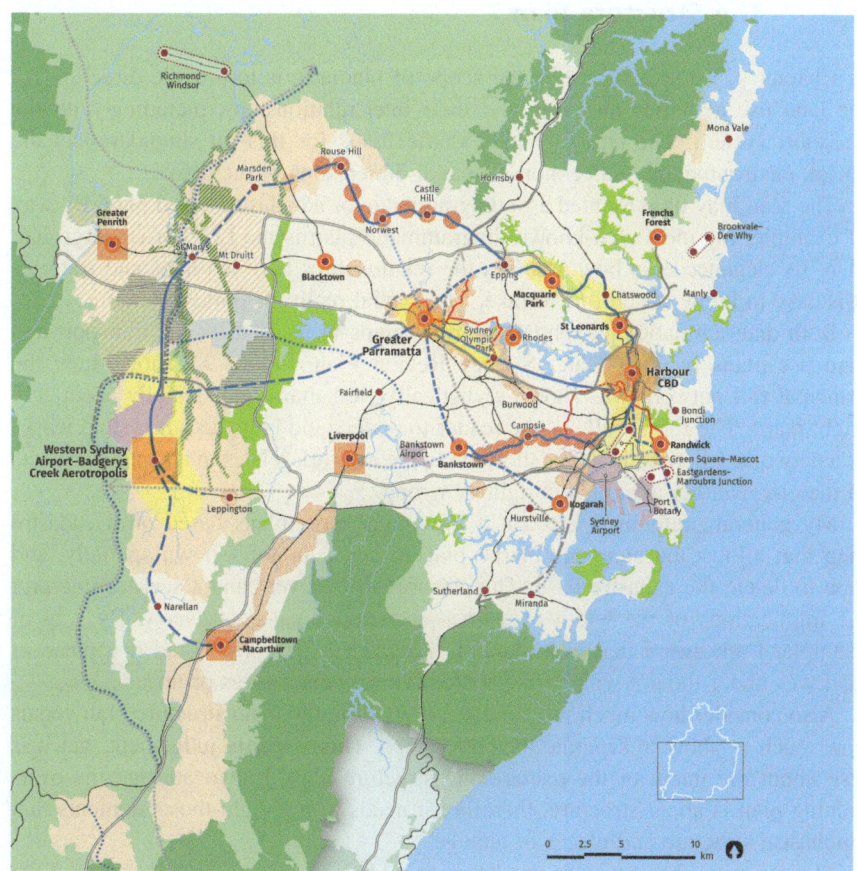

Fig. 9.2 Structure Plan for Greater Sydney
(This diagram is a copy of the structure plan from the Greater Sydney Region Plan. It emphasises the inter-relationships between the principal land use and transport elements. Source: Greater Sydney Region Plan (2018, pp. 14–15) Published with permission from the Greater Cities Commission)

- **Guiding principles for managing growth**, including an indication of the involvement of government(s) in implementation and links to infrastructure delivery.
- **Case studies/links back to community input** to personalise the vision and demonstrate what it could mean on the ground.
- **Detailed priority area or precinct plans** that outline the integration of land use and transport systems as well as urban design outcomes.
- **Diagrams** that show:
  - spatial relationships
  - governance and decision-making structures
  - the plan on a page to accompany the spatial plan.

9.5 The Structure Plan

In Chapter 4, I emphasised that the scope of planning is to provide direction for the land use activities of a city and their inter-relationships, including with the transport system. The structure plan is the focus for this—it should reflect the social, environmental and economic spatial dimensions of the plan.

The plan may be presented as a diagrammatic or a cadastre-based plan. By way of example, the most well-known diagrammatic plan is the London Underground map. Its elegance is in how it shows the relationships between lines and stations. It is easy to know which line to take. The spatial reality is quite different.

Both diagrammatic and spatially correct maps were used for the transport and land use plans in the Greater Sydney Region Plan. Figure 9.3 shows how the principal rail network was shown stylistically (left map) and spatially accurately (right map). The former allows the reader to understand how the rail system works as a network, whereas the latter shows how the network relates to all spatial aspects of the city. Neither approach is right or wrong.

My general preference is to, at a minimum, have plans based on a cadastre map that allows the elements of the plan to be accurately shown spatially, and then to delete the cadastre base. This ensures the viewer cannot seek to interpret the implications of the width of a line—it avoids legal controversy. By way of example, I am aware that in a planning court an expert was asked if a piece of land was under the dot which represented a town centre—yes or no?

Also consider how much information to show on the main structure plan versus how much to show in separate thematic maps. This is partly judgement, but it is also about the intent of the overarching structure plan. I advocate that the overarching plan is about structure, therefore it needs to highlight those elements that emphasise structure and places of change.

The elements that are most important should stand out on the diagram, and the plan should be compliant for those who are colour blind.

In terms of content, I outline a few considerations.

- In areas where major change is foreshadowed, particularly growth areas, consider preparing preliminary concept plans for an area. The agencies affected can provide comment, allowing for an early agreement as to what is generally intended. For example, there are well understood relationships between dwelling numbers and the need for primary and secondary schools. Thus, from the outset the scale of new areas can be agreed to in general.
- Outcomes such as walking, cycling, linear open space and urban tree canopy are increasingly important for cities. These are often lost as, unlike more city-shaping transport elements (roads and public transport), the strategic planning for these elements do not occur until more detailed investigations take place. Consider undertaking early planning to ensure these outcomes can be achieved.

9.5 The Structure Plan

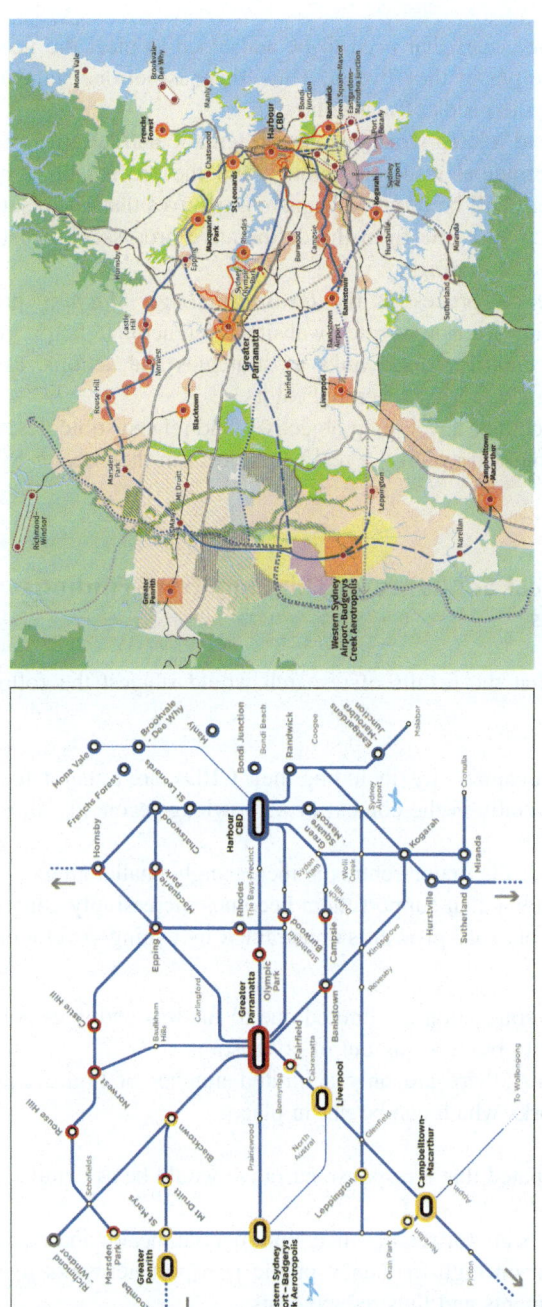

Fig. 9.3 Presentation options: Stylistic and accurately showing the transport network (The diagrams show the proposed rail network in the Greater Sydney Region Plan. The diagram on the left shows to location of stations relative to each other which makes for ease of understanding as to how to navigate around the network. The diagram on the right shows the spatial distribution of the same network in its geographic location, which show, more correctly, the true relationship (distance and location) between stations. *Source* A Metropolis of Three Cities (2018, pp. 88 and 15 respectively) Published with permission from the Greater Cities Commission)

9.6 Finalising Objectives and Strategies

As cities evolve so do the issues that need to be addressed to meet the needs of people, their lives and the places they live in. Thus, there is not one standard set of objectives to adopt for the needs of a specific city.

Finalising objectives and related strategies is a systematic and iterative process that evolves out of the principal research findings and the process of synthesis and direction setting. There will be intuitive leaps to objectives that make sense in hindsight, but most objectives come from the deliberative processes of distilling how to respond to a group of findings.

A toolkit to formalise the process is the *Investment Logic Mapping* process developed by the Victorian Treasury (refer website reference). It helps you to clarify the problem and identify causal links to strategies and actions, as well as assisting in developing key performance indicators.

To best outline the process of developing objectives and related strategies, I outline a hypothetical example followed by a real example from the Greater Sydney Region Plan.

9.6.1 A Hypothetical Sequence of Thinking, from Findings to Objectives

It is plausible to think that the results of research would suggest the following statements:

- The major centres of a capital city, including their CBDs, are a major focus of economic activity especially in the context of a knowledge economy, thus they need to grow and evolve.
- Managing the growth of the major centres is increasingly challenging:
  - as the transport systems that support them becomes increasingly congested
  - as the potential for outward growth is constrained by exiting development.

- Choices for managing congestion are limited due to funding and in established areas it is not possible to build a way out of congestion.
- Equally, due to funding, there are only a limited number of high-frequency public transport networks which can be put in place.

Equally it could be anticipated that a response narrative would be as detailed here.

- Transport planners advocate for retail, office/ commercial, health and education activities to be located on high-frequency public transport networks to focus future transport investments and thus reduce costs.
- The community wishes to reduce the length of commuting trips and want more jobs close to home.

9.6 Finalising Objectives and Strategies

- Transport planners support an increase in walking and cycling trips, but this requires improved networks and more housing closer to centres.
- Local governments and the community are concerned with the quality of development in the centres, including poor human scale and a lack of vibrancy.
- Commercial developers vote through their investments by creating business agglomerations (office precincts).

Consequently, a plan needs to have objectives that address these issues as well as clarity in how these objectives will be applied. Strategies are one way to achieve this. Actions should focus on how the government will directly support the delivery of a tangible outcome, such as transport infrastructure, place-making investments or actions to facilitate investment, such as site amalgamation.

In developing objectives that cover the range of issues identified here, it is evident that no single objective can cover all issues. Therefore, ensure the introduction to a plan and the implementation section note that the plan must be seen holistically, as you cannot rely on the intent of a single objective. With such statements the need for cross referencing, which can interrupt the narrative, is reduced.

9.6.2 A Worked Example

How the hypothetical narrative above may play out in a plan is shown in the text from Objective 22 of the Greater Sydney Region Plan—*A Metropolis of Three Cities* (Greater Sydney Commission, 2018, p. 118).

- **The objective**. The desired outcome needs to be clear. It can be written as a statement, as for Objective 22: *Investment and business activity in centres*, or as a sentence beginning with a verb, such as "to attract …".
  Sometimes objectives can be interpreted in several ways. My time in consultancy emphasised this as I sought to interpret public policy. Therefore, it is important that the objectives are supported by some context which clarifies the meaning.
- **The context**. Firstly, there must be clarity on the issue(s) being addressed. In the context section for Objective 22, five outcomes (benefits) are outlined as the focus for the objective, paraphrased here:
  – Jobs are closer to homes.
  – Significant investment in the public transport network is optimised.
  – Significant investment in health, education, administrative, community and other social infrastructure is optimised.
  – Increased productivity is driven by business agglomerations.
  – A sense of place and identity is enhanced.
  Context sections can also include some of the principal findings to emphasise a point. Objective 22 sits within the productivity theme. In the introduction to the theme, it states (p. 80):

Greater Sydney's major centres, defined as metropolitan and strategic centres in this Plan, account for 50 per cent (2011) of all Greater Sydney's jobs and therefore play a significant role in providing jobs close to home.

In this case the factual information helps build the case as to why an objective for centres is required.

- **Strategies**. My preference is that city plans move beyond guidance and provide clarity as to how each objective is to be delivered.

  Strategies can emphasise the expectations on how to apply the objective. Their benefit, compared to actions, is that they can be applicable in many instances without having to specify each one. In the case of Objective 22, Strategy 22.1 provides guidance as to how centres will be planned. It states: "Provide access to jobs, goods and services by…" and then goes on to list 12 requirements, for example (p. 125):
  - improving the walkability within and to centres
  - completing and improving a safe and connected cycling network to and within centres.

  Additional direction on how to achieve an objective can be provided in the context for the objectives. For example, in the ACT Planning Strategy 2018 (p. 50), the context narrative for "*Direction 1.4: Continue to work with the NSW Government and Councils to implement joint initiatives to understand and manage growth in the Canberra Region*" includes a sentence that states "Key growth management issues for ongoing collaboration include:…" followed by nine points on what collaboration means, such as "protecting the distinct character and setting of the ACT and adjoining council areas".

- **The importance of related objectives**. In the case of Objective 22 it is evident from the initial statement of five benefits that other objectives in the plan are linked, such as:
  - Objective 12. Greater places that bring people together
  - Objective 14. A Metropolis of three Cities—integrated land use and transport creates a walkable and 30-minute city
  - Objective 21. Internationally competitive health, education, research and innovation precincts.

  This is why I emphasise my earlier comment that plans should have a statement upfront that notes the need for the plan to be viewed in its totality.

9.7 Development of Actions

Actions should arise out of the process of developing objectives. They should focus on outcomes of metropolitan or district significance and focus on the activities of state government. In some cases, like the Australian Government's city deals (refer website link), they may involve all levels of government.

9.7 Development of Actions

In developing actions, reflect on the range of tools available, as discussed earlier in Sect. 4.5.2. This may reveal the degree to which outcomes are being supported versus enabled.

For each action there is a need for clarity on:

- the outcome to be delivered and why
- any catalyst effect (private sector investment, job creation)
- the expectations of the task (the scope), with the person or organisation responsible for the action be clear as to what they need to do
- whether the action is linked to the delivery of other actions, a package of projects
- a first order assessment of benefits and costs and potential performance metrics
- delivery risks
- any sequencing and its prioritisation
- sign-off on the action by those responsible for its delivery
- whether the actions will be delivered within current budget allocations or require new funding.

An action generally implies the allocation of new resources to achieve a specific outcome. As resources are limited, actions should be seen as:

- Those fundamental to delivering the vision. Only a limited number will be required, and they will typically be supported by a prioritised listing of infrastructure projects, particularly transport projects. This point is particularly relevant where visions propose a shift in the trajectory of a city. Here a suite of transformative actions, which are whole of government in nature, are usually required.
- Those guided by the objectives which will be delivered by the actions of the planning portfolio and/or other agencies in their day-to-day activities.

There are several additional issues for consideration:

- As city plans are generally directed to long-term outcomes, recognise that their delivery will occur over many budget periods and potentially successive governments.
- The timing of action should reflect budgetary cycles and be beyond short-term priorities. They should be presented in prioritised tranches to be reviewed in future budgetary cycles based on lessons learnt for monitoring and reporting.
- Consider sequencing actions across systems and, therefore, the potential for project packages. We have all seen the situation where roadwork is being undertaken and then soon after completion, a trench is dug across it to lay some pipes. These actions suggest that there was a package of projects for that area that could have been sequenced to either improve the outcome or reduce costs. In city planning there is often a similar opportunity to take a place-based approach to maximise benefits through the collective delivery of related

projects, as well as the benefits of sequencing. Investigate opportunities to identify project packages.
- No plan starts in isolation, on a blank sheet of paper. It is most likely that other agencies have plans in place under thematic issues such as water supply, biodiversity or spatially specific projects such as a health and education precinct. In these cases, there is no need to restate the actions or policy positions already in place. Instead, acknowledge these other plans and indicate their intent.

9.8 Implications for Other Planning Typologies

Several issues need to be considered when applying the approach as outlined in this chapter to the other planning typologies. I outline these in Table 9.3 and consider them in detail in Chapter 12.

9.9 Summary

This chapter covers the principal task for the whole 7-Step Strategic Planning Process—the preparation of a draft plan. The chapter emphasised that this step builds on the earlier work of Steps 2 and 3 and thus should be seen to be part of a continuum of activity and not a single task.

The activities for Step 4 occur in three interconnected phases: plan development, plan refinement and getting ready for exhibition. Some of the principal issues emphasised are:

- the role of a structure plan in articulating the spatial vision for the plan, based on the preferred scenario developed in Step 3
- the need for a deliberative process to identify, develop and review the objectives for the plan
- the benefit in grouping the proposed objectives to assist in identifying the principal narratives for the plan
- the importance of strategies or actions as mechanisms for how the plan will be delivered, particularly for transformative issues in metropolitan areas or districts, usually undertaken by line agencies as part of their business-as-usual activities to minimise the number of actions that need to be resourced as part of the plan
- the importance of collaborating with other agencies in developing the final set of objectives, strategies and actions
- the importance of gaining sign-off for all the actions from the delivery agencies.
- recognising the minimum number of elements that should be included—a vision, structure plan, objectives, strategies, actions, the basis of the plan and an implementation plan

9.9 Summary

Table 9.3 Applying Step 4 to other planning typologies
(This table outlines how the planning activity undertaken for a metropolitan planning project in Step 4: Preparation of a draft plan, needs to be adapted for the other city planning typologies. Additional detail is provided in Chapter 12.)

Planning activity	Local government area plan	Town centre and regional centre plan	Greenfield community plan	Neighbourhood community plan
Delivery levers (actions)	It is likely that some actions will be the responsibility of state agencies, specifically transport actions. Thus, advocacy will be an important delivery lever. In addition, it is critical that any transport assessments reflect investigative approaches of the relevant state transport department.	Some actions, specifically transport related, will potentially require state agencies to deliver, thus the assessment of opportunities should reflect state government processes of evaluation. The need for state agency delivery will mean some actions are about advocacy and thus benefits must be understood. Investment attraction (attraction of specific tenant types) is potentially a delivery tool. Hence, how it will be achieved will need to be understood.	n/a	n/a
Plan elements	n/a	There will potentially be a need for spatial plans to be determined at a cadastre level which will require concept plans to be prepared as distinct from simple conceptual diagrams. It is likely that a detailed understanding of potential new statutory planning controls will be required as enablers of investment.	Delivery is by the private sector, thus plans and guidelines need to allow flexibility for changes in consumer preference and innovation in delivery options. Thus, there needs to be clarity on desired outcomes, such as water quality outcomes, not the method of achieving it. For several elements of the plan, the consequence is outcomes that will still be there in a hundred years, such as roads, most individual lots, parks and town centres and their relationship to residential areas. Thus, the resolution of the structure needs to be tested for its robustness to be deemed to be something deemed to provide future generations with long-term benefits.	n/a

- allowing sufficient time to plan for exhibition and submissions activities and prepare the necessary collateral.

The last task for Step 4 is gaining approval for the public release of the draft document for the purposes of gaining feedback. This exhibition of the plan is the focus of Step 5.

9.9.1 Insights

Insight: Language matters
Jargon privatises your work to a few
Too often, planners, as in many social sciences, get caught up in their own jargon. *A recent example for me was when a communications officer turned to a room of senior planners and asked why they described housing outcomes in terms of phrases such as 'compact city', 'densification', etc.instead of plain language such as, 'where would you like your children to live', etc.—what she called a basket of goodies.*
Equally, different professions have different meanings for the same words. If you a town planner—wish to work effectively with business departments or the community development profession you will need to learn their language. For example, we might suggest we plan for employment; however, business departments argue that we plan/create opportunities for business activity/investment which results in employment.
It's not an academic report, restate in full
At university we are taught to critically evaluate the works of others and distil the relevant issues related to our assignment or research piece. In planning do not paraphrase when reviewing policies related to your project. In my experience the words in policy documents have usually been carefully crafted and reviewed by many. Hence to paraphrase will likely alter the meaning—so write it out in full.

Insight: No such thing as a silver bullet
Actions need to be packaged.
A suite of actions
When systems are interlinked so too are actions. Just because you change a zone to allow apartments, this does not necessarily mean they will be built. Property markets are complex, and change will likely need the right pre-conditions for investment, including, for example, specific infrastructure, site consolidation, etc.
It's not about single pieces. It is about building blocks
While pathways to a future vision may be reasonably simple in a conceptual sense, the delivery of the vision is likely to require the progressive delivery of a series of actions (building blocks). Often, the order in which the delivery of this group of actions happens—the sequencing—matters. In some cases, a detailed investigation of the sequencing of the building blocks is necessary.

(continued)

(continued)

Insights: Informal peer review
You want the future users of the plan to test it
Before a draft version of the plan is released for review, seek an external peer review. Ideally the peer reviewers should come from the cross-section of stakeholders who will use the plans, not external content experts. The peer review focuses on whether the plan hits the mark technically and if future users think it will be useful and able to meet their expectations. Lots of protocols are required here and the easiest is that the reviewers review the document on site. This task can occur multiple times, including early in the planning, when the findings of the research are being brought together, and later when a draft final document is ready after the submissions review.

Outcomes for generations to come
Some actions seek to change the trajectory of the city to provide better walkability and thus deliver better health outcomes, reduce car dependency or enhance opportunities for informal social interaction (to name a few benefits). Some outcomes, however, specifically ones about city structure, usually take decades to deliver as they rely on multiple actions across multiple areas of city planning such as transport and land use. These need to remain in multiple iterations of the plan. How these city-shaping challenges are conveyed is therefore critical because the narrative needs to be long lasting and most likely survive multiple changes of government.

Putting structure to the building blocks and foundation stones
Actions need to be packaged. Within a single system, the ordering of tasks is understood. The challenge comes with considering the inter-relationships with other systems. This aspect is usually left out because it is hard, so if we only describe cities in terms of single systems such as transport, activity, image, etc.then the inter-connections will be lost. Put simply, no system works independently of another; so long as we think they do we will continue to build roads only for cars or subdivide land only for houses.

Sometimes you need to be seen to be doing something
In most cases, the defining elements of a plan—the ones that create systemic change—take time to deliver. To gain the confidence of the community, you need to be seen to be doing something—but this "something" must add value. You need to balance the visible and important (but likely invisible) tasks. The ordering of projects needs to balance the pragmatic with the theoretical, remembering this pragmatic approach may be the difference between success and failure.

Further Reading

Stein, LA. (2017) *Comparative Urban Land Use Planning, Best Practice.* Sydney University Press (A detailed assessment of international urban land use planning practices).

Website links

Australian Government's City Deals initiative. https://www.infrastructure.gov.au/cities/city-deals/
Environmental Planning and Assessment Act 1979 No 203 (NSW) Part 4, Division 3.1, Section 3.3, viewed 16 June 2020h. https://www.legislation.nsw.gov.au/~/view/act/1979/203
Investment Logic Mapping, toolkits. https://www.dtf.vic.gov.au/investment-management-standard/ims-workshops-and-examples
Transport for London, Map of the tube network. Tube and Rail – Transport for London (tfl.gov.uk)
Victorian planning objectives, Victoria Planning Provisions, Planning Policy Framework. https://www.planning.vic.gov.au/schemes-and-amendments/browse-planning-scheme/planning-scheme?f.Scheme%7CplanningSchemeName=vpps
Western Sydney City Deal. Western Sydney City Deal (wscd.sydney)

Australian Capital City and International Plans Website Links

A Metropolis of Three Cities (2018) State of New South Wales. https://www.greater.sydney/metropolis-of-three-cities
ACT Planning Strategy 2018 (2018) Australian Capital Territory. https://www.planning.act.gov.au/act-planning-strategy
Darwin Regional Land Use Plan 2015 (2015) Northern Territory Government, Department of lands, Planning and the Environment. https://planningcommission.nt.gov.au/projects/drlup
Metro Vancouver 2040, Shaping Our Future, 2011, Updated 2020, Greater Vancouver Regional District Board. Regional Planning Services (metrovancouver.org).
OneNYC 2050 Building a Strong and Fair City (2019) The City of New York, Mayor Bill De Blasio. OneNYC 2050: New York City's Strategic Plan – OneNYC 2050 (cityofnewyork.us).
Perth and Peel @ 3.5 million (2018) Government of Western Australia, Department of Planning, Lands and Heritage. https://www.dplh.wa.gov.au/perth-and-peel-@-3-5-million
Plan Melbourne 2017–2050 (2017) The State of Victoria Department of Environment, Land, Water and Planning. https://www.planmelbourne.vic.gov.au/
Shaping SEQ, South East Queensland Regional Plan 2017 (2017) The State of Queensland, Department of Infrastructure, Local Government and Planning. https://planning.dsdmip.qld.gov.au/planning/better-planning/state-planning/regional-plans/seqrp
The 30-Year Plan for Greater Adelaide, 2017 Update (2017) Government of South Australia, Department of Planning, Transport and Infrastructure. https://livingadelaide.sa.gov.au/the_plan
The London Plan, The spatial development strategy for Greater London (2021) The Mayor of London. The London Plan | London City Hall.

Exhibition and a Final Plan 10

10.1 Introduction

Publish or Perish

This chapter covers the last two steps in preparing the city plan before we turn to Step 7, which focuses on the plan's delivery.

After a draft plan is prepared, we hold the public exhibition of the plan to elicit informed submissions. We then assess the submissions to determine what changes should be made to the plan. This second step also needs to include the finalisation of issues relating to the ongoing implementation of the plan.

These steps reflect Steps 5 and 6 in the 7-Step Strategic Planning Process.

10.1.1 Warm-Up Exercise

Again, a small exercise.
The activities for Steps 5 and 6 are fairly straightforward—exhibit the plan, review the submissions and update the plan accordingly. But is it as simple as that? What happens when you get 1000 submissions or more? Is updating the plan the last task or is it more about confirming who to pass the baton to for delivery?

The ability to answer these questions is often linked to the project plan developed in Step 1. Now that you are nearing the end of the process your boss is keen for a successful conclusion to the whole process.

In that context if you had your time again what considerations would you have put in place to ensure a good completion for the finalisation of the plan? Jot down a few points as to how you would respond to the following issues:

- the time, resources and process for the exhibition of the plan, specifically the assessing of submissions
- the process for keeping the decision-makers across the views of *their* principal stakeholders
- the process to manage new issues (desired outcomes) raised by the decision-makers
- the allocation of resources for monitoring and reporting
- the process to assign responsibility for delivery to an agency
- the need for ongoing funding to deliver the plan.

10.2 Step 5: Exhibition of a Draft Plan

> It is a plan for the community, not for the bookshelf; therefore, the community must be active participants. They should not simply read about it in the library.

10.2.1 Purpose of Step 5

The exhibition should maximise the opportunity for people to provide informed formal comment on the draft plan.

It is a unique stage in the planning process as the whole focus is about managing public-facing activities. Consequently, decision-makers will be keen to understand the breadth and depth of the activities, and formal sign-off will most likely be required.

The exhibition period should be the second major engagement step with the community, the first occurring in Step 2 as part of research and analysis. Therefore, your exhibition material and the plan should note how you have considered earlier inputs, with some detail on specific points addressed. This will illustrate to the community and other submitters the benefit of making further comments on the draft plan.

Section 5.3.2 provides context regarding the required community engagement process.

10.2.2 Principal Activities

The exhibition period is one of the few steps with defined start and end dates. The success of the exhibition is influenced by what occurs before and after the exhibition period—see the principal areas of activity, Fig. 10.1.

- **Pre-launch activities.** Step 5 starts with the launch, which relies on the pre-launch activities undertaken in Step 4 to ensure that when the draft plan is approved, and decision-makers have signed-off on the engagement plan and supporting collateral to be released with the draft plan.
- **Exhibition activities.** Design your exhibition activities to inform the community as to what the draft plan is about and to elicit feedback via submissions.
- **Processing submissions.** Processing submissions is a substantial task. It commences straight away by capturing comments and questions from launch activities, although most activity occurs towards the end of the exhibition period when most submissions arrive and continue into Step 6. You'll need to undertake significant pre-planning to ensure it can be managed efficiently and effectively.

10.2.3 First Nations and Exhibition

It is recommended that you work with people you have already partnered with to understand who they recommend should be included in the draft plan exhibition engagement. This is the right time to hear from the broader First Nations communities regarding the proposed change.

Reaching a wider audience requires a targeted engagement approach, which may call for the need to identify a suitable First Nations consultant to support the process. Working with a consultant will assist in identifying the right stakeholders to engage, ensure that conversations are pitched at the right level and allow you to harness existing networks.

Discussing strategic planning and proposed changes with the community requires a sensitive and respectful approach. It is important to manage consultation fatigue and build on research identified in Step 2.

It is important that detailed notes are recorded of meetings and summarised into an outcomes report. This should be shared with the First Nations communities involved in engagement to ensure that their voices are accurately reflected in the final plan.

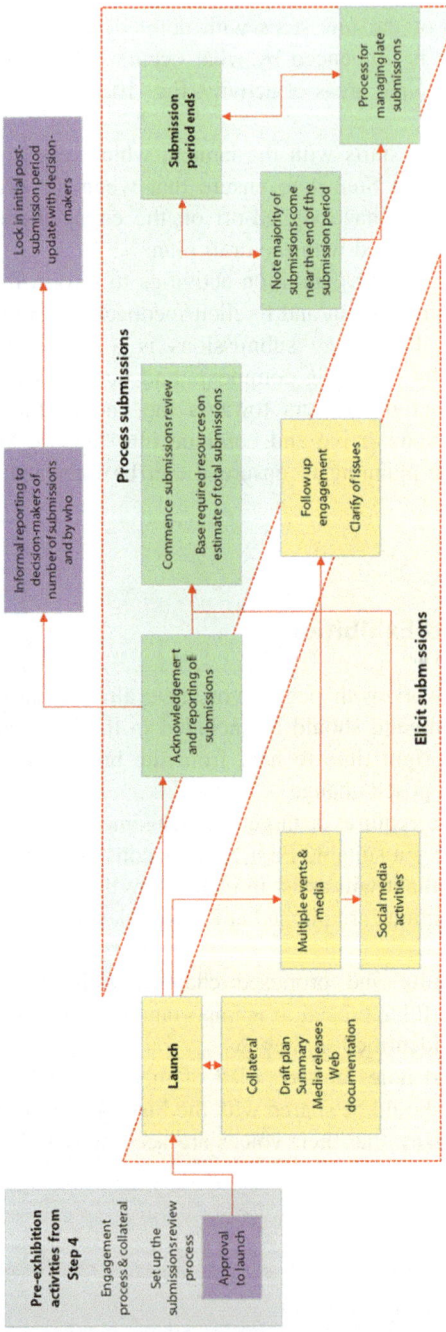

Fig. 10.1 Step 5: Exhibition: Reaching out
This diagram shows the principal activities to exhibit a draft plan. The activities aim to elicit submissions, starting from the launch of the draft plan, then cover the processing of submissions received, which starts with a simple acknowledgement of receipt and leads to the detailed evaluation of their content. This latter task continues into Step 6: Plan finalisation

10.2.4 Pre-exhibition: A Community Engagement Plan

I briefly outlined the pre-launch activities in Sect. 9.3.3. This section provides additional information to present all the information relating to exhibition activities in one chapter.

10.2.4.1 Exhibition Period

Consider the time allowed for the exhibition period. In some jurisdictions, such as NSW, legislation mandates a minimum exhibition time, and this can be longer around holiday times.

The critical issue for local government, peak bodies and community groups is not so much the time available for assessing the plans, rather it is the time available to gain formal sign-off for their submission. Approval times can be three to four weeks due to closing off on agendas, internal briefings to decision-makers, time for decision-makers to review the plan (often a week) and then a meeting to make a decision.

Thus, if an exhibition period is a month, organisations need to finalise their response in a day; therefore, aim for seven to eight weeks. Consider the implications this will have on the total project time, noting that some parties will request more time to submit and others will say the whole project is taking too long, particularly as strategic planning processes generally last at least 12 months.

From time to time, you may need to provide advice to a minister on the issue of how long the exhibition period should last. If the exhibition period is two months, there is little basis for a general extension; however, there may be circumstances where an individual extension may be warranted without delaying the process of assessing submissions.

10.2.4.2 Planning for Exhibition

The internet and social media enhance the ability to inform people of the opportunity to participate, while creating multiple ways to participate in exhibition activities and make a submission or provide informal input.

Ultimately the objective is to elicit *informed* submissions. This requires significant pre-planning as the exhibition period is usually fixed. Short and individual events to support the exhibition require separate plans.

Your community engagement plan, supported by individual event plans and a communications plan, will ensure timely delivery of activities. If ministers are involved, you'll need to plan to meet the minister's needs, including logistics, speaking notes and backgrounding on contentious issues.

The **community engagement plan** needs to cover:

- **The launch**. This is the start of awareness raising. It often involves multiple events to address geographic issues and/or the desire to meet with stakeholder groups such as the development sector or community groups. Launches are usually led by the decision-makers, and thus involve significant logistics in their own right.

There will always be tension between setting the date for the launch and when you can notify people to attend, as launches need to be locked into ministerial diaries, which are fluid. Most stakeholders recognise that the notification time will be short.

- **A website**. All information needs to be available online. From the launch date, the project's website must provide a range of information from the plan and associated background material to instructions on how to make a submission. The site may go live as the launch commences, but the time is flexible; make yourself aware of the time required for the site to become live once the decision to upload is made. I have experienced, several times, the challenge of a minister's office requesting a flexible launch time but also requesting the website going live as they take the floor at the launch.
- **Submissions portal**. This needs to be live alongside the website. Any online facility must cater for multiple types of submissions and be user friendly.
- **Standardised submission forms**. A standardised online submission form may reflect the principal themes of the plan, potentially by chapter. This saves time and improves quality during the assessment process. Also provide opportunities for open-ended responses.

 Also allow for standalone submissions to be uploaded or sent by post.
- **Confidentiality**. To enhance transparency, it is usual that submissions be made public. This requires permission from submitters. Using proformas may require legal advice.
- **Awareness raising**. The initial engagement should utilise multiple media platforms to maximise awareness of the plan and the opportunity to make a submission. The engagement plan should be clear about how different members of the community will be targeted.

Ultimately, you want the planning minister to confidently say they believe all in the community have been given an opportunity to make a submission.

10.2.4.3 Post-Launch Engagement

The community engagement plan needs to address post-launch engagement activities, which may include the following:

- The **traditional 'town hall' meeting** is a combination of awareness raising and providing people and community groups the opportunity to directly meet the planners. These events should be held as workshops where those who participate work through exercises directed to the main issues of the draft plan. In a digital age, fewer people attend town hall meetings and for the work required there are less benefits. However, decision-makers often expect that they will be undertaken.
- **Traditional engagement methods** may not be appropriate for hard-to-reach members of the community, such as those with English as a second language, or the elderly and the young. Consider language translation services and directly engaging with specific communities.

10.2 Step 5: Exhibition of a Draft Plan

- **First Nations communities** are potentially hard-to-reach groups and in line with the discussion in Sect. 5.3.2.5 there are likely to be a wide range of groups to engage.
- **Clarification meetings** are usually directed to local government and peak bodies and held a few weeks after the launch to allow the stakeholders time to review the documents. These help you to ascertain if the stakeholders' interpretation is as you intended.
- Other **innovative methods** include online discussions and deliberative panel sessions.

These activities typically include and/or are led by engagement specialists, with strategic planners providing technical support. Sometimes this mix creates some tension around messaging and language, due to the push to move away from the technical-based narratives of the plan, to 'comms messaging', for want of a better phrase.

When planning for these activities, remember that:

- many activities require significant lead time, and planning needs to occur well before the draft plan is ready
- each activity has logistical issues, particularly resourcing; make sure senior planners are available for each.

10.2.4.4 Submissions Review

In mapping out the logistics around processing submissions, consider:

- a dedicated project manager
- how you'll acknowledge receipt of submissions
- the process for reviewing the content, including whether each reviewer assesses the whole submission, or if different reviewers look only at principal areas of the plan (appropriate if responsibilities for different themes have been given to separate people)

> For the Greater Sydney Region Plan, planning students separated each submission into the themes of the plan. This improved the efficiency of the review process and allowed for quick fact checking when decision-makers sought clarification.

- the process for reporting the findings to the writers of the plan, again collectively or for each issue
- the process and schedule for advising senior officers of issues raised by major stakeholders and local government
- a schedule for informally and formally advising decision-makers of principal issues raised and how they impact the plan
- how the issues will be reported back to the community, including when the submissions report will be released

- sufficient resources, based on an estimate of how many submissions will be received and the time available for the submissions review task
- whether reviewers are experienced planners who can identify the nuances raised in some submissions, especially by the principal stakeholders
- a process for the detailed assessment of complex or contentious issues, including with other agencies
- how you'll provide access to submissions received during Step 2: Research and analysis to establish if previous positions have changed or if new issues have been raised, which will speed up the assessment process.

10.2.5 The Exhibition: Eliciting Submissions

The exhibition period is a short, sharp and intense time. With a well-prepared community engagement plan the expectations for the team should be clear, but as this is a highly outward facing activity, there are several issues for consideration:

- **Monitoring contentious issues**. With an outward facing process and potentially high media interest, keeping abreast of contentious issues raised in submissions or at events will help you to alert decision-makers and prepare responses for their use.
- **Addressing verbal submissions**. Many people will make verbal statements that they will perceive as a submission. Have the resources in place to capture these inputs, even if they cannot be directly attributed to someone.
- **Acknowledging submissions**. Be on top of the process of acknowledging submissions. Besides being the right thing to do, it confirms to the submitter that their submission is in the system, which helps to build trust.
- **Managing requests for further time**. There are nearly always requests to extend the exhibition period. Have a deliberate discussion on the matter with the decision-maker(s) before the exhibition commences so you can quickly manage the issue, when required.
- **Status updates**. Decision-makers will generally require advice regarding the level of engagement, from website visits, social media clicks or event attendees, and they may want this regularly, even daily. They will also want to understand the type of feedback in submissions, including actual numbers, the concerns of the principal stakeholders, and contentious issues (see earlier).
- **Team health and wellbeing** . Exhibition activities may occur after hours and, including travel, that can result in long days. In addition, face-to-face interaction can be emotionally draining and occasionally confrontational. Always monitor the wellbeing of staff; be mindful of the need to potentially change team rosters and have a clear protocol for after-hours travel arrangements and food.
- **Processing submissions**. Processing can start straight away, as there are always a few early bird submitters. However, most submissions arrive in the last week.

- **Late submissions**. Clarify what to do with submissions that arrive after the closing date. While you may allow an extension to individual people or organisations, usually you can let the submitter know that as a late submission it will be considered as far as practical.
- **Back of house activities**. Not all in the team will be involved in the exhibition activities. Use the exhibition period to catch up on a range of outstanding issues.

10.3   Step 6: Plan Finalisation

*Plans are about delivery,
in the absence of an implementation plan,
at best there will be ad hoc activity
at worst the plan will gather dust.*

10.3.1   Purpose of Step 6

Step 6 is the last stage in preparing the plan and all activities are directed towards seeking its approval for public release. Step 6 is about:

- finalising the content of the plan in consideration of the input from the submissions
- preparing an implementation pathway, which requires the allocation of responsibilities for delivering the plan.

10.3.2   Principal Activities

Step 6 requires you to update the plan in line with feedback. It is a deliberative activity that requires a paper trail of proposed changes to allow both confirmation of the changes and to record how the document evolves. Step 6 is also where you finalise responsibilities for delivering the plan and formally handing over responsibility for implementation.

The principal activities for Step 6 are (refer Fig. 10.2):

- **Rapid assessment**. An initial rapid assessment of submissions from the principal stakeholders (including local government) is an early opportunity to keep senior executives and decision-makers abreast of key issues and whether any substantive changes are needed. There is also a benefit from having senior executives undertake the assessment, which at most is a single day activity.
- **Late submissions**. There are always late submissions, the protocols for managing these need to be signed-off before the exhibition period ends.

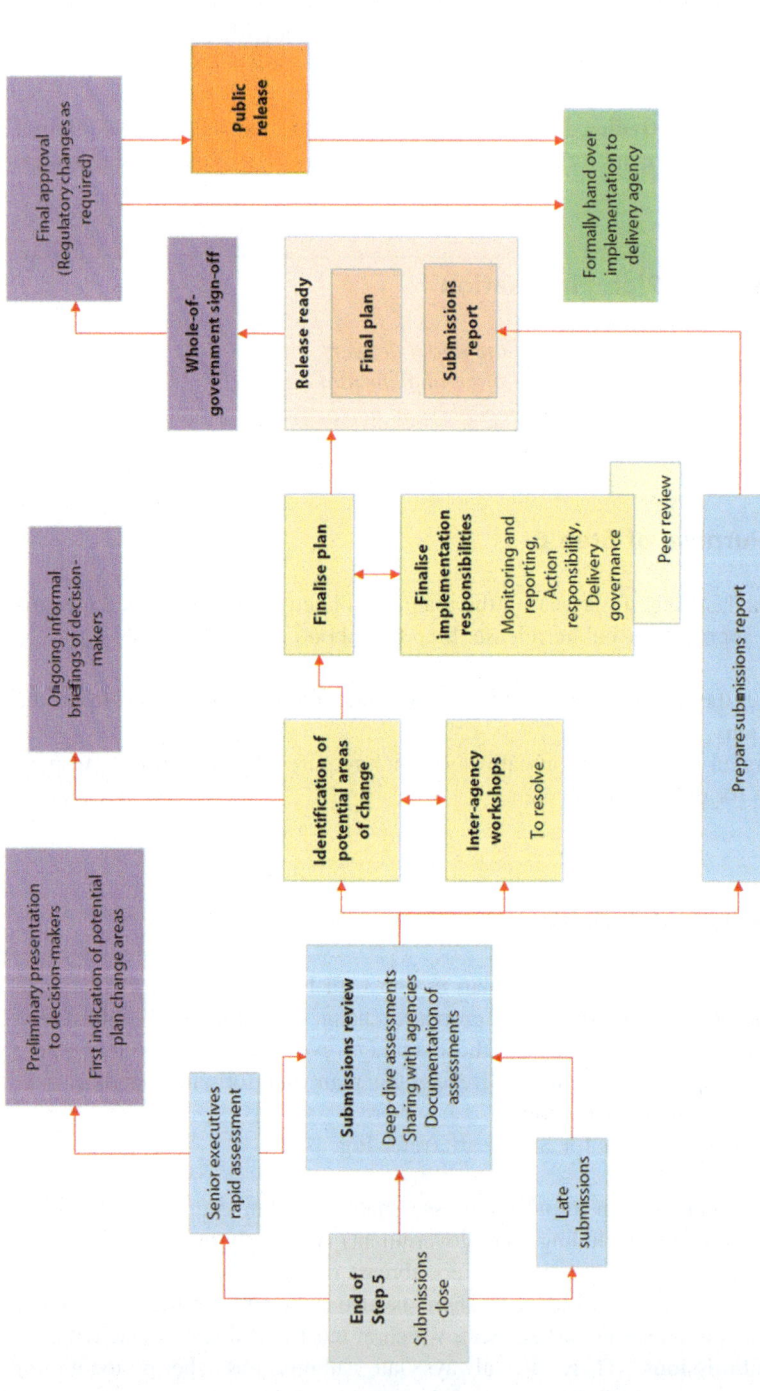

Fig. 10.2 Step 6: Plan finalisation: Principal activities
This diagram outlines the flow of the principal activities required in Step 6: Plan finalisation. This includes completing the review of submissions, advising decision-makers of potential changes and the content of the final plan, updating and finalising the plan, including an implementation plan, preparing the final release documents including a submissions report, final approval and release of the plan, and formal hand over to delivery agencies

10.3 Step 6: Plan Finalisation

- **Submissions review**. In assessing if a suggested change is needed, consider:
  - key reasons why a suggestion will not proceed
  - how you'll distil the change being requested from longer submissions
  - if multiple agencies have been involved, how you'll share relevant submissions with them.
- **Identifying changes**. Consideration classifying changes into four categories:
  a. major changes requiring formal discussions and sign-off
  b. minor enhancements, reporting of which is included in the approval documentation
  c. typos and errors, where there is simply acknowledgement that they have been changed
  d. suggested changes that are not agreed to, with documentation and reporting of more significant issues.

- **Inter-agency workshops**. Proposed changes are likely to cover areas of responsibility outside the planning portfolio, so you'll need to resolve final positions. Provide forewarning of the need for other agencies to review submissions and partake in workshops within a short timeframe, recognising they may have to liaise with their respective ministers.
- **Finalising the plan**. Document the changes in line with the four categories outlined above. Even a simple track change version of all typos is beneficial, and this can occur during the exhibition period. At this point having only one person responsible for approving all changes is an advantage.
  As with the draft plan there is a benefit from a quick peer review process (typically a one-day task).
- **Look and feel**. It is also at this point that the final enhancement to the look and feel of the document will occur from enhancements to graphics to new images. Photos should come from an authorised image library or be commissioned within a clear brief. Each photo should reflect the written words on the page, and each should have a title to identify its location. Photos are heavily scrutinised by decision-makers, so check for bloopers such as the bike rider without a helmet or a construction site without appropriate safety measures.
- **Implementation responsibilities**. You will need to clarify how the plan is delivered and who is responsible for each action. The final implementation chapter requires:
  - affirming the details of all actions, including assignment of responsibilities
  - identifying and approving initial funding requirements
  - finalising a monitoring and reporting plan including responsibilities
  - assigning responsibility for the lead agency that will oversee and drive the implementation
  - establishing the post-plan implementation phase, including governance arrangements
  - formal approval of the handover of responsibilities to the delivery agency.
- **Submissions report**. This is discussed further below.

- **Release ready**. Consider which documents will be published when the final plan is released, such as the submission report and any summary documentation. Thus, as with the finalisation of the draft plan, there are benefits to engaging a production manager.
- **Final approval**. In seeking approval, advise decision-makers of changes since the draft version; the salient points made by principal stakeholders; who is responsible for each action; who will lead the delivery; who will sign-off on the implementation plan; who will report on progress through an annual implementation update; and what is proposed for the launch.
- **Public release**. This is more than a simple statement of finalisation; instead, it is the beginning of a journey that seeks ownership from local government, stakeholders and the community. It signals the start of an educational process to emphasise and clarify the intent and application of the plan.
  This requires:
  – clarity as to the purpose of the plan, such as legislative status
  – an understanding of which agency will lead the implementation of the plan
  – the expectations for local government and the private sector
  – how the community will be engaged going forward, for example, regarding annual reporting.

10.3.3 First Nations and Plan Finalisation

Increasingly it is important to consider how key First Nations stakeholders are embedded into the sign-off process. Many First Nations communities are now demanding a seat at the table and there is an expectation to go beyond providing input from an advisory perspective. Decisions made regarding strategic planning will have a generational impact on Country, community and culture, therefore mechanisms to increase authority in decision-making should be considered.

This is increasingly important as conversations regarding treaties and a voice in parliament evolve.

A copy of the final plan should be sent to First Nations stakeholders that have been involved in the process. They should be informed about how their input was embedded into the final plan.

10.3.4 Submissions

10.3.4.1 Submissions Review
The submissions review process requires considerable resourcing and planning that should commence before the exhibition period starts, as noted in Sects. 9.3.3 and Sect. 1.2.4.4 Exhibition of the draft plan.

Also consider the following:

10.3 Step 6: Plan Finalisation

- Getting the most out of feedback, not just identifying substantive issues of concern but also how the plan can be improved. There will be greater ownership of the plan if the community can see that their feedback was taken into consideration.
- Informing the decision-makers as soon as practical when there are substantive issues of concern and what course of action is recommended. Ideally submissions from the principal stakeholders should be targeted for review at an early initial informal briefing of decision-makers, which will need to be set well in advance.
- During these reviews with decision-makers, identifying if the issues raised differ to any earlier submissions by the stakeholder in Step 2.
- Recognising that word clouds may indicate themes, but that they are simply a voting system based on an invalid sample size.

10.3.4.2 The Submissions Report

When the final plan is released, stakeholders and the community will expect a submissions report. Meeting this expectation is a perennial issue for planners.

The challenge is to establish to what extent the issues raised are addressed. For example, does a submissions report outline how every submission was addressed, noting there could be thousands of submissions, or is it a summary document? I have had senior executives suggest that the final plan is in fact the submissions report, as it outlines what has and has not been accepted from the submissions.

Contentious issues are a challenge; a response in line with a government's general policy positions may be difficult to express when a submission provided detailed evidence.

The submissions report takes considerable resources including time, especially if it seeks to address most issues raised. Ensure decision-makers are aware of the range of issues that come with each submissions report option.

The community will often seek an explanation as to why a decision was made or why their concern was not addressed. Do not put words in the decision-maker's mouth; ensure the submissions report is the only approved wording of how all submissions are responded to in the public domain.

10.3.5 Finalising the Plan

10.3.5.1 Agreement on Changes

In addition to identifying where changes should be made, you must manage the process of gaining sign-off to the changes. There are several considerations:

- develop a clear pathway for sign-off before the changes go to decision-makers
- consider a single point of approval usually by the project director or a collective sign-off by the project control group (or similar) that requires all in the room at the same time with edits approved, via a screen

- report changes in detail, including both text and graphics changes, remembering that track changes can be clumsy to review
- manager version control, particularly when documents have been split up into separate chapters for review.

While the focus is on responding to submissions, also check the wording of the objectives, strategies and policies. Is it clear what you want people to consider/do? My emphasis has always been: if you were asked on a Monday morning when sitting at your desk to do the task or address the policy, would it be clear to you as to what you have to do?

Some changes to the plan may require you to review earlier evidence or undertake last-minute investigations.

Towards the end of Step 6, where the focus has been on reviewing submissions, and some may be negative, there is a tendency for senior personnel to have doubts about some elements when even the slightest concerns are raised about the more innovative and challenging aspects of the plan. This is where senior officers must instil confidence in the document and remind others of the considerable levels of evidence and analysis that underpin the basis of the plan.

10.3.5.2 Inter-agency Workshops

We know that city planning requires collaboration across government agencies and the process of informal and formal interaction must continue. Consider:

- sharing submissions, not just summaries, with agencies
- working through the proposed changes
- re-affirming the details and responsibilities regarding all actions
- notifying agencies of last-minute changes and getting sign-off, where version control is part of the challenge.

10.3.5.3 Quality Control

As you're making changes to the document, have a process in place to manage quality control.

Some of the considerations regarding quality control are:

- There can never be too much proofreading. Bring in staff who have not had previous involvement to undertake the proofreading.
- Editing the document at this point can create challenges, when senior officers are focused on submissions and an editor makes, in good faith, an unfortunate subtle change to the intent of an objective, strategy or policy.
- Working with the typed text version of the plan and the published version, especially as web material will be taken from the typed version. Those who have published documents know the rule—make last-minute amendments to the published document directly at your peril.

10.3.6 Annual Monitoring and Reporting

Monitoring is essential to understand whether the city is evolving as intended and whether actions need to be modified or the expectations of the plan updated.

Underpinning monitoring is an assumption that the expected outcomes of the plan can be measured and that there is a level of evidence that shows a causality between the actions of the plan and the intended outcomes.

The Australian Government's *National Cities Performance Framework* (2017, pp. 27–28) divides performance indicators into:

1. **Performance indicators** that "can be used to assess the complete and final stage effects of a policy, also called outcome or impact indicators."
2. **Contextual indicators** "highlight the circumstances and characteristics of a city on dimensions not amenable to, or appropriate for, local policy intervention. … they can help to understand why a city performs the way it does."

Regarding both:

- There is no shortage of data sources for contextual indicators; many government departments provide access to data sets as does the ABS with Census data.
- Establishing performance indicators requires you to identify the principal outcomes for the plan and then how each outcome will/can be measured.
- In a NSW (Australia) context, the draft *Connecting with Country* framework (p. 34) includes 3 strategic goals as the basis for establishing indicators for success.

In establishing the performance indicators, note that:

- No person, let alone a politician, likes to report that they are not achieving a stated goal. Yet the explicit purpose of a performance indicator is to measure the extent to which an outcome is being achieved. Therefore, the establishment of performance indicators needs to be a journey with decision-makers, as distinct from a last task during the finalisation of a plan so the importance and implications of each indicator can be fully examined.
- There is usually agreement that the best potential indicators will require resourcing to enable measurement. However, at the end of a planning process, seeking additional ongoing funding is often a challenge and sometimes the indicators that can be obtained from existing data sets or related activities are preferred. This is unfortunate and in part why I advocate for a shift to continuous planning where research, including monitoring, is a business-as-usual activity.
- Potentially most importantly, in the short term, it takes time to influence the dynamics of a city. Major transport projects often take a decade from conception to completion. Similarly, creating new housing supply in a specific location can also take up to a decade before we see the construction of new dwellings. Thus,

Table 10.1 Capital city comparison: Monitoring and reporting
(This table highlights the delivery elements for the plans for Australia's capital cities.)

Capital city plan	Monitoring section	Reporting section	Performance Criteria	Governance section	Planned review	Implementation section	Other
ACT	Yes	Yes	No	No	Yes	Yes	–
Adelaide	Yes	Yes	Yes	Yes	No	Yes	(a), (b)
Darwin	No	No	No	No	Yes c)	No	–
Greater Sydney	Yes	Yes	No	No	No	Yes	–
Melbourne	Yes	Yes	Yes	Yes	Yes	Yes	(a)
Perth & Peel	Yes	Yes	Yes	No	No	Yes	(e)
South East Queensland	Yes	Yes	Yes	Yes		Yes	(a), (f), (g)

Notes (a) Implementation responsibilities defined, (b) delivery tools included, (c) no period specified, (d) a separate implementation plan, (e) specifies opportunity for refinements, (f) activities to deliver and (g) implementation program included

Source My review of Australia's capital city plans as listed in the section at the end of this chapter on 'Further reading'

for at least five years It is unlikely that the core objectives of a plan will reveal themselves. In these early years, report on the progress of the actions in the plan that, in theory, will deliver the outcomes.

Ultimately, the principal purpose of setting up monitoring and reporting activities is to establish an implementation framework for the plan. Table 10.1 covers my assessment of the extent that Australian capital city plans address implementation considerations, and it shows a level of variability.

10.4 Implications for Other Planning Typologies

Issues to consider when applying these processes to other planning typologies are outlined in Table 10.2 and considered in detail in Chapter 12.

Table 10.2 Applying the Step 5 and Step 6 approach to other planning typologies
(This table outlines how the planning activity is undertaken for a metropolitan planning project in Step 5: Exhibition of a draft plan and Step 6: Plan finalisation, needs to be adapted for the four other city planning typologies. Additional detail is provided in Chapter 12.)

Planning activity	Local government area plan	Town centre and regional centre plan	Greenfield community plan	Neighbourhood community plan
Implementation plan		Confirming responsibilities for delivery, both internal to the council and by state agencies is fundamental. Hence, the need to clarify benefits, and a general understanding of costs and budgetary cycles, in terms of timing for delivery	The final plan should outline sequencing preferences and the implications and costs of developing out of sequence and who funds the additional costs	

10.5 Summary

This chapter covers steps 5 and 6 of the 7-Step Strategic Planning Process, where the final output is the public release of an approved final plan.

The activities for Step 5 are generally public facing and thus require an engagement plan to coordinate activities and make decision-makers aware of the activities occurring in the public domain. The discussion covering Step 5: Public exhibition of the plan also emphasised:

- the pre-planning activities that need to occur before the exhibition period can commence
- the need for exhibition activities to maximise the number of informed submissions by raising awareness of the exhibition, providing all information necessary to enable informed consideration of the plan, and providing a simple submission process
- the use of a submission template to enhance the legibility and accessibility of submissions by ensuring comments on the separate elements of the plan are easily identifiable
- that the bulk of submissions normally do not arrive until the last week; thus their assessment occurs in Step 6.

For Step 6: Plan finalisation, I emphasised that as the focus of activities is responding to submissions, documentation is required on changes proposed and why. Other issues emphasised for Step 6 include:

- the benefit of targeted activities that allow the early identification of the issues of concern by the principal stakeholder and whether there is a need for any substantial changes
- categorising the proposed changes by type enhances the ability to advise the decision-makers on how the document has changed since its draft form
- quality control
- inter-agency workshops to resolve changes
- a final implementation plan that identifies responsible agencies for each action, the lead agency for delivering the plan and how performance will be monitored and annually reported on.

10.5.1 Insights

Insight: Pre-planning is essential *Remember the race between the hare and the tortoise.* **Post exhibition every second counts** Once a plan has been on exhibition there is pressure to have it finalised as soon as practical. Reviewing a thousand or more submissions takes time and more importantly requires considerable pre-planning, which should start months before the exhibition period starts. The focus here is on both pre-planning and managing expectations. **Insight: The most significant changes are the last** **Changes right at the end don't get changed** *Many years ago, when I was involved in the resolution of a major strategy a colleague emphasised an issue right at the last minute. Those involved were taken up in both the emotion of finishing and the idea being presented. It was included. A lesson in tactics.* **Managing self-doubt at the end of a process** I have seen decision-makers and senior executives, at the end of a long strategic planning process, move from incredibly skilled practitioners to individuals overcome by emotion, with an over-willingness to please the client by making unnecessary changes, which are later regretted.	**Insights: Finalising the content** **The last few weeks are critical—free up your diary** It is the last few weeks where project management is critical at the micro level. This is when the decision-makers give most attention to the plan, and they can potentially raise everything from fine tuning the narrative to new ideas, as well as challenging earlier assumed conclusions. Thus, it is critical at this point for the project manager not to be caught up in the day-to-day working and be free to act as required. The last few weeks are when the second in charge may need to step up and leave the project director free to put out fires. A production manager will bring tangible benefits. **Say it like it is** This is not so much about plain English, but about being clear about the outcome being sought. We often get caught in planning speak and miss the salient point. I find that in ad hoc, relaxed conversation we often get right to the point, as we don't have time to elaborate or put our argument in fancy language—we say it like it is. The consequence of not doing so in the plan is the potential to create ambiguity in a statement, which will allow others to re-interpret your words to their benefit.

(continued)

10.5 Summary

(continued)

Here it is critical for planners to emphasise the journey and past decisions and ensure any last changes are genuinely necessary. After a sustained period of work and reflection, consider whether this sudden requirement for change is valid.

Insights: Finalising the documents
Get a production manager
In the last stages of finalising the plan, hours matter. A production manager in addition to your project manager is essential.

Where your project manager will most likely have weekly meetings with the team, the production manager will introduce daily meetings with daily workplans.

A good production manager will create valuable time when it counts. An extra day at this point of the process is extraordinarily valuable, such as having time for an extra proofread.

Don't edit the 'design' version—you will break this law
The golden rule is to prepare your document in a text document, then transfer it to the publishing software for printing.

Unfortunately, at the end, small changes come thick and fast, and you will be pushed to change the designed version, and you will forget to modify the text document—a critical issue for when you are at the draft plan stage. At this point you unfortunately learn how to say *mea culpa*.

Brief often and brief early
To be successful a plan needs to be owned by the decision-makers and, considering the wide nature of city planning, there are likely to be many decision-makers.

To get alignment, it is my experience that waiting until you have the final document is far too late. Moreover, it is not just the decision-makers you need to brief but their advisors, whether they be the advisors in ministers' offices or senior executives across government departments. They all need to be kept up to speed throughout the process so there are no surprises.

Early in the process, establish who is responsible for briefing and who is providing briefing notes for each step of the way.

Insights: Evidence of success
What proof will there be that the plan is working?
Can you measure it?
In starting to prepare a plan it should be clear why there is a need to intervene; that is, the public policy rationale for the plan. Equally, when putting in place the actions for a plan it should be clear what evidence will indicate that the plan is working.

It is critical to be able to determine the extent to which a plan is heading towards or away from the stated outcomes. Thus, the outcomes need to be measurable. As the future is not static, there will be a constant need to adjust your actions, thus, some way of tracking your path forward is a required minimum.

It's not about absolutes
Too often, we get stuck in the determination of potential performance measures due to concerns about accuracy or, from a political sense, concerns about targets. A starting point is not to see them as absolutes, but as measures that show a relative change—for example, are we moving towards or away from our goal? Such an approach needs to have monitoring, review, and refinement as central elements of the implementation package.

Further Reading

Website links

Australian Government 2017 *National Cities Performance Framework,* Commonwealth of Australia. https://www.infrastructure.gov.au/cities/national-cities-performance-framework/

Exhibition period (mandatory) for a draft metropolitan (regional) plan. *Environmental Planning and Assessment Act 1979 No 203* (NSW) Schedule 1, Part 1, Division 1 Minimum Public exhibition periods for plans, viewed 16 June 2020. https://www.legislation.nsw.gov.au/~/view/act/1979/203

Government Architect NSW 2020 *Draft Connecting with Country.* Draft Connecting WIth Country (nsw.gov.au)

Greater Sydney Commission 2019 *The Pulse of Greater Sydney,* NSW Government. https://www.greater.sydney/pulse-of-greater-sydney-2018-2019

Australian capital city plans website links

A Metropolis of Three Cities (2018) State of New South Wales. https://www.greater.sydney/metropolis-of-three-cities

ACT Planning Strategy 2018 (2018) Australian Capital Territory. https://www.planning.act.gov.au/act-planning-strategy

Darwin Regional Land Use Plan 2015 (2015) Northern Territory Government, Department of lands, Planning and the Environment. https://planningcommission.nt.gov.au/projects/drlup

Perth and Peel @ 3.5 million (2018) Government of Western Australia, Department of Planning, Lands and Heritage. https://www.dplh.wa.gov.au/perth-and-peel-@-3-5-million

Plan Melbourne 2017–2050, (2017) The State of Victoria Department of Environment, Land, Water and Planning. https://www.planmelbourne.vic.gov.au/

Shaping SEQ, South East Queensland Regional Plan 2017 (2017) The State of Queensland, Department of Infrastructure, Local Government and Planning. https://planning.dsdmip.qld.gov.au/planning/better-planning/state-planning/regional-plans/seqrp

The 30-Year Plan for Greater Adelaide, 2017 Update (2017) Government of South Australia, Department of Planning, Transport and Infrastructure. https://livingadelaide.sa.gov.au/the_plan

Plan Delivery and Ongoing Planning 11

11.1 Introduction

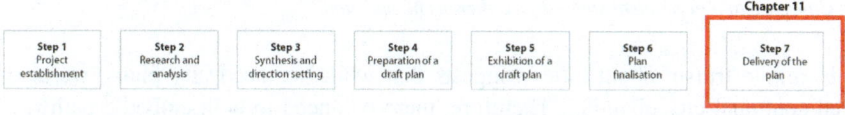

Avoiding creating a white elephant

and

Cities are dynamic, so they need an ongoing dynamic review process

The previous six chapters have focused on the question of how to prepare a city plan. However, in Chapter 3 a principal conclusion was that city planning is about intervention, which by default requires some sort of action. The city plan that is the output of Step 6 is a framework for action; however, it is, in one sense, only a report that just as easily could be placed on a shelf to gather dust. Its delivery requires coordination. The purpose of Step 7 is to outline the activities required for the successful delivery of a city plan.

This chapter begins by outlining the activities to deliver the final approved plan. In addition to coordinating actions and monitoring and reporting, successful delivery requires promoting the plan and the strategic alignment of activities across government agencies and local government.

Importantly I also outline what is at the heart of city planning: an ongoing strategic planning process, where research activities need to be integrated with targeted policy reviews and plan updates informed by the monitoring and reporting activities for the city plan.

© The Author(s), under exclusive license to Springer Nature Switzerland AG 2023
H. Dalheim, *Planning Better Cities*,
https://doi.org/10.1007/978-3-031-33947-9_11

11.1.1 Warm-Up Exercise

Another small exercise.

It's now a year since the plan was finalised so you are now focused on delivery and your team has been split between delivery tasks and other planning teams. You're invited to a joint meeting with your old and new bosses. They let you know they have come from a meeting with the minister and while the minister recognises that the plan is to be reviewed every five years certain events have unfolded and a change to the plan is being requested.

Considering no team exists to do the work you are invited to consider what organisational changes and activities would need to be put in place. What do you suggest? Jot down a few points.

11.2 Purpose of Step 7

Cities are in a permanent state of flux, there is no end state.

This simple truism about cities suggests that while we need city plans, we also need continual city planning. Therefore, there is a need to both embed a pathway for the delivery of the plan as well as a strategic process for ongoing consideration of change across the city.

To this end the joint purpose of Step 7 is to:

- establish a deliberative process for the management of the activities required to deliver the plan, particularly the identification of a delivery lead and governance arrangements to coordinate the actions to be undertaken
- outline the principal activities required to deliver an ongoing metropolitan planning function that complements the activities required to deliver a city plan.

The rationale for establishing an ongoing metropolitan planning function reflects:

- the dynamic nature of cities
- the benefits of responding promptly to the findings of monitoring activities
- the benefits of responding to new policy positions of government as they occur
- the reality that metropolitan planning activities become log jams for new policy issues resulting in some policies being disregarded for convenience not because they lack benefit
- the need to address unforeseen changes such as the COVID-19 pandemic or the Global Financial Crisis, which impact assumptions such as population growth or economic activity
- the opportunity to deal with contentious issues in a more manageable environment.

This approach more correctly sees the plan as a dynamic document that evolves as the city evolves. It also emphasises that the plan is not seeking to arrive at some desired preconceived end state.

11.3 Principal Activities

The activities of Step 7 can be seen to occur in three streams (refer Fig. 11.1):

1. **Delivering the plan.** All the activities required to deliver the approved plan.
2. **Ongoing research.** The research activities (including community consultation) required to understand the dynamics of the city as well as the activities directed to monitoring plan performance
3. **Plan updates.** A coordinated approach to targeted policy reviews and formal updates to the plan.

The latter two relate to the establishment of an ongoing metropolitan planning function that could include the first stream of activities.

11.3.1 Plan Delivery—Principal Activities

To maximise effectiveness, the scope of activities is more than coordinating actions and monitoring performance (refer Fig. 11.2).

- **Action coordination.** The whole of government coordination of actions and the annual reporting of progress.
- **Implementation plan.** An implementation plan needs to build on the implementation chapter of the final plan. It needs to cover annual priorities, governance and an action plan (by type). Each action should identify the lead agency, partner agencies, timing, resourcing, interdependencies with other actions, monitoring and reporting arrangements.
- **Promoting the plan.** The small group of people across government directly involved in the preparation of the plan need to bring others along on the journey. This involves ongoing promotion and masterclass activities to emphasise how the plan influences business-as-usual activities within government agencies, local government and the private sector. This task lasts years, not months.
- **Strategic alignment.** State agencies and local government undertake a range of activities that support and/or enhance the plan's delivery. These activities can be most effective when they are directly aligned with activities of the plan and where the delivery is coordinated in a place-based approach.
  The approval of a new plan can also mean that some policies of other agencies may no longer be consistent with the new directions of government. There is benefit from a review of sectoral policies for consistency.
- **Annual monitoring of performance.** This is covered in the next section.

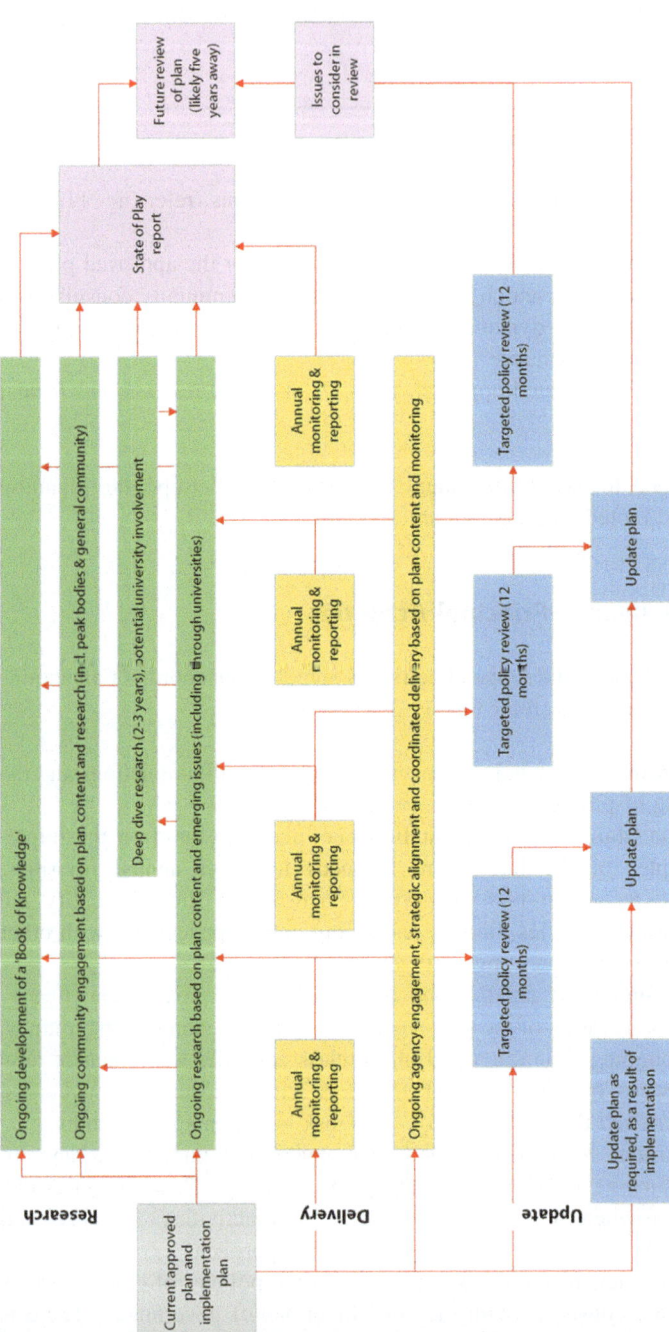

Fig. 11.1 An ongoing strategic planning framework: from plans to planning (This diagram outlines the flow of the principal activities required for an ongoing strategic planning process to monitor and update [including targeted research] the final approved plan. The activities include the establishment of an ongoing research program and book of knowledge, a monitoring and reporting program and a policy review program to update the adopted plan. These tasks lead to a state of plan report to inform the next comprehensive review)

11.3 Principal Activities

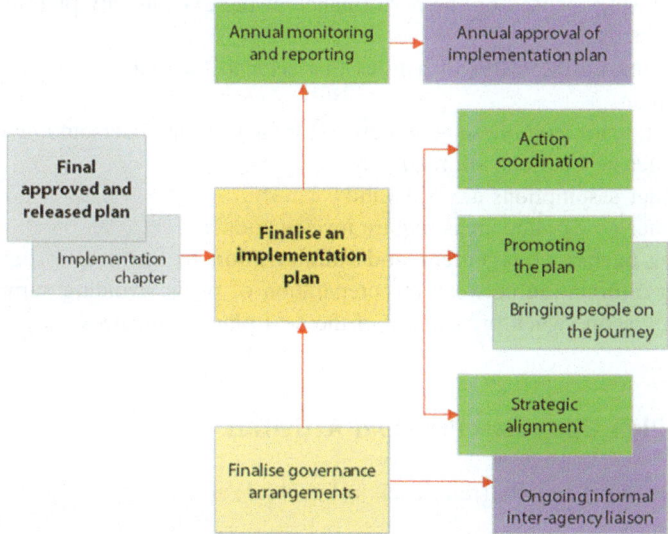

Fig. 11.2 Step 7: Plan delivery
(This diagram outlines the principal activities to deliver the approved plan)

When shifting from plan preparation to delivery, think about how to retain the tacit knowledge gained by staff. As preparation of city plans occurs infrequently, the staff involved often move on to new areas and when a new plan is commenced few, if any, original staff members remain.

Aim to retain a small core team dedicated to metropolitan planning.

11.3.2 Ongoing Research—Principal Activities

There main areas of activity (refer back to Fig. 11.1) are:

- **Ongoing development of a 'book of knowledge'**, a repository of information to inform future strategic planning activities. This requires:
  - **ongoing research**, directed to issues arising from the current plan and emerging issues, including deep dive research pieces (two to three-year initiatives), which may need university involvement
  - **ongoing engagement** with peak bodies and community groups to understand the evolution of community perceptions and aspirations.

  The book of knowledge is the base material for a state of play report that documents the latest understanding of the dynamics of a city on commencement of a new city plan.
- **Annual monitoring and reporting**. This activity was discussed in Section 10.3.6 . It includes:

- monitoring focused on the performance of the existing city plan in meeting its objectives
- reporting on the status of actions that seek to facilitate the delivery of the city plan.

What you learn from these activities will influence the understanding of:
- whether new actions are required
- whether assumptions are still valid
- whether new policy areas require investigation.

- **Ongoing agency engagement and collaboration** to facilitate a share activities and information between the preparation of plans, avoiding surprises and clarifying scope when preparation of the next plan commences.

11.3.3 Plan Updates—Principal Activities

The main areas of activity (refer back to Fig. 11.1) are:

- **Targeted policy review** to address specific policy issues and:
  - reduce time and resourcing during the preparation of city plans
  - manage complex and difficult issues
  - respond to issues to as they arise
  - respond to new assumptions on which a plan is based.
- **Updates to the city plan** to incorporate new policy positions and/or assumptions, which will allow plans to be dynamic documents (as often espoused) and thus allow the public and private sectors to reflect the most contemporary understanding of the city. The intention is to create *flexible certainty*, where formal engagement processes ensure transparency in decision-making.
- **State of play report**. This document is prepared just before the requirement to undertake a review of a plan or prepare a new plan.

11.3.4 First Nations and Plan Delivery and Ongoing Planning

Strong partnerships should have developed throughout the previous stages of developing the plan. This would have highlighted key outcomes and goals of First Nations communities, which offers a strong foundation for partnership during implementation. Frequent and ongoing conversations should be embedded into the implementation process to ensure that First Nations priorities and goals are resourced and become a key focus of delivering the plan.

11.4 Implementing the Approved Plan

11.4.1 An Implementation Plan

The final approved plan will include an implementation chapter that covers delivery responsibilities for each action; governance arrangements, including who is the lead delivery agency; and monitoring and reporting arrangements. This chapter should be converted into a standalone five-year implementation plan that expands on issues included in the plan, specifically:

- final performance measures, including who is responsible for collecting the information for individual measures
- governance arrangements, including a meeting schedule
- an annual action list and forward action priority listing
- agreement in principle to a place-based delivery approach
- agreement to a governance arrangement to strategically align activities across agencies and local government.

As the implementation plan outlines the priorities of government, it should be approved by the decision-makers. Ideally the standalone document is completed at the same time as finalising the plan. However, I've found that the combination of heightened focus on the output of the final plan, and the introduction of a delivery agency that is not the agency responsible for preparing the plan, makes the early completion of an implementation plan elusive.

Also seek agreement on the preparation of an annual update or progress report on the implementation plan. *Plan Melbourne* and *OneNYC 2050* both have clear progress reports.

11.4.2 Plan Delivery

Delivering a plan requires resources. While this may not be difficult for the agencies delivering infrastructure—as they annually seek funds for business cases or delivery—it can be the reverse in planning.

In my experience, the perennial issue is seeking to justify why additional funds are required. Consequently, planning departments are often asked to realign their budget to achieve the actions of the plan that seek to facilitate the outcomes in a plan such as detailed plans for town centres, greenfield areas or urban renewal precincts.

> *I once discussed this with a senior treasury official, who. quickly grasped the issue and suggested that planners need to be able to convince ministers that their actions are akin to buying a train, in that ministers recognise that buying a train needs a separate allocation of funds.*

So, what are planners' 'trains'? In Melbourne and Sydney each year, around $35bn to $50bn (refer to the ABS building approvals website link) goes towards development construction, and planning influences the location of the development, as well as the economic benefits related to a more efficient and productive city. That benefit is our 'train'—over to you urban economists.

11.4.3 Promoting the Plan

11.4.3.1 Bringing Others Along for the Journey

Many parts of the planning or transport portfolios are often not engaged in the preparation of the plan, yet they are important players in delivery. Hence, you need to consider how to keep them up to date during plan preparation and after approval. Consider preparing:

- A simple stump speech for the process and the final plan, for most members of the project team to use
- Simple fact sheets that outline:
  - The purpose, milestones, timing and when their input may be required
  - how policy positions have changed (in the final plan) and how the plan will affect the activities of different departments.

When the Greater Sydney Region Plan was finalised, we gave each local government a document that outlined what the plan meant for them.

11.4.3.2 Promoting the Content and Purpose of the Plan

Most planners in state agencies, and people within planning-related areas in local government, will not have been engaged in plan preparation. Similarly, many in the development sector will have little knowledge of the plan or its basis.

Consider the business-as-usual activities and policy understanding of local government, the development sector and planning profession (including architects, landscape architects and property advisors) that will be influenced by the plan. What options are there for short courses or guidance notes to inform how policy positions have changed and how various aspects of the plan need to be considered?

In a new role for a council, I was asked to comment on a proposed subdivision plan. I advised that the design that had back fences fronting open space was directly against state government policy that had changed many years earlier. I was advised—'that's how we do things here.'

11.4.4 Strategic Alignment

Once a plan is approved you will need to identify and update any policies and/or guidelines that are out of step with the new plan.

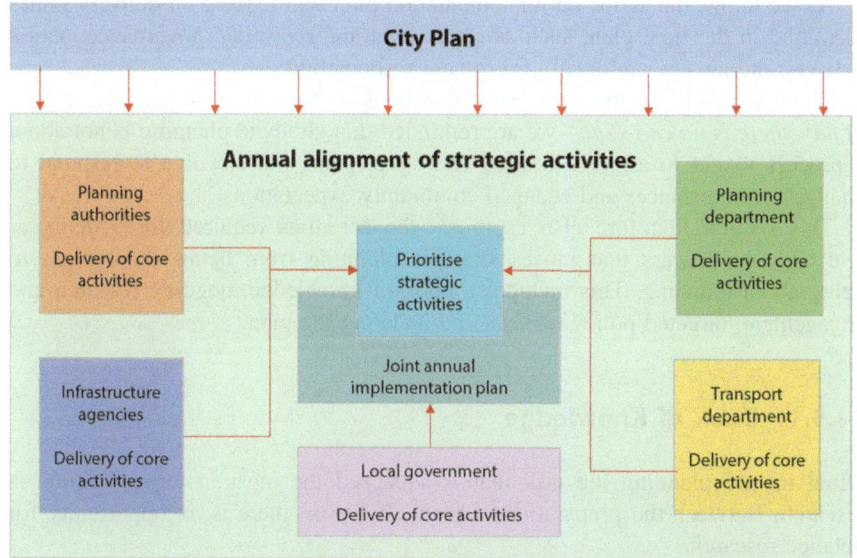

Fig. 11.3 Strategic alignment of delivery activities
(This diagram highlights who should be involved when aligning delivery actions from across state and local government. It highlights that each player will have core delivery activities that will continue to be pursued. The collaboration focuses on coordinating actions that enhance place-based outcomes)

The aligning of infrastructure and planning projects requires a tailored governance arrangement to coordinate activities across state and local government, refer to Fig. 11.3. This arrangement could have a requirement that agencies expressly determine if a place-based program should be developed when a single project is identified.

This coordination of activities could also include the establishment of an annual research agenda linked to the annual reporting of outcomes for the plan.

11.5 An Ongoing Strategic Planning Process

My experience suggests the successful delivery of a plan is enhanced when implementation activities are embedded. The dynamic nature of cities and the impacts of unforeseen events suggests the concept of city plans being prepared only at a single point in time is insufficient to meet the needs and aspirations of the community.

There is no consistency as to how Australia's capital city plans approach implementation, as outlined in Sect. 10.3.5. This section outlines the considerations in establishing an implementation process linked to an *ongoing* strategic planning process.

As we know, the endorsed implementation plan will expand on delivery issues identified in the final plan, such as monitoring and reporting, governance, action delivery and agency and local government responsibilities.

When we consider the subtext for this book—*Cities are in a permanent state of flux, there is no end state*—we are reminded that strategic planning is not about a process to get to arrive a desired end state; plans must evolve to respond to changed circumstances and changed community expectations.

This section therefore also examines the activities required for a deliberative ongoing process that moves strategic planning from being about plans to being about planning. This includes a book of knowledge, ongoing research and engagement, targeted policy reviews and updating the plan.

11.5.1 Book of Knowledge

Often in city planning the task that is squeezed the most in terms of time is research. Between the preparation of plans, however, there is an opportunity for detailed research.

Seek to develop a single repository of knowledge curated by a single group—I call this a 'book of knowledge', refer Fig. 11.4. Its creation will build a culture of knowledge as a resource, where accuracy is paramount and information is easily accessible to maximise consistency, whether for a media release or inputs to a new city planning project.

Considerations in preparing a book of knowledge are:

- developing protocols for vetting and accepting new information
- including narratives as well as facts
- developing a retrieval system based on the advice of users

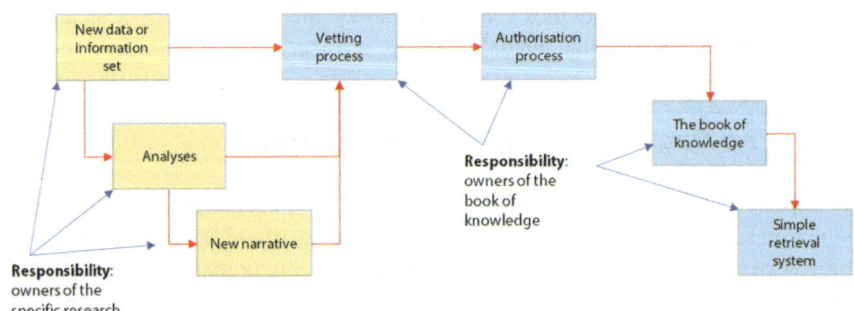

Fig. 11.4 Building the book of knowledge
(This diagram outlines the types of activities required to set up a book of knowledge resource program)

11.5 An Ongoing Strategic Planning Process

- determining what is public facing—for example, the research that informed the Greater Sydney Region Plan and five district plans is available alongside the plans.

In the first instance the book of knowledge should include:

- links to relevant government policies, the ABS Census, and other ABS data sets related to land use such as building approvals data
- data sets used in Step 2: Research and analysis.

Other data sources and research connections can be explored including:

- in-house documents
- in-house research teams and/or libraries
- work of other agencies and stakeholders
- reports from major development applications and/or zoning proposals
- work from local government.

In terms of other important research considerations, Caroline Criado Perez in her book *Invisible Women* (2019) provides an exposé on the male bias in data, which will challenge many people. **I wish such a book had been available 30 years ago.**

Start by considering this issue while data is curated and collected. This requires simple questions that seek to reveal the nature and purpose of data. For example, does understanding the impacts of the journey to work address all travel needs of the community in the morning? Do we know what the other morning trip movements are and how they can be improved? Will improving transport networks enhance the productivity of all members of the community? What monetary value do we put on the activities of running a home?

Further, in 2016–2017, I chaired a research project for the Sustainable Built Environment National Research Centre titled *Scenario Planning Transport Futures: Improved Road and Transport Planning using Digital Scenario Planning Tools* (2017)—you can download multiple documents from the Research Centre's website. The research noted the importance of ensuring, at the outset, that data platforms are available as an open source.

This aligns with the increasing need for transparency of government information. In Australia, the development of the 'digital twin' will create an information system where data from across government is stored in a common platform. The NSW Government's Spatial Services unit states:

> The NSW Spatial Digital Twin (SDT) is a program of work ... which will deliver a cross-sector, collaborative environment that will share and visualise location information, in a 4D model (3D plus time) of the real world, in near real time and will support improved decision making.

At the heart of the NSW SDT is a shared data management and delivery platform that is open to the public and private sector allowing for effective collaboration to accelerate the deployment and uptake of smart and connected technologies across the state.

Source NSW Spatial Digital Twin (refer Website Links)

11.5.2 Ongoing Research

Research between the preparation of plans provides the opportunity to:

- investigate issues that may be contentious and thus difficult to pursue as part of wide-ranging issues pursued for a specific plan
- allow debate on a topic, again unencumbered by work on the myriad of issues as part of any traditional city planning process
- undertake deeper research dives in areas where the research process may take two to three years to complete.

An important consideration here is not so much about methodologies, which will need to reflect the nature of topics, but how you collaborate to get the work done and with whom, such as with:

- universities
- research institutes such as the Sustainable Built Environment National Research Centre, as mentioned earlier
- peak bodies
- organisations receiving grant programs, such as those provided for by the Australian Research Council.

An initial research project may be to work with universities and research centres to understand the breadth and depth of existing research and how it can be accessed or working with the same groups to set up an ongoing research and information exchange dialogue.

Research must be a business-as-usual priority of senior executives. If responsibility is left to the day-to-day planning practitioner, it is likely that tasks will forever be pushed back.

Furthermore, researching is a skill that all strategic planners should have, but as with any skill area the dedicated researcher will outperform the generalist. There is a benefit from using in-house research teams or specialists in this area.

11.5.3 Ongoing Engagement

11.5.3.1 Community Engagement

As cities evolve so do the perceptions and aspirations of communities. Use the time between plans to better understand the values and expectations of the community away from the focus on a specific plan.

The outcomes sought in this area include:

- For the general community, expanding the breadth and depth of knowledge of the expectations as to how people live, work and play
- For peak bodies, expanding the breadth and depth of knowledge of what is important to their constituents as well as issues relevant to the delivery of a plan
- Building ongoing relationships and trust, particularly for working with First Nations communities.

A critical consideration for all activities is transparency.

During this period between plans, seek knowledge as distinct from broad community comment, such as which city planning issues are important to the community. Use engagement techniques such as deliberative panels, focus groups or surveys.

Statistically valid data on community values are not generally targeted in community engagement activities for city plans. You may consider a two-step process for understanding community values, beginning with focus groups to identify issues, then a statistically valid survey.

Local governments also hold data on community attitudes.

When it comes to engaging with the community for a specific project, look at the work of Wendy Sarkissian and Wiwik Bunjamin-Mau titled *Speak Out* (2009). It is a practical book, with a hands-on approach that goes into the detail of what you need including consumables such as pens and contact paper.

> *By way of example, the benefit of thinking about what is needed meant that when at the City of Casey, we created to engagement bags. Two suitcases full of all that is need which meant we were engagement ready at a moment's notice.*

11.5.3.2 Agency Engagement

Keep abreast of the planning activities and actions of other government agencies, such as transport, environment, health, education and utility providers.

It is likely that formal sign-off will be required from other agencies for the data, findings and narratives to be included in the book of knowledge. Formalise this working relationship through a channel such as the senior officers group, as discussed in Sect. 6.4.3.

Most state governments already have many inter-agency working committees. In the first instance an audit of these would be beneficial. The harder part is working out who should have responsibility for leading inter-agency collaboration.

11.5.4 Targeted Policy Review and Updating Plans

Targeted policy reviews provide several city planning benefits:

- Reducing the number of policy decisions required when preparing a city plan, especially across multiple agencies, to avoid important new policies ending up on the cutting floor
- Making city planning a genuinely dynamic process, where issues are dealt with as they arise through an ongoing deliberative strategic planning process, thus achieving my concept of flexible certainty
- Introducing a more explicit notion that policy development is intrinsically interrelated to integrated city (spatial) planning, not independent of it.

The critical process issue here is transparency in the process, particularly the opportunity for community input and formal comment.

The more challenging part is confining the activities to a targeted update only of the policy issue or specific content. Documentation is essential here—those of you involved in zoning changes have experience in targeted changes to regulations.

11.6 Implications for Other Planning Typologies

Several issues need to be considered when applying the approach in this chapter to the other planning typologies—refer Table 11.1 and find detailed information in Chapter 12.

Table 11.1 Applying Step 7 to other planning typologies

Planning activity	Local government area plan	Town centre and regional centre plan	Greenfield community plan	Neighbourhood community plan
Project delivery		Some projects will be delivered by other departments at a council. Thus, ensuring their buy-in to the plan together with an understanding of budgetary conditions will be critical	Monitoring ongoing trends will ensure the timely delivery of infrastructure	

This table outlines how the planning activity for metropolitan planning in Step 7: Plan delivery and ongoing planning can be adapted for the four other city planning typologies. Additional detail is provided in Chapter 12

11.7 Summary

This chapter has covered the final step in the 7-Step Strategic Planning Process. We dealt with the activities to deliver on the final plan and the establishment of an ongoing and dynamic strategic planning processes.

In terms of delivery of the plan, I emphasised:

- the need for a standalone implementation plan prepared by the agency responsible for delivery
- the importance of ongoing promotion of the plan
- the need to align the activities of government agencies and local government to maximise resources, ideally through a place-based approach.

For the ongoing strategic planning process, I emphasised:

- the book of knowledge as a repository for all city planning data and information, including agreed narratives to explain or promote the plan
- how ongoing community engagement will build an understanding of community values as well as trust
- the opportunity for targeted policy reviews on issues as they arise or contentious issues that may be difficult to pursue during a formal strategic planning process
- the opportunity to regularly update the city plan thus making it a truly dynamic document.

11.7.1 Insights

Insight: It's about much more than a plan
Plans need to be delivered
Putting structure to the process of delivery
Much of the process of developing a plan is directed to developing objectives, strategies, actions and a spatial plan. Also consider the elements that influence the delivery of the plan
Early in my career Dr Jeff Wolinski suggested that in terms of delivery we need to consider:
- leadership and commitment of the commissioning government or organisation
- actionable projects, including clearly defined scope, resources requirements, timing and delivery responsibility
- mutually reinforcing projects in contrast to the notion of widespread disparate actions
- prioritisation for projects by time horizon, ease of implementation, scope of benefits and level of private sector participation
- resource allocation
- commitment and resource allocation of delivery partners

Insights: Who delivers the plan? #1
Technocrats can't make it happen
Good advice needs authorisation
It does not matter how good a plan is unless the relevant local, state or federal politicians sign-off on it. Until then the plan is no more than an idea. I recommend testing the expectations of the decision-makers along the way to ensure timely approvals
Governance is important
The development of any plan, and particularly the delivery of a plan, requires good governance arrangements at a senior executive level and at a government level
This requires representation from those that will be required to take ownership of the delivery of the plan, even if they are not directly involved in the policy preparation stage
Delivery is usually by a new team
The challenge is that the new team will potentially read the plan without the benefit of knowing about the research and considerations that informed the plan or the journey required to take it through government
Consider making a 'file' for anyone who comes to review the plan at a later date, so they can appreciate the journey you and the team have been on
I once had oversight of a project where this issue was central to achieving a core outcome
Draft principles had been prepared, supported and released for public comment via *a collaboration between three separate organisations. When it came to finalising the plan, the draft principles were expanded into detailed operational strategies. As this second step started one organisation had a new staff member with no prior involvement in the project; all they could do was read the words as they were written*
This resulted in much debate, which resulted in a stalemate. A mediator was brought in to bring the parties closer together. In the end, agreement was eventually reached, together with a new outlook on a few of the principles and a lesson learnt for the future

**Insights: Who delivers the plan? #2
Don't forget culture**
Governance is important, but it is culture that makes everything happen. Governance does not necessarily infer cooperation, particularly when it comes from above

A culture of cooperation is more beneficial for the development and ongoing delivery of plans than nearly any other task—including research. The benefits include:
- the transfer of knowledge
- gaining access to the knowledge of others
- gaining direct access to others as required
- allowing discussion about any elephants in the room
- a willingness to solve wicked policy problems instead of seeking arbitration through governance

This culture requires leadership from above to encourage partnerships, and new ways of working together where:
- the focus is working groups not simple decision-making meetings
- the working groups meet regularly from the analysis phase through to the end
- most importantly these working groups include staff at the senior officer level

References

Perez, CC (2019), *Invisible Women,* Penguin Random House, UK.
—A must read for all planners.
Sarkissian W and Bunjamin-Mau W (2009), *Speak Out,* Taylor and Francis Ltd, UK.
—Hard to find a better place to start when heading out and engaging with people.

Website links

Australian Bureau of Statistics Building approvals Jun to July 2022, Catalogue. Building Approvals, Australia, October 2022 | Australian Bureau of Statistics (abs.gov.au).
Australian Bureau of Statistics Census https://www.abs.gov.au/ausstats/abs@.nsf/0/B3E6E29390F64923CA257BF10013569B.
Australian Bureau of Statistics Census Community profiles https://quickstats.censusdata.abs.gov.au/census_services/getproduct/census/2016/communityprofile/036.

Greater Sydney Commission, Background reports https://www.greater.sydney/background-material.

Newgate Research (2015) Research Report Community research to support the implementation of A Plan for Growing Sydney (Six reports) unpublished https://www.greater.sydney/background-material.

New York City, OneNYC Progress Report, 2019h https://onenyc.cityofnewyork.us/reports-resources/.

NSW Spatial Digital Twin NSW Spatial Digital Twin - Spatial Services.

Sustainable Built Environment National Research Centre, *Scenario Planning Transport Futures: Improved Road and Transport Planning using Digital Scenario Planning Tools* (2017). Multiple documents are available for downloading https://sbenrc.com.au/category/research-programs/.

Victoria State Government 2019 *Plan Melbourne 2017–2050 Report on Progress*, The State of Victoria Department of Environment, Land, Water and Planning https://www.planmelbourne.vic.gov.au/implementation.

City Planning Typologies   12

12.1   Introduction

Chapter 5 introduced the different strategic planning typologies utilised when planning cities. Chapters 6–11 outlined the 7-Step Strategic Planning Process in the context of preparing a whole of metropolitan area plan.

This chapter outlines how the 7-Step Strategic Planning Process can be adapted for each strategic planning typology.

We begin with the premise that, in general, all seven steps of the 7-Step Strategic Planning Process are relevant for all types of city planning. How the characteristics of a particular typology may require an adapted approach is assessed and outlined in terms of several variables. In each case the issue is whether the differing spatial scale, the nature of the task, or any other matter influence the planning for each specific typology. The variables are:

- the spatial implications of the typology
- the research framework
- the growth and change equation
- community engagement
- levers for change
- governance.

In some cases, additional variables are raised.

The most significant issue for each of the differing city planning typologies is whether a metropolitan plan exists. If it does your task is likely to be influenced by the directions of this overarching plan, such as preparing town centre plans for designated major centres. In these cases, the research areas can be targeted and expectations for success should be clear.

The four city planning typologies assessed are:

- local government area plans
- town centre plans, including regional city plans
- new greenfield community plans
- neighbourhood community plans.

12.1.1 Warm-Up Exercise

An interesting question is to ask if the different types of city plans have differing challenges and/or considerations.

The simple answer is yes—but why? How could different communities of interest, different themes, networks versus place outcomes and managing city shaping versus city serving issues, individually or collectively, influence how we approach different types of city planning projects?

Jot down a few notes on the different types of city planning projects and consider how the challenges for each may differ.

12.2 Local Government Area Planning

The preparation of a strategic land use plan for each local government area is a mandatory requirement for all councils in NSW and Victoria. Planning for local government areas should reflect the high order strategies in place in Australia's capital cities. How they are required to respond depends on individual state planning legislation.

My review of capital city metropolitan plans found the objectives and directions allow for local adaptation, such as where additional housing is to go or how to respond to directions on local character.

The most challenging aspect of local government planning is that metropolitan councils are not islands; regional cities, on the other hand, are. How you address this boundary challenge is essential in adapting the 7-Step Strategic Planning Process for a local government area.

12.2.1 Purpose

In general, plans for local government areas identify the principal spatial and thematic planning outcomes, just like a metropolitan plan, though with greater specification.

In some jurisdictions, legislation outlines the requirements to be addressed. Even so, in NSW, other than ensuring the plan is consistent with any 'strategic' plan (metropolitan or regional), there is no constraint on the issues to be addressed.

12.2.2 Spatial Planning

Several spatial planning aspects for local government area planning can influence strategic planning activities:

- Clear boundaries sometimes mean plans only cover the local government area, not the directly surrounding land.
- That said, the boundary may only be understood by locals, as usually residential, industrial or rural land uses straddle a boundary; for the visitor the boundary appears artificial. In some cases, topographical features like waterways demarcate boundaries.
- The scale of metropolitan local government areas (in Australia) varies in terms of population from 50,000 up to 2 million people and land area from 5.75 to 2447 square kilometres.

These issues remind us that metropolitan councils are not islands. We need to consider many issues beyond the local government boundaries and several spatial dimensions, some related to thematic issues. These include:

- adjacent local government areas
- housing markets
- wider areas with common socio-economic characteristics
- economic networks.

I outline the general applicability of the 12 categories of the research framework (refer Sect. 4.2.2) to these spatial areas in Table 12.1.

Other issues to consider include how each local government area's:

- transport elements fit within the wider transport networks, in terms of capacity and performance
- cultural, educational, health and the arts facilities fit within wider networks
- centres fit within a wider retail hierarchy
- open space networks connect with wider district/metropolitan open space networks
- residents perceptions of landscapes outside the local government boundaries (borrowed landscapes)
- places and people may be impacted by natural hazards from outside the local government boundaries, such as flooding and bushfires.

By considering these issues you can define a common hinterland that extends beyond local government boundaries.

Ideally, cross boundary issues such as open space, public transport corridors and visual landscapes are resolved in metropolitan plans.

Table 12.1 Applicability of research areas to the planning areas for local government areas
This table highlights the relevance or applicability of the 12 research areas of the Strategic Planning Research Framework to the four themes

Research area	Local government area	Housing markets	Wider socio-economic patterns	Economic networks
Characteristics of people and households	✓	✓	–	–
Socio-economic characteristics	✓	✓	✓	–
Characteristics of place and Country	By lot, except physiographic, climate and country		An understanding of structure	
Setting	✓	✓	✓	✓
Needs of people	✓	Only housing	–	–
Quality of life	✓	–	–	–
Needs of business	✓	–	–	Access to customers & suppliers
Growth & change equations	✓	✓	–	✓
Transport & digital accessibility & performance	✓	✓	–	✓
Qualities of places	✓	–	–	–
Needs of urban/suburban communities	✓	–	–	–
City design	✓	–	–	–

Finally, the spatial attributes of a local government area influence the level of detail. For a metropolitan plan, spatial issues are generally simplified and categorised and, while often mapped to cadastre boundaries, they are not shown—the plan is predominately strategic in nature. Local government plans are sometimes a mix of strategic and detailed, with some elements shown at the cadastre level. This reflects the need to clarify the intent of a specific issue.

12.2.3 Research Framework

Many local government areas may seem to be a microcosm of a whole metropolitan area; at first glance the planning objectives appear to match those for a metropolitan plan. However, when you examine this further, you'll find this is not normally the case.

The research areas that need to be considered are influenced by both population and spatial size, as well land uses.

The presence or absence of residential areas (by type), industrial areas, centres, town centres or rural activities will influence how you will examine different issues.

For small local government areas or those with a limited diversity of activity, the community of interest for some activities may originate outside the local government area, like when the shops or entertainment precincts that people use are outside the local government area. In these circumstances, we need to understand these relationships to determine if action is required. This could include enhancing accessibility or facilitating new land uses in the local government area. It can be challenging to deal with the local politic of examining issues outside the council's boundary.

> While employed at a council in the early 2000s, I worked with colleagues from nearly a dozen councils on an economic strategy. We collectively managed to show our respective councillors how each local government area contributed to the economic prosperity of all people in the region. Consequently, my council agreed to fund joint activities across the region.

In a positive way, local government can be parochial in how they value various aspects of their community. The research for the Greater Sydney Region Plan showed statistically significant differences in what communities value across Greater Sydney (Newgate 2015). These differences can influence approaches to and objectives for local planning, and include distinct urban form, topographical values (coastal, estuarine) or heritage/historic elements.

Local government area planning can also be influenced by metropolitan dynamics over which a council has little control, such as greenfield, infill or urban renewal housing growth; demographic life cycles; or economic networks. Understanding how these issues influence local government area planning requires deliberate consideration.

12.2.4 Growth and Change Equation

Growth and change equations for local government areas can differ from state projections. Local analysis is generally based on bottom-up methods that are better suited for small area assessments where more accurate local data is available, particularly for population and dwelling projections. As a result, local government may not seek to align their demographic analysis within a metropolitan wide control figure. This could mean that collated local government results are well out of sync with metropolitan wide projections.

Conversely, employment projections at a local government level can be challenging without considering metropolitan dynamics; employment opportunities are often over estimated.

In all cases, local community pressures, which emphasise local factors and local aspirations, can result in higher or lower projections of population, housing or jobs.

In seeking to counter these issues, while there is often a richer and finer grained understanding of local issues, state governments should share data sets and/or analysis techniques to enhance local assessments of demand and supply for population, housing and jobs.

12.2.5 Community Engagement

Local government is more connected to the community than state government, in terms of the level of activity, and the direct connection between the community and councillors and officers.

Local government is more likely to target their engagement activities to support specific policies such as recreation or community facilities. There is often an opportunity to build on existing data sources, allowing a more nuanced engagement process when developing a council wide plan.

The nature of local government plans can challenge the demarcation of responsibilities between state and local government. When the community is given the opportunity to comment on virtually any issue, the council may be simply seen as the 'government'.

Engagement processes need to recognise the demarcation of responsibilities and consider the importance of advocacy in dealing with some of the issues the community will raise.

12.2.6 Levers for Change

Research in any areas creates expectations that, if an issue is found, there will be a response. For local government, the levers required to respond—such as enhancing public transport networks—can be outside their control. Managing expectations is essential to local government planning.

It can assist to have state agencies involved in the process so you can directly report on the community's need. However, the 'rational feedback' from agencies, which are likely taking a metropolitan view, may not benefit a council that wishes to change metropolitan priorities.

Advocacy is critical when the levers for change rest with higher-level governments. A challenge for councils is how many issues to pursue.

12.2.7 Governance

Local government staff are usually located in the same place. Facilitating working groups can be easier than for metropolitan plans where agencies are dispersed.

Conversely, sometimes engaging with agencies is more problematic due to challenges of distance, particularly when government agencies are in central city locations. When agencies have regionally based offices across a metropolitan area, or across the state, make sure 'head office' is across the issues.

Where communities of interest extend beyond the local government area, consider how to engage with neighbouring councils.

Where metropolitan plans usually require approval of cabinet or a cabinet committee, their preparation is generally overseen by a planning minister. Plans for local government areas, however, generally require engagement with the whole council throughout the process, which can require considerable engagement and actions such as ward visits. This high level of involvement also helps to anticipate the influence of ward boundaries on the prioritisation of actions and/or spatial outcomes when the plan is being finalised.

12.3 Town Centre Planning

Town centre planning is the bread and butter for many strategic planners. Centres have been part of planning policy for both Sydney and Melbourne for more than 70 years.

This can be where young planners cut their teeth on activities ranging from doing surveys to understanding land uses or car parking. This is where you get to do face-to-face community engagement with the people who live and breathe the centre. It is also where you learn the benefits of partnerships, particularly with governments, to influence transport infrastructure and with the private sector which, essentially, delivers much of what is desired.

Interestingly, despite the long period for which centres have been a part of metropolitan policy there is not a universally accepted framework for assessing the performance of centres.

12.3.1 Purpose

The planning for town centres typically revolves around:

- Managing growth and change to enhance economic performance and expand the range of goods and services available to the community, including social facilities.
- Enhancing the quality of the public realm, including built form, to improve the attractiveness of the centre and the user experience.

- Improving accessibility to and within the centre, including for pedestrians and public transport users.

These objectives, in the first instance, are the principal focus of the project. To what degree other aspects of the research framework are addressed depends on the issues of the day, the time available and resourcing.

Achieving these outcomes requires action in:

- **Activity management**, focusing on the roles, mix of activities and structure of a centre.
- **Infrastructure management**, including understanding how the component elements of the transport system intersect with the land use activities.
- **Amenity and design management**, covering the public domain and built form of a centre.
- **Business management**, focusing on operational aspects, such as marketing and tenant attraction, which are usually managed by the local chamber of commerce or a centre manager for internalised centres.

12.3.2 Spatial Planning

In the context of a whole metropolitan area, town centres are small places, generally easy to define in terms of the commercially zoned area to which the town centre plan will apply. I always recommend the study area include the walkable residential catchment.

The greater challenge is to define communities of interests that influence the performance of centres, such as:

- primary, secondary and tertiary retail catchments
- journey to work catchments for all employment activities
- the walkable catchment that reflects where additional housing could be developed.

Accessibility is the central determinant for these issues. We need to determine the extent to which we need to investigate and understand:

- barriers to transport choices for people within the primary and secondary catchments, and the accessibility of competing centres
- the level of off-road cycle networks and open space networks that enhance the attractiveness of the centre for both active transport trips and for leisure and recreational pursuits.

A centre will be influenced by the activities, scale and performance of nearby centres. We need to understand whether there are competing centres and how

12.3 Town Centre Planning

their growth and change might influence the performance of the centre under investigation.

From a spatial perspective, different information is required for the different spatial areas influencing a centre. I outline, in general, the applicability of the 12 research areas (refer Sect. 4.2.2) in Table 12.2.

As with metropolitan planning, town centre planning is about structure, such as the distribution of retail and other commercial activities in an internalised shopping centre or the market-driven co-location of like activities in CBDs (for example, the outdoor clothing and equipment shops in Hardware Street in Melbourne and Kent Street in Sydney). This requires us to obtain information at a detailed (lot) level to gain the best understanding of opportunities and constraints.

Table 12.2 Applicability of research areas to various spatial considerations for town centres
This table highlights the relevance or applicability of the 12 research areas that make up the Strategic Planning Research Framework to five spatial considerations when planning for town centres

Research area	Commercial area	Walkable catchment	Primary retail catchment	Secondary retail catchment	Tertiary retail catchment
Characteristics of people and households	–	✓	✓	✓	✓
Socio-economic characteristics	✓	✓	✓	–	–
Characteristics of place and country	By lot, except country	By lot, except country	Structure	–	–
Setting	✓	✓	✓		
Needs of people	✓	✓	✓	–	–
Quality of life	Influence of the centre on the quality of life of the people in each area			–	–
Needs of business	✓	✓	✓	Access to customers & suppliers	
Growth & change equations	✓	✓	✓	✓	✓
Transport & digital accessibility & performance	✓	✓	✓	✓	✓
Qualities of places	✓	✓	–	–	–
Needs of urban/ suburban communities	✓	✓	–	–	–
City design	✓	✓	–	–	–

12.3.3 Project Establishment

You generally have a high level of knowledge on a range of issues before town centre planning commences. While the plan is still strategic in nature, research and evaluation are detailed so that you understand many issues at the lot level. Assessments are likely to include concept designs.

When preparing the project brief, you'll need to consider:

- **Stakeholders**. The range of activities in centres in addition to retail and commercial can be broad, such as education, fitness, health, entertainment and community services. These potentially require nuanced processes.
- **Study area**. The spatial scale of activities, the proximity to residential areas, barriers (for example, railway lines), topography and the diversity of activities can influence what should be the core study area.
- **Engagement**. Town centre plans can lead to detailed outcomes, such as landscape works and site-specific development proposals. Consequently, notification of all landowners and tenants throughout the course of the project is important.

I was involved in a streetscape project for a small centre and one business advised that if a tree was planted outside their property, they would just cut it down.

12.3.4 Research Framework

12.3.4.1 Context

If a metropolitan plan is in place, a range of research areas may not need to be addressed. Instead, focus on research that supports the objectives of the metropolitan plan. In some circumstances, research may be undertaken if an advocacy role is to be pursued.

The breadth and depth of research will be influenced by the role of the centre and nearby competing centres, as well as the presence of complementary institutional, cultural and community facilities in the centre and in nearby centres or locations. The potential to influence the role of the centre and attract new anchors will be in part influenced by what exists nearby.

For metropolitan planning, design analysis and recommendations are typically at a strategic level, focusing on policies and principles. This reflects the fact that most of the public realm is managed by local government. Thus, for town centre planning, investigations are needed at a concept design level, specifically for initial public realm or landscape plans and often for development where you need to understand functionality (such as access via loading bays).

For a town centre, the local community and landowners will understand the opportunities. You will need a definitive understanding of the level of growth and where it could be located.

12.3 Town Centre Planning

When considering land constraints in town centres, providing direction on growth opportunities often focuses on how to facilitate market outcomes. This requires a high degree of site-specific property economics data and evaluations of benefits, emphasising that many aspects of town centre investigations need to shift from strategic principles to detailed site-specific outcomes.

The consequences of not doing detailed analysis, including what type of interventions are required, can result in undesirable outcomes, such as the shopping centre and/or supermarket that are down the road in a standalone location, subsequently not adding value to the vibrancy and prosperity of the original town centre.

12.3.4.2 Investigation Considerations

Considering the level of detail that directions for a plan may take, the information required can be extensive and detailed:

- **Activity analysis.** Land use by lot, level, defined categories, potentially by precincts and at least about 400 metres from the commercial area. Floor space analysis is similar, but only for the commercial area. Analyse employment by ABS categories, land values by precinct, land ownership and planning controls by lot and age of buildings, as required. Use a cadastre base with topography.
- **Infrastructure.** Understand trunk services and digital capacity issues, and overhead utilities (for informing tree planting options).
- **Community characteristics.** Undertake a demographic and socio-economic analysis of retail primary catchment, prepare population and household projections and survey community values.
- **Economic performance.** Research the history of development approvals and rezoning proposals as well as proposals in the pipeline. Assess the existing planning controls, including general level of compliance, and evidence of effectiveness, including success at tribunals/planning courts. Consider other controls, such as development agreements and covenants.
- **History.** Research the history of the community and area and heritage places.
- **Community safety.** Undertake access and disability audits, a safety audit, lighting audit and community perceptions.
- **Road network.** Understand the hierarchy, performance (including traffic counts and as required over-dimension vehicles), modelling (network and intersection), cross sections, quality and accidents. Check the presence or absence of public footpaths, tree cover and verandahs.
- **Public transport.** Understand provision, frequency, spatial coverage and hours of service. Understand quality issues, including location of stops, information availability, intermodal connectivity, quality of stops (disability and access compliance), and interchange opportunities or functions.
- **Car parks.** Analyse performance by precincts and total numbers, usage, turnover and management; connectivity or accessibility to the road network; pedestrian safety, connectivity and accessibility to activity; and disability and access compliance.

- **Pedestrians**. Network assessment includes hierarchy, volumes, functionality, disability and access compliance, informal desire lines (existing), and walkable catchments to both activity and major public transport nodes.
- **Bicycle network**. Understand the network hierarchy, functionality and informal desire lines.
- **Open space**. Assess the network including hierarchy, functionality, role as it relates to activity and link your findings to the pedestrian and cycle assessments.
- **Design**. Understand the perception of the centre and consider fine grain analysis, visual corridors, edges/nodes, streetscape character, landscape values and street furniture. Define and evaluate the public and private public realm including qualitative assessments linked to pedestrian and open space assessments.
- **Biodiversity and natural systems**. Analyse as required. Any natural values will likely need a management plan, particularly at the interfaces with activity.

12.3.5 Growth and Change Equation

Centre-based assessments help you understand future growth opportunities. They should consider supply issues to ensure the demand can be accommodated. This may require a level of understanding of the feasibility of development.

In addition, understanding barriers to accessibility in the primary, secondary and tertiary catchments will help you determine the maximum potential activity that can be attracted, and, equally importantly, how activity translates to local jobs.

12.3.6 Scenarios and Evaluation

Town centre plans, compared to metropolitan plans, often make recommendations at the lot level. It can become apparent how those recommendations will impact landowners, investors or developers, creating tension.

Consequently, you need a robust evaluation process that demonstrates the benefits, costs and implications of some directions.

If recommendations are likely to be at the lot level, you may need detailed assessments, such as:

- preliminary development feasibility, such as for the redevelopment of a council car park
- concept designs for certain types of development such as for a supermarket to establish if, at a general level, loading bays can work
- all features surveys to inform landscape plans for the public realm.

I learnt the importance of understanding the detail when working as a consultant for a local government. From the initial assessment of opportunities everyone agreed on the benefit of connecting a dead-end street through to a collector road, which would have facilitated a ring road for the centre. However, on detailed examination we established that at the end of the dead-end road was an electricity transformer on a pole, for which the cost of moving was prohibitive. Thus, a proposed statement of intent in a plan had to be dropped.

12.3.7 Draft Plan Elements

12.3.7.1 Component Plans

Town centre plans more than likely have several component plans in addition to a structure plan, reflecting the small spatial scale and expectations of the vision and actions, and hence the need for detailed input. Potential component plans include:

- A traffic and transport plan addressing the road hierarchy, public transport and bicycle network.
- Car parking plan including management issues.
- Landscape plan including a streetscape concept that addresses tree planting, street furniture, signage and street cross sections.
- Urban design framework addressing scale of the built form, character and design issues as required.
- Open space plan linked to walking and cycling networks and objectives for the public realm, with particular emphasis on the issue of fit for purpose for each element of the open space network.

> *On one project, the open space consultant indicated that as the centre was to have a high level of dwellings, half the town park should be developed with soft landscaping and have a playground to reflect the needs of the residents, with the other half hard surfaces and a water feature to reflect the patterns of shoppers and visitors.*

Consequently, town centre planning requires inputs from a range of specialists.

12.3.7.2 Statutory Framework

It is more than likely that a town centre plan will identify the need for land to be rezoned. Consider providing details of the intent of the zone, even a draft outline of exactly what is proposed as part of the exhibition material.

12.3.8 Community Engagement

In a metropolitan planning process, most members of the community will only provide advice as to the area where they live, and often at a level of detail far greater than will go into a plan, whereas the strategic planners will have a good understanding of how the whole metropolitan area works.

For town centre planning the knowledge balance is in reverse. The local community knows far more about the study area than those doing the plan. This potentially influences the engagement process.

At the same time, there may be several stakeholder or community groups with a high level of knowledge but different agendas, such as business, local community, sporting and environment groups. In addition, there will be different user groups, such as students, office workers, shoppers and tourists who utilise the centre for different reasons. It can be a challenge to engage with all these differing groups.

12.3.9 Levers of Change

Interventions to enhance a centre may include transport, expansions of health and education facilities, commercial and retail development and the public realm. Often outcomes required, such as improved transport connections are outside the responsibility of a council. Thus, effective working relationships with state agencies are essential.

12.3.10 Governance

Most major centres have their own governance arrangements through a chamber of commerce, or similar. Large regional' centres, that include a separate shopping mall will have a centre manager. In addition, some landowners, both businesses (for example, a shopping centre owner) and institutional organisations (hospital or university) may own large tracts of land. Consider how to involve these organisations in the project governance, specifically for transparency.

Some centres straddle two or more local government areas. St. Leonards in Greater Sydney straddles three local government areas. Governance arrangements are likely to need input from all local governments.

In regional areas, regional cities are generally managed by one local government. Thus, the competing issues due to a patchwork of local governments do not exist.

State government involvement in supporting planning in town centres across Australia waxes and wanes, When they are involved, the focus is traditionally the major centres (however defined) and often include grant programs for outcomes such as streetscape works. Hence, in the main, local government has responsibility for town centres.

However, you may need state government support for transport enhancements, public transport interchanges or enhancements to hospitals. Therefore, in the absence of direct state government involvement, ensure state governments are represented in governance structures.

12.4 New Greenfield Community Planning

Greenfield development is often maligned, and the derogatory phase 'urban sprawl' is often used to define it. But when you read books on planning for cities 100 years ago you find the same language. Today what we call fashionable inner suburban locations were once regarded as urban sprawl.

> *I learnt a good lesson early in my career when doing a site visit of a public housing estate. One of the residents made a poignant statement to us—what you call a slum, I call my home.*

In this context the planning for greenfield areas should not be seen as a plan for new streets, centres, houses and parks, but a plan for new communities, that will still be around in 100 years.

Typically, planning for greenfield areas is a two-tiered process where, as cities expand, large areas are identified for future growth and some sort of framework plan is put in place. The development of these growth areas usually occurs over many decades. During that time multiple greenfield plans (precinct structure plans) are prepared on a suburb-by-suburb basis; these second-tier plans are the focus of this section.

12.4.1 Purpose

The plans typically identify the principal spatial outcomes supported by principles for specific elements, which can be quite detailed, such as road cross sections that can show pavement widths, or the location of footpaths and cycle paths, trees and utilities. They are likely to include information on how growth will occur in the context of some existing uses, what elements of the natural environment will be protected and managed, and how the area is connected and/or relates to wider transport, land use, open space and environmental networks.

12.4.2 Spatial Planning

Greenfield plans typically cover a defined area that is yet to be developed for urban purposes and is usually rural in nature, though in some jurisdictions it can include forested areas. This core area to which the plan applies also needs to be integrated with the existing urban area, with careful interfaces with remaining non-urban (rural or forested) areas.

This is a perennial challenge for Australia's metropolitan cities as those landowners outside the urban boundary typically perceive their properties as future urban, which creates a range of challenges—not the least inflated land prices that impact the viability of agricultural activities. Some jurisdictions have planning mechanisms to manage this. Melbourne has the most stringent mechanism, the

Urban Growth Boundary, where change requires the approval of both houses of parliament within 10 sitting days of each other.

Regarding the connections to the existing urban area, consider how:

- transport elements fit within the wider transport networks, in terms of the capacity and performance of those networks
- potential cultural, educational, health and the arts hubs will relate to wider networks
- proposed centres fit within a wider centre hierarchy
- proposed open space networks connect with wider district/metropolitan open space networks and/or a hierarchy of active recreation facilities.

For connections to non-urban areas, consider borrowed landscapes outside the greenfield area, in addition to managing urban/rural interfaces.

As the plans for new greenfield communities are about changes in the designation of land use from rural to urban, elements of the plan are provided at a cadastre level to remove any ambiguity.

12.4.3 Research Framework

Planning for a new greenfield community is similar to planning a metropolitan area, in that it is holistic in its nature. The planning is also unique in many ways. Compared to metropolitan planning, greenfield planning is where many final strategic decisions will be made. Some of the unique aspects include:

- When the structure of the community is laid out, many elements will not change, such as (as elaborated on in Sect. 4.5.5):
  - Subdivision patterns, both lots and streets
  - The location of open space and its relationship to the subdivision pattern
  - The general location of centres and their relationship to the street pattern and potentially the rail network.
- The main opportunity is to provide a legacy for how the existing natural systems will be planned for and managed and about the challenging question of what to retain.
- The lot-by-lot details of natural hazards need to be understood, thus principles need to be supported by detailed technical investigations, such as flood modelling.

At the same time, it is not about a clean slate in terms of opportunities. You need to consider connections to existing networks and existing constraints such as incompatible activities (for example, farming that emits odours).

Planning for new communities requires you to understand the status of utility delivery and long-term plans. From this you can ascertain the potential need for sequencing to optimise the roll-out of services, while facilitating innovations reflecting circular economy objectives.

12.4.4 Growth and Change Equation

The growth and change equation is the foundation element of all new greenfield plans. It informs how much land is required to be allocated to each land use type. However, planning for growth areas typically only foreshadows a 20-year time horizon. This can create some limitations to the plans, which is discussed in the next section.

The most difficult area to assess is jobs, historically under-provided in new greenfield communities on a per-capita basis. Yet, at the same time, projections are often very aspirational, reflecting a desire to secure local jobs. Such aspirational objectives need to be supported by an understanding of the levers to achieve the stated ambition.

12.4.5 Temporal Considerations

Several temporal planning issues can influence how the planning for greenfield areas is approached.

It is often assumed that all land will be planned and developed in an orderly manner. However, there can be benefits from keeping some land for the next generation to plan.

> *When working at local government, and as part of the process for preparing a plan for a major town centre, we took councillors on a study tour of other town centres to allow them to see what a future version of their city may look like.*
>
> *At a presentation by the ACT planning department, their officers emphasised the benefit of retaining some land within each centre as vacant until such time as the centre was well developed and its best use could be considered in a future context.*

Also, land is a finite resource and allocating it all to current needs does not consider the needs of all generations. Consider how the needs of future generations can be more explicitly included in evaluation frameworks.

In recent decades the density of many greenfield areas has increased above original planning assumptions; therefore, some infrastructure elements are under-provided for and development contribution schemes inadequate. Consider creating opportunities for such issues to be addressed in sensitivity analysis then revisited in the future for review.

Finally, consider how the area will evolve and reflect on what has occurred in locations that are now established, specifically what challenges they have today that could be avoided. Developing scenarios that reflect the multi-generational nature of how areas evolve over time would inform this.

12.4.6 Draft Plan Elements

12.4.6.1 A Pattern Book
In addition to the preparation of a structure plan, create a pattern book or design guideline to manage day-to-day planning decisions for potentially a 10-year period as development unfolds on an estate-by-estate basis.

In many cases, state planning departments or greenfield development authorities already have a standard pattern book. Be aware that most large corporate landowners (who are also land developers) are likely to have their own pattern books.

> *When I first joined the Victorian state government, I had a land developer present their own pattern book. It was evident that the government planners were unaware of the level of sophistication of the developer's approach to greenfield planning.*

The pattern book needs to balance certainty in areas such as road and open space connections across multiple land holdings, while allowing for innovation in design. Hence, clarity on the outcomes being sought, as distinct from the detail of a response, is the key.

12.4.6.2 Sequencing Plan
The need for a sequencing plan may not simply be about the most cost-efficient roll-out of utility services. It can also relate to community development outcomes, where development is directed to a specific area to ensure the timely delivery of social infrastructure such as schools. When development is dispersed, children in one estate may live next door to each other but have limited contact as they are driven to school and their parents take them to the closest school related to such issues as their own journey to work.

> *I was involved in the advocacy for a school when it was established that in one community the local school-aged children were attending 14 different schools.*

12.4.7 Community Engagement

Community engagement is about planning for a community that does not yet exist. Thus, approaches need to consider ways in overcoming this, including thinking beyond just other communities of recently developed greenfield areas, and also well-established communities.

In some cases, land ownership of the study area may be limited to a small number of people or organisations. The principal consideration here is transparency, as those landowners may wish to be involved in governance arrangements.

12.4.8 Levers of Change

Infrastructure delivery, specifically utilities and roads, are critical development enablers, followed by schools, community facilities and shops. Understand who the infrastructure provider is in each instance and any inhibitors and enablers for investment.

12.4.9 Governance

Considering the significance of infrastructure as an enabler of development, governance arrangements should involve infrastructure providers. This can be complicated when the infrastructure providers are privately owned utilities.

Also consider the involvement of adjacent local governments that are directly impacted by the development.

12.5 Neighbourhood Community Planning

Neighbourhood community planning, designing communities from the inside out.

Special acknowledgement to the then neighbourhood community planning team at the City of Casey:

Greg Bursill, Kerri Elso, Anita Francis, Anna Kijowska, Tammy Sheedy, and Mark Stubbs

Community planning projects are not simply about improved infrastructure, they are about growing the capacity of the community in a range of areas. Hence, they are usually undertaken in areas with high levels of socio-economic disadvantage. The activities do not have the same start and finish nature as infrastructure projects. Thus, they are not short-term initiatives. **Ideally, neighbourhood community planning needs to occur over a five-to-ten-year period**.

As the projects are about the community, they, the community, are also part of the team. Essentially, the community is your secondees; gaining trust is the core ingredient for success. You can achieve this by concurrently aligning the actions of all groups in a common framework directed to common goals.

12.5.1 The Challenge

As I see it, neighbourhood community planning is the ultimate expression of strategic planning. However, it is by far the hardest process and most difficult to manage. Why is this?

Firstly, it is about delegating part of the process to the community, which therefore means releasing part of the control.

Secondly, it is truly holistic—from homework clubs to housing. Thus, it becomes an ongoing balancing act between competing power bases—the community and the decision-makers (the politicians).

Thirdly, it is not so much about a definitive plan; it is more about incremental steps towards some overarching goals and celebrating activities on the way.

Finally, your team needs to be embedded in the community.

A key requirement is ensuring the community, in part, takes responsibility for some of the activities. A natural consequence is the more you seek to engage, the more inclusive your process becomes but also the more difficult it becomes.

My best advice is to jump in. As long as you have your learning hat on and have an enthusiastic and willing team you will survive and by your second and third projects you will not want to turn back.

12.5.2 Purpose

Neighbourhood community planning seeks to blend the objectives of land use planning with community development. Thus, it is as much focused on capacity building as it is on developing a land use vision. In fact, the notion of a fixed land use vision is anathema to those involved in community development.

Hence neighbourhood community planning is about:

- a multi-disciplinary long-term process that involves large teams where many, if not most, are from the community.
- setting up an ongoing process where actions, research and debate, are undertaken with the community
- recognising that community development processes and community engagement are the central strategic planning tools from start to finish
- having partners from external organisations that are a committed part of your core team.

Note also that community planning is not the same as community development—community development is one tool of community planning. In community planning you are seeking to empower the community but also have community input to short and long-term city planning outcomes.

12.5.3 Project Establishment

12.5.3.1 The Project Team

As trust is central, the team for community planning ideally needs to be in the community and be accessible to the community all day—potentially near the main street but not in it, and it will need to allow for space to grow into.

A project team could be a coalition of interested agencies, including non-government organisations from the social sector. State government involvement is also critical when there is social housing in the area, as the community will perceive housing to be one of the questions to be answered.

Core workers include a community development officer, an employment and lifelong learning officer and a project manager. Key support areas are youth workers, maternal and childcare officers, aged care officers and disability support. Behind the scenes is the team working on core strategic planning activities.

12.5.3.2 Timeframe
Most strategic planning projects are a 12 to 18-month process. Neighbourhood community planning has a different timeline. Ideally it is five plus years, as a plan in terms of reporting with a vision and actions is more a minor element. What is critical is the process and taking the community on a journey where the financial and economic independence of households is a principal objective.

12.5.3.3 Executive and Council Support
As the process and timing is different to a traditional strategic planning process, senior executive and councillor support is critical.

> *I was involved in a project at the City of Casey, in the communities of Doveton and Eumemmerring, where the state government, through the housing department, understood the need for long-term support and provided financial support for a five-year period.*

12.5.4 Spatial planning

Spatial planning is usually focused on a discrete area for which the community takes ownership and is typically identifiable as one or a few suburbs. Wider connections are relevant but need to emerge as part of the engagement with the community.

12.5.5 Research Framework

Undertaking neighbourhood community planning projects is underpinned by the community development process. Consequently, there are a range of issues to consider when establishing a project methodology, particularly in terms of engaging and working with the community.

However, what you do and how you do it needs to come from the community. It will often be the case that traditional 'land use' processes are not as relevant, and the community can develop the approach for the research.

Initially it takes a while for the planners to come to terms with what the community determines to be relevant and the focus of activity. Also, there is the potential for the community to revisit an issue that the planners may feel has been resolved, so revisit it you must.

Ultimately, a detailed understanding of traditional land use and transport issues (in line with the research topics) becomes important to investigate as the community identifies issues that need such material to resolve. Importantly, the community must be brought along the learning journey in relation to the issues in their community.

> *When working on a such a project one of my team presented the findings of a neighbourhood character study of the suburb to the housing working group. The research revealed there was a standard set back for all houses. One community representative did not feel this was correct. Though at our next meeting that member indicated that he and his wife had measured all the front setback where he lived and concurred with our findings. This we celebrated—and we thought about how we may have undertaken the task differently next time.*

Thus, neighbourhood community planning is about convergent futures where the needs and issues of the local community converge with wider outcomes sought by local and state governments (refer Fig. 12.1).

An evident challenge is that, while there are usually significant amounts of socio-economic data, there is little time series data on community values.

Additionally, an advantage of working in such locations is the potential to determine the economic benefit to the Australian Government of moving people out of welfare dependency and the savings over the long term, therefore creating an argument for financial support.

12.5.6 Growth and Change Equation

In the first instance the growth and change equation is not so important an issue. The focus is more on understanding the economic costs to governments, from welfare to the wider issues related to the poverty trap of living in such locations. For example, children engaging with other children in the school yard and learning that the parents of many of their friends are both good people and unemployed, therefore, concluding that being unemployed must be an okay life pathway.

12.5.7 Direction Setting

The long-term objective is to blend the aspirations for community development with land use planning. Thus, it is a long-term process of two convergent futures; that is, one where the local communities and the wider city's interests come together over time. This can occur once trust has been built, short-term community outcomes achieved and there is then an opportunity to have a conversation about wider societal objectives and how they may play out at a local level. Equally the community's issues can push their way up and influence wider societal objectives, such as local perspectives on what types of services and facilities are needed.

12.5 Neighbourhood Community Planning

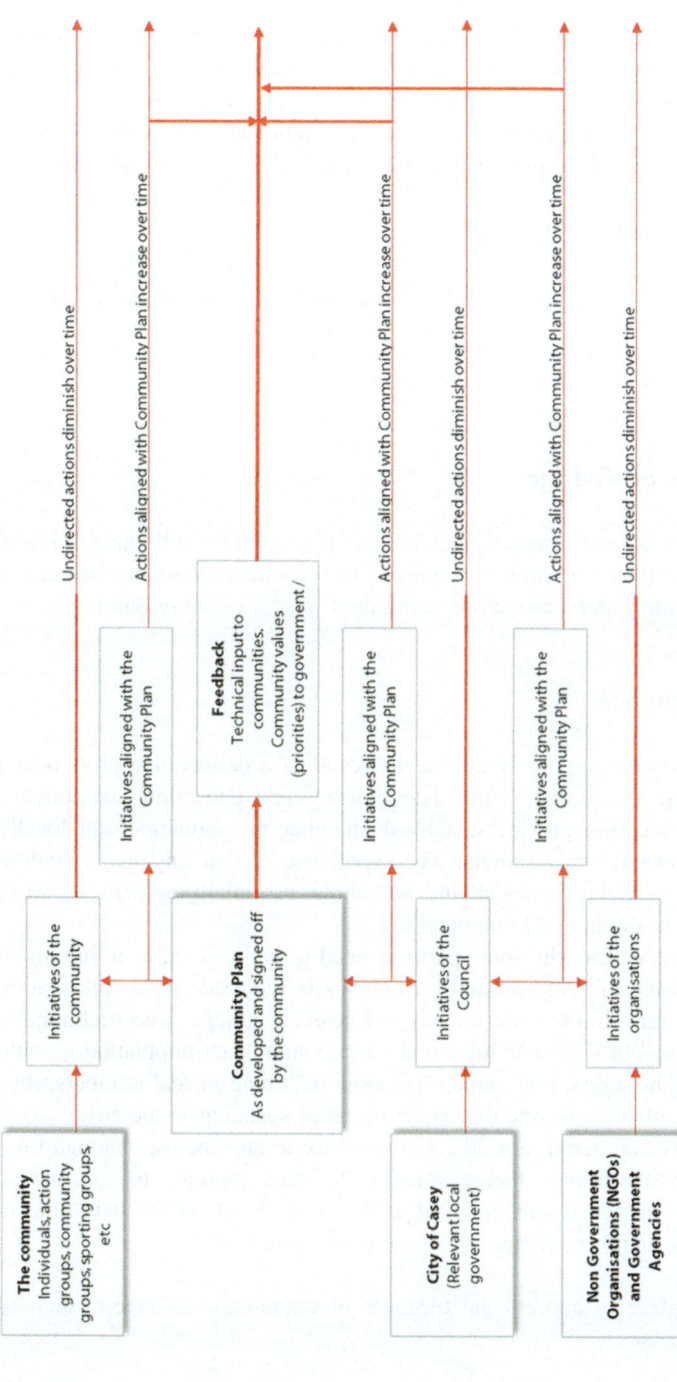

Fig. 12.1 Convergence of community and government activities: Action delivery model
This diagram highlights how the actions for different players in community planning can be aligned over time. (*Source* Unpublished working documents from the Doveton/Eumemmerring Neighbourhood Renewal project, City of Casey [2005]. Reproduced with permission from the City of Casey)

12.5.8 Community Engagement

Engaging with the community is the central theme of how to approach neighbourhood community planning. Engagement is not simply about engaging to get information, comments, or decisions, it is about involving community members in the day-to-day tasks of the project, for which they then take responsibility. Documenting all activities and progress and making the information available to all is critical.

Gaining trust is also a long play.

In the Doveton and Eumemmerring project our employment and learning officer first ran a homework club to gain the trust of the parents before considering approaching the parents regarding to improve their learning skills. In another case, the officer provided music lessons to introduce the adults to a regular learning activity.

12.5.9 Levers of Change

Ultimately neighbourhood community planning will require the full range of levers that any strategic planning project requires. The community themselves are a resource for specific actions as well as being the focus of capacity building.

12.5.10 Governance

Gaining a coalition of support should be the result of a deliberative process and potentially include discussions with state housing and education departments, police, tertiary education providers, a local chamber of commerce and locally based non-government organisations. My experience is that any memorandum of understanding between parties should be simple, essentially agreeing to work together to improve community outcomes.

Gathering evidence for why some partners need to be involved is an important step as a wide range of socio-economic statistics is required. What information is important will vary. In one case we advised business groups, who traditionally may not be involved in such activities, that despite significant population growth, the number of high-income households had been declining in real numbers, thus impacting disposable income and consequently retail spending in the city.

As with any project there is a need for governance arrangements, although for a project with long time frames, I suggest an evolutionary approach to governance. When community members are involved at the start, decide when it is time to move on and new members come in. Consequently, you need:

- processes in place to address the turnover of community members, such as induction processes

- good record keeping of the journey to pass on the history of the project to the next group of community members
- to recognise the project direction will change with new members
- processes for revisiting the basis and process of the project, recognising it will change
- an understanding that what makes sense one day may not be clear a few years later.

An example of an evolving governance structure is shown in Fig. 12.2.

12.5.11 The Plan

In the first instance a plan, in the traditional sense, is not high on the agenda, especially for a process which is to take five to ten years. In fact, talking about a plan in the short term can be disruptive.

Hence, be genuinely clear as to what outcomes you aspire to in the short, medium and long term, when you are involved in a ten-year project.

12.6 Summary of Approaches to Research

This chapter emphasises that while the principal steps and tasks in the 7-Step Strategic Planning Process are generally common for all city planning typologies there are important differences to consider. In terms of research some of these differences are highlighted in Fig. 12.3.

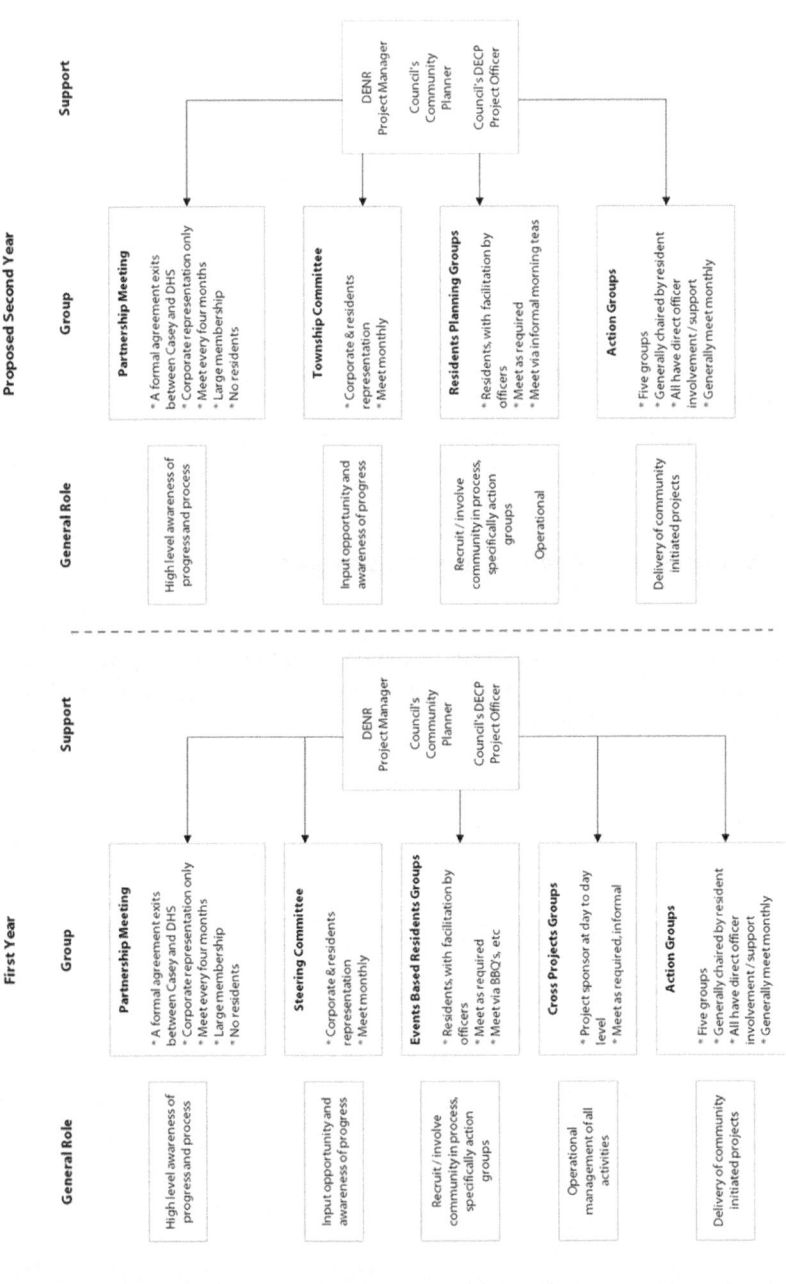

Fig. 12.2 Doveton/Eumemmerring neighbourhood renewal: management framework
This diagram highlights how the governance arrangements evolved as the project progressed. (*Source* Unpublished working documents from the Doveton/Eumemmerring neighbourhood renewal project, City of Casey [2005]. Reproduced with permission from the City of Casey)

	Metropolitan area planning	Local government area	Centres / precincts	New greenfield community
Spatial systems	Metropolitan and district-significant land use and transport structure Centres down to those with supermarkets Open space: general areas of deficiency Urban canopy: general areas of deficiency Connectivity and performance of transport systems Land use structure of hinterland Assets of national significance Journey to work main catchments Principal transport desire lines Topography catchments and barriers Activity precincts of metropolitan or higher significance Socio-economic characteristics (detail at SA1 / mesh block), but patterns at SA2 Car parking as a management tool City design	District and suburb-significant land use and transport structure All centres Open space: specific areas of deficiency Urban canopy: specific areas of deficiency Connectivity and performance of transport systems Assets of district significance or higher Journey to work catchments by district or metropolitan-significant centres Principal transport desire lines Topography catchments and barriers Activity precincts of district or higher significance Socio-economic characteristics (SA1/mesh block) but patterns at SA2 Car parking as a management toll City Design	Land use assessment by lot, including defining the residential edge and potentially an all-features survey Precinct-significant land use and transport structure, including walkable hinterland Open space: detailed assessment Urban canopy: detailed assessment Connectivity and performance of transport systems at detailed level, including pedestrian networks and densities Detailed car parking surveys, including distribution and usage Assets of district significance or higher Topography and barriers Activity precincts of district or higher significance Socio-economic characteristics at SA1 Access and disability audit Safer places audit Streetscape / amenity assessments	District and suburb-significant land use and transport structure All centres Open space: specific areas of deficiency Urban canopy: specific areas of deficiency Connectivity and performance of transport systems, and transport desire lines Assets of district significance or higher Journey to work catchments by district or metropolitan-significant centres Topography catchments and barriers Activity precincts of district or higher significance Socio-economic characteristics (SA1/mesh block) but patterns at SA2 Geology and geomorphology Detailed utilities assessment City design
Thematic assessments	Housing market dynamics/trends by suburb Commercial sectors by district and principal centres trends (jobs and floor space) Industrial land: demand and supply Population and demographic trends by suburb International, national and state economic context and drivers Macro economic context Health and education roles and location by	Housing market dynamics/trends by suburb and/or precinct Commercial sectors by precinct, all centres trends, and proposed development Industrial land demand and supply Population and demographic trends by suburb International, national and state economic drivers Metropolitan economic context Health and education roles all locations	Housing market dynamics by catchment Each commercial sector's district and metropolitan context, centre role, competing centres, trade catchments and proposed development In-home and in-centre surveys (retail focus) Rental/property values Population and demographic trends by catchment Metropolitan economic drivers Roles of health and education facilities	Housing market dynamics/trends by district context Each commercial sector's district context Population and demographic trends by district Metropolitan economic drivers and context Macro-economic context Health and education context by district
Community engagement	Councils individually and by district Peak industry bodies, community, including environmental groups General public via deliberative engagement projects General public, via social media	All councillors, individually State government agencies Local chambers of commerce, Community, environmental and recreational groups General public via targeted deliberative engagement (in person and social media) Site visits with councillors	All relevant councillors, individually State government agencies Local chamber of commerce, Community, environmental and recreational groups All community within walkable catchments General public, via social media Site visits with councillors	All relevant councillors, individually State government agencies As relevant, local chambers of commerce, community, environmental & recreational groups Public via deliberative engagement on social media
Government policy	Commonwealth, state, local Local council narratives	Commonwealth, state, local	Commonwealth, state, local	Commonwealth, state, local Local council narratives

Fig. 12.3 Summary of typical research areas for differing city planning typologies

12.7 Summary

This chapter has outlined why the 7-Step Strategic Planning Process is relevant to all types of city planning activities. As the spatial area of focus and purpose for differing city planning typologies changes, the process needs to be adapted to the characteristics of each type. We examined four different city planning typologies—local government area planning, town centre planning, new greenfield community planning, and neighbourhood community planning.

For each, I discussed several common areas where the required approach would need specific attention. This includes the influence of the spatial scale of each; the application of the research framework; the influence of the project purpose and spatial scale on the growth and change equation; how the make up of the local community may influence engagement approaches; who is responsible for delivery will influence the approach to what levers are considered; and governance.

In some cases, we covered additional variables, such as scenarios and evaluation for town centre planning, temporal considerations for new greenfield communities and direction setting as well as the need for a plan in neighbourhood community planning.

Reference

City of Casey (2005), *Management Framework Years 1 and 2*. Unpublished Working Documents from the Doveton/Eumemmerring Neighbourhood Renewal Project

Website Link

Newgate Research (2015), *Research Report Community Research to Support the Implementation of A Plan for Growing Sydney* (Six Reports) Unpublished. https://www.greater.sydney/background-material

Part III
The 12 Research Areas

Introduction and chapters overview

Chapter 4 outlined the purpose, principal tasks and research areas for the undertaking of Step 2: Research and analysis. We identified 12 research areas and the Strategic Planning Research Framework to understand how they relate to each other.

Part III details the methodological approach for each of the 42 research topics, with a focus on research considerations, research objectives and approaches to research in each case. The research topics keep with the logic of the Strategic Planning Research Framework, which divides the research areas into nine groups within three broad areas (parts A, B and C).

My intent is not to provide a detailed methodology for each research topic. Instead, I want to provide a sufficient understanding of why each research topic is important and what needs to be the focus of the investigation. Many tasks will require specialist input and communicating your needs is critical, as every project is different.

Develop your methodology based on your project objectives and project scope. This will allow you to determine the level of detail required or in some cases, specific research topics will not need investigation and this then should be stated in your project brief, including the reasons why.

The research areas are discussed in three parts in Chapters 13, 14 and 15 as listed here:

Part A: The people and the place – Chapter 13

- Characteristics of people and households
- Socio-economic characteristics
- Characteristics of places and Country
- City setting

Part B: Needs of people and business – Chapter 14

- Needs of people and households
- Quality of life
- Needs of businesses
- The growth and change equation

Part C: Qualities and performance of place – Chapter 15

- Transport accessibility and performance
- Qualities of places
- Urban/suburban communities
- City design

Part 3 Summary

Part 3 concludes the 'how to' technical components of this book. It has focused on the 42 research areas of the Strategic Planning Research Framework initially outlined in Chapter 2 Part 1. Research in all areas will provide a full understanding of the people and places that influence land use outcomes. Part 3 clarifies the expectations of what is needed to research these areas.

Part 3 divides the research areas into three parts in line with the three parts of the Strategic Planning Research Framework:

Part A: People and place. The research areas that will help you understand the context of the place and its people. Four research areas are covered in two themes:

- characteristic of people and households
- socio-economic characteristics
- characteristics of places and Country
- city setting.

Part B: Needs of people and place. Three research areas seek to outline the needs of people and businesses. The findings inform the single most important research area theme 'the growth and change equation'. The equation quantifies the expected change in land use activity that needs to be accommodated by the plan. The three research areas that inform the growth and change equation are:

- the needs of people and households
- the quality of life
- the needs of businesses
- the growth and change equation.

Collectively Part B covers 18 research areas.

Part C: Qualities and performance of place. Part C focuses on the attributes that make places unique as well as our ability to access them. Consequently, the research areas for Part C are diverse:

- accessibility, transport and digital performance
- the qualities of places
- urban and suburban communities
- city design.

Part C covers 16 research areas.

Part A: The People and the Place   13

13.1 Introduction

This chapter provides details on the research areas for Part A: The people and the place. The information for each research topic includes.

- research considerations
- research objectives
- approaches to research.

13.2 Characteristics of People and Households

13.2.1 Demographic Profiles

13.2.1.1 Research Considerations

Understanding the number and profile of the people who live in a city or specific area is invariably the starting point for any land use plan.

The spatial analysis of demographic data is best collected and mapped at spatial scales such as the ABS Statistical Area Level 1 (SA1) to best reveal patterns. This data is most valuable when time series data is available.

When time series data is collected patterns emerge, such as locations that attract people over 65 or young families and differences between mature and new communities. This information can inform how the population of an area may change overtime.

13.2.1.2 Research Objectives
The research objective is:

- to understand the demographic profile of the people that make up a place.

13.2.1.3 Approaches to Research
The *Australian Bureau of Statistics Census Community Profiles* provides the detailed snapshot of these attributes. The ABS also publishes annual estimates of population at a local government area.

13.2.2 Household Characteristics

13.2.2.1 Research Considerations
Understanding the household characteristics such as single person or extended family can provide a range of insights about underlying pressures in a community, such as a concentration of single adult families or whether the dwelling occupied is fit for purpose when the data is cross tabulated with dwelling type. But a word of caution when looking at patterns—for example, in the latter example an empty nest couple may appear to live in a house that is too large, but they may say for the first time they live in a house that provides all the rooms they need, such as a study, craft room or computer room.

The spatial analysis of household types is best collected and mapped at spatial scales such as the ABS Statistical Area Level 1 (SA1), and most valuable when there are time series assessments.

13.2.2.2 Research Objectives
The research objective is:

- to understand the household characteristics of the people that make up a place.

13.2.2.3 Approaches to Research
The *Australian Bureau of Statistics Census Community Profiles* provides the detailed snapshot of these attributes. It is beneficial if the household type data is cross tabulated with dwelling types.

13.3 Socio-economic Characteristics

13.3.1 Research Considerations

Socio-economic analysis for strategic planning helps you understand the qualities of individuals, households and communities that may influence outcomes sought by city plans, such as:

- educational attainment, which influences employment opportunities and the location of businesses (access to skilled labour)
- car ownership, which influences assumptions on the provision of transport
- household age profiles, which influence a variety of areas such as the demand for childcare and primary and secondary schools
- household income, which influences housing choice.

The *Australian Bureau of Statistics Census Community Profiles* provides a rich source of data on socio-economic characteristics and is the starting point for all socio-economic analysis.

Invariably the spatial analysis of socio-economic data reveals clear patterns across a city. Therefore, assessments of socio-economic data are best collected and mapped at small spatial scales such as the ABS Statistical Area Level 1 (SA1), most valuable when there are time series assessments.

Other issues for consideration in analysing socio-economic data are:

- **A crosstab assessment,** where information on two variables is collected and assessed, such as households without cars that live in an apartment. The ABS provides this information, at a small cost, but it can be constrained if it impacts privacy, usually because the spatial area being examined is too small.
- **Linking spatial information** from the ABS Census with other data sets for the same spatial geography, which is most accurate if the other data set is collected around the same time as the Census. Therefore, the information relates to the same community.
- **Creating clear narratives,** which assist the development of a city plan. This is a critical part of the 'why' element of a final plan. In Greater Sydney, one example is the differing levels of employment self-containment across the city.

13.3.2 Research Objectives

The research objective is:

- to understand the qualities of individuals, households and communities that may influence the outcomes sought by city plans.

13.3.3 Approaches to Research

Being able to access, manipulate, analyse and interpret ABS Census data and other data sources is a core skill for strategic planners. The development of narratives and their formatting into easy-to-read presentations takes time. Thus, much of the basic research can occur before projects commence. In actuality, most jurisdictions work to understand the data from the Census as it becomes available, and collate this into one document. Analysis should move beyond the basics to information that reflects the challenges and opportunities for a city.

13.4 Characteristics of Places and Country

This is the most important piece of data collection required for any strategic planning project. The intent of the task is the same no matter the geography; what changes is the level of detail and method of collection. We need to investigate:

1. land use activities and transport networks
2. country
3. built form
4. landform, physiography and climate.

13.4.1 Land Use Activities and Transport Networks

13.4.1.1 Research Considerations

The focus is to identify spatial patterns, typologies and inter-relationships of the land use activities and transport networks across a city and how they change over time. This may be the distribution of centres vis-à-vis the rail network at a metropolitan scale or the co-location of specialised stores.

The intent of the task is the same no matter what the spatial geography; what changes is the level of detail and method of collection.

This task, for most strategic planners, will generally be completed for places with a small spatial geography, such as a town centre. In that circumstance the task is to walk every street and identify all land uses by title and level. For the full metropolitan plan, it is about understanding typologies which require site visits to most major centres, some small local centres and a range of industrial and residential precincts and parklands.

> *Past trends that show how cities change can also be revealing. Many years ago, when I was working in regional Victoria, I undertook a site investigation of Echuca town centre. The drivers of the town's history were evident in the built form and land uses today. Along the river are the remnant buildings of the days when river trade was the focus of activities, now a major tourism area. Up the road beside the railway station are grand old buildings that time has since passed by. They were from the days when the railways took over from the river*

and the railway station became the centre of trade. Between the two is now the new centre of town, a commercial precinct influenced by the advent of the car.

Recognising and understanding such changes helps us understand that there is no fixed vision for a place and exploring a place's evolutionary past can assist in setting the next course for the future.

Site visits are a critical aspect of this work, as they allow you to get a feel for a place and see it for what it is, as distinct from the perceptions of a few or the desktop review of someone else's data.

> Many years ago, I undertook a land use survey of Geelong CBD. In one street, Ryrie Street, I found many homeware shops, all recently refurbished. When I enquired with property agents, they said rents had never been better. However, when I spoke to the council, they said the street was terrible, they reminisced that it was once the focus of high fashion, but they had all moved to a new mall-based centre. The reality was, it was different—places change, and importantly planning should not seek to create museums.

> Another example is a survey I did at a neighbourhood centre which revealed a typical cross-section of activities. If I had just simply written clothing and furniture it would have hidden the fact that they were second-hand shops, and every shop had shutters which were rolled down at night.

13.4.1.2 Research Objectives
The research objective is:

- to identify the spatial characteristics of the land use activities and transport networks and from that identify the functional land use systems and transport networks and their inter-relationships.

13.4.1.3 Approaches to Research
The spatial assessment begins with the gathering of data then moves to a functional land use assessment plan.

The spatial assessment of land uses needs to provide an understanding of a range of spatial land uses/attributes. At the metropolitan scale this would include:

- **Typology of centres**, such as size, major attractors, presence of specialised precincts, such as health, education, office and entertainment.
- **Specialised precincts**, such as health, education, office and entertainment.
- **Open space networks**, ideally assessed by type, size and ownership.
- **Transport networks**, such as road, rail freight, public transport (all modes), principal cycle networks, principal trail (walking) networks, trade gateways, park and ride stations.
- **Housing typologies**, at a suburb or precinct level.
- **Lot sizes**, including time series information.
- **Land values**, including time series information.

- **Government-owned land**, often for specific areas, plus council-owned land as well.

The functional assessment needs to show how the city works strategically as interconnected systems. This information is then used to inform a range of assessments in Step 3. This includes assessing the performance or acceptability of the current spatial distribution in the context of the growth and change equation and identifying the barriers and opportunities for growth and change.

13.4.2 Physiography and Climatic Conditions

13.4.2.1 Research Consideration

Climate and landform not only impact natural systems, but they also influence how we plan and manage cities. Physiographic attributes typically cannot be modified.

Most Australian cities do not have uniform landform or climatic qualities across the whole of their metropolitan area. This is important to understand as these differences may require sub-metropolitan policy positions. An introduction to these issues—including that the landform does not change, climate does—is available in *Physiography of Victoria, An Introduction to Geomorphology* (1975).

For example, in the eastern half of Greater Sydney the topography is such that when you travel through that area you gain the benefits of borrowed landscapes and vistas of water, which are often taken for granted. In Western Sydney specifically the Western Parkland City which ultimately will be home to a population similar to that of Perth, the area is flat, and a two-storey building will hide the views of the nearby Blue Mountains. Thus, we need to understand viewsheds and use careful city design to provide distant views from public places.

The Greater Sydney climate also varies; Penrith has 21 days where the temperature is over 35 degrees Celsius versus just three days for the eastern suburbs. Thus, the expansion of the urban tree canopy is a more significant ambition out west.

Also, when heading west just beyond Parramatta, there is a topographical divide to the land which results in rivers and creeks in that area running north as distinct from a direct easterly path to the sea.

Melbourne has similar landform and climatic differences including a difference in soils. This means that in the outer south east the land is particularly good for intensive agriculture, specifically vegetable growing which creates tensions as to the optimal use of the land—agriculture versus urban expansion.

These few examples seek to emphasise why understanding physiography and climate are important inputs to city planning.

13.4.2.2 Research Objectives
The research objective is:

- to understand the implications of the characteristics of physiography and climate conditions on the planning objectives for a city.

13.4.2.3 Approach to Research
The characteristics of a city, which research activities need to consider, are:

- catchment mapping
- heat wave mapping in addition to trends in climatic data
- viewsheds, which is a sub-element of the discussion on the quality of the city landscape, refer Sect. 15.3.4.
- soil quality, which informs agricultural activities and thus planning in the city hinterland, as well as the viability of differing urban landscapes, and potential natural hazards such as cracking clays
- rainfall, which is linked to the issue of natural hazards (flooding) and particularly the planning of greenfield areas. For example, South Creek in Western Sydney is identified as an intermittent stream; however, when it is fully urbanised, there will be an excess of water run-off, which will create an opportunity for the excess water to be utilised in the landscape. Conversely in the growth areas of outer south east Melbourne a developer sought to have water in the landscape, but in that case the technical advice was that there was not enough water available, with the consequence that instead of having a water feature they would have a mud feature.

13.4.3 Country

Gaining a First Nations' view of Country earlier on in the process is critical if the plan is to:

- respond to cultural landscapes
- achieve culturally responsive design, social infrastructure and public art
- respond to language and place naming.

The research objective is to develop an understanding of the local First Nations people's perspective of the cultural landscape of the area.

How these considerations should be approached is outlined in Sect. 15.3.2.

13.5 City Setting

13.5.1 Research Consideration

The setting for cities is often presented though images of a place, showing housing typologies, striking features such as coastlines or images of a town centre from street furniture to heritage-listed buildings. Consequently, many strategies talk to local or neighbourhood character as an element of a place that needs to be respected and responded to when considering matters of urban design.

In the context of 'city setting' as one of the research topics, it is intended that it be more than the physical attributes of a place. Consider the range of characteristics that make a place distinctive—the sum of the qualities of the people, the place and the activities that occur within it.

> *The task expressing the setting for a city or place reminds me of a conversation I had with a planner as to the vision for a small village community. The person indicated that the vision could have been for any coastal community. From my perspective we had achieved an important goal, that is it was clear that the plan was for a coastal community.*

13.5.1.1 Research Objectives
The research objective is:

- to understand the collective implications of the findings from the three research topics of the characteristics of people and households, socio-economic characteristics and the characteristics of a place which reveal the distinctive qualities of the city or place.

13.5.1.2 Approach to Research
The task of outlining the setting for a city or place is an important synthesis task within the strategic planning research framework. You need to understand the essence of a place and be informed by the perceptions of the community.

> *When preparing the metropolitan plan for Sydney, it became clear, from our engagement with the community, that those in the western part of Sydney do not describe themselves as being part of 'Sydney'—there is a clear emphasis, that they are from 'Western Sydney'. Hence, it is not surprising that there is a Minister for Western Sydney and equally, our nomenclature for Sydney changed to Greater Sydney.*

It should result in providing clarity of a place, including differences such as a mosaic of socio-economic and culturally diverse groups or differing perceptions of a sense of community.

The Victorian Department of Environment, Land, Water and Planning has a planning practice note—*Understanding Neighbourhood Character, Planning Practice Note 43*, which provides a useful context for considering city setting.

It provides a definition that addresses the physical characteristics of a place. The same general approach, as outlined in the definition, is directly relevant to considering how to bring together all the elements which make up a place.

In terms of the definition, *Practice Note 42* states:

> Neighbourhood character is essentially the combination of the public and private realms. Every property, public place or piece of infrastructure makes a contribution, whether great or small. It is the cumulative impact of all these contributions that establishes neighbourhood character.
>
> The key to understanding character is being able to describe how the features of an area come together to give that area its own particular character. Breaking up character into discrete features and characteristics misses out on the relationships between these features and characteristics. Understanding how these relationships physically appear on the ground is usually the most important aspect in establishing the character of the area.

Importantly the analysis should indicate how the findings will influence outcomes and directions for the city.

13.6 Summary

This chapter has sought to provide insights into how to approach the research required to inform the basis of your city plan. Specifically, this chapter provides more detail on the research areas for Part A: Context, the people and the place.

The information provided should in no way be seen as the definitive explanation on how to go about each task. It is rather a starting point for understanding the need to investigate each research area and what questions may be important. In one sense, answering questions is fairly easy, whereas identifying which question to ask is quite hard.

As indicated previously in this book, the individual research areas are not independent of each other, in fact, where they connect are usually the place of most importance. Hence, the last phase of investigation for each research area should be the consideration of what connections exist with other research areas.

References

Sherbon Hills, E (1975), *Physiography of Victoria, An Introduction to Geomorphology*. Whitcombe & Tombs Pty Ltd, Australia
— For those wanting to understand what is behind the maps and data

Website Links

Australian Bureau of Statistics, Australian Statistical Geography Standard. https://www.abs.gov.au/websitedbs/D3310114.nsf/home/Australian+Statistical+Geography+Standard+(ASGS)

Australian Bureau of Statistics Census. https://www.abs.gov.au/ausstats/abs@.nsf/0/B3E6E2939 0F64923CA257BF10013569B

Australian Bureau of Statistics Census Community profiles. https://quickstats.censusdata.abs.gov.au/census_services/getproduct/census/2016/communityprofile/036

Greater Sydney Commission (2018), *A Metropolis of Three Cities, State of New South Wales, Australia.* https://www.greater.sydney/metropolis-of-three-cities

State of Victoria Department of Environment, Land, Water and Planning (2018), *Understanding Neighbourhood Character, Planning Practice Note 43.* PPN43-Understanding-Neighbourhood-Character.pdf (planning.vic.gov.au)

Part B: Needs of People and Business 14

14.1 Introduction

This chapter provides more detail on the research areas for Part B: Needs of people and business. The information for each research topic includes:

- research considerations
- research objectives
- approaches to research.

14.2 Needs of People and Households

14.2.1 Improving the Level of Housing Choice

14.2.1.1 Research Considerations

Housing choice is about what housing options (price, type, tenure and location) are available in any given location in a city. It is not meant to suggest that all options should be available everywhere. Equally, it does not mean there should be only one choice. Finding and delivering the balance is the key.

Few people enjoy seeing their neighbourhood change. Housing policy is one area where social norms have an influence. Therefore, the language we use to describe why, what and how choice is to be achieved is important.

Planners sometimes use their own jargon to describe city outcomes, such as 'compact cities' or 'density done better'. My experience suggests that language needs to reflect the everyday considerations of the community.

I once met with a dozen council mayors who, I was told, wished to challenge proposed housing targets. Being wary of this my opening statement was – Where do you want your children to live? Followed by – What can they afford, and do they own a car? Very quickly there was a discussion about a range of housing types close to rail stations.

Houses are much more than dwellings; they are homes. Exploring housing choice needs to consider people's needs. Our aim is to connect housing choice to a range of other objectives such as access to goods, services, jobs, walkable communities and proximity to amenities such as parks.

I have a longstanding belief that if we wish to understand housing preferences, we should not study housing. What we need to understand is the locational decisions of people when they move to a new home.

To emphasise my point, think about how we choose to buy or rent a house. We first choose a general location, based on needs such as being close to family, friends, work, schools or parks. I have had continual support for this view. Then we look at a house we cannot afford (I always get a laugh, which suggests it is true) and then we fine tune our locational preferences together with a type of dwelling we can afford, whatever type that may be.

Thus, if you want to influence housing decisions, focus on the issues that influence people's location decisions, such as parks, schools, jobs and shops.

In addition, understanding housing choice requires a more explicit statement of what aspects of housing are in question, such as:

- general housing supply and demand, which covers everything from detached dwellings to high rise apartment towers
- affordable housing, as provided through a specific mechanism (such as a planning regulation), and directed to a specific income group
- social housing, as provided by governments
- specialist housing areas, such as student, retirement, rural-residential and culturally responsive housing.

Finally, and importantly, if you push too hard with a simple housing agenda, the community will push back. This impacts the supply of housing, particularly in suburban areas, as we've seen multiple times across Australia.

14.2.1.2 Research Objectives

The research objectives are:

- to gain an understanding of the housing choices available across a city and the drivers of housing supply and demand
- to determine whether there is sufficient housing supply in the short, medium and long term in the context of demand
- to understand the need or role of housing supply on wider societal objectives, such as housing choices for key workers (nurses, teachers, emergency service workers, and police), culturally responsive housing and affordable housing for low and very low-income households
- to determine the actions required to achieve housing choice.

14.2.1.3 Approaches to Research

Understanding housing issues and planning for housing is a core area of city planning. It is one of the more analytical skill areas that also require reasonable numerical skills and understanding. Some areas require specialist input, thus the more a strategic planner understands this area, the better their ability will be to ask the right questions. Several areas require investigation.

Understanding housing opportunities

These spatial assessments of the characteristics of housing choice, undertaken at an ABS Statistics Statistical Area Level 2 (SA2), cover:

- housing mix (type), price and tenure (sources ABS Census and Valuer General data) by location
- characteristics of specialist housing areas, such as student housing and retirement living choices
- housing markets, of which there are a jigsaw of around 18 or 19 in Greater Sydney, compared to Melbourne, where markets appear as wedges emanating from the inner suburbs to the fringe. An oversupply in one market will not necessarily assist another. Identifying housing markets is complex and usually undertaken by housing research teams, consultants or universities.
- housing preferences, which must reflect what a household can afford and is useful at the strategic level. For example, on the Central Coast of NSW, research showed that more than 80 percent of people desired a detached dwelling and it did not matter if it was new or old.

  However, the data can reinforce past preferences and potentially lock in places to historic development patterns. Choice can be considered in different ways—some may choose to trade off having a small dwelling with walking access to goods, services and jobs, for a large dwelling where they will need a private vehicle to access the same. Adaptations to life in response to the COVID-19 pandemic may also be changing people's preferences, which will need to be understood.
- housing choices for low and very low-income groups for rent and purchase in the context of the established housing affordability criteria of housing costs not exceeding 30 percent of a household's income
- culturally responsive housing, such as for First Nations people. In this instance a major consideration is the design of both individual dwellings and how they are clustered. An example is the Auckland Design Manual which includes a Māori Design Hub (refer website link).

These assessments need to be linked to demographic and socio-economic data and ideally as time series assessments.

Understanding housing supply and demand
Most Australian state planning jurisdictions, as well as many local governments, have some sort of housing monitor that provides an understanding of housing supply and demand considerations. In general, they seek to:

- monitor greenfield development and cover change from land designation for residential development through to lots released as part of a developed subdivision, with the focus on annual change
- monitor urban renewal/infill development through databases covering activity from proposals through to completed developments, with a focus on annual change
- monitor take-up rates for redevelopment areas to best understand residual supply.

> *For example, advice once from a colleague was that a specific area that we were seeking to investigate had experienced the same level of annual conversion (redevelopment) in percentage terms year on year, based on the residual existing development. Thus, it was possible to provide a level of prediction of the future supply that would be available.*

Some of the considerations/challenges in these activities include:

- using an assessment method that can identify small changes in supply or specialist areas such as one-for-one conversions, dual occupancy developments, granny flats, retirement villages, student housing and demolitions
- using data sets to identify drivers of change, for example, in Victoria research has shown there is a relationship between supply and various attributes and that the same sized allotment in different parts of the city would yield a differing number of new dwellings
- understanding the development viability of different housing types, including recognising that market feasibility changes with location.

Regarding the last point, the NSW planning department has developed a strategic tool for understanding the viability of differing housing typologies at the suburb level—the Development Capacity Model. Refer to the website links.

The provision of social and affordable housing
Social or public housing in Australia is typically provided by dedicated state agencies, making their planning and delivery usually outside the remit of planning portfolios. City planning for this area is usually driven by the spatial implications of the location of social housing as distinct from levels of provision, which, while important, are generally out of scope.

One issue to be understood is the degree to which the clustering of social housing may reinforce areas of socio-economic disadvantage. The bigger, more significant challenge is to identify how to respond. My direct experience suggests that responses need to take a long-term approach with sustained allocation of resources over many years. In some cases, significant funds may be required to create the opportunity for greater financial, economic and social independence for individuals and households in such areas. As city planners, we need to work with the responsible agencies to identify how to manage the issues in a city plan.

Affordable housing sits at the interface between social housing and market-driven housing. In Australia, this policy area has struggled to gain traction in terms of delivery options.

Based on the definition of need (a household spending more than 30 percent of their income on housing costs), research shows the number of households that need to access affordable housing is far greater than the supply provided.

The challenge has been developing a delivery mechanism that can provide supply at the required levels. The mechanism needs to address the gap between what the housing market can afford to provide in terms of price, versus what the household can afford in terms of income.

The challenge for most city plans has not been about the research required to understand the need, it has been about establishing an acceptable delivery mechanism. In Australia, a consistent and effective mechanism that can deliver the required levels of affordable housing remains elusive.

Increasingly, industry is required to consider culturally responsive housing typologies and models for First Nations communities and other culturally diverse groups. The notion of only planning for nuclear family units needs to be challenged and barriers to a diverse mix of housing outcomes need to be considered.

14.2.2 Enabling the Financial and Economic Independence of Households

14.2.2.1 Research Considerations

The central consideration for city planning is giving all households similar opportunities to advance their lives through access to:

- quality education opportunities, to maximise education and skills attainment and therefore employment opportunities
- a diversity of employment opportunities.

Therefore, we need to consider how we create economic opportunity across the city, as distinct from simply maximising economic output. In this context Glaeser (2011, p. 27) suggests that part of the role of a city is to allow people to move out of poverty into gainful employment. His research of cities in the United States also shows:

> A 10 per cent increase in the percentage of an area's adult population with a BA predicted 6 per cent more income growth between 1980 and 2000.

Moreover, he further states:

> As the share of the population with a college degree increases by 10 per cent, per capita gross metropolitan product rises by 22 per cent.

These findings suggest the importance of accessibility to post-secondary education opportunities.

As to the question of accessibility to a diversity of employment opportunities, economic policies generally seek to maximise economic output that results in a focus of the most productive jobs in central city locations. The Greater Sydney Region Plan's vision, although supporting economic outcomes for the Harbour (Sydney) CBD, is for a metropolis of three cities underscored with a specific and explicit intent on "rebalancing economic and social opportunities" (Greater Sydney Commission 2018, p. 6).

Influencing employment requires several considerations. We often talk about the distribution of jobs, and often how we can get more jobs closer to home; however, we cannot move jobs, but we can influence the locational decisions of businesses, which results in jobs. This point cannot be over emphasised. The principal task is to understand what actions would influence business decision-making, such as improved road and freight rail access to an industrial estate to improve supply chain efficiencies.

A further example is provided in the report *Forecasting the Distribution of Stand Alone Office Development across Sydney to 2035* (BIS Shrapnel 2015, p. A 7) where in Appendix A2 it discusses factors influencing the location of office development.

Influencing education outcomes is outside the scope of city planning, other than to identify and advise governments on the implications of wider economic and social outcomes. For example, there is a significant spatial divide across both Melbourne and Sydney regarding educational attainment. In Greater Sydney there is similarly a significant spatial divide in terms of primary and secondary school education outcomes, reflected by results for NAPLAN (The National Assessment Program—Literacy and Numeracy).

Educational opportunities can be influenced by locational criteria for post-secondary educational facilities and support for health and education precincts, which tend to be distributed across the wider metropolitan area.

We need to recognise the feedback loops in cities that influence people's occupation and skills. For a range of historical reasons, the distribution of the types of jobs across cities is not equal—for example, decisions to influence the location of large industrial areas, ports and airports and the transport networks to support them. It is natural that the areas around these job concentrations potentially attract people with the requisite skills. These decisions to some degree lock activities and people into certain pathways, yet activities and technologies change, and new markets seek to make the best decisions for their business not necessarily for the common good. If we wish to change spatial patterns, we need to understand the

14.2 Needs of People and Households

current and historic dynamics that influence a city, and what is influencing the decisions of new businesses today. We can only understand the required intervention if we understand the nature of the city.

City planning does not typically address the financial and economic independence of households. It does, however, cover the area through a range of other analyses:

- journey to work patterns, which reveal the extent to which people need to travel to gain access to employment which is often expressed as levels of self-containment
  - Research for the Greater Sydney Region Plan showed that 91 percent of people in the Eastern Harbour City lived and worked in that city, yet only 49 percent of people in the Western Parkland City lived and worked in that city.
- socio-economic data, which sets a context for a plan and will often include spatial data on levels of educational attainment, occupations and skills.

14.2.2.2 Research Objectives

The research objectives are:

- to understand the spatial considerations influencing educational outcomes
- to understand the spatial distribution of jobs by type, such as knowledge, industrial, population-serving and health and education jobs (health and education jobs are part of the knowledge group; we separate them as governments have greater potential to influence their distribution and scale).

14.2.2.3 Approaches to Research

Research activities should include:

- understanding the relative differences in access to tertiary educational institutes and employment (breadth and depth), with spatial investigations at the (ABS Statistical Area Level 1 (SA1)).
  - Section 14.2.4 has a more expansive discussion on transport accessibility
  - Regarding employment, a spatial index of what we call effective job density covers private vehicle and public transport modes.
- utilising ABS Census data to understand the relative spatial differences in socio-economic data covering the areas of occupations, skills and educational attainment with spatial investigations at ABS Statistical Area Level 1 (SA1).

We can use this research to understand why actions are required to influence the structure of a city, which can be to create opportunities closer to where people live and/or to improve accessibility to employment opportunities.

14.2.3 Enabling the Economic Self-Determination of First Nations Communities

14.2.3.1 Research Considerations

The Commonwealth Government has a Partnership Agreement on Closing the Gap which commenced in March 2019. The partnership is between the Australian Governments and the Coalition of Peaks. The Coalition of Peaks are national and state and territory non-government Aboriginal and Torres Strait Islander Peak bodies and certain independent statutory authorities which have responsibility for policies, programs and services related to Closing the Gap.

The Partnership agreement is founded on four priority reform areas and 17 socio-economic outcome areas, refer Productivity Commission, *Closing the Gap* Information Repository website.

Socio-economic outcome area 8: Strong economic participation and development of Aboriginal and Torres Strait Islander people and communities has as a target:

- By 2031, increase the proportion of Aboriginal and Torres Strait Islander people aged 25–64 who are employed to 62 percent.

The Productivity Commission's report *Overcoming Indigenous Disadvantage Key Indicators 2020* provides detail on the status of change in education and economic outcome for First Nations people. It highlights that improvement has been achieved but also the need to continue efforts to close the gap. The report states:

> Some of the ways that governments and education and training providers can build on the strengths of Aboriginal and Torres Strait Islander adults and address some of the barriers to their success in post-secondary education and training include:
>
> – providing access to a range of social, cultural, financial and academic supports
> – taking an inclusive approach to the expectations, values and motivations of Aboriginal and Torres Strait Islander communities, particularly in remote areas
> – promoting cultural safety by including Aboriginal and Torres Strait Islander knowledges in post-secondary curriculums and teaching practices (p. 4.75).

Identifying the need for economic outcomes has been included in regional plans across NSW since around 2014, where each plan has as a direction:

- Increase the economic self-determination of Aboriginal communities

Most Australian cities are home to several different First Nations communities. In helping to facilitate economic self-determination for these communities, we need to:

- facilitate and establish processes that build on the land holdings of First Nations communities and determine how cultural values create opportunities such as cultural heritage tours
- recognise that pathways for economic self-determination may involve capacity building as much as land use management
- recognise the need for innovation in how land is used
- recognise that pathways need to both maximise economic opportunities and consider cultural and social needs.

14.2.3.2 Research Objectives

The research objectives are:

- to continue to engage with First Nations communities across the city
- to understand the land tenure of First Nations communities and how planning can influence opportunities
- to understand economic development issues for First Nations communities.

14.2.3.3 Approaches to Research

First and foremost, any approach must be about a dialogue directly with First Nations people and recognising the role of Aboriginal land councils and the range of First Nations people and organisations to connect with, refer Sect. 5.3.2.5. Expect the journey of facilitating opportunities to go well beyond the time allocated for preparing the plan and activities; your approaches and pathways for delivery need to respond to this.

Never under-estimate the role of capacity building on planning matters. I was involved in a NSW Government initiative that sought to provide advice directly to Local Aboriginal Land Councils on the planning status of land they hold as well as capacity building on land use planning.

The guideline, *Recognise Country, Guidelines for development in the Aerotropolis* (2022), states the importance of economic participation as a way to improve social outcomes for individuals and resilient and sustainable communities (p. 30). The guideline also highlights that there are a range of economic development opportunities for First Nations people throughout the life cycle of projects, such as:

- Providing advice and guidance on decision-making for planning and design
- Providing advice on and undertaking caring for Country cultural practices
- Supporting First Nations owned and operated businesses to operate in the Aerotropolis
- Facilitating On-Country cultural experiences and activities throughout all stages of a project including planning and design (i.e. On-Country walks and technical advice), construction (i.e. archaeological investigations) and operation (i.e. cultural tourism experiences). (p. 30)

14.2.4 Urban Amenity: Improving the Level of Access to Goods, Services and Jobs

Accessibility to goods, services and jobs is, in my view, one of the most important considerations when planning a city, yet there is no consensus as to what is acceptable or desirable. This may be because many aspects are private sector-driven in a market economy, and accessibility is a combination of government-provided transport systems and land use planning—it is a three-way tussle (refer Fig. 14.1).

14.2.4.1 Research Considerations

A household's level of access to goods, services and jobs is described as urban amenity in the *Australian State of the Environment Report 2016, Topic Liveability: Urban Amenity* (refer to website reference). Urban amenities cover access to employment, accommodation, educational institutions (childcare to university), retail, leisure, recreation and entertainment, health facilities (from health practitioners to hospitals), culture and the arts and employment (industry, office, warehouse and logistics, agricultural). We also need to recognise that access to goods and services can also be viewed as access to jobs.

Spatial indexes such as the Metropolitan Accessibility/ Remoteness Index of Australia (Metro ARIA) developed by the Australian Urban Research Infrastructure Network (AURIN) provide a standardised tool for measuring levels of accessibility.

The Melbourne and Greater Sydney metropolitan plans each have statements of intent regarding accessibility to goods and services. In line with the earlier comment of a lack of consensus in this area, the two approaches, while similar in dealing with accessibility, are quite different in their approach.

1. In *Plan Melbourne*: Principle 5: Living locally—20-minute neighbourhoods.
   - Creating accessible, safe and attractive local areas where people can access most of their everyday needs within a 20-minute walk, cycle or local public

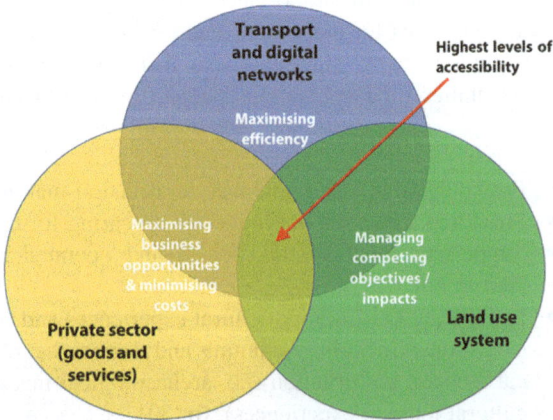

Fig. 14.1 Accessibility: The intersection of a three-way tussle

transport trip will make Melbourne healthier and more inclusive. Due to the specialised and diverse nature of work, many people will still need to travel outside of this 20-minute neighbourhood for their jobs.
2. In *A Metropolis of Three Cities* (Greater Sydney): Objective 14 A Metropolis of Three Cities—integrated land use and transport create walkable and 30-minute cities.
   – Establish a metropolitan transport network which reinforces the metropolis of three cities, particularly the delivery of a 30-minute city where most residents in each city can access their metropolitan centre or cluster within 30 minutes by public transport.
   – Develop a network of 34 strategic centres with jobs, goods and services supported by a public transport, walking and cycling network. This would provide residents with a 30-minute public transport service to their nearest strategic centre seven days a week.

In researching these accessibility issues we need to consider:

- what we mean by accessibility—car, public transport, walk or cycle?
- differences in accessibility levels across the city with a view to establishing if intervention is required
- how to categorise individual areas, such as retail: is it access to any shop or a specific type, such as a department store or supermarket?
- the goods and services provided by the private sector, which raises land use planning issues such as land supply and the need to understand spatial delivery models of different commercial sectors and how to influence the locational decisions of businesses, if required
- the value of different communities place on accessibility for differing goods and services. For example, research for the Greater Sydney Region Plan (Newgate 2015) showed that in the south west area people placed high importance on access to services, at a statistically significant level, compared to the Greater Sydney average.
- the range of attributes or communities of interest of cities such as housing markets, journey to work catchments, shopping centre trade catchments and university catchments
- how trade-offs may influence levels of accessibility such as having fewer large supermarkets (lots of choice and potentially lower prices) where access is predominately by car versus many small supermarkets (limited choice and potentially higher costs) where people can walk, which brings more activity, safer streets and healthier communities
- whether interventions seek to influence the distribution of activities and/or transport options
- any benchmarks for levels of service, noting many areas have operational service levels, such as percent of buses running on time, but it is generally only in education where there is a specified service level relating to the whole population (every child must be found a place in a school, though the size

of schools change). Our research needs to inform a wider assessment on the desired outcomes for a city, such as walkability
- coverage, frequency and travel time to principal destinations; usage patterns show that frequency is important and travel time raises considerations of acceptability and concepts such as the Marchetti constant (a daily travel budget of one hour).

14.2.4.2 Research Objectives
The research objectives are:

- to understand the relative levels of accessibility of households' access to goods, services and jobs across a metropolitan area
- to understand the spatial delivery models for broad categories of goods, services and jobs and the ability to influence their spatial distribution
- to determine if the relative differences suggest the need for intervention to improve equitable levels of accessibility for all.

14.2.4.3 Approaches to Research
Your research will be assisted by geographical information system (GIS) tools. The ABS Census also provides information on the journey to work patterns. Administrative data such as public transport electronic ticketing, which provides information on service usage and the distribution of activities can be obtained from a range of sources.

In the first instance, examine these areas:

- **Retail**, with the principal markers being access to a supermarket and a major centre. The second is judgmental; Greater Sydney, with a population of approximately 5 million people, has 40 major centres. However, the COVID-19 pandemic has revealed that walking access to local centres may be increasingly important.
- **Education**, with the principal markers being an easy walk to primary schools and access to post-secondary facilities. Increasingly the threshold size of primary schools is increasing, which reduces walking trips to schools.
- **Standalone office precincts and health and education precincts**, as they are markers of access to a diversity of employment opportunities.
- **Industrial activities**, so that you can measure people's access to urban services not just industrial jobs. Urban services are defined as a collection of industries that enable the city to develop and its businesses and residents to operate, such as waste management, printing services and motor vehicle repairs (SGS Economics and Planning 2017).
- **Health facilities** are part private (such as the local GP) and public (such as a public hospital). Their distribution, specifically for hospitals, is not simply population driven. Health services and facilities are managed by state health

departments. Therefore, measures of accessibility need to be clear on intent. One area that can be analysed is access to traditional local health services—the local GP.
- **Cultural facilities and activities** are provided by the public and private sectors. In some areas, such as performing arts, an understanding of the hierarchy of facilities is a pre-requisite for any analysis.
- **Open space and recreation facilities**, where a challenge is identifying the role of land designated for open space, which impacts on usability and accessibility, such as bushland versus a tennis court.

Identifying how accessibility to goods, services and jobs can be enhanced is **integrally linked** with understanding the needs of businesses and the ability to improve transport networks. Both issues are discussed later in this chapter.

14.2.5 Improving the Health of Individuals and Communities

14.2.5.1 Research Considerations

An outcome of healthy individuals and communities overlaps with individual and community wellbeing. For this book, the focus for healthy individuals and communities is a healthy built environment, in line with the definition of city planning that identifies planners' scope as the intersection between people's needs and place.

There is a significant body of literature on the topic of healthy built environments. A recent resource is the NSW Government's *Healthy Built Environment Checklist* (2020). In terms of a holistic view, it identifies 11 areas for consideration (NSW Government 2020, pp. 31–88). The health issues are:

- **Healthy eating**. Improving access to fresh, nutritious and affordable food and drink. Research shows that increased access reduces obesity levels, while a high prevalence of fast-food outlets impacts negatively on people's food choices.
- **Physical activity**. Encouraging and creating opportunities for physical activity and providing opportunities to access public open space, where activities can be as simple as walking to catch a bus.
- **Housing**. Facilitating a diverse range of housing to meet the differing needs of households including adaptability and accessibility which can allow ageing in place and housing for those people with a disability. See also Sect. 14.2.1.
- **Transport and connectivity**. Reducing car dependency by providing alternative mode options together with city design that enhances connectivity and improves the quality of the walkable environment.
- **Quality employment**. This directly reflects Sect. 14.2.2: Enabling financial and economic independence. It facilitates upward economic mobility and seeks to improve access to a wider depth and breadth of jobs and access to jobs training.
- **Community safety and security**, with a focus on crime prevention through design. Research for the Greater Sydney Region Plan found that "safety of

people and their property" was the most important aspect of making a good place to live (Newgate Research 2015).
- **Open space and natural features**. Improving access to public open space including green, water and natural spaces as well as quality streetscapes and the sense of identity. See also Sect. 14.3.3.
- **Social infrastructure**. Providing access to social and community facilities that support a diverse population, including their early delivery for new communities. See Sect. 14.3.1
- **Social cohesion and connectivity**. Directly reflects Sect. 14.3.1: Improving individual and community wellbeing and covers facilitating social interaction and community participation in planning.
- **Environment and health**. Covers the quality of the environment we live in such as water and air quality as well as managing the implications of natural hazards. See also Sect. 15.4.2.
- **Environmental sustainability and climate change**. How we respond to climate change, adaptation and mitigation and build environmental sustainability and resilience. See also Sect. 15.3.6.

These themes cross over with many aspects of city planning. In my experience, the best way to address these diverse health outcomes is within the thematic area that they are related to. This will ensure the issue is integrated and managed through the day-to-day activities of that area as distinct from needing a tailored initiative that may not be pursued. That said, a plan will still need a narrative on the healthy built environment, achieved by joining the dots from across the various areas of a city plan.

The community's behavioural responses in adapting to the range of lockdown requirements of the COVID-19 pandemic as set by each state government suggest that the goal of a healthy built environment would benefit from many of the positive behaviours developed by some during lockdown such as people walking in their local neighbourhood and visiting their local centre more often than normal.

14.2.5.2 Research Objectives
The research objectives are:

- to determine which other research topics should include consideration of healthy built environment issues
- to assess the extent, quality and enforcement of guidelines, policies and regulations that support a healthy built environment, which ideally occur outside the strategic planning process.

14.2.5.3 Approaches to Research
A core responsibility of city planning is planning for a healthy built environment.

A fundamental research area is assessing the quality of the urban environment as it relates to structure (such as connectivity), public realm attributes (such as lighting, disability accessibility or shade), provision of public spaces (including recreation and sporting facilities) and provision of cycle networks.

14.2.6 Reducing the Cost of Living

14.2.6.1 Research Consideration
In a statistically valid survey for the Greater Sydney Region Plan, Sydneysiders were asked about the most important aspects of making a good place to live. The research found that the cost of living was the second most important issue (Newgate Research 2015).

However, most factors that influence the cost of living are outside the influence of city planning (as identified by the list of items in the ABS consumer price index). Nevertheless, there are areas where city planning can help to reduce the cost of living, such as determining the spatial relationship between homes and goods, services and jobs (travel costs) together with costs relating to development such as planning processes, development requirements and the efficiency of urban infrastructure provision.

Theoretically, we could argue that a city would be most cost efficient if land was utilised for its highest and best use. However, social norms require the retention of other uses, such as suburban housing forms. If we consider social norms in terms of cost of living and an efficient city needs, we also need to explain to the community the costs of accepting certain social norms.

While we address this in the relevant areas of investigation, we do need to consider equitable outcomes, such as the distribution of jobs. Interestingly the work of West (2018) outlines how there are cost economies of scale for hard infrastructure (utilities) as the population of a city grows.

In addition, the infrastructure costs to governments from different housing options, specifically greenfield versus urban renewal/infill has received significant attention over the years. A general conclusion has been that greenfield development results in higher costs to government (which ultimately is a cost to consumers through taxes), as found in the 2010 study by the Centre for International Economics *The benefits and costs of alternative growth paths for Sydney's economic, social and environmental impacts*.

14.2.6.2 Research Objectives
The research for cost of living occurs as we investigate other areas such as housing, urban development and delivery and transport planning. Therefore, the research objectives are:

- to recognise that inefficiencies in the planning and development of cities impact on the cost of living
- to recognise that cost and benefit analyses must consider societal outcomes, which can be difficult to measure.

14.2.6.3 Approaches to Research

In line with considerations for a healthy built environment, individuals and communities where themes cross over with most aspects of city planning, our best approach is to look into the assessment of the relevant research topic. This will usually require the assessments in that area to use a specific lens to consider the cost of living. It will still be important that a plan has a specific narrative on the cost of living.

14.3 Quality of Life

14.3.1 Improving Individual and Community Wellbeing

14.3.1.1 Research Considerations

The wellbeing of individuals and the community reflects the level of social capital, social cohesion and the delivery of socially sustainable cities. It includes providing for the spiritual, cultural and life cycle needs of the community and contributes to a sense of welcome and belonging—social opportunity.

More particularly from Cred (2017, p. 7–8):

- Social capital refers to connections among individuals—social networks and the norms of reciprocity and trustworthiness that arise from them.
- Social cohesion describes the degree to which a society works towards the wellbeing of all its members, supports inclusive practices and allows individuals to work for upward mobility.
- Social sustainability recognises that individual and community wellbeing are linked, and that by addressing the needs of the most disadvantaged, the whole community benefits.
- Social sustainability is therefore the ability of a social system to support the capacity of current and future generations to maintain a high level of wellbeing.

Moreover, social sustainability should be seen as (Woodcraft et al., 2012, p. 16):

> …a process for creating sustainable, successful places that promote wellbeing, by understanding what people need from the places they live and work. Social sustainability combines design of the physical realm with design of the social world – infrastructure to support social and cultural life, social amenities, systems for citizen engagement and space for people and places to evolve.

Woodcraft et al. (2012, p. 22) identifies four elements as the building blocks to social sustainability.

- **Amenities and social infrastructure**. Amenities and support services provided early in the life of a new community, such as schools, social spaces, transport and community services

14.3 Quality of Life

I have experienced the planning and delivery of suburbs where the school appeared 14 years after the first houses. The result is children are driven to a range of nearby schools, and children in the same street may not get to know each other as their school friends live elsewhere.

- **Social and cultural life**. Shared spaces, collective activities and social architecture to foster local networks, belonging and community identity.
- **Voice and influence**. Governance structures to represent future residents and engage new ones in shaping local decision-making and stewardship.
- **Space to grow**. Flexible planning, housing, infrastructure and services that can adapt over time; meanwhile, use of buildings and public space.

While working in a growth council, the advice from the community development officers was that in the first instance community spaces should be portable buildings to allow the community to establish what their needs are before they assist in designing more permanent buildings.

City planning directly supports these outcomes through city design, community engagement and guidance on the planning of infrastructure for services.

Delivery requires city planners to enhance their understanding of the issues they seek to influence such as social cohesion.

Social capital, with its focus on connections, can be directly influenced by city planning in areas such as designing places for formal and informal connections, community engagement and early delivery of community infrastructure.

14.3.1.2 Research Objectives

The research objectives are:

- to assess how city structure and the public realm contribute to supporting social interaction
- to assess the extent and quality of guidelines, policies and regulations that support social interaction in the built environment, such as pocket parks or pop-up festivals on the road reserve
- to assess the distribution of social infrastructure, education and learning facilities, street life and meeting places and sharing spaces and places, such as community gardens (Cred 2017, p. 26)
- to assess the extent and quality of guidelines, policies and regulations that support social and community infrastructure, including how standard land use planning controls deal with social and community infrastructure. In some Australian jurisdictions, planning regulations push places of worship into industrial areas principally due to car parking regulations, which raises questions as to how we value spiritual beliefs
- to assess the extent and quality of guidelines, policies and regulations that support community engagement. The NSW *Environmental Planning and Assessment Act 1979 No 203*, Division 2.6, outlines requirements regarding community participation, including that all planning authorities must prepare a community

participation plan. Schedule 1 Community participation requirements outline provisions relating to the exhibition of plans, including strategic planning documents.

14.3.1.3 Approaches to Research
When undertaking research consider the following:

- Your first step for each research objective is to identify responsibilities for the city plan and what should be covered by agencies such as health or local government (community development).
- Many elements, such as the assessment of policy positions, should occur outside the strategic planning process.
- Mapping tangible assets that support wellbeing provides a starting point to determine potential issues and questions for investigations, refer Cred (2017).
- Assess regulations, policies and guidelines to determine if they are an impediment to creating opportunities.

14.3.2 Enabling Cultural and Artistic Expression, Participation and Appreciation

Cultural and artistic activities include painting, drawing, crafts, dance, music, photography and film, festivals, parades, cultural heritage and experiential history tours, museums and galleries.

14.3.2.1 Research Considerations
Responsibility for facilitating cultural and artistic expression, participation and appreciation falls outside the planning portfolio and many activities are driven by the private sector and/or are partly funded via government grants. However, planning can enable these outcomes by:

- providing for public spaces to accommodate the activities
- understanding the First Nations cultural heritage of places, which must include First Nations communities and form part of the early engagement approach
- addressing cultural safety in the built environment from and First Nations perspective
- ensuring planning controls allow for activities across a city, from festivals in public places to specific permissible uses that would allow a range of artistic activities, recognising that an approval process may be required, such as for live music
- recognising that some temporary artistic and cultural activities struggle with permissions to operate, when on face value the activity appears benign but may be caught up in definitional issues, such as a pop-up play in a café.

The night-time economy is sometimes a complex issue to manage, as was experienced in Sydney in the five years to 2020, due to violence resulting in deaths in a specific night-time entertainment precinct, which resulted in the introduction of stringent late night access rules for venues. However, city life, particularly nightlife, helps to create a liveable city and therefore requires consideration and resolution. Also, the night-time economy is not just serving those seeking leisure or entertainment activities but also serves the needs of shift workers.

In investigating these issues consider:

- benefits that artistic expression can bring to placemaking
- equitable distribution of facilities and funding of activities (anecdotally and based on real evidence)
- how culture adds to sense of place, as we see in the Chinatown areas of Australian cities that provide a range of Chinese cultural experiences, particularly food
- that cultural activities are a major element in most cities with a wide range of festivals, such as Vivid in Sydney and WOMADelaide in Adelaide
- recognising, respecting and responding to cultural values, specifically including First Nations culture, heritage and history, as we see expressed during NAIDOC week.

14.3.2.2 Research Objectives

The research objectives are:

- to assess the distribution of government-funded facilities and activities and the principles that inform this, such as a hierarchy of performing arts facilities
- to assess the regulatory environment that provides opportunities for cultural and artistic activities
- to identify the issues and/or interventions that can enhance people's opportunities to engage in cultural and artistic activities (from participant to observer).

14.3.2.3 Approaches to Research

Cultural and artistic opportunities are linked with state tourism objectives. You need to engage with agencies for each need to determine how a city plan can advance these goals.

Mapping of cultural and artistic facilities will provide a sense of accessibility. This requires input from state agencies, peak organisations and/or users of the facilities to appreciate operational implications on the distribution of facilities, such as a hierarchy of performing arts facilities.

Engaging with the local First Nations communities is essential to gain an First Nations perspective in the planning and design of public spaces.

In this investigation area, be clear on what is to be investigated and expectations of the anticipated outcomes.

14.3.3 Providing Access to Natural and Developed Public Places

Public spaces refer to publicly accessible dedicated areas, such as:

- natural places: bushland, foreshores including beaches and adjacent water (out to 50 metres) and rivers and creeks
- developed spaces: parklands, sporting fields, public golf courses, floodplains and publicly accessible easements.

For this section, the discussion on public spaces excludes streets, as they are addressed in Sect. 15.3.4.

14.3.3.1 Research Considerations

Planning for natural and developed public spaces—generally referred to as open space—is a core land use planning task and generally referenced at the highest level of planning policy and controls. Responsibility for planning and delivery of open spaces in Australia is, however, spread across multiple levels of government and in multiple agencies. In addition to the planning portfolio, it involves sport and recreation agencies, major parks agencies, acquisition agencies, treasury departments (in the case of government-owned land) and local government. Most open space that the community uses daily is owned and managed by local government.

The principal city planning consideration is the general provision of land; how it is acquired, embellished and managed; and the required policies and planning controls. The development and management of open space is outside the scope of city planning; the task generally falls to specialised areas of state and local government.

Expanding the provision of open space in established areas is difficult due to land costs. Urban renewal projects can manage to create land for open spaces, but in general the overall per capita ratio will not be impacted. In fact, in the established areas of Australian capital cities, were we see most growth, per capita ratios are reducing. Consequently:

- The identification and establishment of a base level of open space in new greenfield communities is critical.
- Innovative ways are continually being identified to create additional open space, such as the use of roof tops.
- How open space is embellished and managed is critical, and should focus on the needs of the local community.

There are several other issues for consideration:

- Calculating per capita provision levels is difficult, due to issues with identifying the spatial geography to which a provision rate relates or the type of open space available (for example, accessible parkland versus inaccessible bushland). I recommend a cautious approach to statements on proximity to open space,

particularly in Greater Sydney where the metropolitan area is surrounded by national and state parks that take up double the land area compared to urban land. Consequently, some local government areas would have high provision rates if the full extent of these parks was included. If we do consider this land, how much should be considered? Equally, how much of the water adjacent to a beach should be 'open space'?
- Cultural issues, such as religious or ethnic values, will influence how open space can be planned.
- Research I have been involved with, in local and state government, suggests that communities desire open space that can fulfil passive needs more than active.
- People's aspirations and needs differ. We need to understand the nuances of these different needs when planning to embellish open space.
- In subdivision processes, the early setting aside of land for open space can be seen as a high opportunity cost. We need strong policies and controls that transparently identify obligations for setting aside land for open space.

This is a real tension area. I have too often seen landowners seeking to designate encumbered land, such as floodplains, for open space which are not fit for sports fields, but are acceptable for linear parks. The challenge is the total level of provision and how costs are apportioned across a new suburb, where some landowners may have no requirement to provide for open space.

14.3.3.2 Research Objectives
The research objectives are:

- to assess the distribution of open space by type and development of an open-source GIS-based database that covers open space owned by all levels of government
- to assess and understand the biodiversity role of land designated for open space
- to assess the effectiveness of planning policies, controls and guidelines to deliver on stated open space objectives.

14.3.3.3 Approaches to Research
Regular audits of publicly accessible open space should occur outside of city planning projects and cover land held by all levels of government. GIS database systems should allow for annual updates, even real time systems, as new land is added.

Local government, state agencies and the development sector should be engaged on the appropriateness of planning controls, policies and other actions that seek to provide, embellish and maintain land for open space.

14.3.4 Protecting the Physical Amenity of Homes

Physical amenity includes safety, noise, privacy, odour, access to sunlight, microclimate (urban heat island effect) and covers both dwellings and private open space.

14.3.4.1 Research Considerations

The physical amenity of households is protected in planning systems across Australia either directly through requirements such as managing the impacts of overshadowing or indirectly, such as requirements to manage industrial noise and odour.

The issues for management have changed significantly over the last 40 years as work health and safety regulations now reduce the impact of many industrial nuisances.

> For example, 35 years ago, when I was involved in my first plan for a town centre, motor vehicle repair businesses were places of noise and fumes; they were an activity you did not want anywhere near a town centre. Thirty years later, on Bridge Road, in Richmond, Melbourne, there is a panel beater in amongst the diverse activities of that street. It does not impact the desirability of the area as a successful main street.

Positive change will continue. For example, electric vehicles will reduce noise impacts when planning for sensitive land uses on main roads. Though, there will be a need to watch which energy source will drive heavy vehicles, such as green hydrogen which potentially will mean noise impacts remain.

At a strategic level, we need to manage and monitor the interfaces between residential and town centre activities and industrial, trade gateway and freight activities. It is a two-way challenge: industrial, trade gateway and freight activities have few options for relocation and intensification, compared to residential development. A central issue here is the separation of activities and ensuring sensitive uses such as residential development do not intrude and/or encroach on industrial activities.

Most planning jurisdictions encourage or allow residential development within town centres, in part to enhance the level of after-hours vibrancy, especially in capital city CBDs. This goal creates a tension in that the desired vibrancy can also create the types of physical amenity impacts (particularly noise) that town centre residents may object to. In these cases, transparency in policy statements and consistency in policy application are important.

A challenge for managing physical amenity impacts is that in most cases the thresholds are social norms. They can be measured, and in some cases international benchmarks can be used, but often they are the result of agreed positions that are influenced by community, or industry, pressure.

14.3.4.2 Research Objectives
The research objectives are:

- to assess the acceptability of interfaces between residential development and noise generating activities
- to assess the acceptability of policies and planning controls which seek to manage the physical amenity of households, that is, residential areas.

14.3.4.3 Approaches to Research
The principal objective is to gain insights from those at the coalface. Thus, engagement with local governments, peak bodies and operators of trade gateways and freight networks will give you a balanced perspective. In some instances, there may also be local community groups involved.

During the plan preparation activities, you may need to revisit the issue to ensure newly proposed activities do not create interface issues.

14.4 Needs of Businesses

14.4.1 Enabling Businesses to Grow, Flourish and Innovate

14.4.1.1 Research Considerations
For city planning to support businesses, we need to understand the spatial implications of:

- levels of business growth, which is core to understanding the adequacy of land zoned for business activities (see Sect. 14.5.3)
- barriers and opportunities to enhance business growth and competitiveness
- locational preferences of businesses and the levers that may influence business decisions.

These issues are influenced by factors such as proximity to customers, population/household growth, international trade, supply chains, proximity to enable business interaction, proximity to freight networks (including trade gateways), 'last mile' freight management, exposure/market perception, access to a labour force, planning controls, agglomeration activities and favourable site characteristics. These forces ultimately reveal differing spatial distributions for differing economic sectors. Planning is generally focused on:

- **retail**, which is population serving and thus dispersed across cities
- **industrial**, which is linked to ports, airports, rail freight, motorways/arterial roads and/or flat land requirements
- **office development**, which is generally footloose with a bias to central city CBDs

- **health and education precincts**, as they are rich concentration of knowledge workers and can be directly influenced by government investment
- **tourism activities**, which are often linked to environmental attributes, central city locations or cultural/sporting facilities
- from time to time, **other specialised areas**, particularly agricultural activities in the hinterland of cities or mining, which is dependent on the geology of the area.

Town centres, including health and education precincts, are a major focus as they can accommodate high numbers of jobs. For example, in Greater Sydney, the top 40 centres account for approximately 50 percent of all jobs across the city, and the top 200 centres account for close to 70 percent of jobs.

A tension in city planning is how to influence the distribution of these activities. When we talk about the objective of 'jobs closer to home, we may consider the notion of moving jobs; however, I do not advocate dictating business locations. The concept of jobs closer to home is a laudable societal objective, but we need to understand the needs of business and use a variety of levers to *attract* business to preferred locations.

14.4.1.2 Research Objectives
The research objectives are:

- to understand the barriers and opportunities to enhance business growth and competitiveness and the levers to support growth and competitiveness
- to understand the locational preferences of businesses, the wider societal benefits for influencing the distribution of businesses and the levers to effect such change.

14.4.1.3 Approaches to Research
Researching activities in these areas requires specialised inputs under the general umbrella of urban economics. A detailed understanding of the city planning issues that influence business decisions and a strong economy are core requirements of any city plan. Central to the task is understanding the needs of the business sector, by engaging with local government, peak bodies, property consultants and urban economists.

14.4.2 The Economy and Spatial Economic Structure

14.4.2.1 Research Considerations
Often, a vision for a place seeks to diversify the economy. The first step to achieve this is to understand the economic structure of existing businesses.

In seeking to influence the economic structure of an area, we need to understand the benefits, and that different sectors have different economic drivers. We need to consider the actions that may influence the location decisions of some sectors; many of these lie outside the traditional realm of land use planning. Hence, our strategic planning may need to move into the detailed areas of trade and investment.

We also need to understand each community's skill levels, as in some cases local jobs may be filled by people coming in from other areas which does little to increase the diversity of employment choices for the local community.

14.4.2.2 Research Objectives
The research objectives are:

- to understand the industry structure of an area and whether concentrations of activities give the area a natural competitive advantage
- to understand the skills of the local community.

14.4.2.3 Approaches to Research
This area requires specialist input. While you may use ABS Census data, interpreting what it means is another thing. Several economic analysis techniques can be used, starting with location quotient assessments, which assess concentrations of activities.

14.4.3 Protecting the Physical Amenity of Businesses

14.4.3.1 Research Considerations
People generally accept that homes need to be protected from adverse impacts such as noise and odours. The flipside is that businesses also need to be protected from the encroachment of sensitive land uses, such as residential development.

This is critical, as businesses like ports and airports may have limited choices for alternative locations, will have made on-site investment, and have a workforce and customer base that reflects the locational advantages of their site.

We also need to protect the physical amenity of public places (particularly from overshadowing), including footpaths in town centres that support businesses by offering al-fresco dining or chance for shoppers to promenade.

14.4.3.2 Research Objectives
The research objectives are:

- to identify locations where operational activities of businesses are being compromised
- to assess the effectiveness of planning controls in managing impacts.

14.4.3.3 Approaches to Research

The interface between business and sensitive uses is linked to protecting the physical amenity of residential areas. Hence, the research focus needs to be engagement with councils, peak bodies and trade gateway operators.

In town centres we can employ several tools to identify the appropriate scale of buildings to address overshadowing issues. A City of Sydney assessment identified a long-term skyline which will allow development and ensure sunlight for major public spaces.

14.4.4 Transport and Telecommunication Access to Support Business Activities

14.4.4.1 Research Considerations

People seek access to a range of activities, which potentially influence decisions on where they live. Access is fundamental to the success of business operations and has many dimensions such as customer access, labour force catchments (the depth and breadth of potential employees), supply chains, freight and logistics requirements (from courier vans to freight rail), and business to business connections (part of the concept of agglomeration economics).

The access needs of businesses relate to all aspects of the transport network and increasingly for telecommunications coverage and quality of service (such as internet speed). In addition, as every trip has two ends, the quality of access provided to business is influenced by factors such as the location of customers—whether they are residents or other businesses—and the location of supply providers, which could be local, interstate or international.

The principal point here is to recognise that responding to the transport needs of businesses is more than monitoring the performance of the transport systems and enhancing their capacity. The focus is on understanding what influences transport outcomes, as well as considerations such as the influence of technology on freight and logistics activities.

14.4.4.2 Research Objectives

The research objective is:

- to understand the dynamics of the many dimensions that make up the transport and telecommunications access to business.

14.4.4.3 Approaches to Research

The details of the approaches to transport access and businesses are discussed in detail in Sect. 15.2.

14.4.5 Protecting Natural Resources

14.4.5.1 Research Considerations

In a metropolitan context, this issue is generally about the management of stone and mineral resources, agricultural activities, and water catchments in the hinterland of the city. It also includes activities that have been overtaken by urban expansion, particularly stone and sand quarrying.

Agricultural activities can be varied and generally reflect soil, topography, rainfall and temperature conditions. Include everything from the intensive activities of vegetable growing and poultry and pig farming to fruit growing and livestock management.

The tension for city planning usually comes from:

- **The outward expansion of cities**. Expansion requires us to resolve whether a specific natural resource needs to be protected versus how we manage urban growth in the context of social, economic and environmental considerations. Adding to the scale of this challenge is the fact that the population of Australia's larger capital cities has doubled over the last 60 years, with an outward expansion of suburb-style development accommodating much of this growth.
- **Competition from lifestyle activities**. On city fringe, people enjoy rural-residential living, which takes advantage of the proximity of the city as well as the amenity of a rural environment. This can impact 'right to farm' issues for the agriculture sector.

The operational activities of stone and mineral resources surrounded by urban development are a challenge, especially if buffer considerations are not adequately dealt with. The operational lifetime for these resources can be well over 50 years—I was involved in the planning for an area which included one site with an expected 100-year operation. Many quarries become waste management sites, which also require buffers.

We also need to consider the separation of responsibilities. The planning portfolio generally has a regulatory role, whereas mining and primary industry agencies are responsible for the activities of each sector.

Our work needs to consider issues from both perspectives.

14.4.5.2 Research Objectives

The research objectives are:

- to assess the values of natural resources and activities in the hinterland of cities and the extent to which they can be exploited
- to understand the operational requirements for natural resource activities and the adequacy of planning controls, policies and guidelines to manage them.

14.4.5.3 Approaches to Research

Understanding the values of mineral resources, agricultural activities and water catchments is part of a wider area of investigation that covers all the activities and resources of the hinterland of cities—see Sect. 15.3.7.

The issues can be complex in some jurisdictions. For example, there are coal and coal seam gas activities in Greater Sydney, and some overlap with water catchments. Our role is to understand the long history behind the management of these activities.

We also need to recognise that there are often a range of agricultural activities that remain within the urban area of cities for a variety of reasons. Local governments are normally best placed to help you understand these situations.

14.5 The Growth and Change Equation

Growth and change present opportunities and challenges. Understanding the nature and scale of change is a key ingredient for understanding if a business-as-usual future is acceptable.

To understand both the scale of activities and projections of future demand and supply, we need to understand the overall objectives and scope of a project.

Typically for a metropolitan area information is required in three areas:

- population and demographics
- dwellings
- commercial activities.

I also discuss greenfield development and health and education precincts in the following sections.

14.5.1 Population and Demographics

14.5.1.1 Research Considerations

The current and projected population for a place influences a range of city planning outcomes.

- **housing**, specifically the demographic aspect of household size
- **social needs**, reflecting the age distribution of the population
- **transport planning**, including the distribution of workers and people of different ages in a city
- **health planning**, including fertility and mortality rates and age groups
- **education planning,** including school aged populations by age cohorts.

Understanding populations therefore requires us to:

14.5 The Growth and Change Equation

- consider total numbers and demographic characteristics, now and in the future
- collaborate with delivery agencies that utilise the data to ensure it reflects their specific planning needs which may vary spatially, temporarily as well as the level detail.

There are differing population projection models that vary depending on the spatial scale of an area and the data available for the geographical area.

For example, the cohort survival population projection model requires fertility, mortality and migration data. Often this data is not available at small spatial geographies, such as the catchment of a town centre. This is when models based on assumptions of current and projected dwellings together with estimates of the number of people per dwelling become useful, as this data is available for small geographies.

Different models and inputs can mean projections for small spatial areas like local government areas do not align with models for a metropolitan area or region. This can challenge discussions between all levels of government on the needs of communities.

Demographers will remind you that projections are not statements of fact, they are simply a projection of what a future might be, based on a range of assumptions. Most modelling processes include a range of scenarios and identify a preferred scenario.

14.5.1.2 Research Objectives

The research objectives are:

- to understand the demographic characteristics of the current population and historic trends, including total size, age distribution (school aged, working age, retirees and over 80), gender differences, household size at a suburb spatial geography or smaller
- to prepare population, household and age cohort projections at an ABS Statistical Area Level 2 (SA2) level at 5, 10 and 20-year levels and for the whole metropolitan area out to 40 years.

14.5.1.3 Approaches to Research

Interpreting population and demographic data is specialised. City planners need a solid understanding of basic methodological principles to interpret and manipulate the data.

The intention is to reveal a range of observations, including:

- trends over time
- spatial distribution differences
- specific age cohort categories, such as school aged, working population, retirees or those over 80
- household characteristics, such as size.

These more nuanced observations can inform the needs of people at the neighbourhood level and allow for targeted actions.

Typically, city planning needs several population and demographic outputs, starting with current and historic time series data at the ABS Statistical Area Level 1 (SA1), including totals and data for age groups. You can find this at the ABS Statistical Geography Standard and ABS Population—refer to website references.

Also seek projections by ABS Statistical Area Level 2 (SA2) for 5, 10, 20 years out, including individual totals, age groups, households and people per household. All models start with data from the ABS Census conducted every five years and the annual update data (known as estimated resident population, or ERP.

Over the last decade, projections by small geographies have been challenged by supply-induced demand, created by the zoning of land for urban renewal purposes. Some population models have difficulty dealing with this issue.

Considering the complexities urban renewal creates for projections, my preference for metropolitan plans is to only use 10-year projections, and utilise scenarios beyond that (20, 30 or 40 years) and to state any assumptions. How far out projections should go is a difficult question. A lesson from the last two plans for Greater Sydney was that by going out 40 years, the data, at the time, suggested continued strong growth into the long term and hence the need to plan for substantial growth, as was the same for Melbourne. History shows, as do the impacts of the COVID-19 pandemic, that assumptions can quickly change. Remember that projections are based on assumptions—we use scenarios to let the users of the projections understand different impacts on their operational needs.

We also need to recognise that transport planners will need population projections at a fine spatial geography, called transport zones (Greater Sydney has around 3000 of these) and that projections need to go out 40 years. Employment projections are also required. This technical information is often not well known by those who emphasise the importance of benefit cost ratios for transport infrastructure projects, which are based on fine grained and long-term population and employment projections.

14.5.2 Dwellings

14.5.2.1 Research Considerations

Residential development has the largest footprint of all land use activities; ensuring sufficient opportunity to accommodate additional dwellings is a central task of city planning. Planning for housing is complex, as we need to connect a diversity of housing types and demands with development choices including greenfield, infill and urban renewal.

Infrastructure providers of utilities and transport need timely data on housing activity. Any disconnect may halt residential development until the required infrastructure becomes available. Consequently, the scale of new greenfield estates can be capped to reflect road capacity, as upgrades from rural to urban roads often lags development. This may be due to unforeseen changes in preferences where demand shifts quickly to a new location.

Thus, as with population data, engage with infrastructure providers and the development sector to understand short to medium-term trends and thus supply data.

14.5.2.2 Research Objectives

The research objectives are:

- to understand the typology of existing dwellings and historic trends, at ABS Statistical Area Level 1 (SA1)
- to prepare dwelling projections at ABS Statistical Area Level 2 (SA2) at 5, 10 and 20-year levels and for the whole metropolitan area out to 40 years.

14.5.2.3 Approaches to Research

Many of the variables that impact residential development activity are well outside the influence of city planning, such as interest rates and the general state of the economy.

In terms of understanding the general state of play of housing as the basis for more detailed analysis and considerations, seek the following data:

- dwelling type and distribution at ABS Statistical Area Level 1 (SA1)
- dwelling density ideally by lot size, which focus only on residential areas and the size of the properties people live in; this provides a richer understanding than assessments per hectare, which requires too many assumptions about what else to include, such as local streets and parks
- dwelling type in the context of household type, size and age of residents (particularly over 80).
- urban renewal dynamics, such as location of change, type of change (horizontal versus vertical), and size of source allotments
- dwelling change in the context of proximity to city features like centres, open space or public transport nodes, so long as this is an identifiable relationship that is statistically valid.

Most data is held in local government and state government databases as well as in ABS Census data.

Projections for total dwellings by the ABS Statistical Area Level 2 (SA2) are also required. A challenge over the last decade has been understanding supply-induced demand, that is supply influenced by government actions such as urban renewal projects or transport investments. Announcing potential supply could make dwelling projections de facto statements of policy (zoning) intent. Equally if future supply projections do not reflect the influence of proposed, but not yet committed, transport projects then infrastructure agencies may be under-providing for a location.

Here we need to remember that housing supply projections need to be transparent in explaining what they include. As with all findings from research, their value is enhanced when we develop simple supporting narratives with maps or diagrams.

14.5.3 Commercial Activities

Understanding the extent and diversity of commercial activities across a city indicates the level of access people have to goods and services. By default, it also informs our understanding of the community's access to jobs, while providing insights as to where new pressure may occur on the transport network.

Understanding changes in the demand and supply of commercial activities is also linked to understanding the needs of business, which is discussed in Sect. 14.4. The extent of data available is variable, as is the role of state governments in guiding commercial activity compared to residential development.

In the main, city planning focuses on three areas: industrial, retail and office. Specialist areas, such as entertainment, leisure and tourism, are usually included in policy directions, although data on the level and distribution of activities are not normally included. In Australia, there are exceptions such as plans for some cities in Queensland and specific local governments where tourism has a greater role.

14.5.4 Industrial Development

14.5.4.1 Research Considerations

As cities grow and evolve, industrial development seeks cheaper greenfield land on the edge of cities with good transport access, as industrial renewal is generally only feasible where activity is intensified. Thus, planning for industrial areas has always been a consideration for planning on the fringe of cities.

Industrial planning, at a city level, generally focuses on levels of land supply, with annual take-up of vacant land an important measure. Aerial imagery can be utilised to monitor annual floor space take up. Most state governments publish data annually on industrial activity.

As industrial areas are usually easy to delineate, we can easily gain information on a range of their characteristics including job numbers from the ABS Census data, dollar values for levels of construction from ABS building approvals data and rental levels from either local governments or through specialist commercial advisory companies. This information informs our understanding of the performance and role of individual industrial areas.

As industrial activity moves to the edge of cities, existing industrial areas have evolved. In many cases these areas become places where the activities provide an ongoing service to surrounding businesses and communities. This issue was explored for the Greater Sydney Region Plan, with a key finding that while more traditional manufacturing and logistics activities locate in large industrial areas in middle to outer suburban areas, smaller mature industrial areas in inner cities supply 'urban services' such as kitchen supplies and car repairs (SGS Economics and Planning 2017).

At the same time, inner-city locations are in high demand for residential development, which can mean industrial areas are turned over to residential development due to price pressures.

Managing inner and middle suburban industrial areas therefore requires a detailed understanding of the types of businesses present, how they are changing, their role and who they serve.

14.5.4.2 Research Objectives
The research objectives are:

- to understand the dynamics of the activities that make up industrial areas and related land use zones that allow industrial uses
- to monitor the supply and demand for industrial and related lands, including changes in the scale of activities.

14.5.4.3 Approaches to Research
City planning needs to:

- explain industrial land supply conditions and what this means at defined smaller geographies such as Greater Sydney's five districts or Melbourne's six regions
- explain the differing roles of industrial areas, including the diversity of activities, job densities and roles that need an urban services location
- identify which industrial areas are part of the rail freight network, including the presence of trade gateways
- identify industrial areas that service trade gateways.

These observations can then inform investigations as to the need to expand or retain industrial land supply, modify planning controls to allow activities to evolve, improve transport connections and protect industrial areas from activities, specifically residential, that impact the operational needs of industrial areas and trade gateways.

14.5.5 Retail

14.5.5.1 Research Considerations
Retail receives much attention in city planning, particularly in the importance of co-locating retail activity with other commercial, community and educational activities in centres. However, governments, particularly state governments, are not inclined to influence retail land supply and leave that to the market, except in greenfield areas we usually identify a network of centres, the scale of the centres and their distribution.

Planning controls manage retailing activities by stipulating differing retail categories and identifying the zones where they are allowed. In some Australian planning jurisdictions, the size of shopping malls is also managed through planning processes that consider the impact of the growth of one centre on the wider network, where simple competition is not a contestable issue.

Other than the desire to co-locate retail activities into centres as a spatial planning principle, the **planning** for retail development (in terms of supply) is generally driven by the private sector's desire to expand a facility. This occurs at the centre level.

Existing data is generally developed and published annually by peak bodies. City-wide retail databases can help us to understand the comparative accessibility of people to goods and services. As mentioned, this also means access to jobs. They are a challenge to prepare, however; Greater Sydney, for example, has approximately 1,350 centres ranging in size from the Sydney CBD to a collection of a few shops.

As centres are generally well defined, job data can be obtained for larger centres on employment levels for centres from the ABS Census.

Behavioural changes influenced by the COVID-19 pandemic lockdowns shifted many people's attention to their local centre. Ensuring local centres are not limited in the activities they can provide will allow these centres to best serve their communities.

Another way to consider retailing is to think about the areas that governments may wish to have a public policy interest. In this regard, consider four areas:

- **Supply**. Providing sufficient supply of land for retail activities is the area of most debate, particularly regarding the impact of new retail supply on existing centres, where simple competition is not a reason for preventing supply.
- **Innovation**. Retail will continue to evolve. For example, historically most clothing was made to order whereas now most clothing comes in standard sizes. These changes affect retailing activities so planning controls also need to evolve to allow ongoing innovation.
- **Infrastructure efficiency**. Governments often locate facilities and services in centres and provide transport services to connect people to centres. Consequently, planning controls can be structured to prevent the disbursement of activities to ensure the efficient delivery of a range of government infrastructure services, such as public transport. A related issue is centre vibrancy, where it is argued that the disbursement of some retail attractors, such as a supermarket, reduces the attractiveness of a centre and thus its vibrancy. The disbursement of retail activities is a contested policy area.
- **Support the public realm**. Large shopping malls have internalised pedestrian places—creating a private 'public' realm, which can be a contested policy area. While on a 40-degree day the benefits are understandable, we need to consider how these malls connect to the public realm and whether they add value through their connection.

14.5.5.2 Research Objectives
The research objectives are:

- to understand the characteristics of centres in terms of their size, role and distribution
- to prepare projections of demand for retail floor space by broad category type
- to identify the barriers to growth for centres, including regulatory constraints on the functioning of local centres.

14.5.5.3 Approaches to Research
As retail planning is driven by the private sector and as it is usually a major element in centres, we can easily seek out technical advice on growth and change in centres. Our aim is to understand:

- total level of retail, by centre and local government area
- per capita provision rates, ideally by retail type such as department stores, supermarkets and large format retailing
- projections of total additional retail demand at district/local government level
- changes resulting from online retail activity.

The latter point informs whether we need to investigate and facilitate change at the local level as distinct from a statement of an accurate projection. Preparing projections is a technical task and usually requires input from specialist services.

In addition, and linked to the discussion on offices in the next section, there is a benefit in understanding trends in employment for centres, including projections. Again, this is for the purposes of understanding the need to investigate and facilitate the growth of centres.

14.5.6 Offices

14.5.6.1 Research Considerations
For office development, as with retail development, the focus of city planning is normally on the principle of co-location in centres. The detailed planning often falls to local governments to manage as part of individual town centre plans.

The limited distribution of office development across a metropolitan area has often been a challenge. A report that informed the Greater Sydney Region Plan (BIS Shrapnel 2015) provides some good insights as to what to consider when seeking to influence the location of office development.

A related approach, based on advice I received from a commercial advisory company, is that if a developer wishes to undertake suburban office development, do all that you can for this to happen, as it will enhance the perception for the market that a suburban location is acceptable. It is better to have office development in the wrong location in the suburbs and thus closer to where people live, than not at all. This is especially the case in Norwest and Macquarie Park in Greater Sydney where standalone office parks have evolved, over a long period, into more mixed-use precincts.

Anecdotal advice I have received is that an office precinct needs around 100,000 square metres of floor space before it is perceived as an office precinct. We have yet to determine what the trend for working from home will mean for office development.

14.5.6.2 Research Objectives
The research objectives are:

- to identify the distribution of standalone office development and historic patterns of growth
- to prepare projections on the demand for standalone office development
- to identify the barriers and locational preferences for office development and the levers that may influence their distribution
- to monitor the implications of working from home.

14.5.6.3 Approaches to Research
Peak bodies, as with commercial property advisors, have solid databases on the extent of standalone office development. The ABS Census also provides data on employment that can usually be identified for individual office precincts. Unlike retail activity, which is distributed across cities, standalone office development is often restricted to a limited number of locations and/or areas.

Research I undertook at a local government level suggests that, when there is an absence of standalone office development and offices are sprinkled through centres, for every 200,000 people you get about 25,000 square metres of offices (research circa 2000).

In assessing the supply of commercial activities, be aware of the limitations of differing data sources. For example, the ABS Census occupation data allows estimates of the number of office workers but does not distinguish the type of workplace. The office worker category can include those in manufacturing premises, education and health facilities as well as standalone offices.

Many years ago, I commissioned two pieces of research - one to establish total office workers, the second to identify total office workers in standalone buildings. The latter was half the former.

14.5.6.4 Greenfield Planning
When planning for office development in greenfield areas, land supply is not an issue in one sense, yet we need to understand how many houses, shops, jobs and community services are needed. This is difficult to calculate when there is no

one there to ask, so you rely on understanding the growth and change in recently completed greenfield areas nearby. Hence, the recent past influences the future.

However, a bigger challenge is how to allow for growth into the long term, in that the planning for greenfield areas is often based on 20-year projections of people and jobs with some allowance for an understanding of long-term capacity.

However, experience suggests that places change over time and growth continues. In that context it was once put to me that for a new centre we should mandate very low-density housing around the centre, which can be further subdivided at a later stage—an innovative suggestion.

> *I once took the councillors of a Victorian growth area council on a study tour to Canberra and Sydney, to help them understand how their local government area would evolve. The council at the time had close to 200,000 people and was forecast to grow beyond 350,000 – akin to the size of Canberra. The advice from the planners in Canberra, noting land development is a bit different, was that they always retained vacant land adjacent to each centre to be utilised when it was more mature.*

Therefore, planning for greenfield areas needs long-term thinking. Other examples of growth and change from other parts of the city are a way of gaining insights as to how greenfield areas may evolve.

It is my understanding that for the 1909 Royal Commission into the city planning needs for Sydney, rather undertake population projections, the planners of the day looked at comparable cities around the world to see how they had changed and used what they learnt as the basis for their projections, which I understand were robust.

14.5.7 Health and Education Precincts

Activity in health and education precincts is significantly influenced by actions of state governments and the Commonwealth Government. They have high concentrations of employment and activity and are often part of a wider town centre precinct, or policy encourages them to be so.

Research for the Greater Sydney Region Plan suggests health and education precincts can be categorised in a continuum from simple precincts where there are purely adjacent facilities, to complex innovation districts that include a range of public and private activities and research institutions, and where there is collaboration between organisations. As precincts evolve into complex innovation districts, and not all can, there is a greater economic dividend than if activities are dispersed.

Health and education precincts must be a focus for city planning. Seeking advice from relevant government agencies and institutions will maximise opportunities. A principal area for understanding is the barriers to growth; local governments are well placed to understand opportunities in that area.

14.5.8 Agriculture and Mining Activities

Historic settlement patterns usually mean that agricultural activities occur in a city's hinterland. The extent to which they remain reflects natural values (soils and rainfall). With agricultural output significant nationally, state primary industry departments have detailed data on the economic output at a reasonably fine grain and by categories, such as intensive horticulture or intensive animal husbandry.

Mining activities naturally reflect the presence of minerals. Extraction is influenced by the need to maintain buffers to allow for the operational needs of specific types of mining activities. Sand mining and the quarrying of rock materials for construction are highly sought after, considering the cost of haulage. Thus, the location of these natural resources is usually well known and in some cases protected by planning controls. Sub-surface mining does occur, as in Greater Sydney, and consequently planning needs to consider subsidence. This is why there is a Subsidence Advisory NSW organisation in NSW.

As with agricultural activities, there is typically good information as to the economic value of mining activities in the hinterland of cities. There is also good information on the extent of available resources. A challenge is whether all the natural assets should be extracted.

14.5.9 The Growth and Change Equation

Being able to understand the likely level of change is fundamental to any plan, even if it means no growth or negative growth. Collectively this change can be expressed as:

$$GC = P + D + C(I + R + O)$$

Where:

- GC is growth and change.
- P is population change.
- D is dwelling change.
- C (commercial) is a combination of I (industrial), R (retail) and O (standalone offices).

This may seem pedantic, but I have read many plans where it is difficult to locate the assumptions regarding changes in these areas.

The growth and change equation should cover both the level of demand and the ability to facilitate supply.

Our aim is to identify issues through the data, such as the existence or not of a land supply gap. Subsequent steps in the 7-Step Strategic Planning Process can determine the interventions required.

Also remember to look behind the data, such as lessons we learnt during preparation of the Greater Sydney Region Plan. We received advice that indicated:

- There was no relationship between dwelling growth and population growth for 20 years preceding the plan, potentially due to behaviours such as staying at home and group housing.
- Changes over time to the amount of office floor space per person meant that an existing developed area could see increases in employment as a result of operational changes of businesses.

14.6 Summary

This chapter provides insights on how to approach the research that will form the basis of your city plan, particularly the research areas for Part B: The needs of people and business.

This chapter is in no way to be seen as the definitive explanation on how to go about each task. It is a starting point for understanding why there is a need to investigate each research area and what questions may be important. Answering questions is fairly easy; identifying which questions to ask is difficult.

As indicated several times in this book, the individual research areas are not independent of each other, in fact, where they connect are usually the places of most importance. Hence, the last phase of investigations for each research area should be the consideration of what connections exist with other research areas.

References

Glaeser, E (2011), *Triumph of the City*. Pan Macmillan, UK.
—A must read for anyone interested in urban economics.
Marchetti, C (1994), *Anthropological invariants in travel behavior*, Technological Forecasting and Social Change, vol. 47, no. 1, pp. 75–88.
Markus, A (2019), *Mapping Social Cohesion, The Scanlon Foundation Surveys*, Monash University, Caufield East, Victoria, Australia
West, G (2018), *Scale, The Universal Laws of Life and Death in Organisms, Cities and Companies*. Hachette, Australia.
—Based on the research of hundreds of cities, this book outlines that there are relationships between the scale of cities and various attributes of cities.
Woodcraft, S, Bacon, N, Caistor-Arendar, L & Hackett, T (2012), *Design for Social Sustainability a framework for creating thriving new communities*, Social Life

Website links

Auckland Council, Auckland Design Manual: Māori Design Hub, Te Pokapū Whakatairanga Tikanga Māori - Auckland Design Manual

Australian Bureau of Statistics, Australian Statistical Geography Standard, https://www.abs.gov.au/websitedbs/D3310114.nsf/home/Australian+Statistical+Geography+Standard+(ASGS)

Australian Bureau of Statistics Census, https://www.abs.gov.au/ausstats/abs@.nsf/0/B3E6E29390F64923CA257BF10013569B

Australian Bureau of Statistics Consumer Price Index, https://www.abs.gov.au/ausstats/abs@.nsf/mf/6401.0

Australian Bureau of Statistics Estimated Residential Population, https://www.abs.gov.au/AUSSTATS/abs@.nsf/Lookup/3101.0Main+Features1Sep%202019?OpenDocument

Australian Bureau of Statistics Population, https://www.abs.gov.au/Population

Australian Government Productivity Commission *Closing the Gap*, Information Repository, Dashboard | Closing the Gap Information Repository - Productivity Commission (pc.gov.au)

BIS Shrapnel (2015), *Forecasting the Distribution of Stand Alone Office Development across Sydney to 2035* Unpublished, https://www.greater.sydney/background-material

Centre for International Economics (2010), *The benefits and costs of alternative growth paths for Sydney's economic, social and environmental impacts.* Unpublished, http://www.thecie.com.au/wp-content/uploads/2014/06/CIE-Final-report_NSW-Planning_-Alternative-growth-paths-for-Sydney_10-December-2010.pdf

Cred Consulting (2017), *Greater Sydney's Social Capital Its Nature and Value,* Unpublished, https://gsc-public-1.s3.amazonaws.com/s3fs-public/social_capital_report_-_cred_-_october_2017.pdf

Greater Sydney Commission (2018), A Metropolis of Three Cities, State of New South Wales, Australia https://www.greater.sydney/metropolis-of-three-cities

Newgate Research (2015), *Research Report, Community research to support the implementation of A Plan for Growing Sydney*. Six reports North, South, Central, West Central, West, and South West Districts, https://www.greater.sydney/background-material

NSW Department of Planning, Industry and Environment, Urban Feasibility Model, https://www.planning.org.au/documents/item/3357

NSW Government (2020) *Healthy Built Environment Checklist,* NSW Ministry of Health https://www.health.nsw.gov.au/urbanhealth/Pages/healthy-built-enviro-check.aspx

NSW, the NSW Environmental Planning and Assessment Act 1979 No 203, viewed 25 July 2020 https://www.legislation.nsw.gov.au/~/view/act/1979/203

NSW Department of Planning and Environment, Regional plans, web page, Regional plans - (nsw.gov.au)

NSW Department of Planning, Industry and Environment – Research, https://www.planning.nsw.gov.au/Research-and-Demography/Research

Productivity Commission (2020), Overcoming Indigenous Disadvantage Key Indicators 2020, Overcoming Indigenous Disadvantage: Key Indicators 2020 - Report (pc.gov.au)

Recognise Country, Guidlines for development in the Aerotropolis (2022) Recognise Country Guidelines for development in the Aerotropolis (amazonaws.com)

SGS Economics and Planning (2017), *Sydney's Urban Services Lands – Establishing a Baseline Provision* Unpublished, https://www.greater.sydney/background-material

State of the Environment report, https://soe.environment.gov.au/ Part C: Qualities and performance of place

15. Part C: Qualities and Performance of Place

15.1 Introduction

This chapter provides more detail on the research areas for Part C: The qualities and performance of place. The information for each research topic includes:

- research considerations
- research objectives
- approaches to research.

15.2 Accessibility, Transport and Digital Performance

Since the first cities emerged 6,000 years ago, accessibility has been about physical mobility; for most of that period it was about walking.

The industrial revolution changed all that. It brought motorised travel, including travelling in space. Motorised travel has allowed cities to expand and still allow reasonable access to goods, services and jobs. Motorisation did not, however, change one of the underlying principles of how we plan cities—that is, creating transport systems that connect people's place of residence with places that provide goods, services and jobs. How well we have done so is debatable.

This basic approach to laying out cities is being challenged by digital technology. In 1984, 1G digital infrastructure was introduced, which has and is continuing to evolve, with 5G introduced in 2019. This virtual connectivity changes many aspects of our lives.

Further, the impacts of the COVID-19 pandemic on physical mobility accelerated our understanding of the opportunities to access goods, services and employment without the need to travel. The implications are yet to be fully understood though it is clear that we are approaching a tipping point where we have choices that did not exist a generation ago.

Thus, the question of accessibility and cities now needs to consider both transport and digital infrastructure.

15.2.1 Transport Network Performance

Transport planning is integral to city planning. All city planners need to understand the basics of transport planning and be prepared to collaborate.

While most technical advice will come from transport planners, city planners must be able to interrogate and challenge the assumptions and conclusions.

Transport is a means to an end. Therefore, to understand transport accessibility and performance, we need to understand the purpose of trips (refer Sects. 14.2.4, 14.4.4 and 15.2.1) as well as the expectations about the trip, such as quality and travel time.

City planning can influence the performance of networks so long as we consider all the variables. This includes thinking about transport networks as single integrated multi-modal networks that include:

- roads
- road-based public transport, including on-demand services
- passenger rail (heavy rail and light rail)
- freight rail
- footpaths (including access for wheelchairs and similar transport options)
- cycle paths (including for e-bikes, which raise separation considerations from pedestrians)
- trade gateways (air and sea)
- freight intermodals (road and rail).

15.2.1.1 Research Considerations

Network performance needs to be understood and monitored to inform the need for capacity or efficiency enhancements. There are many variables to consider:

- **Trips have two ends, an origin and a destination**. We can influence travel time by influencing land use decisions that bring people and/or businesses closer. While working on a new transport plan in Melbourne many years ago, it was clear it would be virtually impossible to augment the rail network to satisfy the projected passenger needs for the morning journey to work identified in the transport model. This was a concern, as all potential transport capacity enhancements had been exhausted. However, this thinking was focused on building a way out of congestion; the land use planners suggested actions to create employment close to the origin of the trips, which changed the whole approach.

- **Trip modes.** For much of the second half of the twentieth century it was assumed transport access was about cars. This is no longer the case, though walking and cycling are still small players, and historic data tends to support this. However, the COVID-19 pandemic-related patterns of behaviour suggest walking and cycling require greater attention. Perceptions also need to be challenged. For example, when the additional lane was added to the inner section of Monash Freeway (in Melbourne) cycling advocates noted that the volume of people in the new lane for cars was similar to the volume of people in the bike lane below and that maybe an alternative would have been to enhance the capacity of the bike lane which would probably have been cheaper.
- **Trip friction.** Whether it is about express public transport routes or freeway trips, travel times are impacted by the level of 'friction' along a network—the interferences such as rail stops or road intersections. It can be a challenge to balance the competing priorities of access versus time and cost.
- **Network capacity.** Transport planners can advise on the theoretical capacity of networks for all motorised modes.
- **Complexity.** Transport networks cannot simply be categorised by the different modes—most have multiple sub-networks. For example, rail has freight and passenger networks and passenger rail has inter and intra city networks. If one single network provides for the needs of sub-networks, efficiency is impacted, as we see when freight trains running on passenger lines and reduce the frequency of the passenger service.
- **Network structure and land use consequences.** These are most evident when you look at rail lines built when walking was the only real alternative, meaning stations are generally spaced within walking distance. With the advent of the car, station separation increased and car parking and drop off points became part of station design. Rather than being corridors of accessible homes, rail lines create islands of accessibility. Travel time, of the train, is often put forward as the reason why, but the consequence has been the entrenchment of car-based communities.
- **Land use impact.** Transport networks not only provide a means of travel they also have the potential to change the dynamics of cities by influencing land use activities (SGS Economics and Planning 2012).
- **Technology, innovation and adaptability.** These areas require support and consideration when we want to improve the efficiency, quality and capacity of transport networks. For example, as research and development goes into autonomous vehicles, and cars based on sustainable energy are no longer an over-the-horizon consideration, we are now in a transition phase. Other changes such as e-bikes are changing where and who can use bikes; hills are no longer an issue. The e-bike could also mean cycling is part of the principal transport choices in new greenfield areas, so long as safety issues are addressed.
- **Car parking.** The provision and pricing of car parking can act as a deterrent to car use and/or a catalyst for behaviour change to another transport mode. When intended as the latter, alternative travel modes must be available to provide

a reasonably comparable service. For town centres, planning for car parking requires a range of assessments, often by sub-precinct.
- **Interchanges.** People's trips are not always confined to one mode or a single trip. Travel time is influenced by the efficiency of timetabling and the layout efficiency of interchanges. Importantly, as interchanges usually have multiple routes and higher levels of activity, they are also potential nodes for a greater mix and density of land uses.
- **Disability access.** All jurisdictions in Australia are improving accessibility to those with a disability, including ambulatory and visual. This work is essential to inclusive accessibility. There may be significant costs and in some areas, such as railway station upgrades, delivery is over a long time period (decades).
- **Transport networks as barriers.** Road and rail networks can act as a barrier to walking or cycling, particularly in growth areas, where, over the last 50 years, efficiency and a desire to quickly move people from the fringe of cities to the centre has been the planning objective. Consequently, freeways, six-lane arterials and railway lines impede cross movements for walking and cycling.
- **Performance enhancement.** The performance of the network can be influenced by:
  - demand management, including user pays systems
  - user information such as access to real-time data on congestion or real-time timetable updates
  - road network management, such as signals on ramps to a motorway.

15.2.1.2 Research Objectives
The research objectives are:

- to understand the relative performance of the network, such as congestion (travel time), delays (compared to timetables), coverage and frequency (equity in access) and accessibility (including to those with a disability) and the inhibitors and enablers to better performance.
- to understand how transport networks can be city-shaping (influencing land uses) or city-serving (supporting community access to goods and services).
- to ensure new transport networks are inclusive for all in the community.

15.2.1.3 Approaches to Research
Transport planners normally assess network performance, though many a land use planner has surveyed pedestrians or cars in car parks as part of the data collection. For strategic planners, we need to understand the types of activities being undertaken so we can understand the implications of the assessments in the context of wider research activities.

Research needs to:

- assess the performance of the network by manually or automatically counting or collecting user data (passenger trip data)
- model future scenarios based on differing population and network (infrastructure) assumptions
- assess options using a variety of cost benefit tools.

The influence of these assessment areas on the transport network is in part influenced by the underlying approach.

For example, in NSW there has been a significant paradigm shift in how transport planning is conceptualised. It has moved from the historic 'predict and provide' approach (those who have get more), to a 'vision and validate' methodology. The latter seeks to identify a network to support the needs of the city at the end of the planning horizon (such as 20 to 40 years), working backwards using the most efficient approach; the former stays in the 'today' and seeks to enhance the network based on current usage patterns plus the impact of growth. Thus, new infrastructure supports the status quo, in the context of growth, not necessarily a future vision based on the needs of the whole community.

15.2.2 Transport Service Provision

From my experience, only one area has a service model that provides an outcome which is the same for all—education. Every child must have a desk to sit at, noting the travel time to get there may not necessarily be equitable. All other agencies traditionally assess service performance in the context of the network they have or some delivery outcome, such as a waiting time for a specific service.

Transport has such an approach, such as the level of congestion (roads or public transport) or performance against a stated outcome (such as a bus timetable). It is not the case that all in the community have equal access to the same level of service, such as access to public transport within a set distance for a set performance.

The NSW *Future Transport Strategy 2056* (2018, p. 35) is moving to this approach by stating a service performance objective:

> Customers will be able to travel to one of these cities or to their nearest strategic centre within 30 minutes of where they live by public or active transport.

15.2.2.1 Research Considerations
Research activities for transport service provision should consider:

- **The quality of the travel experience**. This is critical if we are to maximise people's mode choice. Personal safety for users is a starting point, whether that be urban design considerations to create safe public places, including safe car parking areas for people using public transport, or safe roads for cars, people and bike users. In addition, all elements of transport networks should be a positive experience, down to the bus stop (Alexander et al. 1977).

We also need to consider the provision of services for all in the community, especially women. For example, to what degree should journey to work trips be called men's journey to work trips. *Invisible Women* (Perez 2019) notes that transport models generally seek to solve the simple home direct to work trip, despite many women undertaking a daily work trip that can involve school drop offs, shopping or both.

- **End of trip amenities**. Showers, lockers and safe bike storage are recognised as required infrastructure if you wish to encourage people to ride. Consequently, many planning jurisdictions require such facilities just as much as car parking. Another insightful issue was put to me by a Dutch expert, who contended that if you want people to walk or ride to work, particularly in the case of the office worker, you should accept their clothing which reflects how they travel to work.
- **User pays transport systems**. These are accepted as a given for public transport and acknowledged, though often reluctantly, as necessary for some motorway projects, particularly those delivered for government by the private sector. In Australia, road pricing is yet to be used as a moderator of travel behaviour, as occurs with congestion taxes. An inherent challenge for user pays systems is that of equity, for example, where people have little mode choice and essentially must pay a toll to reach their place of employment or travel on very congested routes with a significantly longer travel time.
- **Acceptable travel times.** This is a challenge given the outward expansion of Australia's capital cities and the traditional response of augmenting transport networks that connect growth areas to jobs in inner city areas. The alternative of influencing job location has generally not been employed, with productivity being the basis for supporting the status quo (central city jobs are technically more productive). However, community need requires more than an assessment of productivity. The issue of acceptable travel time raises, for some, the Marchetti constant (a daily travel budget of one hour) as a basis for addressing city structure (Marchetti, 1994).
- **Frequency not just travel time**. The frequency of public transport services is often influenced by network capacity (trains per hour) and patronage. I've seen time and again that passengers prefer increased levels of service before faster travel times, when services are not walk up and go. Frequency enhancements are usually more complex than saying there is a need for more services. They can potentially require a range of actions such as increased rolling stock (trains, trams, buses), duplication of single rail line, increased operating costs, enhanced signalling, enhanced stations or bus stops, additional line capacity or allocation of dedicated bus lanes.
- **On-demand digital services**. Digital technologies have dramatically changed on-demand transport options, particularly services to rival the on-demand role of taxis. Transport authorities are trialling on-demand bus services and we can expect these to provide for more local transport functions.

15.2.2.2 The Research Objectives
The research objectives are:

- to identify accessibility issues for people and businesses that may impact the service provision of road, rail, bikes and walking networks.
- to identify the inhibitors and enablers for enhancing service levels.
- to consider spatial (coverage) equity.

15.2.2.3 Research Approaches
Service provision is linked to network performance. The research focus is not on operational matters; rather, it is understanding how changes in coverage and provision can increase mode share away from private vehicle usage and create equity.

The method of assessment and objectives sought will influence solutions. 'Predict and provide' approaches will unlikely result in recommendations for new services in greenfield communities, especially where there is no evidence of demand. Thus, objectives need to consider a wider range of issues such as reducing the need for households to have multiple cars, recognising that once a car-based behaviour is in place it is difficult to alter.

15.2.3 Trade Gateways and Freight

15.2.3.1 Research Considerations
Nearly every activity in a city is connected to freight activities in some way. The demands for freight are increasing, as online activities grow and the economy moves away from manufacturing towards a knowledge economy, which requires increasing imports of goods. Freight activities also impact many aspects of how people live, in terms of as noise and safety.

We need to recognise several aspects of freight activity, especially that, like all transport, freight activity is a means to an end. Several considerations are briefly outlined here.

International connections. For Australia, as an island, air and sea transport are essential for global logistics operations and business to business activities. Ports and airports need to operate as major intermodal facilities for a variety of commodity types, such as containers and specialised activities such as chemicals/fuels and cold storage. In addition, given time differences, airports need to operate 24/7 to be internationally competitive.

Scale of activities. The scale of an investment required for ports and airports is such that the planning for new facilities typically takes decades. The development of the Western Sydney Airport was first mooted in the 1960s and initially proposed in 1986. It was finally committed to in 2014 and opening is scheduled for 2026.

Operational activities. Airports and ports are noisy and need to ideally operate 24/7 and ports can have lighting running all night. Both have safety considerations to manage such as buffers for hazardous goods for ports. Airports have large buffers for noise as well as controls that manage the heights of buildings around the airport as well as more difficult issues such as bird strike.

Road and rail freight. Trade gateways and road-rail intermodal terminals require connections to end-of-trip destinations. Within Greater Sydney, 90 percent of freight trips from the port have destinations within 60 km (Transport for NSW 2018, p. 28). Efficient management of local freight trips is challenging considering freight activity has to compete with other road and rail-based activity.

15.2.3.2 Research Objectives

The research objectives are:

- to understand the operational activities of trade gateways and intermodal terminals.
- to understand the long-term growth needs for ports and airports.
- to understand the effectiveness of road and rail connections for supporting trade gateways and intermodal terminals.

15.2.3.3 Research Approaches

Both airports and ports are required to have operational management plans approved by the Commonwealth and/or state governments. Thus, city planning focuses more on the activities around them that may impact operational effectiveness—although some may see the reverse—that the activities of the airport should be curtailed.

Therefore, to protect the operational activities of ports, airports and intermodal terminals, we need to understand land use change around them as well as the effectiveness of planning controls in managing change. We also need to understand the effectiveness of road networks to ensure efficient movement of freight.

In addition to any regulatory agencies, seek input from the operators of the ports and airports and relevant local governments.

15.2.4 Digital Coverage and Performance

15.2.4.1 Research Considerations

The considerations for digital connectivity are similar to transport coverage and performance.

- **Market driven.** Many see digital infrastructure as an essential service, despite there not being a requirement for its provision to households and businesses. Digital services are provided by the market based on demand, raising concerns

about a digital divide in low-demand locations. Some jurisdictions require the provision of 'clean pipes' which will allow future service provision.
- **Performance needs**. Pre the COVID-19 pandemic, many users of digital services sought high download speeds to enable streaming of movies and games. Working from home created demand for better upload services. Into the future the demands on performance will increase with emerging technologies such as autonomous vehicles.
- **Infrastructure needs**. Many elements make up the full suite of digital infrastructure from mobile phones to sensors. With digital services being market-driven, the principal infrastructure consideration is providing a conduit that will enable fibre optic cabling to be provided later. We also need to ensure different providers are not duplicating hard infrastructure such as pole-based infrastructure.

15.2.4.2 Research Objectives
The research objectives are:

- to understand the hard infrastructure requirements for digital connectivity, such as pole-based transmitters and 'clean pipes' (conduits)
- to understand the coverage and performance of digital services.

15.2.4.3 Research Approaches
City planners need to understand how planning controls and development approval requirements are leveraging the provision of hard infrastructure, such as clean pipes in new greenfield estates.

With digital services being market driven, the challenge is understanding coverage and performance. Another challenge is the speed at which things change, including that some opportunities deemed impossible become possible.

A future consideration will be minimum service levels, just as the provision of clean water and sanitation is a minimum requirement when developing land for homes and businesses.

15.2.5 City Structure—Spatial Equity and Mode Choice

The recognition of spatial inequality across a city (such as urban slums) is not new. Plato raised the issue 2,500 years ago when he noted "any city, however small, is in fact divided into two, one the city of the poor, the other of the rich" (cited in Glaeser 2011, p. 69). Mumford (1961, p. 61) states that "on the negative side, the citadel introduced class segregation."

Furthermore, Glaeser (2011, p. 81) contends that part of the role of cities is providing for upward mobility, and in that context, he states: "If an area has become the home of default for poor people who are staying poor, then that area is failing".

This challenge still resonates. For example, the vision for the Greater Sydney Region Plan (2018, p. 6), *A Metropolis of Three Cities*, states that:

> As the population of Greater Sydney is projected to grow to 8 million over the next 40 years, … rebalancing economic and social opportunities will leverage that growth and deliver the benefits more equally and equitably across Greater Sydney.

Spatial equity raises the issue of a just city, as raised by Fainstein (2010, pp. 172–175). She states that city planning for a just city, particularly at the local level, requires principles that further equity, diversity and democracy.

An observation. In 1880s England, as in the 1940s and 50s in Australia, and recently for remote Aboriginal communities in Australia, housing is often seen as the problem for those in poverty, as distinct from employment and wider socio-economic issues such as levels of educational attainment and health.

15.2.5.1 Research Considerations

We are seeking multiple outcomes for the individual that also benefit governments, such as reducing dependence on private vehicles, reducing transport costs, improving physical health and increasing independence for those who cannot drive or do not have access to a car. In addition, environmental benefits are likely.

The principle of an equitable city sits at the heart of this issue. In this context I remember being told when working in an urban fringe growth area, with limited bus services, that you need a business case with a positive outcome to get a bus service; however, without a service to benchmark from, it is difficult to develop a business case—it's a *catch-22*.

I acknowledge that many parts of suburban cities where business cases are required are not conducive to public transport services. We are, however, getting innovative in our responses, such as the use of on-demand services.

Conceptually enhancing people's mode choices is also linked to the principle of the Marchetti Constant, the daily one-hour travel budget that many planners utilise as a basis when considering the structure of cities. The issue here is the available travel modes. Interestingly, Glaeser (2011, p. 167) suggests that sprawl started many centuries ago when people used something other than their own two feet to travel.

We can give people more choice in travel mode by changing the distribution of land uses and/or public transport, walking and cycling networks. Therefore, this issue of mode choice is linked to the research activities for Sects. 14.2.4 and 15.2.

15.2.5.2 Research Objectives

The research objectives are:

- to assess the relative levels of mode choice across a city, considering the frequency and coverage of public transport networks; walkability (lighting, disability access compliance, shade); and cycle networks

- to assess the relative levels of accessibility to goods, services and jobs, which is an area of investigation outlined in Sect. 14.2.4.

15.2.5.3 Approaches to Research
The required assessments will occur as part of research areas already identified. Make sure those research activities deliberately consider relative levels of mode choice.

15.2.6 The City in its Region

15.2.6.1 Research Considerations
In addition to hinterland areas, we need to understand how a city interacts with its wider region, and identify what that region is. This is primarily a transport question, but can include biodiversity values. The issues for consideration are:

- **Connected communities of interest**. Communities may connect to a city for a range of reasons, from the need to access high order goods and services to business to business connections. Levels of interactions vary, from the Melbourne to Sydney air service (the third busiest in the world) to lifestyle or tourism connections. My observation from working on regional plans for Victoria suggests community connections, from Melbourne, can extend to about three hours by car.
- **Environmental considerations**. These occur when the ecosystems framing a city extend for significant distances, creating biodiversity corridors that connect multiple ecosystems. The area around Central Coast (just north of Sydney), for example, forms complete corridor of ecosystems from inland plains, across the dividing range and through to the coast.
- **Freight connections.** As Australian capital cities are generally coastal cities, freight connections from primary sources to markets and trade gateways extend well into the heart of Australia.

15.2.6.2 Research Objectives
The research objective is:

- to understand the interactions between the city and its communities of interest and what may influence those interactions.

15.2.6.3 Research Approach
The focus is to understand how the quality of transport connections can influence economic and liveability outcomes for the city and its community.

15.3 Qualities of Places

The qualities of places can imbue a sense of community, place and history; attract business investment; enhance real and perceived levels of safety; and help people understand how land is central to Country, community and culture for First Nations people.

15.3.1 A Sense of Place and Community

15.3.1.1 Research Considerations
A sense of place and community covers how individuals and communities value and perceive places. We can consider this at various geographies and for various groups, from the school community to a cultural community, each with different social connections and different spatial or physical markers (such as the school gate or a purpose-built facility).

Therefore, a sense of place and community is directly influenced by city design. It is about responding to and protecting cultural places and natural features and creating recognisable places from clear urban breaks between suburbs to protected viewsheds and landmarks. Examples include the view down Mercer Street to the spire of Saint Mary of the Angels Basilica in Geelong and the green hilltops that are a strong design philosophy for Canberra and South Morang and even the front gate of a school.

I have found the work of Bacon in the *Design of Cities* (1967) provides a useful introduction to the concept of how city structure can be influenced over time. He uses the work of Pope Sixtus V in Rome as an example.

15.3.1.2 Research Objectives
The research objectives are:

- to identify the spatial attributes of a city that can support or enhance a sense of place and community
- to identify design principles to guide evolutionary change that will enhance a sense of place and community.

15.3.1.3 Approaches to Research
Metropolitan plans only deal with this issue occasionally; it is more often considered at smaller spatial geographic scales. Despite this, we often speak enthusiastically about places where there is a strong design expression such as in Canberra, the central areas of Melbourne and Adelaide, or in views to and from landscapes or landmarks, such as the Sydney Opera House and Harbour Bridge.

Seek advice from landscape architects and review findings around community values. The COVID-19 pandemic travel restrictions resulted in many people re-connecting with their local neighbourhood, providing a better opportunity to understand people's perceptions of place, which may help to inform a metropolitan view.

15.3.2 First Nations Country, Community and Culture

15.3.2.1 Research Considerations

Across Australia, government agencies support First Nations people and communities in terms of education, health, housing, economic development and cultural activities. State and Commonwealth legislation protects Aboriginal places and objects.

My review of seven capital city plans across Australia, however, shows they all, other than the South East Queensland plan, primarily focus on heritage matters relating to artefacts or rock art. I found little direction on how planning can support outcomes for Aboriginal people.

Outside Greater Sydney, the nine regional plans for NSW include a common direction to strengthen the economic self-determination of Aboriginal communities (I did not assess regional plans from other regional areas). I covered the issue of economic self-determination in Sect. 14.2.3.

Thus, there appears to be an opportunity to enhance the narratives and responses in capital city plans beyond that of protecting places, to city plans that support outcomes such as enabling economic self-determination and identifying how First Nations Country, community and culture can be incorporated into city planning.

15.3.2.2 Research Objectives

The research objectives are:

- to establish partnerships with local First Nations communities
- to learn about cultural landscapes
- to learn about culturally responsive design, social infrastructure and public art
- to learn about language and place naming.

15.3.2.3 Approaches to Research

Policies and guidelines addressing First Nations communities and city planning are only just emerging. My recommended research approach is informed by the NSW Government's 2022 report *Recognise Country, Guidelines for development in the Aerotropolis*, specifically Part 2: Recognise Country Guidelines.

Begin by identifying if there are guidelines for researching First Nations issues of Country, community and culture within your own jurisdiction. I also suggest seeking specialist advice to guide you.

A range of activities are required:

- **Meaningful engagement**. Engaging with local First Nations communities should aim to develop a partnership. Section 5.3.3 outlines considerations for engaging with First Nations communities.

  This task is about enhancing cultural awareness. The essential task of Walking on Country is essential to inform your understanding of the issues outlined below.

  Be sure to establish whether relationships already exist between local First Nations communities and relevant local governments or your state government.
- **Starting with Country**. *Recognise Country* states:

  > Country is central to the identity and wellbeing of Aboriginal communities. ... Country will likely be expressed differently depending on the individual or group and therefore there is no single way of defining Country. P21

  Only through engaging with the local First Nations community and Walking on Country will you obtain a genuine appreciation of the cultural landscape.
- **Cultural landscape**. Start by assessing existing reports of cultural values including historical and contemporary values, oral stories and mapping. Augment your desktop review with an on-Country review with Knowledge holders who can share values of Country and insights into place.

  Research in this area covers significant sites, traditional movement corridors, view lines, landscape, flora and fauna, waterways, cultural practice, caring for Country and narratives of Country.

  Caring for Country is deeply embedded within First Nations culture and is an expression of custodianship for a First Nations person's Country.
- **Built form**. Aim to understand the context of moving from the cultural landscape to the built form. *Recognise Country* highlights:
  - culturally responsive design, which, in an Australian context requires a holistic approach to respond to Country, along with the consideration of all cultural landscape elements outlined above (p. 44)
  - culturally responsive social infrastructure, which "incorporates the facilities, services and spaces that are used for the physical, social, cultural or intellectual development and welfare of the community" (p. 47)
  - culturally responsive public art, whereby "Aboriginal cultures, knowledge and history [are] communicated and shared orally through storytelling and song, as well as visually through dance and art. Art is an important form of cultural expression for Aboriginal people, using traditional symbols and patterns to convey stories which provide vital information about events, culture and Country" (p. 50).

Furthermore:

> The *International Indigenous Design Charter* emphasises the importance of respecting copyright, moral rights and cultural rights. It also emphasises the need to understand the importance of appropriate acknowledgements and credits, as per the legal requirements of the country in which the cultural knowledge resides. (p. 50)

- **Language and naming**. First Nations place naming is central to language revitalisation as it helps reawaken, preserve and grow First Nations languages. Since 2001 the NSW Government has supported a dual naming policy for geographical features and cultural sites, refer to the Geographical Names Board website. Wayfinding strategies are one way to utilise First Nations place names.

For each of these research issues, *Recognise Country* includes generic targeted questions to start a conversation of learning.

By documenting engagement and research activities, you can help to build trust. *Recognise Country* includes a template for documenting the research activities. In general, the outputs cover project overview, engagement planning, walking on Country, cultural values research, engagement activities, key outcomes and a First Nations stakeholder statement. Refer the NSW Government web page Western Sydney Aerotropolis Development Control Plan Phase 2.

15.3.3 Post-European Contact Heritage

15.3.3.1 Research Considerations

The history of places can provide insights as to how cities have evolved, as distinct from the simple extrapolation of population, transport and other data.

A valuable piece of research I commissioned was a history of retailing in Melbourne. It revealed that growth and change in retailing was more than an evolution of retail zones. It also revealed the complexity of the suburbanisation of retailing—this could only occur with the invention of the refrigerated truck and pallets to freight goods, but was also spurred on by the reality that Melbourne CBD was bursting with people on a Saturday morning. Of course, there was also the car, but it was not just the car. This information gives much more meaning to Melbourne's first supermarket at North Balwyn and first discount department store (K1), at Burwood.

When thinking of heritage, therefore, consider the history behind the heritage.

> When I was at the City of Casey, officers of Heritage Victoria told me heritage assets should reflect the history of the area rather than be considered old buildings. Consequently, we found out that 100 years earlier parts of the city were internationally famous for dairy farming, so it was fitting that one of the city's heritage buildings is the Cheese Factory.

All Australian jurisdictions have legislation to identify and protect post-contact heritage—city planning starts in that context and can add value to legislative requirements. For example, we can examine how the history of a city can inform city planning opportunities where the future is the sum of the achievements of past, present and future generations. The adaptive reuse of heritage buildings provides an economic incentive to protect and preserve heritage.

Enhancing connections with the history and protecting and maintaining heritage recognises its "capacity to enrich lives and provide a sense of connection for locals and visitors" (Northern Territory, Department of Lands, Planning and Environment 2015, p. 54).

When considering recent histories (post 1788) it is important to recognise that there are important First Nations stories to be told of this time—truth telling. To collaborate to deliver a better future we must acknowledge the past.

15.3.3.2 Research Objectives
The research objectives are:

- to identify how the history of the city creates opportunities for city planning and provides a context for understanding the heritage assets of a place
- to identify opportunities for truth telling regarding colonial narratives and events.

15.3.3.3 Approaches to Research
State governments heritage agencies can provide information on heritage matters. Historians can prepare tailored research, and my advice is to commission early.

If you've not been involved in heritage matters, I recommend reading the Burra Charter (The Australia ICOMOS Charter for Places of Cultural Significance, The Burra Charter 2013). It guides the conservation and management of places of cultural significance. The NSW Government's 2022 report *Recognise Country, Guidelines for development in the Aerotropolis*, specifically Part 2: Recognise Country Guidelines provide a starting point on how to engage with local First Nations communities.

15.3.4 Quality, Aesthetics (Beauty) and Amenity

15.3.4.1 Research Considerations
We need to focus on how people experience and perceive the city when walking, cycling, driving or as passengers going about daily activities. We deal with public spaces such as parks in Sect. 14.3.3. Also consider rail corridors given thousands of people view these corridors every day. Therefore, the quality, aesthetics and amenity of streetscapes are about:

- the visual landscapes (viewsheds/corridors), including the 'borrowed' landscapes of private land for which we have little control
- urban structure, including topography, street patterns and open space networks
- the interface between public spaces and the private realm
- the design of buildings, individually and collectively.

Many textbooks cover this area, and I recommend the following:

15.3 Qualities of Places

- *The Image of the City* (Lynch 1960) outlines how the image of the city is influenced by how people interact and perceive several essentially simple elements: paths, edges, districts, nodes and landmarks.
- *A Pattern Language: Towns, Buildings, Construction* (Alexander et al. 1977) notes the importance of creating a positive experience from every element of a city by focusing on detail, right down to, for example, a bus stop.
- *Great Streets* (Jacobs 1995) covers what is important to make a great street.
- *What Makes a Great City* (Garvin 2016) focuses on the public realm as a quality that makes great cities.
- The City Assembled, The Elements of Urban Form Through History (Kostof 1992) provides a detailed historical analysis of the elements that make urban form.

Of the many challenges for quality streetscapes, the principal one is competition for land. In the absence of an integrated and strategic view, opportunities are lost. The specific issues are:

- **Traffic**. Nearly all streets are designed for vehicles. The role of the road affects speed restrictions, which then impacts the perceived amenity of the street for pedestrians. For example, if a main street shopping environment is also a major truck thoroughfare, pushing a pram in front of two large trucks at a pedestrian crossing can be intimidating.
  Also, in many jurisdictions the speed limit sets a clearance zone (where no obstacles are placed) adjacent to driving lanes to prevent collisions. This can be problematic. For example, in some greenfield areas the standard cross-section for a four-lane dual carriageway with an 80 km per hour speed limit means the clearance zone prevents trees from being planted.
- **Utilities**. Power, telecommunications, water, sewer and drainage, whether above or below ground, all potentially impact the ability to landscape a street.
- **On-street car parking**. This can impact cyclist safety (opening doors in front of an oncoming cyclist). Space is also required for easy egress curb side of a main street, which may impact the location of alfresco dining.
- **Footpaths**. Their width needs to accommodate wheelchair and pram users, including for passing; the volume of people; the needs of the visually impaired; and of course, provide lighting, shade and quality surfaces.
- **Interfaces**. We need to consider interfaces between land uses and the streetscape; retail, residential, office, factory, health and education uses have a different influence on the pedestrian experience. We therefore need to understand the objectives for any given part of the street, whether this is about active street fronts or the need for 'eyes on the street' in residential areas.

> *Regarding the latter, when working in greenfield areas we found it was a challenge to design a single level house on a 500 m^2 allotment without a garage ending up at the front of the house—creating a 'garagescape' rather than a streetscape. Developers and councils agreed that such a lot size was inappropriate, and instead we needed a mix of 400 m^2 and 600 m^2 lots.*

- **The scale of buildings**. This is also considered in terms of street width, with much already written about this topic (I recommend Jacobs 1995 and Alexander et al. 1977, there will be many others). While many tall buildings directly address the street, our role is to consider *how* they address the street and expectations of sunlight on the street. Kostof (1991) provides insights how the skyline of cities has evolved over time. Reflecting up to recently the ideals of governments, to now, a privatised element of the city.
- **Costs**. Retrofitting places to enhance amenity can be costly, with most costs falling to governments.
- **Private public space interfaces**. Many town centres include private arcades and shopping malls. When temperatures go over 30 degrees or on rainy days the value of such places to the community is self-evident. The critical policy and design issue is how these private 'public' spaces interface with the streetscape, and whether they add value to the public streetscape.

Many jurisdictions now provide better guidance on all these matters, including identifying typologies for different parts of a city.

I also recommend looking into the background to the city of Celebration in Florida, in the United States, which was developed by the Walt Disney Company. After investigating many aspects of town design, they shifted driveway crossovers along the street to rear access, after finding these impeded pedestrian movements due to concerns for personal safety. They also required all houses to have a front veranda, at a height, so that a person sitting would have eye contact, at the same level, as a person walking along the street.

> When Jan Gehl visited the university where I studied town planning he observed that in Melbourne, the small private space at the front of a terrace house allowed a person to stand in their private 'room' and have an informal contact with a passer-by in the public space of the street—the solution to a challenge in design he had been searching for.

15.3.4.2 Research Objectives

The research objectives are:

- to assess the extent to which planning controls and policies provide direction on how to enhance the quality, aesthetics and amenity of streetscapes
- to assess the qualities of the streetscapes of metropolitan importance such as major thoroughfares and those in major centres and consider how to fund improvements.

15.3.4.3 Approaches to Research

This research area overlaps with a sense of place and community, Sect. 15.3.1. City planning investigations that address the quality of streetscapes should focus on areas of metropolitan importance that can add value to a sense of place and community.

On-site assessments are essential and you'll likely require expert advice (landscape architect, urban designer, architect) to guide or undertake the research. Be sure to provide a clear brief that sets out the exact information you seek.

15.3.5 Healthy Natural Systems

Natural systems include terrestrial and aquatic habitats and cover issues such as the water quality of catchments, rivers and streams and other waterways. Managing biodiversity covers identifying, protecting, enhancing and managing natural systems.

15.3.5.1 Research Considerations
We need to consider healthy and natural systems **in and adjacent** to cities in terms of identifying biodiversity values, then protecting and managing habitats, including individual species such as orchids.

Identification can be challenging when investigations must pick out specific species. For example, investigations into the Golden Sun Moth can be labour-intensive processes and can only occur for a few days of the year, generally in December.

In the last decade, a more strategic approach to investigations has responded to the requirements of Commonwealth legislation, specifically the *Environment Protection and Biodiversity Conservation Act 1999.*

The earlier investigations can occur the more likely management plans can be prepared to protect biodiversity values. If this occurs at the development phase, expect contested views and, as a worst-case scenario, illegal removal.

Early identification is relevant in the hinterlands of cities where there is the potential pressure for urban development (real or perceived).

The protection and management of biodiversity values come at a cost and most jurisdictions have processes to manage these costs. Management relates to the nature of urban areas, such as public access; invasive pests (such as weeds that have been thrown over a back fence); and predation of native species by foxes, dogs and cats.

Ultimately, how we manage the biodiversity values within an urban area is influenced by how we see nature and the city. For example, if viewed as a 'city in its landscape' the overriding philosophy of city planning begins with a consideration of physiographic and biodiversity values, how urban development responds to these values, and how natural systems connect to systems outside the city. Alternatively, a 'scorched earth' approach places little value on biodiversity within a city, with biodiversity values retained outside the city, in its hinterland. This approach can sometimes bleed out into the hinterland as the urban area seeks to expand.

15.3.5.2 Research Objectives

The research objectives are:

- to assess the performance of planning controls and policies in managing biodiversity values within and adjacent to the city
- to assess the extent and effective coverage of biodiversity assessments for the city and its hinterland.

15.3.5.3 Approaches to Research

All jurisdictions have agencies directly responsible for the stewardship of natural systems. The planning portfolio usually manages processes related to development and biodiversity values and creates regulations and policies in that regard.

Identifying and protecting biodiversity values requires management plans that take time and should occur outside city planning processes. City planning should focus on the status and effectiveness of these activities, except where expansion of the urban footprint is being considered. In those instances, timing is everything.

15.3.6 Responding to Climate Change

15.3.6.1 Research Considerations

For metropolitan planning, considerations include:

- whether infrastructure can be adapted to threats such as flooding on roads or coastal inundation on drainage outfalls
- the influence of extreme weather events and their influence on natural hazards such as bushfires
- the influence of changing weather conditions such as more or less rainfall or hotter temperatures
- the impact of sea level rise on coastal settlements.

Many of these changes, like sea level rise, are slow to reveal themselves, yet the long-term impacts are significant as responses are costly. Some impacts are highly localised and thus do not result in systemic policy changes, meaning local communities end up taking responsibility.

The impact on communities and natural systems has increased awareness and activity in resilience planning for communities.

The way we manage activities such as transport (therefore, the distribution of land uses) and energy sources for homes and businesses can contribute to zero carbon emission targets.

The diversity of areas influenced by climate change suggests we need responses within individual policy areas, such as infrastructure, housing, commercial development and coastal management. Our objective is to understand how climate

15.3 Qualities of Places

Table 15.1 Assessment of the scope of climate change issues addressed in capital city plans

Issue	ACT 2018	Adelaide 2017	Darwin 2015	Melbourne 2017	Perth & Peel 2018	South East Qld 2017	Greater Sydney 2018
Achieve net zero emissions	✓	-	-	✓	-	-	✓
Reduce carbon footprint	-	✓	-	-	-	✓	-
Adaptation and resilience	✓	-	-	-	-	✓	✓
Natural hazards	-	✓	✓	✓	-	✓	-
Heat island effect	-	✓	✓	✓	-	-	✓
Green infrastructure	-	✓	-	-	-	-	-
Circular economy	-	✓	-	✓	✓	-	✓
Renewable energy	✓	✓	-	✓	✓	-	-
Protection of natural assets	-	-	-	-	-	✓	✓
Design policies	-	✓	-	✓	-	-	-

Note I have excluded statements in narratives. Some plans have multiple initiatives for the one issue
Source My article from the September 2021, (Issue No. 128) of *New Planner*. Reproduced with permission from the Planning Institute of Australia

change is impacting those areas and what responses can be included in business-as-usual activities.

We also need an overarching appreciation of climate change issues to guide the collective mitigation and adaptation activities and public resources. This responsibility typically sits outside the planning portfolio.

15.3.6.2 Climate Change and Capital City Plans

This section draws heavily from my article in the September 2021 edition of *New Planner* (Dalheim, 2021), the journal of the NSW and ACT branch of the Planning Institute of Australia, which examined how climate change is being addressed in Australia's capital city plans.

I identified a range of mitigation and adaptation responses to climate change and little consistency, refer Table 15.1. Only four issues are consistently addressed in four of the plans.

Table 15.2 Variability of wording for common issues in the capital city plans

Issue	Direct wording from capital city plan		
Achieve net zero emissions	To keep us on track to achieve net zero emissions, Government has set firm interim targets based on advice from the ACT Climate Change Council. (ACT 2018)	Transition to a low-carbon city to enable Victoria to achieve its target of net zero greenhouse gas emissions by 2050. (Melbourne 2017)	A low-carbon city contributes to net zero emissions by 2050 and mitigates climate change. (Greater Sydney 2018)
Renewable energy	Provide the opportunity for neighbourhood-level alternative energy supplies, which may include embedded and distributed renewable energy, co-generation and smart grid/green grid technology. (Adelaide 2017)	Facilitate the uptake of renewable energy technologies. (Melbourne 2017)	Incorporate affordable renewable energy, low emissions technology and energy efficiency measures into the planning and development of communities, buildings and transport systems. (Perth & Peel 2018)

Source My article from the September 2021, (Issue No. 128) of *New Planner*. Reproduced with permission from the Planning Institute of Australia.

In terms of common issues, we need to recognise the variability in the phraseology for each issue—see the examples in Table 15.2. This influences interpretation and thus, delivery outcomes.

The wording is also both high level and not definitive in terms of mandatory outcomes. Delivery challenges are amplified in that only the ACT and Adelaide plans had a suite of actions to guide delivery. The plan for South East Queensland has one, the rest have no stated actions.

Table 15.3 illustrates my assessment of which issues include metrics for each of the capital city plans. The inconsistency in terms used also applies to metrics. For example, even though three jurisdictions outline sources for greenhouse gas emissions, all three utilise different categories.

In few cases, the metrics describe the benefit of actions, such as how increasing canopy cover decreases ambient temperatures.

15.3 Qualities of Places

Table 15.3 Assessment of the scope of climate change metrics addressed in capital city plans.

Metric	ACT 2018	Adelaide 2017	Darwin 2015	Melbourne 2017	Perth & Peel 2018	South East Qld 2017	Greater Sydney 2018
Greenhouse gas emissions	Source of emission	-	-	Source of emission	-	-	Source of emission
Natural hazards	-	-	Coastal inundation mapping	Coastal inundation mapping	-	-	-
Tree cover	Canopy cover over 3 m	-	-	-	-	-	Tree canopy mapping
Urban heat	Surface heat mapping	-	-	Urban heat island profile	-	-	-
Target: emissions	Interim targets and net zero by 2045	Net zero by 2050	-	Net zero by 2050	-	-	-
Target: renewable energy	100% by 2020	50% by 2025	-	40% by 2025	-	-	-

Note Some plans have multiple metrics for one issue and Table 3 excludes data in background reports.
Source My article from the September 2021, (Issue No. 128) of *New Planner*. Reproduced with permission from the Planning Institute of Australia.

15.3.6.3 Research Objectives

The research objectives are:

- to understand how a city plan can help to mitigate climate change
- to identify how different thematic policy areas can contribute to climate change adaptation and mitigation.

15.3.6.4 Approaches to Research

Begin by understanding the objectives and approach of government to tackling climate change, and the areas where city planning can help mitigate the effects of climate change. An example of this is *Exploring Net Zero Emissions for Greater Sydney* prepared by Kinesis (2017), which informed the Greater Sydney Region Plan. You will also need to work with partner agencies to understand how their policy area is responding to climate change.

15.3.7 City Hinterlands

15.3.7.1 Research Considerations

I describe hinterlands as the towns, villages and rural lifestyle communities, agricultural activities and national and state parks that are near cities. These areas provide the food, water and natural resources that cities need. Their rural and natural amenity attract people who seek a rural-residential lifestyle.

Cities influence activities in hinterlands, which can have positive and negative impacts (see Sect. 14.4.5, which covers the management of natural resources).

The spatial extent of hinterlands varies. The ABS uses journey to work information to define the outward reach of cities and thus the spatial delineation of Australia's greater capital city statistical areas. For example, the ABS identifies the Central Coast as being part of Greater Sydney. Utilising this economic descriptor may show one economic relationship, but it is not necessarily a determinant of what defines a sense of community—only the community itself can define that.

As Australian cities continue to expand, the resultant land speculation increases land values, which in turn impacts the viability of agricultural activities. In Melbourne, the Urban Growth Boundary is a planning control that seeks to manage this—it can only be changed with the approval of both houses of the Victorian Parliament within 10 sitting days of each other. Creating stability in rural land prices requires consistent decisions of no change by both sides of politics for a sustained period. I have a personal interest in this, as I led the last major change to the boundary back in 2010.

The Urban Growth Boundary is based on natural features and long-established policy positions including the protection of Mornington Peninsula and the Yarra Valley.

As city planners, our task is to identify and manage the values of hinterlands. Values may be influenced by the presence of small communities or towns, biodiversity, natural resources, scenic landscapes, agricultural land or natural hazards.

Management can be complex—for example, can we allow the natural growth of a small settlement without it becoming an urban satellite town, or can limited levels of development be used as an economic tool to fund biodiversity outcomes.

15.3.7.2 Research Objectives

The research objectives are:

- to articulate and identify hinterland values and how they will be managed
- to articulate how the outward growth of the city will be managed.

15.3.7.3 Approaches to Research

This task requires classic land use mapping combined with assessments of values based on qualitative and quantitative assessments of the mapped elements, such as the value of biodiversity based on recognised criteria, soil quality to assess agricultural value and established buffer distances to protect intensive agricultural activities such as poultry farms.

15.4 Urban/Suburban Communities

Managing the individual needs of households and businesses requires consideration of a range of issues that in the context of their spatial influence.

15.4.1 Urban Infrastructure

Urban infrastructure includes water, sewer, drainage, energy, waste management, telecommunications and green infrastructure.

15.4.1.1 Research Considerations
Across Australia large agencies plan and provide the utilities infrastructure required to enable development. There are differing models in terms of the ownership of the agencies, from public to private entities. Some areas such as energy have different players for differing parts of the system—generation, distribution and retail.

City planners need to understand the strategic aspects of the various networks and delivery issues:

- **Delivery and funding mechanisms and what they mean for development.** Seek to understand the ownership of utility authorities (public and private) and that jurisdictions have differing powers with regard to funding. This means you'll see varied perceptions of equity across jurisdictions.
- **Development thresholds.** Understand what level of development will require capacity augmentation.
- **Spatial needs.** Consider what different utility networks need any opportunities to coordinate activities and or share easements.
- **Lead times.** Know the lead times for delivery—for example, it could be many decades in the water sector.
- **Easements.** Consider whether easement can be incorporated into a city and any encumbrances to public access and embellishment.
- **Greenfield areas.** Consider these as an opportunity for large-scale innovative solutions, while understanding capacity constraints for urban renewal, particularly town centres. Remember that in greenfield areas you may be second-guessing the next development front and the rate of development. Many developers may be required to provide temporary works that are then decommissioned, all at their cost.

I directly encountered these issues in a fully planned area that was well into development. The energy provider advised a new transmission line was required to build resilience and wanted to build in the road reserve. This would have prevented tree planting. Fortunately, we negotiated an alternative.

- **Green infrastructure**. Identify opportunities for:
  - bushland and waterways—for habitat and ecological health
  - urban tree canopy—for climate change adaptation and resilience
  - parks and open space—for people.
- **Decentralised systems.** Consider these systems as well as on-site delivery such as solar panels and water tanks—all are changing the way development can be serviced. Consequently, utility planning and delivery increasingly considers ecologically sustainable development and risks related to climate change.
- **Waste**. While minimising waste and supporting recycling, reuse and safe disposal of toxic wastes are mainly managed by local government, though often in regional groupings, city planning needs to protect existing and potential waste management sites.

15.4.1.2 Research Objectives

The research objectives are:

- to gain a temporal understanding of development thresholds for the different utilities requirements to enable urban development and the consideration required to enhance capacity from broad costs to funding mechanisms
- to understand delivery options such as trunk services versus decentralised services and the spatial needs for the principal utilities in the short and long term
- to understand the funding mechanisms available to support infrastructure provision.

15.4.1.3 Approaches to Research

The planning and consideration of the utility requirements for a city requires a three-way conversation between the utility providers, the development sector and state and local government. Focus on bringing together information and on understanding strategic issues, and undertake technical peer reviews as required.

This requires an understanding of detailed technical issues and the ability to develop simplified strategic approaches and narratives.

15.4.2 Natural Hazard Risks

Natural hazards include bushfires, floods, wind (for example, cyclones), coastal inundation, heatwaves and acid sulphate soils.

15.4.2.1 Research Considerations

Natural hazards are a real threat to life and property as recently experienced with the bushfires along the east coast of Australia from Victoria to Queensland (2019–20) and the Brisbane floods in 2011 and the NSW and Victorian floods of 2022.

They have a direct impact on city planning, as I saw when involved in the last major change to Melbourne's Urban Growth Boundary. One location rejected for urban development, was impacted by the Black Saturday fires of 2009.

Issues to consider include:

- how to manage threats in cities or hinterlands due to past planning decisions, and identifying adaptation options (ranging from reducing a threat to relocating settlements) and potential costs
- the impacts of reducing the threat of bushfire hazards such as vegetation removal and subsequent loss of biodiversity
- the desire of some people to live near a natural hazard due to amenity values (forest, coast and rivers) when the threat is invisible
- agreeing on risk values and their implications on development for different threats, including the implications of climate change on those threats, to determine levels of acceptable risk to life and property
- heat stress as a natural hazard, for example, the *Report on Department of Health's January 2009 Heatwave in Victoria: An assessment of Health Impacts* (2010) identified that potentially 374 people died from heat-related conditions (over a week) at the same time as the Black Saturday bushfires resulted in 173 fatalities
- the ability for urban tree canopies to mitigate against heatwaves, given that every 10 percent increase in tree canopy cover can reduce land surface temperatures by 1.13 degrees Celsius (Greater Sydney Commission 2018)
- in light of these issues, how to balance conflicting or difficult trade-offs to manage existing threats or prevent new threats.

15.4.2.2 Research Objectives

The research objectives are:

- to spatially identify natural hazards (including heatwaves) and the implications of the threats on urban development, with threats based on risk assessments and policy positions
- to understand the implications of existing and future hazards on development growth and change.

15.4.2.3 Approaches to Research

Responding and planning for natural hazards is a core input to strategic planning. Planning departments or emergency services agencies will likely hold significant data on the location of threats and response policies. Emergency services agencies need to be part of the investigations in this area.

The activity required is classic spatial sieve mapping.

These can be sensitive issues; clarify your findings, narratives and way forward when briefing decision-makers. Assessments may exclude certain areas from potential development and/or require specific development conditions (buffers) that may be perceived to be a cost on development for landowners.

15.4.3 Choice in Local Neighbourhoods

15.4.3.1 Research Considerations

The design of new communities or major urban precincts needs to facilitate choice in what is accessible. You can enable a choice of goods, services, parks and jobs through a combination of land use and transport principles. Many jurisdictions, and land developers, have design manuals that provide guidance in this area.

The recent amplification of walkability—with more people working from home and wanting easy access to the local shopping centre—has come alongside revelations that some cases offer poor walking environments.

Behavioural shifts can be the impetus to reimagine the design of new neighbourhoods or retrofitted urban areas. I call this designing from the 'inside out', where we start our planning for a location from the perspective of the pedestrian on the street.

This does not mean every street has activity, it means we need to consider:

- where activities are located, to create community corridors
- how to establish bikeways for daily commutes
- the amenity of walking and cycling environments—lighting and shade
- permissible uses for home-based businesses to enhance opportunities to work from home and create active places
- opportunities to grow and enhance the vibrancy of local centres, not just major employment hubs
- the micro aspects of planning local streets, such as the relationship of houses to the street and the role of the street—as noted earlier, this is highlighted in the research for Celebration in Florida
- how planning for places responds to the natural landscape—designing with nature and taking advantage of view corridors and natural and built landmarks.

Once you've considered all these elements, then you can think about the cars.

These considerations are relevant to greenfield and existing urban area planning. They will help you to address what has been a challenge for the planning of new communities—their mono-dimensional nature—while also helping to build a sense of place.

Ultimately, city planning should put local planning issues on the table. This will influence the interventions that can support a 'return to local' (including significant capital expenditure), while considering benefits such as physical health, wellbeing, improved productivity and reduced travel demands.

15.4.3.2 Research Objectives
The research objectives are:

- to gain initial insights into opportunities in existing urban areas and new communities to reimagine the local neighbourhood and the policy guidance and interventions to support and enable change
- to facilitate the necessary collaborations across government agencies through this new approach to local planning and delivery.

15.4.3.3 Approaches to Research
Local governments and local residents are best placed to understand and identify opportunities to reimagine local neighbourhoods. Many of the major land developers can also help you to understand opportunities. For example, some developers already provide purpose-built homes designed to accommodate home offices.

15.4.4 Adaptation, Change and Innovation

15.4.4.1 Research Considerations
The transport sector is transforming with innovation including electric vehicles, autonomous vehicles, on-demand private services and car sharing.

Innovation is also occurring around utility services where water and power (solar) can be harvested from rooftops and waste can be managed on site, thus enabling industrial precincts to be completely independent from traditional utility services. However, in many jurisdictions, sites cannot be developed unless water is available through traditional means.

The virtual delivery of education and business to business activities continue to evolve. Equally, young people are increasingly not seeking their driver's licence and instead walk, cycle or use public transport. All these behavioural changes reduce demand on road transport systems.

Smart technologies can meet a range of infrastructure needs, such as charging electric cars or optimising the efficiency of motorways through signalised on ramps.

All these adaptations, emerging technologies, behavioural changes and innovations allow us to plan, deliver and manage cities without traditional infrastructure interventions.

The role of governments in this area includes kickstarting (from legislation to piloting) new activities, such as on-demand transport, before the market ultimately delivers.

15.4.4.2 Research Objectives

The research objectives are:

- to understand emerging ideas in the management of cities
- to explore technology options that extend the utility of infrastructure and behaviour changes to reduce demand
- to review policy and legislation to enable innovative change.

15.4.4.3 Approaches to Research

The concept of smart cities means many organisations are exploring ideas of how cities could operate/be managed. Begin by engaging with these organisations. In addition, many governments are establishing groups to explore smart city concepts, specifically for the transport sector.

This area is therefore a classic research exploration piece. An example of the right approach that still resonates with me was listening to the then new CEO of the Western Sydney Airport authority. He was talking about creating the world's first digital airport from scratch and explained how his team was investigating what emerging innovations were on the drawing boards of research institutes, to avoid pursuing a specific digital future that could be a dead end.

15.5 City Design

15.5.1 Introduction

At various points in time, design has been central to city planning, whether that be through the geometry of renaissance cities such as Palmanova in Italy; the Garden City and City Beautiful movements of the early twentieth century, as we see in Canberra, Australia's capital; or more recently the philosophy behind new urbanism (noting that the latter has not been put forward as an underlying design philosophy for contemporary city plans, at least in Australia).

My assessment of capital city plans suggests the design philosophy is more inwardly focused on local character rather than seeking some understanding of the city design in totally, except for the strategy for Melbourne—refer Table 15.4.

This is an interesting predicament considering there is no shortage of literature on the topic as already discussed in Chapter 2 on great cities.

This section differs a little from the others in Part 3, as it seeks to outline the case for city (strategic) design rather than the process for its undertaking. My underlying objective is to reawaken strategic planners to the importance of city design as an integral part of 7-Step Strategic Planning Process, particularly Step 3.

Hence this section is more a marker to challenge your thinking, so that design becomes a genuinely strategic consideration rather than a series of incremental urban design exercises dealt with as a city develops.

15.5 City Design

Table 15.4 Comparative assessment of the approach to design for Australia's capital cities plans (This table outlines the design policy statements included in the metropolitan plans for Australia's capital cities)

Strategy	Guidance
ACT (2018)	**Direction 4.5**: Encourage high quality design, built form and places for a changing climate **Action 4.5.1** Investigate a range of processes to improve the design and quality of our buildings and public places, including: … **Action 4.5.2** Investigate policy and planning mechanisms to improve streetscape design for better tree canopy cover and improved verge design of streets that includes: … **Action 4.5.3** Integrate policy and planning mechanisms to enhance the living infrastructure for the planning and design of residential areas in our neighbourhoods. Consider: …
Adelaide (2017)	**Principle 5**: World-class design and vibrancy Eight policies under the heading 'Design quality', including: **Policy 30**: Support the characteristics and identities of different neighbourhoods, suburbs and precincts by ensuring development considers context, location and place
Darwin (2015)	Not included
Greater Sydney (2018)	**Strategy 12.1**: Using a place-based and collaborative approach throughout planning, design, development and management, deliver great places by: recognising and celebrating the character of a place and its people
Melbourne (2017)	**Outcome 4** Melbourne is a distinctive and liveable city with quality design and amenity **Policy 4.1.1** Support Melbourne's distinctiveness **Policy 4.1.2** Integrate place-making practices into road-space management **Policy 4.1.3** Strengthen Melbourne's network of boulevards **Policy 4.1.4** Protect and enhance the metropolitan water's edge parklands
Perth & Peel (2018)	**Section 7.3 Design**, provides direct reference to the draft *Design WA* package, and states the intention to—'Elevating the status of design considerations in planning policy and procedures …'
South East Qld (2017)	**Element 3: Inspiration from local character**. The communities of SEQ demonstrate a strong respect for their heritage, distinct context and local character **Strategies** 1 Identify and conserve local landscape, heritage and cultural assets, including Indigenous landscape values, and where appropriate, integrate or adaptively reuse them in building, streets and spaces 2 Work respectfully with natural topography to create development that contributes positively to the environmental and visual experience of a place 3 Explore the appropriate use of building materials to create contemporary design that adds to a local area's character and diversity 4 Work with the characteristics, traditions and values of the local community to create a distinctive local character and contributory community value

Source My review of Australia's capital city plans as listed in the section at the end of this chapter on 'References'.

15.5.2 A Definition

I suggest a concept of city design in the context of strategic planning process for a city or place, which is why I put it forward as one of the 42 considerations for research, not as a central overarching principal to guide all others. Equally, it should not be viewed as an afterthought to be considered at the detailed design phase of city development where most urban design considerations take place.

- In this book, I define city design through two lenses: parameters as to its scope, and an understanding of place.

In examining city design through these lenses, consider that:

- We experience a city at different speeds. Bacon (1967, p. 252) emphasises that pre-rail, cities were experienced at one speed; with many modes of transport we now experience the city at multiple speeds. This needs to inform our design thinking.
- In terms of city structure, we need to distinguish between essential and non-essential elements (Bacon 1967, p. 253).
- The city provides a series of experiences; thus, city design is about creating the experiences (Bacon 1967, p. 23).

15.5.3 City Design Scope

I suggest five considerations to provide parameters as to the scope of city design:

- **Mass—activity—space**. Design as a discipline is sometimes described in terms of the relationship between mass and space (Bacon 1967, p. 15). For city design, I believe the element of activity should become the central consideration connecting and informing the relationship between mass and space. The elements of mass and space also emphasise the need to view cities in three dimensions and, at times, what happens below ground, such as the web of underground lanes and eat streets in Sydney CBD.
- **Quality of life**. Critically, city design thinking must extend beyond the physical dimensions of a city and consider the quality of life elements, as discussed in Sect. 14.3. This includes the areas of:
  - individual and community wellbeing
  - cultural and artistic expression, participation and appreciation
  - access to natural and developed public spaces
  - the physical amenity of people's homes.
- **Scale**. The scope of strategic planning changes with the scale of the place we are planning for, from a metropolitan area to a town centre, as we discuss in Chapter 12. This recognition is equally relevant to city design.

- **Structure.** Many spatial assessments of a city are about structure—this is why spatial plans are often referred to as structure plans. When we think about city design compared to urban design, we focus on structure and try to understand the significant elements that need to be either enhanced, created or ameliorated to inform detailed urban design. Bacon's (1967, pp. 140–161) expose on the plans of Sixtus V for Rome and the use of a series of obelisks to set up a long-term design approach to the city is a good example of how understanding structure can influence city design.

15.5.4 Understanding Place

The foundation of city design is understanding place. Here, I make the following comments:

- **A deep analysis.** McHarg (1976, pp. 103–115) uses his analysis of Staten Island, in the Borough of Richmond, US, to emphasise the importance of understanding all the elements that make up a place. His assessment covers climate, geology, physiography, hydrology, pedology, vegetation, wildlife and land use.
- **Community values.** A comparison of Staten Island today compared to the vision proposed by McHarg (1976, p. 114) shows land use outcomes evolve and include elements not considered in earlier plans. Garvin (2016, p. xxvi) discusses the benefits of understanding the history of a place in terms of why certain elements exist. This suggests that a community's values evolve; thus, documenting what the community values is important, as it also allows future planners to understand the evolution of community values.

  Work to understand how a community values the elements that make up a place.

  > In the late 1980s I was involved in a plan for the Geelong foreshore. The council sought a vision that could include a range of foreshore activities, and that one area - Steampacket Gardens - was sacrosanct as a piece of open space and thus any design needed to respect that. Thirty years on it is pleasing and interesting to see that the space is still intact.

- **A framework for perceiving the city.** Lynch's seminal work *The Image of the City* (1960) identified that as we move around a city our perceptions can be simplified into a few concepts—paths, edges, districts, nodes and landmarks. Having a structured framework for analysing the landscape elements of a city is therefore important. The analysis required here is usually undertaken by experts such as landscape architects.
- **Image of the city.** This considers public realm viewsheds and their importance from a design and/or sense of belonging perspective. It may include a public building framing a vista or the view of a landscape or landscape feature from a public place. An example is the protection of the vista to the spire of the St Mary of the Angels Basilica when viewed down Mercer Street in Geelong or

the protection of Canberra's hilltops from development, so a green landscape remains the city's backdrop.

Understanding image requires us to see the city through the eyes of the people who live there.

> *I sought to explore the views of the community on the Casey Foothills project. A planning control said the area had a valued landscape without defining what was valued. We gave 40 community group representatives a camera, with instructions on how to report on their photos. Interestingly, they all included a photo of the same spot – a view across some farmland – the essence of what they valued. This allowed us to brief a specialist visual consultant to provide advice as to how to retain that quality.*

- **Structure**. Implicit in understanding structure is understanding the design opportunities created where different networks intersect.
- **Country**. First Nations people see the environment, people and stories as intrinsically connected. Country refers to the natural systems of the land, water and skies that bind us together, which humans rely on to live and function. Responding to Country requires engagement with local First Nations communities from the outset and a shift in our thinking where planning for Country is embedded in all aspects of our plans.
- **Scope of issues**. The issues within the research topics that can influence design outcomes include:
    - Characteristics of places and Country
        - the characteristics and evolution of land use systems and transport networks
        - the cultural landscape
        - the characteristics of the physiography and climatic conditions
    - City setting
    - Quality of life
        - individual and community wellbeing
        - cultural and artistic expression, participation and appreciation
        - access to natural and developed public places
        - the physical amenity of homes
    - Qualities of places
        - a sense of place and community
        - First Nations Country, community and culture
        - post-European contact heritage and history
        - quality, aesthetics, and amenity of the urban fabric of a city and its hinterland
        - natural ecosystems, biodiversity and resilience
        - responding to climate change
        - the values of the city's hinterlands.

15.6 Summary

This chapter provides insights on approaching the research required to form the basis of your city plan. Specifically, this chapter provides more detail on the research areas for Part C: The qualities and performance of place.

The information provided is in no way to be seen as the definitive explanation on how to go about each task. Rather, it is a starting point for understanding why you need to investigate each research area and what questions may be important. In one sense, answering questions is fairly easy, whereas identifying which questions to ask is quite hard.

As indicated several times in this book, the individual research areas are not independent of each other, in fact, where they connect is usually the place of most importance. Hence, the last phase of investigations for each research area should be a consideration of what connections exist with other research areas.

References

Alexander, C Ishikawa, S & Silverstein, M (1977), *A Pattern Language: Towns, Buildings, Construction.* Oxford University Press, New York
—Detailsall the elements that make up places, from cities to bedrooms, and their interrelationships, including that every element should be an experience including a bus stop.
Bacon, EN (1967), *Design of Cities.* Penguin Books, Ringwood, Australia.
—From my university days and where I learnt about the power of city design (structure) and the art of communication.
Dalheim, H (2021), Climate Change: Where do our capital city plans stand? *New Planner*, September 2021, Issue No. 128.
—Comparative assessment of the degree to which capital city plans address climate change.
Fainstein, S (2010), *The Just City*, Cornell University Press, Ithaca, New York.
Garvin, A (2016), *What Makes a Great City.* Island Press.
—The public realm as a quality that makes great cities.
Glaeser, E (2011), *Triumph of the City*, Pan Macmillan UK.
—A must read for any interested in urban economics.
Jacobs, A B (1995), *Great Streets,* MIT Press
—As per the title, what makes a great street.
Kostof, S (1991), *The City Shaped, Urban Patterns and Meanings Through History* Thames & Hudson, London, UK
—A detailed exploration of urban form and what drove different structures.
Kostof, S (1992), *The City Assembled, The Elements of Urban Form Through History* Thames & Hudson, London, UK
Lynch, K 1960 *The Image of the City*, The MIT Press.
—Insightful understanding of how we experience a city.
Marchetti, C (1994), 'Anthropological invariants in travel behavior', *Technological Forecasting and Social Change*, vol. 47, no. 1, pp. 75–88
Mumford, L (1961), *The City in History*, Penguin Books, Australia.
Perez, C. C (2019), *Invisible Women,* Penguin Random House, UK
—A must read for all planners.
SGS Economics and Planning (2012), *Long run economic and land use impacts of major infrastructure projects* Unpublished.

—Outlines the findings of four case studies on the economic impacts of transport and land use projects, relevant for those wanting to understand what is behind the maps and data.

Website links

Australia ICOMOS Incorporated (2013), *The Burra Charter*, https://australia.icomos.org/publications/charters/

Celebration, Florida, United States, https://celebration.fl.us/

Environment Protection and Biodiversity Conservation Act (1999), https://www.environment.gov.au/epbc

Department of Planning and Environment (2022), *Recognise Country Response Template*, Western Sydney Aerotropolis Development Control Plan Phase 2 | Planning Portal - Department of Planning and Environment (nsw.gov.au)

Exploring Net Zero Emissions for Greater Sydney, https://gsc-public-1.s3.amazonaws.com/s3fs-public/exploring_net_zero_emissions_for_greater_sydney_-_kinesis_-_october_2017.pdf

NSW Geographical Names Board, Dual naming - Geographical Names Board of NSW

NSW Government, *Western Sydney Aerotropolis Development Control Plan Phase 2*, Western Sydney Aerotropolis Development Control Plan Phase 2 | Planning Portal - Department of Planning and Environment (nsw.gov.au)

NSW Government (2022), *Recognise Country, Guidelines for development in the Aerotropolis*, Recognise Country Guidelines for development in the Aerotropolis (amazonaws.com)

Transport for new South Wales (2018), *NSW Freight and Ports Plan 2018–2023*, TNSW Freight and Ports Plan 2018–2023.pdf

United Nations (2022), IPCC Sixth Assessment Report, Climate Change 2022: Impacts, Adaptation and Vulnerability, Climate Change 2022: Impacts, Adaptation and Vulnerability | Climate Change 2022: Impacts, Adaptation and Vulnerability (ipcc.ch)

Australian Capital City Plans Website Links

A Metropolis of Three Cities (2018), State of New South Wales, https://www.greater.sydney/metropolis-of-three-cities

ACT Planning Strategy 2018 (2018), Australian Capital Territory, https://www.planning.act.gov.au/act-planning-strategy

Darwin Regional Land Use Plan 2015 (2015), Northern Territory Government, Department of Lands, Planning and the Environment, https://planningcommission.nt.gov.au/projects/drlup

Future Transport Strategy 2056 (2018), Future Transport Strategy 2056 (nsw.gov.au).

Greater Sydney Commission 2018 (2018)), A Metropolis of Three Cities, State of New South Wales, Australia, https://www.greater.sydney/metropolis-of-three-cities.

Perth and Peel @ 3.5 million (2018), Government of Western Australia, Department of Planning, Lands and Heritage, https://www.dplh.wa.gov.au/perth-and-peel-@-3-5-million

Plan Melbourne 2017–2050 (2017), The State of Victoria Department of Environment, Land, Water and Planning, https://www.planmelbourne.vic.gov.au/

Recognise Country, Guidlines for development in the Aerotropolis (2022), Recognise Country Guidlines for development in the Aerotropolis (https://www.amazonaws.com)

Shaping SEQ, South East Queensland Regional Plan 2017 (2017), The State of Queensland, Department of Infrastructure, Local Government and Planning, https://planning.dsdmip.qld.gov.au/planning/better-planning/state-planning/regional-plans/seqrp

The 30-Year Plan for Greater Adelaide, 2017 Update (2017), Government of South Australia, Department of Planning, Transport and Infrastructure https://livingadelaide.sa.gov.au/the_plan

Afterword

When I was in Year 11, I designed a city based on a circle. I guess I knew then—and this has been reinforced throughout my career—that the variety of choices and opportunities available depends on where you live in the city.

My career commitment has been to push for better choices and opportunities for all households. To do this, I have immersed myself in all aspects of the qualities of cities. I see every city as a mosaic and to learn about that mosaic you need to ask questions of those who know about each piece. I describe myself as a specialist at being a generalist—a city planner who understands how to put the pieces together.

This book reflects my journey of learning about the pieces that make up a city and how to achieve better city planning. The foundation of the 7-Step Strategic Planning Process (Sect. 5.2) was the decade of deliberative and systematic technical training I received under the watchful eye of my first boss, and enduring mentor, Dr Jeff Wolinski. Jeff also instilled in me a passion for learning and new ways of thinking.

And after Jeff and I both attended lectures by Edward De Bono, we realised we both drew to record our thoughts, rather than take written notes.

For me, my decade in a strategic planning consultancy opened my eyes to a diversity of projects. I could start to visualise the complex mosaic of cities as I learnt to trust the process of a disciplined and structured approach.

The catalyst for delving deeper into how to effect change in cities came during my master's studies. In one subject, called systems planning, I learned about complexity theory (Sect. 5.3.10). For the first time I felt I was learning about a concept (positive returns) that explained how systems evolved towards a future state, though not necessarily in the interests of all. This view of systems led to Geoffrey West (2018) identifying laws for the growth of cities.

As a result, I started to explore how cities change and how to influence that change. This led me to a discussion with Lyndsay Neilson, who introduced me to a structured approach to understanding five levers of intervention. I have continually evaluated these and the five have evolved into a conceptual framework of 11 levers (Sect. 4.5).

© The Editor(s) (if applicable) and The Author(s) 2023
H. Dalheim, *Planning Better Cities*,
https://doi.org/10.1007/978-3-031-33947-9

My time at the City of Casey brought me to the coalface with the community. After years of preparing plans that focused on the short, medium and long term—without any real basis for what those time periods meant—I started to think about planning for three communities: the current community, the next generation and the legacy for future generations (Sect. 4.2.3).

Working at a council, I noticed the phones always rang, and residents turned up at the front desk. Engaging with the community can happen daily (Sect. 5.3.2). Putting structure to that was hard. For us at Casey, Wendy Sarkissian not only led the task, she arrived with the goal of building capacity. It's from this foundation that I developed a more structured and inclusive approach to community engagement.

A joy of working at council is being an active player in delivery. You learn the importance of collaboration and engaging with those that will *deliver* not just those that *plan* (Sect. 6.4).

This was the same as I moved into urban economics. Instead of being an adviser, I was sitting face-to-face with developers and local businesses to help create a better environment for investment and business attraction (Sect. 14.4). Seeing the world from their perspective helped me to understand the levers that support economic development.

As I've moved through my career, I've come to realise that whether a vision has been established by a national, state or local government, they must be delivered at the local level. I've led and worked in teams that need to actively achieve tangible outcomes; I learned quickly about the timing and cost for everything from main street landscaping to footpaths to connect new communities—and the need to understand where the funds come from. This involves advocacy and funding agreements to gaining decision-maker (councillor) support (Sects. 4.5.4 and 5.3.5). My daily interactions with the community, and the councillors who represented them, brought these ideas to the surface.

After I worked on a major town centre plan, at Casey, I started on the journey of writing this book. During a holiday break I started jotting down the lessons learnt, and insights gained—initially from the plan I'd just completed, and then from my previous experiences. These initial thoughts now form for the insights' sections of Chapters 6 through to Chapter 11.

Importantly, as I jotted down my insights my desire for structure saw the 7-Step Strategic Planning Process emerge as an organised concept. It was initially a six-step process; the seventh and final step came after my time in state government leading metropolitan plans.

For several years I continued to jot down ideas, especially after Marcus Spiller encouraged me to continue, as he saw the benefit of a book based on a practitioner's insights on strategic planning. What we read today is enriched by my work in both the Victorian and NSW planning departments, where I led numerous metropolitan plans, with oversight of many regional plans.

This work reaffirmed the need for a structured approach to city planning, regardless of the location, so long as that approach could be adaptable—for example, a structured approach needs to address local considerations and the scale of the task at hand (Chapter 12).

I also became even more convinced of the importance of informal collaboration. From that belief I established senior officers' groups (Sect. 6.4.3) in both jurisdictions. The NSW group remains in place today.

However, my biggest area of learning in government is the importance of governance, specifically the task of gaining approval for a plan and all that is required to achieve that approval. An approval journey could involve multiple portfolios and multiple ministers. The time required for a government decision will evolve around a clear governance process and can take around a month (Sect. 6.8).

Interestingly, the onset of the COVID-19 pandemic created a window of opportunity for me. I took a sabbatical and started to turn my notes into a structured manuscript.

This opportunity to write a book was also created by Emeritus Professor Peter Phibbs and the support of the Henry Halloran Research Trust. I particularly appreciated the support from my supervisor, Dr Michael Bounds, who helped me to structure my thoughts, think about the audience and clearly convey my ideas.

Part 1 is the outcome of my discussions with Dr Bounds. The task of structuring my experiences of preparing a plan led me to question what planning is about and its purpose. Those questions led me to explore contemporary plans in Australia and internationally (Sect. 3.3) and to digest contemporary planning textbooks on planning systems and issues for consideration.

From this work, my Strategic Planning Research Framework (Sect. 4.2) emerged. I am proud of this framework, as it gives structure and detail to the early work when embarking on a new plan. I am keen to receive feedback from fellow city planners so I can improve the framework.

My involvement with the Henry Halloran Trust also opened doors for the beginnings of a new part time role in academia, where the opportunity to teach some of the ideas in the book has helped in refining some concepts. It is through teaching that I have had the opportunity to listen to guest lectures by Elle Davidson and continue my own learnings on First Nations Country, community and culture.

As I come to the end of this journey, I hope you gain some insights and adapt what I have outlined in the book so we can all look to create better cities.

I firmly believe city planning is on the cusp of achieving better, innovative outcomes for cities by utilising methods that I could not have even dreamed about when I was a young city planner.

Here's just one example. Just as the emergence of the knowledge economy catalysed the revitalisation of capital city CBDs in the early 1990s, I believe city planning can help to re-imagine suburbs and regional cities. These opportunities will be technology-led, whether they come from hybrid work arrangements to autonomous vehicles.

Most importantly I hope there is a shift in what we value as important when we make decisions about cities. I want to see the profession elevate community and individual wellbeing to be an equal consideration to economic outcomes.

Digital technologies will open new doors to the next generation of city planners, as will the tools available and the methods of community engagement. More and more, we will seek the input and advice of the community, including First Nations people—this is essential if we're to plan cities for people today and the future. Embrace and experiment with the many new ways that will allow you to do this.

Cities are living, breathing and complex organisms. They require our full and deepest attention if we are to meet the aspirations of communities. I hope this book is a platform for all of us to go about the task of planning better cities.

Index

A
Acceptable travel times, 398
Accessibility, 33, 36–37
  to goods, services and jobs, 90, 91, 364
Accessibility, transport and digital performance, 399
Achieve net zero emissions, 413, 414
Acronyms, 13
Action coordination, 297
Action development, 254, 262, 270, 273
Activity analysis, 323
Adaptation and resilience (capital city plans), 413
Adaptation, change and innovation (urban and suburban communities), 422
Adelaide plan, 56, 60, 110, 260, 290, 413–415
Advisory panels, 183
Advocacy, 53, 105
Aesthetics and amenity, 95, 410
Affordable housing, 354
Agency engagement, ongoing, 300
Agency workshops, 171. *See also* Inter-agency workshops
Agricultural and mining activities, 94, 376, 379, 390
Airports, 399
Amenities, 368
Amenity of places, 49, 54, 57, 411
American-inspired functional model, 50
Annual monitoring and reporting, 290, 299
Architectural vision, 24
Arterial roads and motorways, 220
Asset management, 107
Auditing the planning content, 165
Australian capital city plans. *See also* specifics, e.g. Greater Darwin plan
  aligning infrastructure with growth, 109
  approach to design, 422
  climate change issues/metrics, 414
  common policy issues, 63–65
  insights, 56–57
  monitoring and reporting, 276
  nomenclature, 238
  principal elements, 261
Australian Capital Territory plan, 56, 110, 274, 294, 428
Australian metropolitan planning
  evolving planning eras (chronology), 46
  federalism impact on, 46
  reflections on planning eras, 46–52
Australia, planning systems, 123
Autonomous vehicles, 74
Awareness raising (about the exhibition), 280

B
Back of house activities, 175, 283
Base case, 9, 228
Basis of the plan, 262
Benchmarking, 9, 37
Bicycle networks, 324
Biodiversity, 220, 221, 324, 403, 411
Blue-green grid, 9, 220
Book of knowledge, 299, 304–306
'Book of truth', 183
Bringing others along for the journey (plan promotion), 302
Broadacre land, 11
Burra Charter, 408
Business and community development, 53, 107
Business-as-usual, 9
  assessment of, 224
  base case, 228
  is it acceptable?, 85, 218
Business community, 185
Businesses
  economy and spatial economic structure, 377

enabling them to grow, flourish and innovate, 375
needs of, 92, 198, 378
physical amenity of, 377
and protection of natural resources, 380
transport and telecommunications access to support, 378

C

Cadastre, 10, 316, 323
Canberra plan. *See* Australian Capital Territory plan
Capital city names, 10
Capital city plans. *See* Australian capital city plans; International city plans
Car parking, 325, 395, 409
CBDs, and work from home, 73
Centre-serving corridors, 205
Championing the vision, 215
Changes. *See also* Levers of change
 agreement on (plan finalisation), 287
 identifying (following submissions), 285
 the most significant changes are the last, 292
 planning for, 143–145
Choice
 enabling, 96
 in local neighbourhoods, 421
 specialisation and innovation in cities through, 22–23
Circular economy, 10, 413
Cities. *See also* Great cities
 definitions, 20–21
 emergence of, 20–21, 23
 first cities, 22–23
 insights for a strategic planning framework, 30
 more than the people who live in it, 185
 nature of change in, 144
 through the ages, 23–24
 urban form of, 24–29
 where change is the constant, 3
 why and how to plan, 5–6, 15–40, 43–77, 83–111
the City as a diagram, 25
'City beautiful', 49, 54
City design, 24, 97, 200, 426
 Australian capital city plans, 424
 definition, 426
 scope, 426
 understanding place, 428
City edge, 29
City hinterlands, 95, 96, 376, 417
City in its region, 95, 403

City leader boards, 37
City of Casey, vision diagram, 242
City of Waverley, 220
City planning typologies, 3, 120–122, 313–337. *See also* specific types, e.g. Town centre planning
 applying Step 1 to, 179
 applying step 2 to, 204
 applying step 3 to, 243
 applying step 4 to, 271
 applying Step 5 and Step 6 to, 291
 applying Step 7 to, 308
 summary of approaches to research, 337–340
City plans*See also* Australian capital city plans; International city plans
 principal elements, 260
City-serving corridors, 205
City setting, 91, 197, 350–351
City-shaping corridors, 205
City structure – spatial equity and mode choice, 403
Clarification meetings, 281
Climate change, 52, 71, 96, 366, 412
 and capital city plans, 414
 variability of wording in capital city plans, 414
Climatic conditions, 90, 196, 348–349
Codified societal norms, 136
Collaborative working arrangements, 159, 162, 255
Collective understanding of the basis for the plan, 215
Commercial activities, 94, 380
Commissioners, 203
Communities
 characteristics, 323
 connection to cities, 402
 perceptions of change, 143
 what are they?, 127
Community and individual wellbeing, improving/supporting, 61, 92, 368
Community engagement, 125–133, 187. *See also* Stakeholder engagement
 engagement approach, 128–130
 engaging with First Nations communities, 130–131
 general considerations, 131–133
 insights, 211
 local government area planning, 204, 314
 neighbourhood community planning, 204, 331
 new greenfield community planning, 204, 340

Index 435

ongoing, 307
purpose, 125
regional cities planning, 204
role of community in decision-making, 137–138
role of planners, 126–127
sticky note planning, 194
town centre planning, 204, 319, 326
town centre planning, 327–328
using experts, 131
what is meant by 'the community', 127
Community engagement activities
approach and general considerations, 202
coordinating the activities, 202
purpose, 201
Community engagement plan
post-launch engagement, 281
pre-exhibition, 282
preliminary, 158
Community groups, 127, 128, 130
Community needs, 85–88
Community perspective, 39, 51, 62
Community planning, 121. *See also* Neighbourhood community planning
Community safety and security, 323, 365
Community values, 99, 425
Competition from lifestyle activities, 379
Complexity
cities and a systems view of planning, 142–143
and laws for cities, 142
Complexity theory and its relevance to city planning, 142
Component plans, 325
Confidentiality, 138, 280
Confirming the requirement for the plan, 157
Consultants, 184
Consumption pattern changes, 48
Contemporary city planning, 56
insights from Australian city plans, 56–57
insights from international city plans, 58
Content control, 203
Contentious issues, monitoring, 282
Contested decisions, 136
Context
creates meaning, 57
draft plan, 258
and need for the plan, 86, 157
town centre planning, 321
Contextual indicators, 289
Contingency planning, 172, 203
Continual improvement, 2
Coordinating research activities, 189

Core plan elements (draft plans), 263
Cost of living, reducing, 92, 368
Costs to enhance amenity, 410
Country, 10, 115, 130, 133, 162, 220, 404. *See also* First Nations peoples, culture, heritage and Country
access to, 92
characteristics of, 90, 346, 426
designing with, 98
COVID-19 pandemic, 52, 54, 69, 71–73, 75, 122
Creating opportunities or improvements for society, 59
Creating places, 99
Crosstab assessment, 10, 345
Cultural and artistic activities, 92, 365, 371
Cultural landscapes, 196, 199, 218, 405
Culture of cooperation (plan delivery), 311

D

Dark restaurant, 10, 72
Darwin. *See* Greater Darwin plan
Data analysis, 193
Data collection, 193
Decentralised systems, 418
Decision-makers, 10, 177
engaging with, 158
reporting principal findings to, 190
Decision-making
challenge of multiple portfolios, 137
and community, 138
hierarchy of, 177–178
and negotiation, 138
within government, 137
Deliberative engagement methods, 129
Delivering change, 144
Delivery (evaluation measure), 230
Delivery levers, 52
other planning typologies, 270
Delivery of city plans, 55, 56, 58, 103–110. *See also* Plan delivery and ongoing planning (step 7)
funding, 107–110
intervention levers, 105–107
the issues, 103
recognising the things that do not change, 110
selected strategic intervention, 104–105
Delivery tools available to planners, 55
Demographic profiles, 89, 196, 343. *See also* Population and demographics
Design, 66, 324
Designated project director, 177

Designated project manager, 177
Design policies, 243
Desired outcomes
  distilling the, 218
  varied nomenclature for, 237
Developed public spaces, access to, 92, 373
Developing the report structure, 215
Development contributions, 108
Development thresholds, 417, 418
Digital accessibility and performance, 72–74, 94, 106, 199, 393
Digital coverage and performance, 95
Digital technology, 128
Direction setting, 215, 241
  approval in principle, 240
  developing the objectives, 238
  neighbourhood community planning, 331–337
  preferred scenario, 240
  varied nomenclature for desired outcomes, 237
  vision statement, 241
Disability access, 396
Distribution systems, 72
Diverse places, 57
Documenting the journey, 175
Doveton/Eumemmerring Neighbourhood Renewal, management framework, 335
Draft plan
  exhibition, 120
  preparation, 120
Draft plan elements
  core plan elements, 263
  new greenfield community planning, 327
  optional plan elements, 262
  other planning typologies, 270
  principal elements (capital city plans), 261
  town centre planning, 319–326
Drivers of change in the 22nd Century, 71–76
Dwellings, 382

E
Easements, 417
Economic context of the plan, 93
Economic performance (towns), 323
Economic self-determination of First Nations communities, 91, 361
Economy, 93, 374
'Eddie Barron case', 108
Education precincts/planning, 364, 376, 380, 389
Emergence
  of cities, 21, 23
  of structure, 23
Employment scenarios, 236
Enabling choice, 96
End of trip amenities, 398
Engagement approach, 128–130
Engagement outside of government, 165
Engagement plan, preliminary community, 158
Environmental sustainability, 366
Environmental value, 55
Environment and health, 366
Evaluation framework, 219, 232
Evaluation measures, 230
Evaluation options, 243, 247
Evaluation process (scenarios), 224
Evolving policy considerations, 57
Evolving scope of planning, 54
Executive and council support, neighbourhood community planning, 333
Exhibition activities, 277
Exhibition material, 257
Exhibition of a draft plan (step 5), 120
  eliciting submissions, 283
  and First Nations communities, 281
  implications for other planning typologies, 290
  pre-exhibition: a community engagement plan, 282
  principal activities, 277
Exhibition period, 276, 277, 279, 282, 283, 285
Exhibition planning, 276
Exhibition-ready, getting, 256
Existing systems, insight, 208

F
Federalism, 46
Final approval, 286
Finalising individual research briefs, 189
Finalising objectives and strategies, 268
  hypothetical sequence of thinking, from findings to objectives, 266
  worked example, 268
Finalising the plan (step 6), 120, 292
  agreement on changes, 287
  annual monitoring and reporting, 289
  finalising the content, 283
  finalising the documents, 293
  and First Nations communities, 286
  implications for other planning typologies, 290
  insights, 293

Index 437

inter-agency workshops, 288
principal activities, 286
purpose, 283
quality control, 288
submissions, 287
Financial and economic independence of households, enabling, 91, 359
Financial arrangements, 106
First cities, 22–23
First Nations communities
  enabling economic self-determination of, 91, 361
  engaging with, 130–131
  and exhibition of draft plan, 276
  meaningful engagement with, 130, 158, 165, 406
  pathway for developing a response, 241
  and plan delivery and ongoing planning, 300
  and plan finalisation, 283
  post-launch engagement, 280
  and preparation of draft plan, 253
  and project establishment, 162
  and research and analysis, 190
  synthesis and direction setting, 221
First Nations peoples, culture, heritage and Country, 5, 52, 95, 130–131, 162, 195, 219, 254, 407. *See also* Country
  access to Country, 92
  built form, 406
  characteristics of Country, 90, 351, 426
  considering project life cycles with an Aboriginal perspective, 134
  cultural landscapes, 199, 218, 405
  language and naming, 407
  oral traditions of First Nations Knowledges, 224
  pathways for connecting, 134
  Recognise Country guidelines, 130, 134, 135, 254, 405
  starting with Country, 406
  strategic planning response, 135
Footpaths, 409
Formal executive working group, 177
Formal project control group, 177
Formal sign-off, 176
Formal steering committee, 177
Formation of towns and cities, 26
Fortifications, 23, 24
Framework for perceiving the city, 425
Freight, 220, 400, 403
Frequency of public transport, 398
Functionality versus liveability, 54
Funding mechanisms, 53

Funding the delivery of city plans, 107–110
  aligning infrastructure with growth, 109
  development contributions, 108
  value capture, 107–108
Future generations, planning for, 89

G

Gaining trust, community engagement, 336
Garden city concept, 44–46, 55
Garden suburbs, 45, 54
Garnaut, Christine, 44
Garvin, A., 34–35
Gathering the evidence. *See* Research and analysis
General public, 127
Getting exhibition-ready, 257
Gig economy, 72
Glossary, 12
Governance, 53, 105
  applying to other planning typologies, 178–180
  delivery of the plan, 309
  local government area planning, 317
  of metropolitan areas, 11
  neighbourhood community planning, 331–337
  new greenfield community planning, 327
  sign-off and project management, 176–178
  town centre planning, 321
Governance arrangements, 177
Governance structure, 159
Government
  challenge of multiple portfolios, 137
  decision-making within, 137
  deliberative agendas, 136
  establishing informal working relationships with, 163
  identifying project partners across, 163
  politics and planning, 136–137
  positives for the, 136
Government-owned land, 348
the Grand Manner, 25
Great cities, 30–39
  Accessibility, 33, 36–37
  and great streets, 30–33
  insights for a strategic planning framework, 38–39
  and public spaces, 34–35
  what are?, 19–40
  what makes them great?, 30
  who defines 'great'?, 38
Greater Darwin plan, 56, 110, 260, 290, 413, 415

Greater Golden Horseshoe (Toronto) plan, 58, 68
  policy themes, 69
  principal elements, 259
Greater Sydney Region Plan, 38, 56, 60, 107, 128, 140, 167, 229, 259, 283, 319, 365, 367, 369
  accessibility, 36
  approach to design, 423
  championing the vision, 215
  climate change issues/metrics, 413
  finalising objectives and strategies, 268
  funding the delivery, 107
  overlay of economic data sets, 222
  plan on a page, 239
  responding to community values, 99
  spatial equity, 402
  structure plan, 262
  submissions review, 281
  transport network, 241, 265
Great streets, 31–33
Greenfield community planning. *See* New greenfield community planning
Greenhouse gas emissions, 414
Green infrastructure, 11, 66, 417
Grid pattern, 25
Groups, working directly with, 128
Growth and change equation, 11, 94, 199, 224, 389
  importance of, 230
  local government area planning, 317
  neighbourhood community planning, 331
  new greenfield community planning, 328, 372
  physical equation, 389
  town centre planning, 322

H
Hall, Peter, 30, 45
Hamnett S. and Freestone R., 46–52, 136–137
Have your say days, 129
Health of individuals and communities, improving, 92, 367
Health precincts/planning, 363, 376, 389
Healthy eating, 365
Healthy natural systems, 61, 96, 324, 412
Heat island effect, 413
Heritage and culture, 57, 63, 66, 407
Heritage assessment, 95
Hinterlands, 96, 379, 417
Homes, physical amenity, 92, 375
Households
  characteristics, 89, 196, 344

  financial and economic independence, 91, 359
  needs of, 91–92, 197
Housing, 48, 49, 220, 365, 380
Housing affordability, 61
Housing choice, improving the level of, 91
Housing demand, 94
Housing development data, 225
Housing opportunities, 355
Housing scenarios, 234
Housing supply and demand, 356
Housing typologies, 347
Howard, Ebenezer, 44–45

I
Ideal project timeline, 172
Image of the city, 425
Imagery, 241
Implementation plan, 182, 286, 297, 301
Implementation responsibilities, 285
Implementing the approved plan, 301
Independent advisory committees, 203
Individual and community wellbeing, improving, 61, 92, 366
Industrial development, 235, 385
Industrial revolution, 24
Informal input, 129
Informal working group, establishing, 177
Infrastructure, 323, 382, 400, 401
  aligning with growth, 109
  funding, 108
Infrastructure plan, 254
Infrastructure projects, 245
Infrastructure section, 259
Innovation (retail), 386
Innovative methods (post launch engagement), 281
Innovative ways to gain community input, 129
Insights
  Australian capital city plans, 56–57
  international city plans, 58
  plan delivery and ongoing planning, 301–302
  plan finalisation, 287
  preparation of a draft plan, 252
  project establishment, 182–185
  project management, 147
  research and analysis, 211
  synthesis and direction setting, 248
Insights for a strategic planning framework
  cities, 30
  emergence of modern planning, 53–56
  great cities, 39

Integrated place planning, 99–103
Integrated regional and metropolitan strategic plans, 51
Integrating the findings, 218
Integration of the findings and search for inter-dependencies, 221
  groupings to assess, 220
Inter-agency workshops, 285, 292
Interchanges, 396
Interfaces, 408
International city plans
  insights, 58
  nomenclature, 238
  principal elements, 259
International freight connections, 395
International, national and regional connections, 262
Internet of Things, 122, 129
Intervention levers, 105–107. *See also* Levers for change
Interventions, 59, 61, 76, 83–85, 95, 96, 104
  public benefits sought through, 83
  selected strategic, 104, 105
  since the 1880s across the globe, 53
Investment attraction, 106

J
Jacobs, Allan B., 31–33
Jurisdictional context, 4, 57

K
Kostof, Spiro, 21, 25–30, 37, 39

L
Land use activities and transport networks, 90, 346
Land use segregation, relevance of ongoing, 54
Land values, 347
Language matters, 272
Late submissions, 283
Launch (of exhibition), 279
Lead times for delivery, 417
Legislative requirements, 63
Levers of change
  local government area planning, 315–316
  neighbourhood community planning, 336
  new greenfield community planning, 327
  town centre planning, 322
Linking spatial information, 345
Literature reviews, 193
Liveability versus functionality, 54

Local amenity, 54
Local government area planning, 3, 179, 180, 204, 243, 271, 291, 314–319
  community engagement, 318
  governance, 326
  growth and change equation, 329
  levers for change, 318
  purpose, 314
  research framework, 315, 316, 320
  spatial planning, 315–316
  typical research areas, 339
Local neighbourhoods, choice in, 421
London Plan, 58, 68
  policy themes, 69
  principal elements, 259
Look and feel (final document), 285
Lot sizes, 347

M
Managing change, 143
  for communities, perception is reality, 143
  delivering change, 144
  nature of change in cities, 144
Managing the client, 183
Managing urban and suburban communities, 96, 200
Marchetti's constant, 11, 232
Mass – activity – space (design), 424
Melbourne plan. *See* Plan Melbourne
Mercer's Cost of Living Survey, 37
Mesopotamia, 22, 23
Metropolitan area planning. *See also* Australian capital city plans; Australian metropolitan planning; City planning typologies; International city plans
  typical research areas, 339
Metro Vancouver plan, 58, 59, 68
  policy themes, 69
  principal elements, 261
Mining activities, 94, 376, 390
Minister's office, liaising with, 159
Mode choices, 95
Modern planning, emergence of, 47
  Australian experience, 46–47
  insights for a strategic planning framework, 53–56
  reflections on planning eras in Australia, 46–52
  response to urban ills, 44–46
  suite of delivery levers, 52
Monitoring and reporting, 290
Multi-criteria analysis method, 227

Mumford, Lewis, 20–21, 23

N
Narratives
 creating clear, 345
 distilling research findings into, 205
 importance of presenting findings as, 224
Natural hazard risks, 86, 418
Natural public places, access to, 92, 93, 372, 373
Natural resources, protecting, 93, 380
Natural systems/natural environment, 61, 96, 324, 410–412
Needs of business, 92, 198, 380
Needs of people and households, 91–92, 197
Needs of the community – a research framework, 85–88
Negotiation, and decisions, 138
Neighbourhood character, 351
Neighbourhood community planning, 3, 121, 179, 180, 204, 243, 331–337
 challenge of, 331–332
 community engagement, 332
 direction setting, 334
 governance, 336–337
 growth and change equation, 334
 levers of change, 336
 the plan, 337
 project establishment, 332
 purpose, 332
 reserach framework, 333–335
 spatial planning, 333
 timeframe, 333
Net community benefit, 233
Network performance, 94
New greenfield community planning, 3, 8, 121, 179, 180, 204, 243, 271, 291, 327–331
 community engagement, 330
 draft plan elements, 330
 governance, 330
 growth and change equation, 317, 387
 levers of change, 331
 purpose, 327
 research framework, 328
 spatial planning, 327–328
 temporal considerations, 329
 typical research areas, 339
New South Wales, planning objectives in legislation, 63
New York City plan. *See* OneNYC plan
Next generation, planning for, 89

O
Objectives/objectives setting, 237, 243, 252, 254, 261
Office development, 235, 358, 375, 389
On-demand digital services (transport), 398
OneNYC plan, 58–60, 68
 policy themes, 69
 principal elements, 261
Ongoing agency engagement and collaboration, 300
Ongoing development of a "book of knowledge", 299
Ongoing engagement, 299, 308
Ongoing research, 297–299
 principal activities, 297–300
Ongoing strategic planning framework, 298
Ongoing strategic planning process, 303–308
 book of knowledge, 298–300
 ongoing research and engagement, 303–308
 targeted policy review and updating plans, 304
Online retailing, 72
On-street car parking, 409
Open space, 324, 365, 366
Open space networks, 347
Operational needs of business, 93
Operational versus strategic objectives, 57
Opportunities for informal input, 129
Optional plan elements (draft plans), 262
Orderly and coordinated development, 61
'Organic' patterns, 25, 27
Outward urban expansion, 48, 379

P
Participatory processes, 136
Pattern book, 330
Peak environmental and social bodies, 127, 165
Peak industry bodies, 127, 165
Pedestrians, 323
Peer review (of draft plan), 273
People and the place, 90–97, 343–351
Peoples and households
 characteristics, 90, 343
 needs of, 91–92, 197
Performance (evaluation measure), 230
Performance indicators, 289
Perth (Perth & Peel) plan, 56, 60, 110, 259, 292, 415, 416, 425
Physical activity, 365
Physical amenity
 of businesses, 377
 of homes, 92, 375

Physiography, 90, 196, 348–349
Piazzas, 29
Place-based planning, integrated, 99–103
Places
   amenity and diversity of, 49, 54, 57
   characteristics of, 90, 196, 346–349, 426
   creating, 99
   defining, 98
   planning for, 97–103, 195
   qualities and performance of, 86, 200, 427
   qualities of, 95–96, 417
   responding to community values, 99
   what is important?, 89–97
Plan delivery, 297, 299
   principal activities, 297
Plan delivery and ongoing planning (step 7), 120, 295–308
   First Nations communities, 300
   implementing the approved plan, 303–305
   implications for other planning typologies, 308
   insights, 311–312
   ongoing strategic planning framework, 298
   ongoing strategic planning process, 305–310
   principal activities, 298–301
   purpose, 296
   putting structure to the process of delivery, 310
   who delivers the plan?, 311–312
Plan development, 252, 255
Plan elements, 263
Plan finalisation (step 6), 120, 290, 292
Plan Melbourne, 51, 110, 230, 260, 294, 362, 413, 416, 422
Planners, community engagement, 126–127
Planning and decision-making, 137–138
Planning, as very reactive, 136
Planning context, auditing, 165
Planning delivery authorities, 55
Planning for change, challenges of, 143–145
Planning for cities, 43–78
   in the beginning, 182
   as a challenge, 61
   emergence of modern planning, 44–47
   every starting point is different, 183
   implementation: the end at the beginning, 182
   interventions. *See* Interventions
   perspectives, 38–39
   rationale, 59–62
   scope of, 56, 58, 62–77
   why do the plan?, 182
Planning for exhibition, 279
Planning for future generations, 89

Planning for places, 99, 195
Planning literature, 55–56
Planning paradigms coming in and out of favour, 46
Planning systems, 123–124
   Australian context, 123
   international context, 124
   principal elements, 123
Plan refinement, 252, 255
Plan updates, 295, 300
   principal activities, 300
Policies, 53, 105
Political process, do not participate in, 137
Politics and planning, 136–137
Population and demographics, 94, 382
Population growth, and urban expansion, 48
Ports, 399
Post-European contact heritage, 408
Post-exhibition, 292
Post-launch engagement, 281
Pre-exhibition activities, 282
Preferred scenarios (direction setting), 240
Preparation of a draft plan (step 4), 120
   core plan elements, 263
   development of actions, 270
   finalising objectives and strategies, 268
   and First Nations communities, 254
   implications for other planning typologies, 270
   insights, 273
   optional plan elements, 262
   principal activities, 258
   report role, structure and content, 263
   structure plan, 264
   supporting activities, 258
Preparing and reviewing existing plans, 182
Pressure for early answers, 203
Principal elements, 262. *See also* Draft plan elements
   Australian capital city plans, 259
   international metropolitan plans, 261
Principal findings, 190
Principal issues to be addressed in the plan, 168
Principal stakeholders, 11, 176
Privacy, 75
Private public space interfaces, 410
Private sector delivery of cities, 54
Problem statement, 157, 158, 160, 161, 165, 166
Processing submissions (from the exhibition), 277, 281
Procurement, 140, 173, 174, 190
Project brief, 155–157, 159–161, 184

applying to other planning typologies, 178
essential tasks, 159, 160
inputs and outputs, 161
iterative process, 159–160
outputs for, 167, 169, 176, 177
Project brief sign-off, 159, 160
Project delivery. *See* Plan delivery and ongoing planning (Step 7)
Project establishment (step 1), 120, 155–185, 324
   auditing the planning content, 165
   developing the project methodology, 169–176
   establishing the project objectives and scope, 167
   establishing working relationship, 162–165
   and First Nations communities, 162
   governance, sign-off, and project initiation, 176–178
   implications for other planning typologies, 178–180
   insights, 182–185
   neighbourhood community planning, 331
   principal activities, 157–162
   the process, 183
   town centre planning, 325–326
Project flexibility, 171
Project initiation, 176–178
Project management, 139–140, 147
Project methodology, development, 158, 169–176
   agency workshops, 171
   applying to other planning typologies, 178
   approach, 169
   back of house activities, 175
   documenting the journey, 175
   overall methodology, 171
   procurement, 174
   research areas for Step 2, 170
   resourcing, 173, 183
   risk management and quality control, 173
   timing, 171–172
   what are we seeking to achieve?, 169–171
Project objectives, establishing, 158, 167
Project partners, identifying across government, 163
Project risks, 140
Project scope, 155, 156, 158, 176, 179
   applying to other planning typologies, 178–180
   establishing, 167
Project team, establishing, 172, 184, 332
Project timeline, 172
Promoting the plan, 295, 302

Public benefits sought through intervention, 83
Public housing, 11, 356
Public places, 28, 31
Public realm, support of (retail), 386
Public release (of the final plan), 286
Public servants, 126
Public spaces, 34, 39
   characteristics, 34–35
   positive and negative experiences when walking in, 99
Public transport, 323, 394, 397, 402, 421
   frequency, 398
   user pays, 397
Public works, 53, 105
Purpose of strategic planning, 83–111
   is business as usual acceptable?, 85
   it's about delivery, 103–110
   needs of the community – a research framework, 85–88
   planning for places, 100
   temporal considerations, 88
   what is important to people's lives and places?, 89–97

Q

Qualities and performance of places, 86, 200, 426
Qualities of places, 95–96, 414, 426
Quality, aesthetics (beauty) and amenity, 95, 410
Quality control, 173, 246, 288
Quality employment, 365
Quality of cities, 49
Quality of life, 92, 97, 198, 375, 424, 426
Quality of travel experience, 397

R

Rail freight, 220, 400
Rail revival, in city planning, 51
Rapid assessment of submissions, 283
Rationale for planning cities, 59–62
Recognise Country guidelines, 130, 134, 135, 254, 405, 408
Recreation facilities, 365
Reduce carbon footprint, 413
Reduce or prevent negative externalities, 59
Re-emergence of cities, 24
Reflections on planning eras in Australia, 46–52
   each historical trend has brought new ideas, 49–50
   events from 2000 to 2020, 51–52

Index

evolving planning eras, 46–49
  notable events, 1890 to 2000, 50
  we have seen it all before, 46–49
Regional areas, relocation to, 73
Regional cities planning, 3, 120, 179, 180, 204, 243, 271, 291, 308
Regulations, 54, 106
Release ready (final plan documents), 286
Renaissance, 24
Renewable energy, 413–415
Reporting period, 203
Report structure, developing, 215
Research, 185
  approaches to, 8
Research activities, 193, 204
  overview, 197
Research and analysis (step 2), 120, 211. *See also* Strategic Analysis Research Framework
  community engagement activities, 202
  coordinating the research initiatives, 203
  distilling research findings into narratives, 205
  finalising the research briefs, 195
  and First Nations communities, 190
  implications for other planning typologies, 205
  insights, 211
  principal activities, 191
  purpose, 188
Research areas
  approach for each, 195
  city planning typologies, 337
  needs of people and business, 353
  people and the place, 344–351
  qualities and performance of place, 393, 430
  for Step 2 (project methodology development), 170, 181
Research briefs, finalising, 195
Research findings, distilling into narratives, 205
Research framework. *See* Strategic Planning Research Framework
Research initiatives, coordinating, 203
Research methods, 194
Resourcing, project methodology, 173, 183
Retail, 235, 362, 375, 387
Reviewing existing background material, 166
Review of existing plans, 182
Risk management, 173
Road freight, 220, 397
Roads/road network, 23, 220, 323

S

Safety (cities), 23, 75, 323, 365
Sanitation, 23
Scale (design), 97, 424
Scale of buildings, 410
Scenario development and evaluation, 215, 233
  base case: business as usual, 228
  evaluating options, 243, 247
  evaluation framework, 232
  evaluation process, 224
  importance of growth and change equation, 230
  multi-criteria analysis method, 228
  net community benefit, 233
  town centre planning, 325
Scenario typologies, 237
Scope of city planning, 56, 58, 62–77
  common issues from Australian contemporary plans, 60–65
  definition, 76–77
  drivers of change in the 22nd Century, 68–77
  legislative requirements, 63
Selected strategic interventions, 105
Senior Officers Group (SOG), 164
Sense of place and community, 95, 404
Sequencing plan, 330
Service provision, 95
7-Step Strategic Planning Process, 7–8, 99, 116–122
  common threads and considerations, 122–145
  conceptual framework, 116–118
  implications of differing city planning typologies, 120–122
  the model, 119–120
  from plans to planning, 122
  principal insights, 117
  rationale for a framework, 116–118
  relationship between fundamental elements, 119
  step 1: project establishment, 120, 155–185
  step 2: research and analysis, 120, 211
  step 3: synthesis and direction setting, 120, 248
  step 4: prepare a draft plan, 120
  step 5: exhibit a draft plan, 120, 280
  step 6: finalising the plan, 120, 287
  step 7: plan delivery and ongoing planning, 120, 295–311
Sign-off and exhibition ready, 253, 257
  exhibition material, 257
  getting exhibition ready, 258

implementation section, 256
Social and cultural life, 368
Social bodies, 127
Social capital, 368
Social cohesion and connectivity, 366
Social equity, 61
Social housing, 11, 354
Social infrastructure, 66, 92, 199, 330, 366, 368, 369. *See also* Quality of life
Social media, 128
Social needs, 380
Social sustainability, 368
Societal norms, meeting, 61
Socio-economic characteristics, 90, 196, 346
Socio-economic characteristics, 345–346
South East Queensland (SEQ) Regional Plan, 52, 56, 60, 110, 120, 260, 290, 414
Space to grow, 369
Spatial development patterns, 66
Spatial economic structure, 93, 377
Spatial planning. *See also* Structure (spatial) plans
  local government area planning, 315–316
  neighbourhood community planning, 331
  new greenfield community planning, 327–331
  town centre planning, 319–326
Specialisation and choice (cities), 22–23
Specialised precincts, 347
Specialists, for community engagement, 131, 132
Sporting, leisure or recreational groups, 127
Stakeholder engagement, 115, 122, 125, 132, 253
Stakeholders, 120, 126–128, 130, 136, 140, 322
Standalone office development, 235, 388
Standardised submission forms, 280
Standard State Zoning Enabling Act (SZEA), 124
State of play report, 300
Status updates (about the exhibition), 282
Statutory framework, 325
Sticky note planning, 194
Strategic alignment of delivery activities, 48, 303
Strategic planning
  nature of, 2
  purpose, 83–111
  what do I need to know?, 185
Strategic Planning Research Framework, 8, 86, 87, 89, 170, 192, 194, 195, 197, 199
  applicability to local government area planning, 315, 317

applicability to new greenfield community planning, 328, 340
applicability to town centre planning, 319–326, 340
context, the people and the place, 197
needs of people and business, 199
planning for places, 195
qualities and performance of place, 200
what is important to people's lives and places?, 89–97
Strategic versus operational objectives, 57
Strategies (plan development), 252, 261, 262, 268
Streets, 29. *See also* Great streets
Structure
  emergence of, 23
  of city plans, 56, 58, 96, 424
Structure (spatial) plans, 12, 252, 259, 262
Study area, identifying, 168, 322
Submissions
  acknowledging, 282
  eliciting, 283
  late, 283
  managing requests for further time, 282
  processing, 277, 281
  rapid assessment, 283
Submissions portal, 280
Submissions report, 281
Submissions review, 282, 285, 287
Suburban communities, 96, 200, 422
Success
  evidence of, 293
  what constitutes success, 158
Supply of land for retail, 386
Surveys, 129
Sustainability, 51, 140
Sustainable infrastructure, 66, 67
SWOT analysis, 12, 218
Synoecism, 26
Synthesis and direction setting (step 3), 120, 248. *See also* Direction setting
  and First Nations communities, 221
  implications for other planning typologies, 243
  insights, 248
  principal activities, 214
  purpose, 217
  scenario development and evaluation, 233
  scenario typologies, 237
  supporting activities, 215
  synthesis of the research findings, 215, 224
Synthesis of the research findings, 215, 224
  importance of narratives, 224
  integration and inter-dependencies, 221

principal activities, 214
Systems thinking, 142

T
Targeted engagement, 129
Targeted policy review, 300, 304
Targeted research, 106
Team health and wellbeing, 282
Technology, influence on cities, 74
Telecommunications access, 93, 378
Temporal considerations, 88, 329
3D printing, 75
Timeframe, neighbourhood community planning, 333
Time lag from issue identification to response, 54
Time requirement for formal approval, 172
Timing, project methodology, 171
Today's community, planning for, 89
Toronto plan. *See* Greater Golden Horseshoe (Toronto) plan
Tourism activities, 221, 376
Town centre planning, 3, 121, 179, 180, 204, 243, 271, 291, 308, 319–326
  community engagement, 318, 325–326
  context, 322
  draft plan elements, 325
  governance, 326
  growth and change equation, 317
  investigation considerations, 324–325
  levers of change, 326
  project establishment, 322
  purpose, 319
  research framework, 324–326
  scenarios and evaluation, 324
  spatial planning, 321–322
  typical research areas, 339
Town planning, UK, 44–46
Towns and cities, formation of, 26
Trade gateways and freight, 400
Traditional engagement methods, 129, 280
Traditional 'town hall' meetings, 280
Traffic, 409
Transport networks, 24, 26, 90, 94, 96, 97, 204, 347, 365
  access (insight), 209
  and land use activities, 346–348
  and land use consequences, 395
  Greater Sydney Region Plan, 262
  narratives, 204
  to support business activities, 378
Transport planning, 37, 66, 380
  and land use planning, 65

Transport scenarios, 237
Transport service provision, 399
Tree cover, 415
Trips, 397
Typology of centres, 347
Typology of city plans. *See* City planning typologies

U
Understanding place (city design), 426
Understand the expectations as to the type of actions (project objective), 168
Unforeseen events, 122
United Kingdom, planning systems, 124
United States, strategic planning controls, 123, 124
Unwin, Raymond, 45
Updates to the city plan, 297, 300
Urban amenity, 91, 365
Urban communities, 96, 200, 421
Urban divisions, 28
Urban form of cities, 24–30
  elements of, 28–29
  evolution, 26
  rationale behind, 27
  social outcomes, 27
  unintended outcomes of controls, 27
Urban heat, 415
Urban ills, response to, 44–46
Urban infrastructure, 96, 418
Urban patterns and meanings, 25–28
Urban process, 28
Urban renewal/urban renewal plans, 3, 12, 121
Urban skyline, 25, 27
Urban tree canopy, 221
Urban typologies, 25
User pays transport systems, 398
Utilities, 409

V
Value capture, 107–109
Value management, 140, 255
Verbal submissions, addressing, 282
Victoria, planning objectives in legislation, 63
Virtual reality activities, 73
Vision statement, 241, 261
Voice and influence, 369

W
Walkability, 36, 66
Waste management, 417

Website (about the launch and plans), 280
Wellbeing, individual and community, 61, 92, 367
Why and how to plan cities, 5–6, 15–40, 42–77, 83–111
Work from home, 72
Working groups, 177
Working relationships, establishing, 158, 162–165
   engaging outside of government, 165
   identifying your project partners across government, 163
   importance of, 162
   informal working relationships, 163
Worship, 23
Writing the plan, 215, 246

Z
Zoning, 27, 52, 53

The manufacturer's authorised representative in the EU is Springer Nature Customer Service Centre GmbH, Europaplatz 3, 69115 Heidelberg, Germany. If you have any concerns regarding our products, please contact ProductSafety@springernature.com

Printed and bound by CPI Group (UK) Ltd, Croydon, CR0 4YY

25/03/2026

02078170-0006